Making My Own Luck

By Harvey Thorneycroft

Text © Harvey Thorneycroft Ltd. 2011,
Weston Grange, Weston Green Road, Thames Ditton, Surrey, KT7 0HX

Designed, Typeset and Cover design by Jake Burdess & Daniel Bravo

The right of Harvey Thorneycroft to be identified as the author of this work has been
asserted by him in accordance with the Copyright Designs and Patents Act 1988.

First published 2011

British Library lkCataloguing in Publication Data
A catalogue record for this book is available from the British Library
ISBN 978-0-9569710-0-5

Printed in Great Britain by CPI Antony Rowe

Website
Please visit www.makingmyownluck.co.uk for more information about this book.

Table of contents

Acknowledgements

I would like to thank the following people for allowing me to use the photographs contained within this book, The School Wellingborough, Northampton Saints Football Club, The Rugby Football Union, Northampton Chronicle and Echo, Jake Richardson, The Richardson Group, John Scott , Tim Rodber, Matt Dawson, Ben Cohen, Martin Hynes, Keith Barwell, Ian hunter, Paul Grayson, The Public School Wanderers, The Barbarian Football Club, The Cafe Royal, Federico Méndez, Pat Lam, Joel Stransky, John Inverdale, Phinda Game Reserve, Getty images

I have no idea why when I walked to Twickenham that night with Matt Dawson, that I would decide to write a book the following day, about my wonderful memories. They seem as vivid today as they did when I was living them. Daws you were the catalyst that gave me the confidence to get going on this very cathartic journey. You are living proof of what can be achieved if you have a common purpose and I thank you for initiating the latent desire I had to undertake this journey.

Dad, Mum, Nicola you laid the foundations that I needed to stride forth on this voyage of discovery. It was Joy, Grandma and Nan alongside you that provided me with the stability that I needed to realise my desire to travel and meet people from all parts of the world, knowing that my roots were very firmly entrenched in my beloved Northampton.

To Graham Garrett, for allowing me the chance to study at Wellingborough. Mike Askham for nurturing my sporting ability and providing me with encouragement on the other facets of the school curriculum.

To the institution that is Northampton Saints and for everyone who has enjoyed watching the men that have worn the Black, Green and Gold. You provided me with more than I could ever repay in just over a decade that I spent in these wonderful colours.

To life after rugby and the partnership that I had with Tim Rodber, who helped me manage what could have been a difficult transition. To Alice Bufton who took the baton over from Rodders to become my best friend and my wife. I love you Alice with all my heart and the two children that we have brought into this world, Scarlett and Harry. You are the wind beneath my wings and without you I wouldn't have been able to have met Francesca Heslop, who believed that this was a story worth telling. Thank you for your encouragement and support throughout. Lastly to Patrica Julie Allen (Mum) who continues to inspire me with her spiritual presence.

Prologue

It's 6:00 p.m. on Friday 27th June 2008 and I get a call from Matt Dawson asking to stay the night with Alice and me in Twickenham. I get back to close the day with my beautiful little girl, Scarlett, when in walks Mr Dawson armed with an overnight bag and a ticket to watch Bon Jovi live in concert at Twickenham Stadium. It was one of those beautiful summer evenings that you want to go on forever and I suggested that we go for a beer at the White Swan before he went off to the concert. There are very few places that I would rather be on a Friday night in London than the White Swan. The setting is idyllic – you are transported to a different era. The pub perches on the side of a high pavement down a winding lane over-looking the Thames and Eel Pie Island, and you can imagine yourself back in the seventeenth century without any trouble. Sitting on the terrace, watching the swans drift past, Matt invited me to join him in the Sky corporate box at the concert and it is whilst walking to Twickenham Stadium with Matt that I decide to write this book.

His invitation was unexpected. The chance to go to this concert was more about the enjoyment of living the moment and being spontaneous than a passion for a pop group from the 1980s. It was a realisation that by being there I could enjoy the passion of a group that despite having sold 140 million albums around the world had, until this evening, passed me by.

I have been very lucky to have lived a life that was spur-of-the-moment and until the birth of my first child, a baby girl, largely a selfish one. Throughout my life I have been extremely lucky. Luck is that thing which you cannot predict. I had never planned to be lucky. I put myself in a position where I was able to take advantage of every opportunity. Isn't it odd that lucky people always seem to be in the right place at the right time? I have been lucky, and in the right place at the right time. This way of living has taken me on adventures that I could never have imagined. I want to share some of these experiences with other people. This book is about a period of time that I will never get back and would never consider reliving. It represents a remarkable epoch. It was a time where I was care free and receptive to anything and witness to some extraordinary changes happening in rugby and to countries around the globe. It didn't occur to me at the time but on reflection I realise that I have been extremely fortunate.

My life now is about sharing with other people the knowledge I gained during those years and continually striving to learn more. After all, life is all about discovery. I love reading autobigraphies of successful people and the business books that adorn the shelves of bookshops. However, I can't help thinking once I have read them that they are all saying similar things. The authors are just using different metaphors to describe their personal journey. Now I would like to share my own journey with you. If, when I was thirteen, someone had described the life that I was going to lead I wouldn't have believed them. I still pinch myself when opportunities present themselves and never take them for granted. I hope you enjoy this extraordinary journey – I have.

Chapter 1

The roots to grow and wings to fly

The Number 52 United Counties bus pulls out of the village of Old Duston, Northamptonshire, to take me on a journey that will change my life forever. Up until this point I had spent the first thirteen years of my life in and around Old Duston. In 1982 it was a village on the outskirts of Northampton. I lived on the corner of Berrywood Road and Main Road, and you could be in the heart of the town or country within 15 minutes in either direction. We lived in Doctor Rutherford's House, next to the surgery. It was a detached house in its own grounds. We were very proud of the house and loved its garden. It stood on a hill at the far end of the village and within walking distance of everything that I did.

People who lived in Old Duston were proud of its heritage. The main local employer was British Timken, which had been part of the local economy since 1942, making bearings mainly for the car industry. This American owned business had a factory set in immaculate grounds with a cinder athletics track and one of the best football grounds complete with its very own stand. It felt like Wembley. Every budding athlete in the vicinity was desperate to play on the pitch and run on this track

Duston was a great place to grow up in. The village had its own bakery, butcher, post office and 'The Squirrels' Pub. I attended Millway Middle School, newly built in the grounds of an old quarry. The school was very optimistic about its future; you could smell progress in the fresh plaster. The headmaster, Fred Harrison, lived in the village and he was a strict disciplinarian. The school loved sport and so did its teachers, Mr Butler, Mrs Lockwood, Mr James and, of course, Mr Townsend. The sporting activities of Millway Middle School reached high standards in Northampton, particularly in the areas of atheletics, football and rugby. It was Mr Townsend who had a passion for rugby and through his passion created one of the best sides in the county for Under Thirteens. He bucked the trend in the Duston area as most of the schools were producing great soccer players.

Millway didn't have huge grounds, just enough room for a rugby pitch, football pitch and cricket square. Because the grounds were part of an old quarry before a match, we would have to walk the pitch and pick up the Northamptonshire sandstone that lay on the surface before we could play the game. In the summer, we didn't have a large enough ground for the conventional 400-metre track for sports day, we had a 300-metre running track which created its own problems for both the competitors and spectators but we produced some great athletes.

At this point in my life I loved soccer more than any other sport. During my enchanted childhood the only pressures I had extended to whether my team would be able to win the three football matches I played in at the weekend. I played on Saturday morning for Millway School, Saturday afternoon for the 7th Northampton Boys Brigade and on Sunday afternoon for the Duston Magpies or Venturians.

I played sport constantly. Duston Upper School, which was the other end of Berrywood Road to where we lived, had its own twenty-five-metre pool, in which I spent the long summer months. In this swimming pool, I passed all my Amateur Swimming Association survival awards and the Swimming Teachers Association distance awards. Ryeland Middle, which was next door to Duston Upper School, had a teacher called Mr Austin who was passionate about sport. He ran the local gymnastics club and I would often perform displays at local fêtes throughout the county with his team.

I attended The Boys' Brigade every week on Sunday. Its motto was 'sure and steadfast', and I loved the brigade and everything about it. Brian Thorpe was the Captain of the 7th Northampton, which was based at St Andrews Methodist Church on the Harlestone Road. Every Sunday I attended Sunday school and once a month we would have a parade. The parade involved dressing up in a uniform, blue blazer, black trousers, a cap, lanyards and belts. These had to be cleaned and maintained regularly and you were inspected on the condition of your uniform before any parade. As a military organisation, marching featured heavily in the form of drill. This was often performed to music, which was led by a marching band. We played bugles, drums and other brass instruments. I loved parading around Duston on Sunday mornings and The Boys' Brigade was very popular in the village. You were either in the 7th or the 11th. I remained loyal to the 7th although I lived closest to the 11th.

My peer group was made of people from the local school, The Boys Brigade and Duston Magpies football team. Nonny May, Michael Dillon and Ashley Starmer were the people I respected at this stage of my life. All the girls thought they were great – they were trendy and sporty. They were the cool lads who everyone aspired to be friends with. We all lived locally and aspired to play on the British Timken ground in the local football cup final. This world was perfect in every way.

I had a perfect home life, surrounded by my Nan, who also lived in the village, my Grandma, Sister, Dad and Mum. They were everything to me and they supported me in all I did. My sister had a passion for riding and owned two horses, Flicker and Gentleman James. They were stabled in a farm at Upton and she spent all her time riding around Duston and the surrounding fields, long before the arrival of Junction 15A of the M1 Motorway, the A45 and the huge developments that have now made this land of my childhood into a concrete jungle. Whilst she was riding, I was playing sport. We had everything on our doorstep. I didn't go anywhere unless Mum took me on the bus to town or Nan took us out in her blue Escort for a day trip. Mum didn't drive, so we were reliant on Nan to take us to exotic places like Wicksteed Park in Kettering. This was the equivalent of Alton Towers with flying chairs, a rollercoaster, a railway, and a 30-acre lake where we would have picnics. The star attraction for us was the water chute.

Mum, Nicola and I loved going into town to go shopping in the ancient market square, which was very vibrant in the 1970s. We would always finish in Lawrence's in St Giles Street, which at the time was in Egon Ronay's guides. It had won awards for the best afternoon tea and whenever I go back to Northampton I try to get in for a tea there. It is a place where Mum loved to go.

Dad worked long hours in his business and so as a family we went on very few holidays until I got much older, but every summer there was a Boys' Brigade Camp to places like Dawlish Warren in Devon. These were a real highlight of the year. The other summer adventure was that Nicola and I would go for a week in Southsea with my grandma, to give my mum and dad a bit of a break. These were happy days. I didn't want for anything. I was loved, my parents loved each other. They had a passionate relationship so there were arguments, but they would always kiss and make up.

Mum was the matriarch in our family. I didn't know it at the time, but many of the family outings and parties that we had were because of Mum and her desire to keep the extended family together. She was one of three children and she made sure that her tribe all saw each other. Christmas was a great time for family parties and it was always either at our house or my Uncle Rick's.

I biked or ran everywhere. I had a Raleigh Commando. It was a poor man's Chopper but I spent my life on it. This was replaced by a racer, The BSA "Tour of Britain", which was a Raleigh. It was good, but the bike everybody thought was best at the time was an Eddy Merckx bike, named after the man considered by many to be the greatest bicycle racer of all time. Dad always bought me great football boots,

Puma Kings and my all time greatest boots, a pair of Michel Platini's. In 1982 I watched one of the greatest footballers ever in the World Cup and these boots were named after him. I still have these boots today, carefully stowed away in my box of memories.

I was very fashion conscious (if you could call it this). We all wore Fred Perry T-shirts and V-neck Jumpers, Farah Sta-Prest trousers, white socks and slip-on leather shoes to the village Youth Club on a Friday night. Life was bliss. Whilst hanging out at the Youth club, Gaynor Bedford, Kay Wallace and Caroline Walters were the girls that I hoped would notice me. Sadly, it was all about to change for good.

Millway was a school that we were very proud of, but my dad had decided that Duston Upper was never going to be the school that I was going to attend as a secondary school. I can remember being physically dragged off the football pitch by my Dad to study with a private tutor, Dougie Young, a former master at Northamptonshire Grammar School. My dad and Dougie helped me revise for an entrance exam for a totally different school to the one that my peers were about to attend. I still remember the angst when I think of having to study when all my mates were playing sport and I was toiling upwards through the night with Dad. I was on a very steep learning-curve and I had no idea why. I was content with my world. It was only when I started visiting the senior schools that Dad wanted me to attend, and saw with my own eyes an altogether different world, that I started to realise the opportunities that existed beyond Old Duston.

At thirteen, you are oblivious to your purpose. It's up to your parents to recognise your potential and place you in the best position to enable you to realise it. I am very grateful that they did what they did. My dad had been educated in a grammar school system in Cambridge and wanted a similar education for me. Sadly, the only way this was going to happen in Northamptonshire was through the private school system. My mum and dad made some personal sacrifices for me to gain this advantage. Even at thirteen I was aware of this and never wanted to let them down.

I look back now and all my memories of Old Duston are happy ones. It holds a unique place in my memory, and rivals all the exotic locations that have since tried to jostle it from top position in my mind. Despite all the amazing journeys I have been on, incredible places I have visited and people I have met, Old Duston still holds my heart. The people I grew up with there were good people. It was a secure and reassuring place where everyone knew everybody. Families were immersed in each others' lives. School, church, The Boys' Brigade and sport brought us all together. Some of my greatest sporting triumphs could not replace the euphoria that I felt winning a rugby match for Mr Townsend at Campion, Bugbrooke for Millway, or the school relay on the track, or scoring a goal on the equivalent of Wembley at Timken.

If you have any kind of ambition, you always strive to achieve your potential. However, there is something very remarkable about being content with the life that you have and enjoying each moment. I had everything I needed and was comfortable with myself and my family and friends. I didn't need to know about anything else, because I lived for the moments that each day provided. This was about to change.

One day, late in the summer term, I was left in the playground with a few other pupils. I saw the rest of my year group walk up the slope in the direction of Duston Upper School for an open day. I had very mixed feelings. On one hand, I would not be able to see my mates that I had grown up with every day and who formed a significant part of my life. However, I had been given a sneak preview of another life by my father on those school visits and I wanted to find out more about what it could offer me. The irony was that in my head I told myself that if the next journey didn't work out then I could go back to my old life. The number 52 bus took me away from Old Duston and transported me on a voyage of discovery that would change my life forever. Andrew Collins, a Duston boy wrote a book called *Where Did It All Go Right*, where he describes in great detail growing up in a happy home in the 1970s. I read his book and felt how fortunate we were; he was few years older than me, but it seemed that there were so many similarities between his life and mine.

I still have an overwhelming need, deep inside me, to go back to this time. A fear exists of not ever being able to return home, to a time when it was always sunny and I didn't have a care in the world. A time when Nicola would be out riding, Dad and Mum would be at home and I would be coming back to find everything just as it always was and always should be. Andrew Collins remembers in his book waiting for his mum to shout, telling him that tea is ready. "Findus Crispy Pancakes followed by a Supermousse". As I write this I have 'something in my eye' which I can't get out, and maybe never shall.

When I was thirteen, my Dad made a choice for me that would enable me to realise any ambition I might have. I was to attend a very different school from Millway and from the secondary school that all my mates were off to in the autumn. I boarded the bus in the late summer of 1982, armed with a metaphorical suitcase containing the moral code and a huge awareness of the opportunity given to me by my parents.

What would follow would eventually lead me to people and places that I had no idea even existed. However, it was the principles that had been instilled in me by my parents that would prove to be the most valuable lessons that I could ever learn. I look back with great affection at this moment in time. It is a moment that I will never be able to relive and one that I will never forget. Without realising it, I was poised on the brink of a new life.

The change in school life was dramatic in many ways. I was about to be a day boy at a boarding school and had no idea what to expect. The length of each school day increased significantly. Each morning I dressed in a charcoal grey suit and Loake shoes. I caught the United Counties bus outside my house at 7:15 a.m. bound for Greyfriars Bus station in Northampton whilst all my mates would still be in bed or doing a paper round. I then had to catch the school bus, which left Abington Square, ten minutes walk from Greyfriars, at 8:00 a.m. for a forty-minute journey to school. There was no margin for error. Just to get to school gates each day was quite an ordeal. Fortunately, it was so early in the morning that there was never much traffic. The school bus returned at different times during the week, depending upon what activities we had each day, but I was very rarely home before 6:00 p.m. Every day-boy was expected, like the borders, to do their 'prep'. This was seen as an essential part of the day's learning and was a time to consolidate and reflect on the day's events. My new school day would end at about 9:00 p.m. when I had finally finished my prep.

I soon realised that I was on catch up. I was placed in DD, the bottom set. At Wellingborough there were four sets in each year, A to D, based on the likely grades that the teachers anticipated you would get at that stage of your academic career. On reflection, it seems rather harsh that each boy would automatically know what the teachers' thought of his academic ability. There were no concessions made to self-esteem.

At Wellingborough, the third year was called the Shell Form and all Shell formers were placed in houses, something that I had never had experienced before. I was put in Parkers House, which consisted of a central common room full of old chairs and sofas on the first floor, and changing rooms and showers on the ground floor. It was not attractive in any way. As a Shell former, you were expected to perform tasks for the Head of House, who was a school prefect, and other house prefects. If you had not performed your house duties correctly then you had to report to the house prefects at break time to talk to the light bulb. This was a very odd form of punishment and one that we hated and the school prefects loved.

Each house had a House Master. The House Master for Parkers House was Mr Askham. He helped me through a difficult transition in those early days as I adjusted to my new way of life. He was a former graduate of Loughborough College and the Head of PE. Sport was one thing I was good at, but I was by no means the best. The school was full of great talent in every sport, none more so than the most talented soccer player I have ever seen for his age, Jarrad Isherwood. He was asked to sign up by many professional clubs after he left

Wellingborough. Jarrad and I played up front for Wellingborough and we were soon playing representative sport through the encouragement of Mike Askham. Jarrad was spotted as a player for the future when representing South East Region Public Schools against Arsenal Under 15s. I have no idea why we would have played this fixture but we did. We were 4–1 down at half time. Jarrad came on and scored three goals and we eventually beat them 6–5.

The thing that struck me most forcibly in the first few weeks of Wellingborough was how talented the majority of students were within the school. It was a high performance arena and boys were there because they wanted to get on. Founded in 1595, Wellingborough School was the place where I would spend the next five years of my voyage of discovery. Wellingborough broadened my horizons and equipped me with the tools that I would need for the next phase of my life.

The school year was split into three terms. Michaelmas term started in early September and ran through to late December. A long holiday would follow for Christmas, before resuming again in mid January for Lent term, which would finish in late March. Trinity term started in late April and then finished in late July. We had huge holidays compared to my mates at comprehensive schools; however, the activities that were packed into term time certainly made up for the free time you got in the holidays. For the first time in my life I had Saturday school. At thirteen this was a huge change, but one I came to terms with very quickly and learned to love.

It was difficult to get a complete understanding on how many things beyond the academic curriculum took place. Sport was on three afternoons a week on playing fields extending to over 50 acres. This included nine football/rugby pitches, five cricket squares, two grass hockey pitches, five hard tennis courts and five grass tennis courts, five netball courts, two squash courts, a rifle range, a grass athletics track and a nine-hole golf course. In the academic year that I joined, a sports hall was opened by Lieutenant General Sir Peter Hudson who had been educated at Wellingborough during World War II.

On Wednesday afternoon we had CCF (Combined Cadet Force) and I elected to join the army section. This was taken very seriously at school and provided me with one of my first truly life changing experiences. It's funny how little preparation you get for seismic shifts in your perception. The things that tip you from child to adult occur without any fanfare or warning.

It was the school holidays and it was one of the first times, apart from The Boys' Brigade camp, that I had been away from my parents. We were taken on army camp to Warcop Training Area in Cumbria. The camp was established in 1942. It is in an area of outstanding natural beauty and was the place where most of the armoured formations that took part in the D-Day landings trained. We spent the week doing a mixture of activities that included firing 303 rifles, assault courses and military exercises. At the end of the week we were being transported back to camp in convoy by some young recruits in ten-tonners. These are big trucks designed to transport troops in the army. Sadly, one of the vehicles over turned on the narrow tracks trapping a young boy underneath. He was alive until the truck was jacked off his chest, but the pressure from the release resulted in him having a cardiac arrest. This shocked everybody at the camp. The incident made the national news. It was the first time in my life that I was that close to death. This brush with mortality shocked me.

Institutions like Wellingborough, whose motto is *Salus in Arduis* (fulfilment through challenge), provide superb opportunities for children to unlock their true potential. It was the headmaster, Graham Garrett, who gave me the opportunity to attend after a dreadful entrance exam. I don't know whether you can call it serendipity, but he just happened to be walking across the quadrangle as my dad was consoling me and he made it his business to introduce himself and give me another chance to re-sit the paper I had just failed. Luck, as

I mentioned earlier, is that thing that you cannot predict and this was one of the luckiest moments of my life. Graham may not remember this act of thoughtfulness; however, I do and I will always be grateful for the opportunities that he gave me.

Each day school started with a Chapel service, in a beautiful building built in 1906, located in the very heart of the school surrounded by tennis courts and solid red brick Victorian buildings. The masters and school prefects wore academic gowns. All the boys got their news from a board called the Hot Board. One note that Mr Croft the classics master left on the Hot Board to deter boys from sunbathing in the playing fields was particularly memorable: "Naked Torsos are Taboo."

Boarders came from all over the country and from countries that I had never heard of. One of my great friends was Sam Leadsom. He lived in Chobham in Surrey and often talked about the lawns being the feature of his house. It wasn't until I visited Chobham House in the school holidays that I realised what he was talking about. The lawns were indeed large and the house had medieval origins. It was part of Chobham Park, built in a Queen Anne style. The people I mixed with at Wellingborough were very different to my mates in Old Duston.

The whole school would sit down together to eat lunch in the dinning hall. The headmaster would always start lunch with the whole school standing with the prayer *Benedictus benedicat*, which means 'Be blessed by Him who is blessed'. A house prefect would serve dinner whilst boys sat at trestle tables. There was a top table where the headmaster and teachers would sit. It wasn't as grand a hall as Hogwarts dining hall, but it had a very similar lay out and feel. If you can imagine yourself sitting down to supper in Hogwarts dining hall, you are not very far away from what every meal was like for me at Wellingborough.

The school produced pupils that had a wide diversity of skills. It was academically geared to producing candidates that would go on to Oxford and Cambridge, but it was about more than just academic achievement. It encouraged sport, mainly soccer and cricket, and had a huge range of thriving pupil communities. Students became involved in musical theatre, orchestras, chapel choir, public speaking, debating, drama, young enterprise, the Duke of Edinburgh's Award Scheme and the CCF. You couldn't fail to be impressed with the people Wellingborough produced as a result of all this effort.

The school theatrical production each year was very professional and its cast included many of the talented pupils that I started with at Wellingborough. I never really got to know them until the sixth form. Two productions that I went to see were outstanding. *The Fire Raisers*, a play by Max Frish, and *Criminal Proceedings, Including The Real Inspector Hound*, by Tom Stoppard. Sam Leadsom played Moon in *The Real Inspector Hound* alongside Rupert Higgins (Birdboot), Emma Hulmes (Lady Cyththia Muldoon) and Nick Cole (Major Magnus Muldoon.) These pupils were perfect examples of the type of all-round pupil Wellingborough was trying to produce. Each of them went on to be head of house in the Sixth form. Emma became the first ever Head Girl at Wellingborough. Emma eventually went on to Oxford and Rupert to Cambridge. Sam was a boarder and captained the rugby team; Rupert is now a barrister dealing with all aspects of property and commercial litigation with a large element of professional negligence work for Hardicke. Nick Cole is very senior at Oracle and Sam Leadsom produces Barclays Premier League World at IMG.I was lucky enough to join these "bright young things" as Head of Parkers House and as a school prefect.

I am painting a rosy picture of life at Wellingborough. Not everyone was a model pupil. There were scandals in the school, but these were minor compared with the world outside Wellingborough. The seedy side of Wellingborough revolved around The North End. This was where pupils went to smoke. It also happened to be the school urinals and toilet block, but this didn't seem to deter the smokers from hanging out here. The North End was next to Parkers House. This meant that everyone in Parkers House knew who the smokers were. They performed what we called The Walk of Shame across the quadrangle towards The North End, and as they did Jonnie Potter, Dick Smith and James Cousins and I all applauded. The smokers' Walk of Shame always caused a stir in Parkers House. It was a bit of daily theatre. The smokers would walk to The North End directly opposite the teachers as they walked to their common room. We could see all sides and would clap our hands at exactly the same time as a teacher and smoker were in eyesight of each other. The North End was also the location where fireworks in the form of rockets were let off from the windows, in the direction of the dinning hall, barely missing pupils in their path. It seemed to be at the root of all that was forbidden and anti-establishment.

A car once appeared in the centre of the dinning hall. It was owned by the art teacher Duncan Ellison and usually sat outside Platts House growing mould on the windows. It was never used and was slightly rusty. One morning, when school began, it had taken pride of place in the centre of the dining hall. It has been painted vibrantly and was multi-coloured on the outside, and full of plants and flowers on the inside. It had been mysteriously taken during the night and sabotaged by boarders. It looked better than it had ever done before.

These pranks were harmless fun in a school full of bright and creative people. The school was a cocoon on the edge of the town of Wellingborough where we were known locally as The Plum and had very little contact with the surrounding area. At lunchtime or after school, we were given permission to go down to town.

The town had been a pretty market centre that was sadly blighted with some awful developments such as the Arndale Centre in the late 1970s. Much of the town centre was developed during the 1970s, when the town grew dramatically, based on London "overspill". It looked a little tired and weary and the only reason we went to town was to go to the shops and cafés. The Wimpy in the Arndale was the height of luxury for us. That was until it was banned because too many pupils were being what was known as 'taxed' by the locals. Wellingborough was a boarding school and often, after school, pupils would go down town dressed in casual gear. The fashion at the time was to be a Casual. This style started on the terraces at football matches. 80s Casuals became a burgeoning culture, where all that mattered was having the latest trainers and continental sportswear, like Fila, Stone Island, Fiorucci, Pepe, Benetton, Sergio Tacchini and Ralph Lauren. The kids in our school obviously followed fashion and came from wealthy backgrounds, where they were able to buy the latest clothes. This was obvious to some of the locals in Wellingborough who 'taxed' the kids of their clothes, wallets and anything else of value. This once almost happened to me and my friends. We were accosted by two rather large guys in the town who demanded our money, as they were not interested in our two-piece charcoal grey suits. I wasn't prepared to give them any money and we legged it back to school before they could mug us.

There was a good music scene in the school and always lots of parties in peoples' houses. Pete Murphy, the vocalist of the rock group Bauhaus, lived in Wellingborough. Bauhaus were considered to be the first gothic rock group and there was a huge following in the school, because of their local connections. Their influence was seen in small pockets around school. It was cool to be a goth, with black dyed hair, black lips and black clothes. The school's big claim to cool fame was to have Richard Coles as a pupil. Richard formed The Communards with Jimmy Somerville in 1984, whilst I was at school. In three years the band had three top-ten hits, including *Don't Leave Me This Way*.

I loved the tradition and the fabric of the buildings at Wellingborough, but it was the eccentric teachers that made the place really special. Many of the teachers during my time at Wellingborough had been at the school for many decades. Every teacher had a nickname that was passed down from year to year. Mr Elbourne, who was my maths teacher, was called 'Weeble'. There wasn't a teacher more committed to the school than he. He ran the CCF, taught rugby and compiled computerised printouts for the inter-house athletics standards. In 1985 this was a rare thing to have, and he processed several thousand results for the benefit of the pupils. He was well liked, but every time he walked past, someone from somewhere would go "UH-UH" – the noise the computer makes in *Family Fortunes* if you get the answer wrong – which drove him nuts. Mr Gordon was known as 'The Bear'. He was a scary maths-master who liked to throw calculators out of the window and blackboard rubbers at pupils. Mr Lingfield, or 'Sweaty', was my history teacher. We found it highly amusing when we watched a video on twentieth-century history in his study. The VHS video had a remote connected to it and Mr Lingfield thought the only way to operate the video was to continually point it at the video player, which he held up in the air for the whole duration of the video. 'Bugsy' Burrell was the school chemistry teacher and one of the worst-dressed members of staff, adopting the tie outside the jumper look. Mr Ashworth, AKA 'Cherry', was the head of The CCF and wore a maroon red beret (hence his nickname) as he had been part of the parachute regiment before joining the school. 'Bendy' Butcher was the school vicar. Mr Nugent, affectionately known as 'Hairy', was the German teacher. 'Drunkie' Duncan was the art teacher and, as his name suggests, was not averse to the occasional tipple.

Out of this universe of stars, two teachers left the greatest impression on me. Mr Croft and Mr Flex ran the Classics Department. I still think of the multitude of voices that Mr Croft produced as he read Homer's *Odyssey* to us during lessons on the ancient world. He brought this story to life in a way that no other master could have done. His attempt at Penelope will live in my memory forever. Mr Flex inherited the nickname of 'Flogger' and a deep affection for the school from his father, who was the vicar of Great Doddington and served on the staff part-time during World War II. 'Flogger' Flex junior joined the school in 1951 and was one of its great servants. I had a huge affection for him, he loved sport and taught rugby and was president of the Old Wellingburian rugby club for many years.

As master for my Ancient History A-level, he brought the past alive. Gordon Whateley Flex was a gregarious person and his lessons were often riotous and out of control. He actively encouraged participation and we were often asked to read out loud. He was like an older version of Robin Williams in *Dead Poets Society*. He rarely got pissed off. That was until one day when Sean Chamberlain mentioned innocently, when doing some Roman history, how he loved Italian women, until they got older and then they got fat. To our bemusement Flogger grew incensed and quickly cut him down. What we did not realise was that Flogger had a deeply romantic side. He had been a typical bachelor schoolmaster until, at the age of forty eight, he decided to marry his beloved Lole, an Italian nurse whom he met at the Isebrook Hospital in Wellingborough. It wasn't poor Sean's fault – he could have never had known the secret that Flogger was nursing. He never really recovered from the dressing down that Flogger gave him that day. Flogger had a stock of bizarre stories about military life, ancient history and mysterious references to his Mafia contacts throughout Sicily.

One story was particularly vivid, and helped to build this man in our collective imaginations as we sat through his ancient history lessons. He told us about how his brother-in-law had rented him a holiday home for the summer. It was in Sicily, and Flogger became annoyed by the contant blasting from his next-door neighbour's stereo. He mentioned in passing to his brother-in-law that he was having trouble with his neighbour who was reluctant to turn his music down. Gordon's brother-in-law, who was reputed to have Mafia connections, paid the hapless neighbour a visit and told him politely that if he didn't turn it down, he would have his house blown up. We were enthralled, his anecdotes added to the "richness" of the man in our minds. He got me through my A-level, but the fun I had being taught by this remarkable person was far more rewarding than the qualification.

Flogger was well travelled and probably the first person that actively encouraged us to travel to see the places that we were studying. He brought them to life uniquely, with flair and humour. He had a disregard for the Japanese and felt that some of the best places of the ancient world were spoilt by Japanese tourists and the constant clicking of their cameras. He assumed that all his students were from very wealthy backgrounds. He always started a story by making reference to the motorcar that you might arrive in. It was either a Lincoln Zephyr (which was a mid-size, entry-level luxury car from the Lincoln division of the Ford Motor Company), a Mercedes or a Pontiac. I think he had a burning desire to own one of these cars; sadly, on a teacher's salary, it was probably never going to be possible.

One of the members of our ancient history class, Paul Hannah, passed his driving test at seventeen and his parents bought him a Porsche 944S to celebrate. He wrote this car off and was then given a BMW E30 325i Sport. One winter's day he wrote this car off as well, as I followed him to school in an old Austin Metro. I was the first to arrive on the scene and was able to pull him out of the car. He had lost control on the ice as he accelerated up a hill and hit a Cavalier coming the other way. Fortunately everyone survived the crash. In a strange twist, whilst we were in the ambulance being taken to the local hospital, we were hit by an oncoming car, so everybody had to wait for another ambulance to arrive before taking all those involved in the first car crash along with the shocked ambulance men from the first ambulance to hospital. Paul Hannah's next car was a 4X4. His parents gave him something a little less temptingly quick, and hopefully the rest of his driving career was uneventful.

I passed my driving test whilst I was at Wellingborough. My amazing dad waited in the park next to the school, so I could show off to my friends the morning I passed my test. I stood outside the car with the keys in my hand as my mates came out of lessons. This was the ultimate in street credibility, standing next to my Dad's car, which we were very proud of in 1987. Looking back I don't know whether I could have looked that cool standing outside a chocolate brown Volvo Estate. However, I felt like a god.

I loved Wellingborough, but it was all consuming and left little time for anything else. I loved going home to tell Mum and Dad all about the things we were doing, especially when it came to sport. At Wellingborough School I was able to develop my fervor for sport.

My two great loves were football and athletics, probably because I showed a natural aptitude towards them and because it gave me an opportunity to travel. Wellingborough had a strong fixture list that took us to schools all over the UK. It was exciting to travel on a coach to different schools, generally in and around London. These were some of the best soccer schools in the country, each set in their own grounds with magnificent buildings. This included Alleyn's in Dulwich, Westminster in the heart of central London next to Westminster Abbey and the Houses of Parliament, Highgate School in North London, next to the burial place of Marx in Highgate Cemetery, Charterhouse in Godalming and Aldenham in Elstree.

We travelled further afield, to places like Owestry in Shropshire and Repton in Derbyshire. These schools had unbelievable facilities. One of my favourite places was Kimbolton on the Cambridgeshire/ Northamptonshire Borders. This was set in the grounds of Kimbolton Castle, which was originally a medieval castle that had evolved into a stately palace. It was once the home of Henry VIII's first queen, Catherine of Aragon. As I visited these schools I got a true idea of how privileged I was to attend a public school and all that went with it. It was life changing, I was mixing with some of the most fortunate children in the country and I was part of one of the best public school teams in the country in 1985. Jarrad Isherwood, Steve Oakenfull, Pete Rowse and I were playing in the 1st XV in the firth year alongside fellow sixth formers. We were undefeated, having won eight of our eleven matches, and were regarded as one of the two teams of the year, according to George Chesterton, the schools' football writer for The Times.

One memorable fixture was in the Public Schools Six-a-Side tournament at Brentwood School in Essex. The night before the tournament our team stayed in accommodation close to Euston Station in London. We decided that it would be a good idea to experience the bright lights of the big city, and so the eve of a significant tournament was the first time that I drank a spirit. We got as far as a bar in Euston Station and Nick Tuckley, our captain who looked far older than us, went to the counter to buy Cinzano Red. There was something brave and daring about our captain striding up to a barman in the centre of the metropolis and ordering something that seemed forbidden, glamourous and deeply sophisticated. There couldn't have been a worse drink than this. It was disgusting and put me off spirits for life. A drinking session the night before our match seriously affected our accuracy, coordination and reaction times on the pitch at 10:30 a.m. against King's Chester, so much so that we lost the first match. We were a team that didn't lose and we were shocked to the core. We ended up group H runners up and so were entered into the plate competition. We got the alcohol out of our system and ended up winning the plate.

I never played in a side at school quite like this again. After O-levels, Jarrad Isherwood left and went on to have trials with professional clubs. He was the glue of the team and one of the best soccer players I ever had the chance to play with. Whilst Jarrad was a great player, he had a mullet like all footballers in those days. I'm sure he had it permed at the back and straight at the front. Our school team beat Repton and the whole school was awarded a half-day's holiday to celebrate the 1st XI triumph over the old enemy. This was a hugely significant event in the school's sporting history and one that we were very proud of.

It was through sport that I developed a passion for meeting people. In a short time I had gone from playing for Duston Magpies made up of children from my local area, to a team consisting of some of the most privileged kids in the country. One such teammate on the day that I played in a match for South England Public Schools was Obi Asika. He was the first and only son of Ajie Ukpabi Asika, an erudite scholar, university lecturer and ex-Administrator of Nigeria. Obi had attended the then-famous Ekulu Primary School, Enugu, in Nigeria, before attending Eton College. We couldn't have had more different educations and backgrounds, yet on the 5th March 1985, Obi and I played together in the same team for Southern Schools Under 16s. He later went on to run a record label (Storm Records) and did television shows. He was a club promoter, a DJ and a sports analyst on television.

Why did he stand out from a team that included players from Malvern, Westminster and Charterhouse and other leading public schools? The reason is very simple. Obi was from a country that I knew nothing about and he was a player who went on to follow his passion, which so many of us neglect. He captured my imagination and inspired me to look for friendships and take lessons from everyone I met.

The following year I was selected to play in the Southern Schools Trial which was held at Eton College on the 12th October 1986. The school was in a beautiful location, north of Windsor Castle. Eton is one of the original nine English public schools was a world apart from Wellingborough. On that day there were two sides selected to play each other which contained one Wellingburian, me, and four Etonians. What I could not have predicted was that four years later, Andy Lee and I, who played that day, would also go on to represent England Under 21s in Fontainebleau against the French Under 21s in Rugby Union. Andy was at Chigwell and one of the most natural sportsmen that I have ever met. He went on to play for many years for Saracens, and he and I sit alongside each other in an office over twenty years later.

Back in October 1986, I was given access to the inner sanctum that was Eton College. Eton is one of the most exclusive schools in the country. The uniform sets the tone. Boys wear a three-piece tail suit with a white shirt, the Eton collar, disposable ties and collar studs. The school is on the Thames near Windsor Castle, surrounded by beautiful grounds. I was amazed by the architecture of Eton College Chapel and the twenty-four houses that the boys lived in, but even more impressed by the fact that the sixth form boys were able to drink alcohol during lunch. Wellingborough was not the best public school in the country. In fact, friends of mine from neighbouring schools like Uppingham, Oundle, Stowe and Oakham would often taunt me, describing it as a fee-paying comprehensive. It was much more than this. It produced individuals that were well-rounded and better equipped to enter the normal world, and it introduced me to people and places I could never have had exposure to if I had remained in Old Duston.

I did try to keep up with old friends in Duston, but apart from attending The Boys' Brigade and playing soccer there was not much time to do anything else. I started to experience some resentment towards me from my old friends because of the school I went to. I have no idea why they resented me and I felt very hurt by some of the things that were happening to me in the place where I had grown up. One Friday night, I attempted to attend my old stomping ground, the local youth club in St Andrews Methodist Church. Before I had a chance to have a drink or meet anyone, the local lads chased me out of the door with a view to kicking my head in. They didn't catch me but I ran scared up Cotsworld Avenue, pursued by kids who only a few years before were friends at Millway. "What comes around goes around." I remember exactly who my tormentors were and some years later I would spot them at Franklin Gardens on the terraces supporting the Saints team and chanting my name. You can imagine the frisson of pleasure I experienced in seeing people who had made my life a misery shouting my name in support rather than as part of a taunt.

Their behaviour didn't stop me wanting to stay friends with the boys I had grown up with. Soccer provided me with a platform to play with Mickey Dillon, Neil Taylor, Andy Burrows and Ashley Starmer, who were the stars of Duston football. I held them in huge admiration because they had a very strong work ethic and tirelessly worked on their core skills because they wanted to be professional footballers. We were all selected to play in the Midland Youth Counties Youth Competition, which was held at Wellingborough School. This is the first time they had seen my school it was very odd to be on the 1st XV Pitch with them. They were good footballers and the cream of Northampton Youth at the time. I did very well to be selected to this squad, and the team ended up coming third place to Shropshire and Birmingham.

At the same time as participating in soccer I also represented the County Under 16s on the wing at rugby with Rob Jones, the late Richard Brookes and Jim Cousins from Wellingborough School. I ended up playing for Northampton Saints Youth team during the school holidays, which was the senior club in the county and the club where I had been a ball boy. I was seventeen years old and playing rugby for the Saints Youth in my school holidays and just a few months later I was selected to play for Northamptonshire in the Midland Counties Youth Championship at Irthlingborough Diamonds Football Ground. This fixture was on the eve of my A-level exams on Sunday 26th April 1987. I made a conscious decision after this game that rugby was the sport that I wanted to pursue. One of the big attractions was the social scene that unfolded after the game had been played. Rugby people hung around to drink and went out with each other afterwards. This was very different from football. I loved football and still do, but my heart had been won by rugby and the community that went with the sport. This turned out to be one of the best decisions that I ever made.

I left Wellingborough in the summer of 1987 with four A-levels. Wellingbrough School provided me with the tools that society judges as the prerequisites for future success. However, my school also helped me gain an understanding about people that I now feel was the most valuable part of my education. Wellingborough gave me the academic, cultural and sporting understanding that was part of their mission statement, but I felt that nothing could ever truly educate me in the way that travel could. I needed to find a vehicle that would take me to West Africa to see first hand the world that Obi came from. Sport provided this in a way that I could never have imagined.

Chapter 2

Naked torsos are taboo

Up until now Rugby had taken a back seat and been a sport that we only played in the Lent term at Wellingborough. The grounds of the school were magnificent, and during the soccer and cricket term you couldn't have played on a better surface. Harry Neal, the groundsman, was an obsessive cricket fan. He would periodically insist on calling off rugby fixtures to protect the surfaces for the cricket season. Northamptonshire Cricket Club used to play one fixture a year on the cricket square, which was known as "The Grove". In August 1986, I watched Ian Botham hit six sixes and score 175 runs not out for Somerset against a side that included Alan Lamb.

My rugby initiation at school and beyond was not particularly auspicious, but epitomised a sport made for all shapes and sizes and all social classes. Frank Hawtin, our local village shop owner, recruited me to the Men's Own Rugby Club in the village of Ashton. The club was my introduction to senior rugby and regularly ran three senior sides and a Colts side, which I played for in the school holidays before playing for Saints Youth. I loved playing for the Colts with some old mates from Duston that I used to play soccer with. Rugby then was a strictly amateur sport. You paid five pounds, known as "subs", to play and drink until the early hours with people who were passionate about the sport and everything it gave them. On a Saturday night in Ashton after a game it didn't matter what you did for a living – people drank at the bar and bonded together through their passion for the sport. People looked after each other at clubs like the Men's Own. Rugby was more than just a sport for them. It represented a way of life. Families joined the boys at the club for social gatherings. Children ran around scrounging change from the pockets of the players to buy

Refreshers, crisps and Coca Cola. The players would always wear a blazer and tie after the game with the clubs crest emblazoned on the front of it. You knew your place. You respected the 1st Team Players. They were kings of their hallowed turf and you aspired to their lifestyle. Every Saturday night there would be a function and the bar would be open as long as there were people there to drink. There was always an army of volunteers who would drum up great after-match meals on a minuscule budget and everyone would be fed before they ventured into town for a curry or a kebab. The chairman, Jim Atwood, was afforded the reverence that he deserved by everybody at the club. He dedicated his life to Men's Own.

The end-of-season dinners were deeply memorable. They represented a mixture of tradition and bawdy good fun with loyal toasts, awards and a couple of local strippers thrown in for good measure. If one could criticise Wellingborough School, it could be because it didn't really prepare you for a Men's Own end of season dinner. The clubhouse would be packed with trestle tables covered with cheap tablecloths that came in big rolls. The dinner was always oversubscribed by past and present players in search of a great piss-up. The evening would start in quite an orderly way, but very quickly disintegrate into a food fight, and no-one ever left early because the highlight was not the awards: it was the sight of a bit of naked flesh in the form of the local ladies of the night. I never knew how I got back from the clubhouse, which was in the village of Aston, miles from Northampton, but there was always someone to help me home. It was this club that provided me with my first run-out at Franklin's Gardens, the home of the Northampton Saints Rugby Club, in the Final of the Oceanic Cup in 1986. It was the year before I was due to leave school.

Northampton was a rugby town and Franklins Gardens was its hallowed turf. I shouldn't really have been in the final XV. It was slightly unfair on some of the players that had played all season. I had just been drafted in with another player called Andy Collier. The team was made up of many of the boys that I knew from my Duston days, largely because Frank Hawtin (or "the Dungeon Master" as he was affectionately known, because of his similarity to the character in the animated television series *Dungeons & Dragons*) had recruited them. Frank ran the local butcher and convenience store in the village of Old Duston. He was a rugby fanatic and talent-spotted the youths who visited his shop, recruiting players like Josh Johal, Joe Hood and John Tyrell. Most of the players had not gone to private school. In fact, the players who went to Duston Upper School in the 1980s had seen rugby cut from the curriculum. Players had to go elsewhere to clubs like Men's Own to follow the passion they developed because of their teacher Mr Townsend at Millway Middle School. Mr Townsend left Millway to join a local prep school called Spratton Hall. He was, for many, the inspiration at Millway. He encouraged people to want to continue playing rugby, even though Duston Upper had let them down. Mr Townsend was a great teacher; all these years later, he now has his own Facebook appreciation page set up by grateful pupils.

I was oblivious to the significance of my first run out at Franklin Gardens and how it would go on to shape the rest of my life. It was the first time that I had played in front of a large crowd and gone on to win silverware. I can remember the night as if it was yesterday. I was under floodlights at the same ground where I had been a ball boy as a kid with Snowie. Snowie represented the heart of the Saints for me in those days. If I wanted some extra pocket money then I would knock on his door and he would give me my duties. Even now I can feel the anticipation of this first big game and desperately not wanting to let anyone down. That night I subconsciously registered something that I was keen to repeat. I was hooked. To quote the *Chronicle and Echo*, "the star that night was the flamboyant French style fullback Andy Collier, scoring the winning try for the Men's Own."

I had made my first team debut for Northampton Saints at the tender age of eighteen, just six months after leaving Wellingborough School. I was oblivious to the significance of this event. Northampton Saints was a club founded in 1880 that had been one of the giants of the game. It had sadly fallen upon tough times, languishing at the bottom of the second division. The idea of a league system first came to fruition in 1987 after decades of the RFU rejecting calls for a league. It had been felt that a league encouraged foul play and professionalism, and instead preferred friendly matches like the EDF Energy Cup, the County Cups and the County Championships. However, a league was finally formed with the advent of the Courage Leagues in 1987. 108 divisions were organised, covering more than 1000 clubs.

My selection to play for the Saints was low key. The fixture secretary at the time, the legendary RB Taylor, invited me to play after Northampton had just lost to Llanelli on the 5th December 1987. Bob was a former England and British Lions rugby player and a legend from Northampton's rich rugby past. He was an uncompromising flanker who captained England in one of his 16 caps. "Piggy" Powell, a former Saints coach, captain, England and Lions Player, had seen me playing for the youth team and mentioned to him that I was worth a punt. I was totally unaware of the pedigree of both these men. In fact, I couldn't name one England player at the time. My rugby knowledge extended to the people I was playing with and no further. Bob approached me, beer in hand, in the Sturtridge Pavilion in Franklin's Gardens. Bob wasn't a man of words and cut to the chase immediately: "We were wondering whether you might like to play for the 1st XV next Saturday as Frank Packman got injured today." I thanked him and duly accepted and then proceeded to get drunk, which was the way in those days – "win or lose on the booze".

It was only when I was travelling back on the 52 bus from Northampton to Old Duston that I realised the honour that I had just been paid. The headline in the *Chronicle and Echo* proclaimed, "Saints opt for powerhouse Harvey", and the programme notes read, "Frank Packman is replaced in the Saints side today by a man who has been playing in the Youth Side. I hope he can make the transition successfully." That Saturday I played against a strong London Irish side that boasted Hugo Macneil, the Irish fullback. I was a bag of nerves before the game, which was not helped by the fact that I could not remember any of the back moves. Paul Larkin, my fly-half, walked me onto Franklin's Gardens before the game. Now you would call it visualisation – the mental rehearsal you do before the game to improve your performance, which is part of the larger science of sports psychology. We didn't know anything about sports psychology or visualisation in 1987, it was just a time-honoured tradition that a senior player would walk you on to the pitch before your first ever game for the club and relaxed your nerves by pointing out what it would be like when the ground was full. In those days the main stand was wooden and rocked when the crowd got going. Playing on the pitch with a large crowd in full throat was a bit like being in the hull of a wooden boat being shaken by a storm. Directly opposite was the Gordon Terrace, which was the place to be if you wanted to savour the atmosphere of Franklin Gardens. Despite some poor years Northampton still got a good crowd. This was what I was looking forward to more than anything – performing on a big stage in the town where I grew up. Nothing could get much better than this.

My chance at Northampton Saints had come at a time when I was doing a management development program for Natwest Bank. My role within the bank was on the counter as a cashier. I had taken the job as a fall back to not being able to get a university place. I knew it wasn't for me within two days of entering the doors of The Drapery in Northampton. Dad told me that I should give it more time. Sadly, I only lasted a few months and it was obvious once I had been picked for Northampton Saints that my days were numbered at the bank. I couldn't understand why people with better A-level results than me would not go to university, instead opting for the safety of the bank. I led a personal crusade to try and change a few minds but without much success. This was a time when a job at a bank was considered to be a job for life. The nail in the coffin for my career in retail banking was when the head cashier asked me to wear a Father Christmas hat whilst serving customers. I have sticky-out ears, and a Father Christmas hat was not very becoming for a young man with sticky-out ears. I wrote the resignation letter and handed it to my boss. He accepted and I was released from my shackles. I sprinted home that night and vowed that I would concentrate on rugby before going off to university.

That first encounter for Northampton Saints seemed like a very natural thing for me to be doing. I had no delusions of grandeur, but I had dreamt of playing for the Saints from when I was a ball boy with Martin Lee at Millway School. Snowie looked after us and gave us pocket money for helping out at the club. Jacko Page was the player I wanted to be more than any other when watching the games in the 1970s, He played for England between 1971 and 1975, winning 5 caps. He was the star scrum-half at the heart of all the action. I had no real background in rugby. I had only played for Men's Own, Saints Youth and the School XV. In the context of the modern game my progression would have been impossible. I did possess raw pace and was very powerful; these strengths made up for my deficiencies. I couldn't catch a high ball and my passing off the left hand was hit-and-miss. I can't believe that I got so far in such a short space of time, but I think that it was meant to be.

Having a chance to playing for the 1st Team was amazing, but it was some months before at Cut Throat Lane, the home of Wellingborough RFC, that something happened that was to change my life forever. A trial for the East Midlands Under 19s rugby team went very well and afterwards in the clubhouse we were told that one of the squad of players assembled that day would go on and represent England Under 19s on a tour of Italy. I decided that I would be that player. I had no reason to think that I had a special right to take this place in the same way that I had felt about playing for Saints. I had no experience of representative rugby but I did have natural speed and a passion to succeed. Spurred on by the promise of a free trip to Italy, I was determined to be the one that was chosen. I have never worked so hard for anything in my life as I did to get on that tour of Italy. It was like a modern day *X Factor* for the best Under 19s rugby players in England. It all started with the East Midlands, who would play Leicestershire, Warwickshire and counties such as Nottinghamshire, Lincolnshire and Derbyshire. At the end of every match each player would be marked out of ten. These scores would be added up over the course of five games and players were then invited to a Midland Trial, which was made up of the best players from all the teams that had just played against each another. Miraculously, I did not put a foot wrong in these games and never got less than 9/10 in any of them. The same applied to the divisional trials where my team played the North, the South West and London. After these games, the selectors chose the best players in the country to attend an England Colts training weekend at Birmingham Rugby Club.

This is when it became serious and, like *X Factor*, over a series of weekends the players met until the very best players were invited to a final weekend at Loughborough University, to play against the Freshers XV. The highlight of this stage was being awarded a V-neck acrylic grey sweater for getting into the final squad. It sported an England rose with the immortal word "Squad" embroidered below it. The Loughborough weekend in March 1988 was the make-or-break weekend, when the selectors told you whether you would go to Italy or not and awarded you your stash, which at the time seemed like gold dust. The stash was purple Nike tracksuits. Everyone wanted to wear that purple tracksuit. I did get picked in that final squad, which I consider to be one of my greatest achievements. I will never forget hearing my name being called out. I worked very hard to put myself in a position to be chosen for England Colts Squad. The mountain that I had to climb to achieve my goal was huge. It had taken five years at Wellingborough to teach me that anything is possible, as long as you apply yourself. The task of being in the bottom academic sets in 1982 and then ending up with four A-levels, Head of Parkers House and Victor Ludorum by 1987 was the same as the task I was presented with at Cut Throat Lane.

Keith Picton gave me an opportunity and I just needed to break down, game by game, how I was going to meet his expectations. I could never look further than each game or each training session because the task was enormous. I concentrated on the things that I could influence, not the things I couldn't. I didn't worry about the opposition or my lack of skills. I just honed the raw qualities that I had and someone gave me a chance. This was the chance to enter the world of elite sport with some of the players who would eventually go on to win the Rugby World Cup in 2003.

One such player was Neil Back, born in January 1969, just over a month before me. He personified the dedication that you needed to succeed. He was my age, but had a determination that was different to any of the players that I had played 1st XV rugby with up until then. His work rate in the games leading up to the tour was extraordinary. In fitness tests, he was the fittest member of the England squad and was someone I looked up to and spent a lot of time with. We were both odd ones out. I had no rugby pedigree, and Backy was probably one of the only members of the squad who had not attended a public school. Schools rugby was very much about what type of school you had attended, and Backy was very resentful of this and wanted to prove everyone wrong. Colts was different. The selection process was open to any player. I had come from obscurity and a school that did not play rugby as its first sport, and was able to get on the plane with Backy to Italy.

He taught me simple skills that I should have learnt at a very early age, such as switching the ball. Neil was very competitive in nature and refused to compromise. He once played against a prop for the Midlands Colts v the RAF who kept dropping the scrums. Backy warned him that if he did it again then he would dislocate his arm. The prop repeated his antics once more and left the field with his arm in a sling. We couldn't have been more different but I had huge respect for him. He knew what he wanted. He had a reason for being that set him apart from the rest of us. The rest of us had goals and objectives, but he had purpose.

Failure to Neil Back was not achieving his long-term purpose, which was to be the best player in his position in the world. He had experienced repeated setbacks and failures, even at the tender age of nineteen; however, these were all short term. He was a different kind of sportsman to the people I had met before. Jarrad Isherwood had his talent, but he didn't have anything like the same level of dedication or desire to achieve. He was the best player and the first person that the selectors would have picked for their squad. I, on the other hand, was just happy to be in the company of the other players. Neil Back had dedicated his life to reaching this moment, he had already represented England at Under 18s level and this was one more step along his path to play for England and the British Lions. I was just pleased to be going to Italy, the country I had spent two years of my life studying at Ancient History A-level with Flogger Flex. This was a chance to meet people and travel and I used sport as my vehicle. Neil Back was one of the first people that I met who was totally driven and relentless in the pursuit of excellence, but for Neil and me the dream of playing rugby for England Colts nearly ended before it began.

The England Colts Tour of Italy lasted one week and consisted of two games.

We were based in the town of Prato in Tuscany. Prato is now the centre for the slow food movement, with many local culinary specialties, including *cantucci*, a type of biscotti, sold by local bakers. This was the first international rugby tour that I had been on and there was a certain degree of trepidation about what to expect. I had got to know many of the players over the weekends that we had spent together. We were a mixed bag of people from all walks of life, from all over England but with one common vision – to represent our country as the best players of our age in the country at Under 19s level.

In 1988 Rugby was strictly amateur, and part of touring included getting to know the country you were visiting as well as being shown places that you would not ordinarily be given access to. During our stay we were invited to play a Presidents XV on the Wednesday before the main international. There seemed nothing strange in this, although today you wouldn't want to risk that we were able to go out drinking after the match, three days before the international. You wouldn't have imagined that Neil Back and I would have been walking around the Bacchino fountain in Prato dressed in number ones at 11:00 p.m. at night having had a skinful of beers. We must have been the worse for wear because a local policeman reminded us that in Italy they carry guns and kindly escorted us back to the hotel, where the England Colts management team was awaiting our arrival in the reception of the The Art Hotel Milano.

Neil and I were both summoned to the manager's room the following morning to be informed that our behaviour was unacceptable. I think I could have very easily lost my place in the International if Backy had not been involved, but they did not want to lose their secret weapon in the back row so we were let off. That day was a rest day and we were told that we were going to visit Florence and the Leonardo di Vinci Museum.

For a lot of the players the thought of visiting a museum was not high on their list of priorities. For many of us this was the first trip abroad away from our parents and staying at a hotel where MTV was playing 24 hours a day seemed more appealing than traipsing around a dusty museum. It seems odd that watching music videos all day long would be more appealing than the opportunity to visit Florence. I was clearly in the minority, I was desperate to see Florence and explore the Museum at Vinci. The whole essence of why I had trained so hard to get picked for the England Colts side was so I could travel. I hadn't any idea of the importance of Florence in history and the people that had been part of its culture. My basic knowledge at the time extended to knowing Michelangelo's *David* from the General Studies A-level I had taken at Wellingborough. I couldn't wait to get my education first hand by experiencing the city for myself.

Florence was full of beauty, grandeur and history, and memorable for a story that involved Neil Back. Some years later I was reading Backy's autobiography, called *Size Doesn't Matter: My Rugby Life*. In the book, Backy recalls that he decks me in the Vatican City's Sistine Chapel. He said it was one of the best punches he had ever thrown. The single blow was delivered because I accused Jason Hoad, our teammate, of dropping my camera on the floor in the chapel, having left it precariously on a church pew. Imagine my surprise upon reading this, not because the story of the punch wasn't accurate, but the Sistine Chapel is in The Vatican City, and the one where he knocked me out in was the Basilica di Santa Maria del Fiore, the cathedral church (Duomo) of Florence. This all happened the day after I had been drinking with him and walking around a fountain. Such was the strength of our relationship. I can only imagine that over the many years of rugby he had forgotten where he was on tour due to too many blows to the head.

It was at the Stadio Comunale di Prato on Saturday 19th March 1988 that I first pulled on an England rugby shirt and sang the National anthem. There was something very symbolic about wearing the white shirt with the red rose of England emblazoned upon it. This was the time when England shirts were all white and the red rose was the only badge embroidered on your chest. The ground was a football stadium and the Italian rugby federation had done a great job promoting the game. The stands were full and there was a real atmosphere. As we entered the changing room, there were the shirts on the coat pegs, together with the shorts and England socks. Graham Smith our coach was a passionate Cumbrian man and articulated the importance of this moment. Howard Lamb, our captain, set the right tone, having played at various England Levels before this match. We had been together, as a squad, for a few months and were part of an elite group of players in England at Under 19s level. We were reminded of how many players had taken part at county level, divisional level and had made the final trial but not got this far. There was one player, Dave Sims (a second row for Gloucester, who had not been selected to play Loughborough Freshers because he had been dropped out of the squad at Moseley), who we all thought of at this moment. He did eventually go on to play for England on the Tour from Hell, where he made three appearances.

The changing rooms were underground and you had a heightened sense of anticipation when you came through a tunnel out of the darkness onto the pitch. You emerged from the dark tunnel into the white glare of the pitch with your teammates around you and the roar of the crowd. It was surreal. This was the first time that I was to sing the national anthem in front of a foreign crowd and I loved it. It was a moment that I had worked very hard for and to finally get the opportunity to play for my country was magical beyond words.

Before the game we, were asked to write about what being selected to play in the game meant to us on a flip chart in the changing rooms. I wrote, "Every man should make his niche in history, this is my contribution." This was a quote from Solon that I remembered from my Ancient History A-level. The ancient Greeks considered Solon to be one of the Seven Wise Men. He was a poet, politician and law maker, and helped to found democracy in Athens. You can imagine the reception that my comment got from the other players who were less philosophical in their feeling for this game. The England Colts team was made up of men from all walks of life. I had turned to Flogger Flex for inspiration but I doubt many of those players would have had the pleasure to study under such a man. We had a bludgeoning pack made up of some nasty forwards. Neil Back, Neil Ashurst, and Rob Hardwick are the three players that I would single out. I have spoken about Backie, he had a ruthless streak in him which you saw on the pitch when he was destroying his opposite man. Neil Ashurst seemed to have no pain barrier, he came from a rugby league background and was hard as nails; and then there was Rob Hardwick, straight from Coundon Court Comprehensive and probably one of the most uncompromising prop forwards you could ever meet. He ended up playing rugby for England and had a professional career spanning 19 years from its beginning in Coventry in 1987 until it finished at London Irish in 2006. Another of those players was Lee Rick of Rotherham. His trip to Italy had been difficult because most of the meals were pasta based and Lee had specified right from the start of the trip that he refused to "eat any of that foreign muck." Instead, he would only eat steak and chips. England Colts was made up of a hard set of boys who were picked because they were the best in their positions at the time in the country. The Italian side could not live with the pace of our team and we destroyed their forwards. Our backs had sublime skills and in Jason Hoad we had one of the best kickers of his age in the country. I was part of a team that would be together for only a short three-match period, but the memories I have of them are vivid and the team we created that day in Prato was indestructible.

ach took different souvenirs home from our trip to Italy. For me, it represented the culmination of months of hard work. Before that tour I could not have imagined running out for my country as I did that day in Prato. I had come a long way from Cut Throat Lane and can still remember the words that Keith Picton uttered that day. I was indeed that one player from the East Midlands that went on to play in the starting XV, and this opened my eyes to a world that I wanted more of. Returning victorious from Italy with England Colts was a bit of an anti climax. It wasn't immediately life changing and it didn't affect the way people treated me by any stretch of the imagination. In fact, I started work at the Danes Camp Leisure Centre as a lifeguard on the Monday morning after I returned. It was very much back to life as it had always been. It was as if Prato and Italy had been a strange dream. Rugby was low profile even in the rugby town of Northampton and I settled down into every day life.

It was deeply fashionable at the time to carry a filofax, which was a leather bound, six-ring loose-leaf binder system carried by yuppies in the early 1980s. The term yuppie (short for "young urban professional" or "young upwardly-mobile professional") was only bestowed upon a relatively small group of people in Northamptonshire and by the time I got to own a filofax, they were being given out by Barclays Bank and were made of PVC. I loved my filofax and still have it today – a token of all I was trying so hard to achieve in terms of what it represented in my mind of success and power.

The first time I appeared on television was in the next game of the England Colts v Wales Youth, at the Gnoll Ground, Neath on Saturday 9th April 1988. For some odd reason, *BBC Rugby Special* had decided to cover the match in Wales and it was then shown on BBC2 on Sunday afternoon. This was the match that launched my career because I scored a hat trick. Phil Bennett, who was part of the BBC Wales commentary team, described me as a player for the future. It doesn't get much better than this, when a sporting icon singles you out on national television. Phil Bennett made eight Test appearances for the British Lions, whom he captained in New Zealand in 1977 (only the second Welsh player to have led the Lions) and 29 Welsh Senior Caps (8 as Captain). The thing that I remember him most for was being part of the most famous try of all time for the Barbarians against the All-Blacks in 1973. It was also the humility of the man that most resonated with me when I met him. He had achieved every level the sport had to offer and yet had an unassuming nature. I was privileged to be in his company and listened his words of wisdom.

I discussed his humility and kindness with one of my coaches at the time and his response was simply, if you are that good you don't need to prove anything to anyone. The name Phil Bennett was written in folklore in Wales, with other outside-halves such as Barry John, Jonathan Davies, Cliff Morgan and Cliff Jones. I was nineteen years old and couldn't believe that I was meeting people who had traits that I admired and wanted to emulate. Phil Bennett was the first true legend that I had met, but looking back I didn't have the presence of mind to realise the importance of that meeting. I did not understand the significance of that meeting because I didn't understand his standing in rugby. My lack of education in rugby let me down. I knew very few players and had watched very little rugby. If I could have that time again, I would ask him many more questions. I would give anything to have the opportunity to talk to a man that I now know commands the utmost respect within the rugby world. Despite the failure of this meeting in one sense, it ignited my fascination for the psychology of success and what made Phil Bennett and others like him go on to achieve greatness.

My mum and dad saw the game on *Rugby Special*. I phoned them on the way back from Neath on a pay phone, at Birmingham New Street Station and they were so excited. We were not a rugby family, so it was unusual for them to watch *Rugby Special* – they must have been waiting to watch *Antiques Roadshow* or *Songs of Praise* and stumbled across their son running down the wing for England Colts. They were so proud, and this lifted my mum at a time when her health was poor.

It was the first time that my name had appeared in headlines in the national sporting press. I happened to notice my surname on the back page of the *Daily Express*, which was being read by a rather cute passenger called Jo Tyer; needless to say I used my short-lived notoriety to try to chat her up. I took the name-tag off my kit bag, which had my full name and address (and more importantly telephone number) on it, and tucked it inside one of the papers that I had been reading. I handed it to her when I got off, hoping that she would contact me. Sadly, not even headlines in the *Times*, *Observer* and *Express* were good enough to win this Berkhamsted girl over.

The last game in the series was against the French Juniors Team at Bristol. The vanquished side was sadly not the French. This was unexpected given the strength of our side and the fact that we were on home soil. It was also very sad because we had set ourselves extraordinary high standards and we felt like we had let our coaches down that day. This was the point when I developed a dislike for the age-old tradition of rooming a back with a forward as part of the team bonding before an international.

I had the misfortune the night before the French International of sharing with Peter Walton. He was a bullock of a man, a farmer's son who played for Alnwick RFC. Alnwick was in the heart of Northumberland, on the border of England and Scotland. He was another forward in the bludgeoning pack we had that year. Peter could have played for both England and Scotland because he was educated at Merchiston Castle School, one of the leading Boys' Schools in Edinburgh. This brute of a man was not the sort of person you wanted to spend the night with prior to an International. In your pre-match manual there was a reference to getting a good night's sleep, but no reference to listening to snoring all night long. I did manage to check myself into another room rather than spend the night with Sleeping Beauty, who was totally oblivious to his nighttime behaviour. Peter eventually decided, like many players who had dual nationality, that the lure of international rugby was so attractive that he decided to play for Scotland rather than England. He ended up winning 24 caps playing in the back-row for the Scottish Rugby Union side between 1994 and 2000, and played club rugby with me at Northampton Saints and then eventually Newcastle Falcons before he was forced to retire due to injury in June 2000. Another player who played rugby in that England Colts side went on to do the same. This was Andy Reed, who was born in Cornwall but had Scottish grandparents and a mother who was born in Edinburgh.

We departed that weekend knowing that we would never play together again. It seemed very odd given the hard work that had gone in from Graham Smith and his team to put us together. This is rugby – there is not much room for sentiment. However, I will always think fondly of this time and the players that I was lucky enough to play with under Howard Lamb's captaincy.

Returning from England Colts duty to Northampton was a very easy transition. The sport of Rugby Union was strictly amateur and the players played for their love of the sport not for the financial rewards. I had begun my career during a golden period of rugby. There was no incentive other than the incredible camaraderie and the occasional perk like a beer token after the match – but you would have to pay extra for the packet of crisps and the pickled eggs that came with it. Saints consisted of people with a passion for the sport and who were willing to put a serious amount of time in for no financial reward. The players were strictly amateur, running careers alongside their sport. This meant that they were only truly accountable to themselves. It was up to them whether they performed or not and the club was made up of players who largely lived in the county.

In 1987 support for the club was still strong, despite dwindling fan numbers. The club was amateur in every way. Off the field it was run by former players who cared deeply about their club but were simultaneously holding down careers and caring for families. The president of the club was Don White, probably the greatest ever Saintsman for four-and-a-half decades and a totemic figure at Franklin's Gardens, as a player, captain, coach, administrator and president. He made his Saints debut as a sixteen-year-old schoolboy in February 1943. It was an inauspicious start to a glorious career that spanned eighteen years, 448 appearances (placing him second in the all-time list), 116 tries and 930 points as well as 14 England caps. He was captain of the Saints in 1949/50 with the team that would go on to dominate English rugby for a decade with other rugby legends – Ron Jacobs, Jeff Butterfield and Dickie Jeeps. Don was one of the very first men that I met in the changing room after my first appearance and someone who I respected for his achievements as a rugby player and his ability to run a successful business. He was born in Earls Barton, the Northamptonshire village that was home to his family shoe business for which he worked all his life. He was Managing Director and Chairman. I had met him as a boy because one of my great friends, Richard Smith, lived in the village and Don was often discussed at the Smith's breakfast table. He was old school and his aura reflected that of a man who had spent most of his life achieving. He was commanding; when he spoke, people listened. Sadly, unbeknown to me his world was about to change, along with the other committee men that had served so proudly for so long at the club.

There is an expression which is "no man is bigger than the club." If there was anyone who might dispel this myth then it was Don White. He was a giant of our local community. However, on July 6th 1988, his tenure at the club came to an end when a gang of seven local business men displaced Don and the committee at Northampton Rugby Club. These seven men could not match Don White in terms of his rugby calibre; but their intention was to try to make the Saints great again.

I had been asked to attend this meeting of the great and good of rugby in Northamptonshire by Jon Raphael, a charismatic local doctor and ex-player. I attended the meeting out of fascination rather than any understanding of the implications of this night in the history of Rugby Union in England. That night the Sturtridge Pavilion was packed to the rafters for this Extraordinary General Meeting. The seats in the room were occupied by members of the club who probably attended most AGMs. In 1988 people attended these meetings in blazers and ties, and there was an air of anticipation and expectancy amongst the people who attended. I stood at the back and watched proceedings unfold. The amateur committee was overthrown by a very professional group of businessmen who wanted to revive the club. Murray Holmes, one of the gang of seven, addressed the hoard that night. It was like Mark Antony's funeral speech in *Julius Caesar*, when he swayed the crowd. 1987 was a pivotal year for Northampton Saints. The advent of the league structure in 1987 and the decision to not have relegation from the second division was crucial. That night the actions of those seven men ensured that the club would never slip away and was to remain alongside Leicester as one of the forces of English Rugby in the Midlands. Fortuitously, this momentous event occurred right at the start of my career. Northampton realised that to become successful they had to take a more professional approach to the running of the club. Don White became a victim at that Extraordinary Meeting at Franklin's Gardens, but even he could not have predicted how his sport was to change within a very short period of time.

Chapter 3

Start of life in the black green and gold

As a young player I was oblivious to the fact that many of the players I had made my debut with were demotivated and seeking change. Later in life I realised that change is inevitable and you have to learn to adapt to it. Sadly, Northampton Saints had not been a club that liked change. However, with the advent of the league structure and the installment of the new committee, there was a new sense of hope that Northampton could become a force in rugby once again. Northampton town loved rugby. The Northampton faithful were entirely egalitarian. Whether you were a worker in one of the shoe factories or you were from the landed gentry, everyone loved the sport for what it gave the town. Even when Northampton was at the bottom of the second division, diehard crowds would be present to support their team.

One of the first acts of the new committee was to remove the committee room in the Sturtridge Pavilion. It was felt that this small room was elitist and represented a bygone era. It was restricted to use of the committee members (those that ran the club) for meetings and for entertaining visiting committee members on match days. Many clubs had these sorts of rooms in 1987 and they were traditionally an area where the players were forbidden access.

The "them and us" culture was alive and well. Whilst the current players respected the former players who formed part of the new committee, we felt that they were no longer great athletes – just old men basking in their former glory. I always thought that it was very sad that once-great players were destined to languish on the sidelines of a world that they had once been the epicenter of. During their playing careers they would have experienced the adulation of the crowd, and retiring from the game must have been difficult, However, the prospect of becoming a committee man was one that filled me with dread, and seeing the faces of those that were removed from office that night in Franklin Gardens was enough to put you off ever taking office, however much good you knew you were doing for the club.

The removal of the committee room was received well by members and players alike. After the match, as players we were encouraged by the new breed of committee member to go and drink in the members bar because this is where they would be after a game. This bar was typical of any rugby club of its type. It boasted a trophy cabinet, with a lack of silverware in 1988, faded team photographs going back decades and, of course, international shirts in frames donated by players. There was also an area made up of photographs of all the past internationals of the club. This became the place to drink after the game, and this brave new era created an atmosphere of openness and egalitarianism. The irony is that when a new stand was erected in 2000, a directors' box was created. It took twelve years for the new guard to transform into the establishment.

I learnt an important lesson that night at Franklins Gardens when the old guard were overthrown, which was never to rest on your laurels. Northampton Rugby Club had been founded in 1880 and many players would pass through it enjoying their unique experiences. However, all they were doing were holding a baton for future generations and no-one had a divine right to think otherwise. It was my intention to enjoy the club for as long as I was fortunate enough to be able to wear the club colours. It was Northampton Saints that made me who I am today and provided the opportunities for many incredible experiences and took me on journeys that I could never have imagined. My careers officer at Wellingborough School, a slightly shabbily dressed chemistry teacher called Bugsy Burrell, could not have prepared me for the career that I was about to embark on a the tender age of nineteen.

Rugby was still strictly amateur and I decided that I should pursue a university education, with a view to furthering my career prospects. I decided to go to Trent Polytechnic, to pursue a vocational course in Urban Estate Surveying. I chose the vocational route because I wanted a course that related to the specific trade of becoming a chartered surveyor. I only picked this course because my friend Andy Collier was training to be a surveyor whilst working for Berry Brothers in Northampton, He drove a company car and had an All Star petrol card, which at the time seemed so attractive that I thought that is what I would like to do. Some of the best rugby players in the country including Rob Andrew, Gavin Hastings, Marcus Rose and Andy Harriman were chartered surveyors. This career and rugby seemed to go hand in hand in 1988.

It was the education I gained through rugby that was to lay the foundations for the rest of my life. I didn't know this at the time and, having just come fresh out of Wellingborough, I still thought that sport was a hobby and my career should come first. I was never faced with a decision that many of the young rugby players of today are faced with. Rugby was amateur and we played it because we loved it. A full-time career in sport was never a consideration and I thank my lucky stars for that. There was value in the fact that the sport was amateur. The joy of participation and personal friendships were rewards in their own rights. Sadly, within a few years, this ethos was to be eroded, dismantling the very fabric of the sport and what it stood for. I am pleased to have experienced the last few years when the sport was still amateur. This quickly changed and it was impossible to predict what was just around the corner for the last major sport in the UK to succumb to professionalism. The changes were so quick that you needed to be able to adapt, and I became very adaptable throughout a career in a sport that underwent a complete metamorphosis in two decades.

Rugby is played in more than 100 countries across five continents and is rich in history, traditions, camaraderie, high standards of behaviour, community involvement and the feeling of pride it evokes.

I was lucky to recognise at an early age that if I continued to maintain the standards that England Colts had given me and that Neil Back had shown me, I could enjoy a long career in the sport. My teammates in England Colts had given me a benchmark for excellence and a desire to be one of the team's achievers. Frank Dick, who I met some years later, one of the best coaches of his generation and one of the best motivational speakers, described these people as mountain people in his book, *Winning: Motivation for Business, Sport & Life.* Neil Back was a mountain person and every mountain he climbed was just preparation for the next bigger and tougher mountain.

Whilst I enjoyed climbing metaphoric mountains, I did enjoy the view when I got to the top. I enjoyed the people I met and the places where the challenges were enacted. I wanted to play rugby for Northampton and England, because it provided me with opportunities to meet people and visit locations that my career as a trainee chartered surveyor would never have provided. I had to maintain my degree as a fallback, but rugby was my passion.

How many people do you know who spend their life doing something they are passionate about? I made this choice consciously at a very early age and the catalyst for that choice was Neil Back. I didn't want to be Neil Back, although I admired his dedication and will to win. I wanted to do enough to be allowed to eat at the top table with the "mountain people" and be considered worthy of being there. I would always enjoy each moment, which could be considered by the true mountain people as something of a weakness. I have come to realise that mountain people very rarely enjoy the moment. They are never deeply satisfied. As Frank says, they are always looking for the next mountain to climb. Inevitably, when you enjoy living each moment in your life, you get to see the detail and appreciate the essence of each experience.

The driven people that I have come across in my life very rarely celebrate small victories; they only truly get complete satisfaction when they have conquered their mountains or met their goals. It is at this point that they then set other mountains to conquer without ever looking back at the view. This is a quality that I admire in those incredibly talented mountain people that I have met. For me playing rugby for England was not the dream that I had visualised from a young age or my whole reason for being. I had stumbled across it after I left school. You may want to call it serendipity and I would agree with you. However, at the age of eighteen I was fifteen stone and ran sub-eleven 100 metres, so this helped me in my quest to play rugby – but I would not have followed it at any cost. Neil Back sacrificed everything to pursue his purpose. I had many debates with him about this on bus journeys and never really understood the quest he was on until much later in my career. Backie never really needed to be told how he would become number one in his sport. He understood what he had to do and the behaviour he needed to maintain to be world-class. Most of this work was not achieved on the coaching field with his teammates, it was on his own at home.

Daley Thompson was a hero of mind when I was younger and I later found out that he used to train on Christmas Day, but not for a single session. He trained twice, just in case Jurgen Hingsen, one of his competitors, had decided to train on Christmas Day. Backie was like this he understood the extremes that he could put his body through from a nutritional and psychological point of view. He worked with Darren Grewcock, on strength and conditioning well before any of us were doing weights and fitness. He was ahead of his time and transformed my thinking about how to get the edge in rugby.

After England Colts, the next time I pulled on an England Shirt was at England Students Level. Apart from full honours there was no other level to work towards and this seemed to be a realistic mountain to climb. There was no fast track as there is today to the full England Squad. England had experienced the first rugby World Cup in New Zealand and Australia in 1987, and in 1991 were joint hosts with Ireland, Scotland, Wales and France for the second Rugby World Cup. This was a great period to be involved with the sport.

Chapter 4

The fall of Ceausescu

On the 11th May 1989, England Under 21s played its first ever fixture against Romania as a warm-up match prior to England's full international against the national team and Mr Back scored a hat-trick. We travelled with the England Team to Romania and were given the same privileges as them. We stayed in the beautiful surroundings of Richmond upon Thames the night before we flew from Heathrow to Romania. This was the first time that I had visited a communist country and there could not have been more of a contrast between waking up in the Richmond Gate Hotel and arriving later in the day in Bucharest, the capital of Romania.

We were given a briefing the night before we left by Chris Thau, a Romanian who was a writer for *The Times* and *Rugby World*. I thought that this was going to be a very odd place to play rugby. It was more like entering a war zone than going on a rugby tour. Chris had detailed knowledge about what was happening in his country, but, because of his passion for rugby and the desperate need for us to visit Romania, he did not tell us the whole truth about the atrocities that were taking place in one of the most brutal communist regimes in Europe. If he had given us the full picture then I am sure that the rugby football union would not have let us travel there. In modern day terms it would be like an international side visiting Zimbabwe. The speech that this Romanian gave that night in the hotel in Richmond really made the players aware of what they were about to encounter, although there was no way it could have prepared us for what we were about to witness. The journey to Bucharest needed two planes and we eventually got there courtesy of Aeroflot, the Russian airline. We travelled with the England team and all the committee. It was Jeremy Guscott's first cap, I sat in the aisle next to him on the plane and he did not mutter a word to anyone. Instead, he was engrossed, listening to his Walkman.

The streets of Bucharest seemed full of unhappiness. The faces of the Romanians were striking in that they were so sorrowful. The people didn't smile. While we were on the bus from the airport all the players caught sight of a pretty girl walking along the street. We caught her attention as only lads can do and the girl was flattered and waved back to us. However, this wasn't the best thing she could have done, because shortly after we had passed by we saw her being accosted by two men and taken from the street into a car. We never knew why or where she had been taken, but that memory will always stay with me. We were told that she may have been taken by the Securitate, the secret police who everybody lived in fear of. People could be arrested and imprisoned for the most trivial reasons.

In 1989 in Bucharest, food and fuel rationing meant a life of endless queuing and shops with empty shelves. This was a country that was extremely fertile and possessed enormous reserves of oil and minerals. These were exported to obtain hard currency to repay mounting debts from overseas and the average Romanian never benefited. We saw buses, trucks, cars and taxis with methane gas tanks on their roofs in huge queues waiting to fill up at petrol stations. Life was very difficult

The contrast between "them and us" could not have been more extreme. We traveled to Romania knowing full well that we would have our own food served to us because food was not readily available, even in the mainstream hotels aimed at foreigners. We were encouraged to take snacks and drinks with us, because there was nothing to buy in the shops. I was expecting Bucharest to be like some of the other major European cities that I had visited, but I was shocked when I saw the state of some of the construction that had taken place. Many of the older buildings had been destroyed by war, earthquakes and Nicolae Ceausescu's program of systematisation, which since he had come to power in 1965 had had a major impact on the city. Rural communities were practically destroyed when people were encouraged to relocate to cities. This led to a lot of the older buildings being replaced with multistorey, "modern" apartment flats. The reputation that Bucharest had of being the Paris of the East was fast fading because of the demolition and reconstruction that had taken place. Tragically, eight square kilometers in the historic centre of Bucharest were leveled, including monasteries, churches, synagogues, a hospital and a beautiful Art Deco sports stadium. 40,000 people were evicted with a single day's notice and relocated to new homes, to make way for the Centru Civic. I saw many Communist-style, high-rise apartment blocks that were put up as part of this program. It is tragic to think about what these shabby blocks represented, not only in terms of the lost history and fabric of Bucharest but also the destroyed lives of a whole generation of Romanians.

The day after we arrived we were police-escorted through the streets of Bucharest to the British Embassy for a welcome drinks party. As I got off the coach at the steps of the Embassy I felt quite sick. We had passed people who looked physically and mentally downtrodden. The greyness and desperation of their lives left me feeling shaken. Upon entering the embassy we were greeted with the most opulent surroundings you could imagine. The contrast with what was outside on the streets of Bucharest was almost too much to take. As guests of the ambassador, Hugh Arbuthnott, we were treated to canapés and miniature Cokes, and you would have never thought that there was anything wrong beyond the confines of this secure building.

I had never met an ambassador before or been in an embassy. It felt overwhelming and unreal, given that outside the compound people waited in food queues and the country was in complete disarray. Many of the players at the time felt uncomfortable and couldn't wait to get back to the hotel. Hugh Arbuthnott and his staff were not responsible for the hunger and misery of the people or the corruption and vandalism of Ceausescu's.regime. It had reduced the population to abject poverty whilst a grandiose palace was erected for the megalomaniac president. Whilst we travelled about, we were were protected by a shield that only permitted us to see what the Romanian authorities wanted us to see.

The match took place in the ancient stadium, which was used by FC Steaua Bucureşti. This was the first ever England Under 21s match ever played. We were the warm-up match to England's full international, where Guscott scored a hat-trick of tries at the age of twenty-three. The atmosphere within the stadium was very subdued. We thought that this was because both the Under 21s and the England side convincingly beat the opposition. We later found out that the spectators were probably forced to go to the stadium. They were also forced to line the streets for some time after the match to clap us as we left the stadium. Whilst we felt very honoured, the body language of the people suggested that this was not something they had done of their own volition. Whilst we were euphoric in victory, the people that lined the streets for at least a mile from the stadium were like robots.

That night we were invited to join the England side at the famous Athénée Palace Hotel, which had a reputation for its sumptuousness, but also because the Communist government bugged every room, tapped every phone (and every pay phone within half a mile) and staffed the entire hotel with informers. We were treated to a traditional evening with Romanian bands, when really all the boys wanted was a nightclub. Sadly, by the time the function had finished Bucharest was under curfew. The government issued an order for people to return home before 10:00 p.m. to maintain public order. Romania was under national curfew as it was beginning to slowly unravel, just a few months before the collapse of the regime.

The only place you could get a drink was at the hotel, or so we thought. David Pears and I struck it lucky. We stumbled across two young girls who were from the Canadian Embassy and had permission to be out in the evening. We asked them if they knew any where we could get a drink in a city under curfew. Imagine our surprise when they invited us to their embassy social club. This was like an oasis in the middle of a dessert.

The journey home from Romania will stick in my mind forever. The sight of the full English rugby team, standing up at the front of the plane, enjoying themselves, drinking beers and singing songs was incredible. At no point did any one ask them to sit down or stop drinking. Their behaviour was typical of any rugby team enjoying themselves, yet this was the national side, made up of iconic figures on a public flight. This was the spirit of rugby.

It was 1989 and we were not being paid to play but we were having fantastic fun. The full English side were letting their hair down before returning to their day jobs the next day. I had a long drive from Heathrow to Nottingham, to take my first year university exams. Sadly, for the people we left behind, things were to get progessively worse before they would get better. In the spring of 1989, Romania was already falling apart at the seams. Ceaucescu's grip on his country was loosening and all over Eastern Europe communism was under pressure. 1989 was to be the year communism in Eastern Europe died. Poland became the first country to fall, closely followed by Hungary in October 1989. In East Germany, the Berlin Wall had stood since 1961, a stark reminder of the Cold War. In November 1989 the wall finally crumbled, signalling the destruction not only of an entire system of government but the end of a million individual tragedies as families and lovers and friends were finally reunited after decades of enforced seperation.

The delusional Nicolea Ceausescu stood firm in office believing his people still adored him and that Romania would remain the last bastion of Communism in Europe. In late November 1989, he was re-elected to another five-year term. He was oblivious that he was the target of the demonstrations in Timisoara on the 17th December 1989 and his efforts to suppress his critics backfired when he was booed at a mass rally in Bucharest on the 22nd December 1989. Fighting then broke out between street crowds and the secret police, in which 1000 people were killed and parts of the city destroyed. On 25th December 1989, Ceausescu and his wife were tried by a court set up by the newly created National Salvation Front. The trial lasted fifty-five minutes during which time they refused to accept any responsibility or accept their trial and were sentenced to death. They are taken outside and shot by a firing squad. Romania was the only Eastern Bloc country to overthrow its Communist regime violently or to execute its leaders. I read the newspaper reports and couldn't believe that I had witnessed the fall of communism and had visted the location where Ceausescu and his wife were killed.

On 9th December 1989, sixteen days before the fall of Ceausescu, I watched a match at Murrayfield when Romania played Scotland and lost 32–0. Raducanu, a six-foot-six-inch forward who was capped at the 1987 World Cup aged nineteen, had quietly slipped away from Rowan's, a bar in Edinburgh. This bar had become a local haunt for the Scottish players and visiting teams. The only difference on this night was the presence of secret police as unofficial doormen. Luckily for Raducanu, they were not familiar with the maze of ancient tunnels running beneath the streets of this old part of Edinburgh. The Tron Tavern offered an entry into the labyrinth. So while the secret police guarded the pub, Raducanu was bundled through a hatch and emerged into the Edinburgh night a few hundred yards away, introduced himself to a policeman and asked for political asylum. Apparently Raducanu's father was a high-ranking official in the Romanian military and he had been told to defect for his own safety ahead of the country's imminent revolution. There are suggestions, too, that British security services had advance knowledge of his plans and had representatives of their own keeping tabs on the two teams that night. What is now clear is that Raducanu made his escape only days before the most turbulent events in his country's modern history. A number of rugby players died in the uprising, including internationals Florica Murariu and Radu Durbac

Chapter 5

Dutch courage

I cannot explain why I decided to leave Northampton Saints in the summer of 1989 and join Nottingham Rugby Club. It remains one of the worst personal decisions I have ever made and one of the best rugby decisions that I have ever made. I knew from the moment I walked into the changing rooms at Beeston that I would not be there for more than one season. I had the opportunity to play with some of the best players in the country and of being coached by one of the best coaches in the country, Alan Davies. Pulling on an England Under 21s shirt in Romania had made me want to step beyond the comfort zone of my hometown, who were then playing in Courage League Two and into League One.

At Nottingham the club facilities were second rate; the 1st Team pitch had a good playing surface, but the rest of the ground was poor. It was difficult to break into this side and I was clearly an outsider. The team consisted of some great players who knew each other very well. One such player was Gary Rees who began playing for Nottingham RFC in 1977 and gained 23 England caps in an International career spanning seven years. Another England teammate was Simon Hodgkinson who I had seen make his debut against Romania in Bucharest after our fixture. Gary Rees, Brian Moore and Simon Hodgkinson were the bedrock of a great Nottingham side coached by Alan Davies, who went on to be Wales Coach but before that coached the English B side between 1986 and 1988, and assisted Geoff Cooke in the English Tour of Australia and Fiji in 1988. It was a great place to learn how to play rugby and be part of a team that also included four players who went down the road to join the Tigers, Neil Back and my old teammate from England Colts Wayne Kilford, Stuart Potter and

Steve Hackney. Neil moved to Nottingham RFC from Barkers Butts, a good local junior club side in Warwickshire, a year before me and was another reason why I joined the club.

At this time Nottingham were a much stronger side than The Saints. I represented Nottingham against my beloved Saints at Franklin's gardens and we beat them convincingly. Ironically, I played against Frank Packman, the person I had come in for on my debut. I came off second best that day. I made a decision that afternoon to return to Franklin's Gardens the next season. I didn't acquit myself well at Nottingham. I got on the bus with my kit bag to go to a first division game to discover that I had brought no boots, wash bag, towel and kit. Instead I had brought my files from the lectures that I had been in the day before. This didn't go down very well. I played against Bath in a league match and got the sole of my boot ripped off during the course of the game. The club didn't keep spare boots in 1989 and I left the field of play to attempt to find some boots in the changing rooms. I was joined by Simon Hodgkinson, who I thought had come in to help me; instead, when I asked him whether he had any spare boots, he replied with true Nottingham RFC dry humour, "What colour?" I ended up playing the rest of the game in one trainer and one boot.

Northampton Saints treated their 1st Team players very well and whilst we were not paid to play we still had many benefits. The nail in the coffin for my career with Nottingham came after a 1st XV game. It was traditional to be given a meal voucher and a beer ticket to redeem when you got to the club house. Instead of a beer, I desperately wanted an orange juice and lemonade. Sadly, the beer voucher only allowed you to redeem beer, so I ended up having to pay for my orange juice. I was a poor student who hankered to be back at his old club house and not at Ireland Avenue, Beeston.

Playing for Nottingham certainly enhanced my chances of playing further representative rugby with appearances for England Students and two for England Under 21s against Holland and France. My mum, who had been poorly for some time, was well enough to make the trip to see me play against Holland in Hilversum near, Amsterdam, where she stayed with my Dad and some of the other players' parents.

You can't visit Amsterdam without going to the red-light district and my conservative mum and dad were no exceptions. As a child I was brought up in a household where my parents rarely swore and if a program came on the television that had any sexual scenes, Dad would immediately turn it off. What they made of this area of Amsterdam, I will never know. Even then, when I was twenty-one, it was not discussed. I think Mum was shocked when she saw the prostitutes displaying their wares in the windows of the old city. Amsterdam was beautiful despite the debauchery taking place inside these tiny rooms. The red-light district is in one of the oldest parts of the city, overlooking the tree-lined canals. Hundreds of years ago it was frequented by sailors docking in need of some female company. The district was not populated exclusively by the sex industry. In fact, many of the beautiful 300-year-old gabled buildings were occupied by doctors, lawyers and plenty of families. There were also theatres, shops, museums, restaurants, bars and coffee shops where smoking marijuana was totally acceptable.

As players, we were confined to barracks and had a boring trip. We had a strong side and played Holland who were not exactly a world force in rugby. It is odd that in the early stages of England Under 21s we ended up playing lesser nations of world rugby. Two weeks later, I was back in Amsterdam for the 1990 Heineken Amsterdam Sevens. I was invited by Stoneygate Rugby Club, a junior club based in the village of Scraptoft, Leicestershire, and went with Ian Hunter, who two years earlier I had convinced to join The Saints. We were drafted in to strengthen the side and whilst we were keen to enjoy the rugby, we were also keen to experience Amsterdam's nightlife. The decision to go to this tournament was a difficult one because I was in the middle of my second year exams and should have been concentrating on these rather than being on a rugby tour. I will never regret the decision to go, and whilst there I was studying for an exam on architecture that was due to take place when I returned. The big debate at the time was the controversy that had been caused by a speech given by the Prince of Wales at Hampton Court Palace in May 1984. Prince Charles had launched an attack on modern British architecture when describing an extension to the elegant facade of the National Gallery to be "like a monstrous carbuncle on the face of a much loved and elegant friend." I found myself, on the Saturday night after the Sevens, studying the speech he gave and how he prompted a great national debate, making many architects and those who commissioned them think differently about their designs.

That night I arranged to meet some players in the red-light district who had played for The Netherlands two weeks before for England Under 21s. They were both playing in the Sevens and kindly agreed to give a local's tour of the best nightlife. Armed with the address of my hotel and some local currency, I headed into the night. The night could have been like any other, except on this occasion the group that I was drinking with contained someone who was known throughout The Netherlands. I was totally oblivious to this. I made the fatal call to inform this group of revelers of why I was late joining their party. I mentioned Prince Charles and his famous speech and the exam I had coming up. This was immediately punished with a concoction of drinks which I had to down in front of my new found Dutch friends. Through the haze of alcohol and the roar of my new friends, I noticed that one of the party seemed to be surrounded by men looking after his welfare. This individual did not ridicule me for staying in to study. Instead, he was able to offer some great insight into the subject and spoke at great length about the reason why Prince Charles had kicked off this debate. He offered a very informed view of the whole debate on modernism versus classicism, which I was able to use in the exam that I took the following week. I later realised why he knew so much about the subject. He was Prince Constantijn, the son of Queen Beatrix of the Netherlands. I only discovered his identity because I was told off in the bar's loos by one of the locals for being disrespectful. I had noticed that as we sat chatting people were looking over at us and would often stare when they went by. The reason he knew so much about Prince Charles was because he had discussed the subject of modernism/traditionalism with him at great length on one of their Royal visits. I had been introduced to him by the captain of the Dutch Under 21s side who he was studying with at University. I wasn't fazed by my drinking companion's background and we carried on into the night, despite the fact that the people who had joined us in the bar had left, leaving me alone with the Prince and his bodyguards. I had delusions of grandeur brought about by a bit of "Dutch courage". I asked audaciously whether it might be possible to have a lift home to my hotel. My lasting memory of that night is sitting in the back of the car with the Prince and arriving at my hotel. That night I slept in a tiny room with Hunts whilst the Prince returned to the Royal Palace for the night. The following morning over breakfast, I explained my night to the boys who didn't believe it. I remember a magazine on a coffee table in the reception of the hotel and on its front cover was the Dutch royal family, and dressed in full regalia was the prince I had been drinking with the night before.

It felt like Rugby was opening many doors for me whilst the work that I was doing with my degree felt incredibly mundane. Despite being away from Nottingham a great deal in my second year playing rugby, I did pass my exams. I worked hard to make sure that I was able to progress onto the fourth year of the course, but I wasn't enthralled by the subject matter. I enjoyed some aspects of my degree and realised that it was offering me a good foundation in preparation to become a chartered surveyor.

This year was a means to an end on both a rugby and an academic level. The most important thing it taught me was to follow my passion. Passionate people tend to achieve things. This doesn't mean that that everything you do has to give you complete satisfaction, but it should help you on your way to following your dreams and achieving your purpose. My rugby and academic career improved in this year and I used this foundation to propel me into the next phase of my life.

Before I could complete the fourth year, I had to complete a third year placement in London. This was an exciting opportunity to live in a big city and take advantage of all it had to offer. There seemed no point in staying at Nottingham RFC. Northampton Saints became Courage Division Two Champions and the desire to return home was much greater than the lure of London Wasps, who were captained by Rob Andrew and had won their first Courage Division One trophy in 1989/90. I was a Saints man and had realised that I didn't want to be anywhere else. The prospect of playing again at Franklin Gardens was compelling. I had known from the first moment I entered the Nottingham changing rooms that I had made a mistake. I felt totally the opposite emotion when I agreed to return home to Northampton Saints. It wasn't just the rugby that was important to me in my life, I had a whole support system in my family in Northampton. I missed going to my Nan's and Grandma's for tea before training. I missed being able to swing off the M1 motorway from Nottingham at Junction 16 of the M1 for a cup of tea with my mum and sister. Life was good for me in Northampton. I felt physically different when I saw its fields and villages. I still do. The old expression you can take the boy out of Northampton but you can't take Northampton out of the boy is true in my case. I was at university studying to be a chartered surveyor, but my heart was in Northampton.

I had a summer to enjoy before joining the club for pre-season. This summer was a long hot go-between summer of all our childhood memories. It was the summer of parties and twenty-first birthday celebrations. I had turned twenty-one in February and we had a great party at the Buckby Lion in Long Buckby. However, a birthday party that will stay in my memory was the twenty-first birthday party of Giles Wilson. Giles was the son of a great man called Lynn Wilson who was an excellent role model to us growing up. He had helped build a property firm called Wilson Connolly into a leading construction company; he was also the president of Northamptonshire County Cricket Club and very active in Northampton Saints rugby club. I had a huge amount of respect for Giles and his family, and we would sit around the kitchen table at the Grange listening to his father talk. They were an unassuming family despite their success. The only time that I saw any indication of their wealth was at Giles's twenty-first. Up until now I had attended few events that took place in a marquee and this marquee would have been one to rival any other of its time in the country.

Giles was a gregarious character who was liked by all and his twenty-first proved to be a huge affair, with friends and family from the world of sport, Oakham School and Aberdeen University. I cannot imagine how much this must have cost but it was a superb drunken night. The marquee was joined to his house, which had a swimming pool that I found myself in late at night. No-one needed to go home. Beds had been set up in the marquee and all over the house.

Giles had a very large bedroom, with walk-in wardrobes that were big enough to sleep in. Beds had been laid out on the top and bottom shelves, and I bunked down on the top shelf. I was joined in the night by a very drunk bloke with a handlebar moustache. I had no idea who he was until I got up in the morning. I got off the top shelf and stood on his hand, causing him considerable pain. This wouldn't have been great for anyone, however this individual had earned a reputation using the very hand I stood on. It was Dennis Lillee, the Australian cricketer rated as the "outstanding fast bowler of his generation".

The Richardson family was another family who I respected a great deal for their ability to mix business with pleasure. They had built a very successful pharmacy, hairdressing and property business in Northampton, and were about to venture into the leisure industry in 1990. They owned a former paint factory in the centre of Northampton next to Lloyds Bank, which they had converted into a hairdressing salon, a gym aptly named Georgie Porgie's and a jazz club called the Black Bottom Club in 1981. The Club was tucked away in a courtyard in George Row and was an institution to those quietly in the know. Jake and Jarvis, who I played rugby with at the Saints, decided to open a private members' bar with a difference, which became the place to drink for many years to come. Auntie Ruth's was born and we loved it. It became the place to drink in Northampton for our friends, and often we would finish playing the percussion instruments with the Ginger

Pig Band late into the night. Ten years later we would celebrate one of Northampton's great sporting triumphs at Auntie Ruth's.

Everyone knew everyone in Northampton in 1990, and Colin and John Richardson (Jake and Jarvis's father and uncle) had played alongside Lynn Wilson in my junior club, The Men's Own. Colin Richardson was Lynn Wilson's best man and, ironically, Jake would later become my joint best man. It was men like Lynn, Colin and John who I respected as I grew up. They were people who lived life to the full. They loved sport and had grown great businesses, but they also liked to party hard. I had some treasured evenings listening to some of the best live bands in the Black Bottom Club with a fascinating crowd of people from very different walks of life.

Auntie Ruth's became the place to meet. Jake had a great eye for art and the walls of this old paint factory were adorned with some superb modern art. The bar was made up of old counters from Lloyds Bank. In the midst of the modern art was a picture of a slightly rotund sportsman called Colin Milburn. It looked slightly incongruous and I never knew why it was there. Colin's picture would look down at us as we drank at the bar and, although I knew his name, I had no idea what this great man had achieved. The people of a generation who knew him would remark that he was a legend in Northamptonshire cricket folklore. He was a great cricketer, a charming and humble man, and a rowdy raconteur. John Arlott, the cricket commentator, who was regarded as the "voice of summer" described Colin Milburn as, "a great gust of North-East fresh air and one of the best liked cricketers of modern times." He played nine tests for England with an average of 46.71. The irony was that it was booze that eventually killed him a few months before Auntie Ruth's was opened. This picture was a tribute to him.

Chapter 6

International jet setter

That summer I travelled to two new countries. I visited Namibia and Canada back-to-back with only two hours and a shower at Heathrow between flights. Before my departure to Namibia I was introduced to my mentor at The Saints, Tony Hewitt, who lived in Holcot. Rugby was amateur, but the club operated a mentoring system for its young players. This meant that a member of the local business community was appointed to look after you and make sure that you were given the right tools to succeed in your professional life beyond the club. Tony had experience in the commercial property market, which was the career I was about to embark on, and had served on the board of two public companies. He was the first businessman that I was to know properly.

Tony made sure that I was able to go on the two summer tours. He had an important role in my life at a time when I was playing First Division rugby and for England Under 21s. I would visit him at his offices at Wilson and Partners, which were in a fine old rectory. There wasn't a significant commercial property deal in Northampton that went on without Tony and his fellow partners having some sort of interest in it. This was the company to work for and I was being fast-tracked to have a career with them when I finished university. Tony gave me great advice and helped me to take advantage of the overseas trips that I was offered. In return I would tell him how I was progressing and from time to time, when I stepped out of order, it was Tony who put me right. The business community maintained the players who were to revive the glory days. We certainly didn't have to pay for our orange juice and lemonade at Northampton Saints. The two most promising youngsters at the time were Tim Rodber and Ian Hunter.

Tim Rodber was one of the players on a fast track to play for the National side. Despite playing for the Saints in Division Two, he was able to make his England B debut in France and was picked to tour with England in Argentina during the summer of 1990. Ian Hunter and I went to Namibia and Canada to discover new experiences and improve our rugby pedigree with the blessing of our mentors, who were keeping a close eye on us.

It is true that none of us got any cash for paying rugby, but we were loaned cars and given accommodation by friends of the club. The first car I was given was a Ford Capri MK2 – 3 litre Ghia. I was very proud of my "hot hatch" at the time, despite the word "elegance" being plastered down the side of it. This was until the gear stick came off in my hand on the way back through Leicester for training. Ian Hunter and Tim Rodber were given free accommodation courtesy of Persimmon Homes. Sadly this was as bad as the Ford Capri for street credibility. Their accomodation was a bungalow that had been bought to unlock the access to some land in the village of Collingtree in Northampton and should have been condemned. The house had mould growing up the walls and was home to two of the country's best players for a time. By the end of this decade much would have changed for players of the standard of Tim and Ian.

The prospect of travelling on a long haul flight seemed to me beyond the realms of possibility, yet in the summer of 1990 I got a chance to go to Africa. I had no idea the effect that travelling to this continent would have on my life. I had no understanding of the magnitude of this land, the 54 countries that occupied it, the extent of its cultural diversity and, more importantly, the impression its people would leave on me for many years to come. I had no idea of the history of South Africa, or Namibia, which had only just gained independence from South Africa. The unknown was beckoning me and I felt a huge sense of anticipation.

Many teams including Wales and England Students were invited to go and play against the Namibian side and other provinces in the area. This was a big decision because up until that point no teams were prepared to go anywhere near this part of the world. The 1969–70 rugby tour of Britain by an all white South African team was one of the first occasions when the British public showed their disapproval of invitations to sports teams from countries under apartheid rule. I had only ever come across the mention of apartheid when I was at Wellingborough during a presentation given by Natwest Bank. They had come to convince us to open an account with them and when we were asked if we had any questions, one of the more articulate pupils piped up with a bit of a curve-ball question, "Can you tell me what Natwest's policy is in South Africa and their view on apartheid?" I can remember asking one of my mates what apartheid was and he hadn't got a clue, and I did not come across the word again, until I had to address the question as a rugby player in Namibia.

Apartheid was an evil system of legalised racial segregation enforced by the National Party government of South Africa in 1948 and public opinion in the UK was strongly opposed to it. During the South African tour of Britain, the Anti-Apartheid Movement organised demonstrations outside rugby grounds. On the field, matches were interrupted; off the field, demonstrators protested outside the team's hotels. The AAM urged that the world should boycott teams from apartheid countries. South Africa was excluded from all international competitions at the time we went to Namibia. This was not an official tour sanctioned by the RFU. It had been organised by Derek Morgan, who became the President of the English Rugby Union in 2002. He had very close contacts in South Africa and when we arrived they welcomed him with open arms. Our coach on this tour was Brian Ashton, who became the England Head Coach in 2006. Brian was a great coach and led the tour with distinction. The players respected him as a former player and he couldn't have imagined that he would be at the centre of a debate on apartheid when he agreed to conduct this tour. Brian was a softly spoken Lancastrian schoolteacher and we felt very fortunate to have him with us.

Our flight out to Namibia touched down in Johannesburg and we were given a tour of one of its gold mines, before taking part in a training session at Ellis Park, the home of the Springboks. Back in 1955, this stadium had played host to the largest ever crowd at a rugby game in South Africa, when 100,000 spectators saw the Springboks go down 23–22 to the British Lions. It was rebuilt in 1979–80 and we saw the changing rooms of this very historic ground and trained on the pitch. The Springboks were revered in their country and the changing room was a shrine to the players, with individual wooden changing areas and memorabilia on the walls that exalted the home team. I had entered the inner sanctum to which very few people were admitted.

Our tour wasn't going to involve playing South African sides, but the South African authorities had only just released leading anti-apartheid campaigner Nelson Mandela from prison after 27 years on the 11th February 1990 so this tour by an English Team was quite historic, although never officially sanctioned by the Rugby Football Union.

Namibia was regarded as the fifth province of South Africa and became subject to apartheid laws after 1948. It wasn't until after the elections held in 1989 when Sam Nujoma became president of Namibia that it gained independence, just a few months before we arrived in the country. The country had a strong rugby tradition and had played in the Currie Cup as South West Africa. I hadn't got a clue of any of this history and yet we had to face the question of whether we should play rugby in a country that had been subjected to apartheid. There were some highly educated players on this trip who were informed about how a country that had suffered under apartheid might look. It was beautiful country, but there was not much to do for twenty-five rugby tourists. I didn't have any pre-conceptions about Namibia. I was starting this trip with a blank canvas. I wasn't well read and judged every situation as I found it. I hadn't been let down by life; in fact, the reverse – I positively loved soaking it up. Before we landed in Nambia, I think I could have been described as reassuringly naïve with a rather romantic view of life. Along with my kit bag I had brought a leather travelling suitcase that I had found in an antique shop, which had the initials of a former traveler on it. I felt I was breaking down new frontiers by travelling to Africa and, of course, I needed a travelling case that befitted this mindset. This provided huge amusement to the rest of the tour party, but I was my own man on my private journey.

Our first port of call was Tsumeb. We arrived during carnival time, so it was lively. We were there for three nights and on one of these nights we witnessed hundreds of black miners protesting about poor pay. This was quite unlike the UK Miners' Strike of 1984–85. The workers paraded through the streets singing, the sound of which could only be likened to that of the group Ladysmith Black Mambazo. It was a very peaceful march and formed my first impression of Africa and its amazing diversity. I had no idea about what these people had suffered over the years in their country. The German seizure of Angra Pequena in 1884 was one of the first incidents in the European scramble for Africa. The tribes that had occupied the arid coastal strip of the Namib desert which became South West Africa suffered some of the harshest experiences of modern colonial history at the hands first of Germans and then South Africa. Tsumeb was the gateway to the Etosha national park, one of the largest game parks in Africa. We visited Swakopmund, a pretty seaside town, full of colonial buildings and a dramatic dune-lined coastline. The country had great diversity and we saw it all by bus on this tour. It was the first time that I experienced an African hunting trip. The players were invited by a local farmer on one of our days off to travel to his farm in a remote part of the bush, to experience what it would be like to hunt a springbok, which ran wild on his farm. The extent of his land was immense and included mountains and river valleys. It took us nearly half a day to get to his farm and we returned after nightfall to the Safari Hotel in Windhoek. The memory is still vivid, travelling around in open sided land rovers across rough terrain in search of a brown and white gazelle who was oblivious to the fact that she was just about to be felled by a single shot from the one of the rifles we had on board. I winced when the fatal shot was fired and the beautiful animal brought down, even though I knew that we would be eating it later on a *braai*.

The player who was given the task of shooting the animal from a long distance with telescopic lenses had only managed to wound it, which meant that we were then duty-bound to follow it to put it out of its misery. It seemed like such a cruel and unnecessary way to die, just to give a few rugby players an experience. Travelling through the bush in a land rover made me feel exhilarated, but I could have done without the kill. However, this didn't stop me tasting springbok, which had a wonderful texture not unlike lamb.

We were due to play one of the matches on tour in a black township in Walvis Bay that hadn't been given up by South Africa and remained under their sovereignty. We had trained on a pitch that was an oasis in the middle of the Namib dessert and formed part of a black township. Getting off the bus in a cloud of dust, we met some of the most lovely people and were greeted by hoards of children who thought one of our players, Adel Kardooni, was Diego Maradona. Maradona's fame had spread even to this isolated part of Africa. The pitch had been watered daily in anticipation of our arrival and we felt very humbled by the whole experience. At this stage we were oblivious that Walvis Bay was still under South Africa's sovereignty and quite frankly I wasn't bothered, I was more moved by the human experience of going to a black township and seeing first-hand how people lived and how lucky we were to be welcomed into their inner sanctum. Derek Morgan took all the players aside at a beach barbeque, to decide whether we should go ahead and play the game in Walvis Bay. This game became a huge issue on our tour. We had been invited to a barbecue on a beach. The sun was setting over the Atlantic Ocean and our host waded into the water with a fishing rod, which he cast and five minutes later caught a huge tuna that he promptly put onto a grill. This was the freshest fish that I had ever eaten.

My decision to play the game was based on a conversation that I had had that afternoon with one of the local men from the township. After we had trained on the pitch, I chatted to him about what it was like to grow up in Nambia and the importance of this game to the local community. We were two people from completely different backgrounds but shared a common love of rugby that brought us together that afternoon. I cannot tell you what he looked like, his name or the position he played in rugby. However, his comments fundamentally changed my perspective on life. At the end of our conversation, he thanked me and said that this was the first time in his life that he had had a conversation with a person with blue eyes for more than five minutes. This shocked me and made me determined to play the game. Very few of our squad refused to play the game and for those who did we respected their decision. I couldn't understand until much later the significance of his comments. But the way that people treat each other and the brutality of man to man shocked me to the core. The history of Namibia was a litany of violance.

The country was sparsely populated. In between towns, we visited some of the biggest and oldest dunes, the largest national park, the oldest desert (Namib) and the oldest petrified forest in the world. We had to make our own entertainment and one night in the coastal town of Swakopmund, we were successful in removing a fully stuffed zebra from the forecourt of a local garage and placing it in Derek Morgan's bed. Derek was always attending drinks parties whilst we were stuck in the hotel in preparation for games. Imagine his surprise when he returned from a night on the beers to find that his bed companion was a Zebra. The theft of the animal made headline news in Namibia and Derek had to eat some humble pie on our behalf.

The final test against Namibia in Winhoek will not be remembered for the rugby but for the post-match activities. We all attended the after-match reception, which was a traditional dinner dance. This was an incredibly old fashioned event, very much like something out of 1950s Britain. The players were dressed in blazers and ties, and the ladies were in ball gowns. It was like an African version of the Beagle Ball. The after-match dinner was important in rugby in 1990; speeches were the norm, the players would thank the opposition for the game and the management would be present to award man of the match and souvenirs for the home and away teams. If you wanted to dance with the females, you literally waltzed around the room in one big circle.

In Namibia this was normal, in our culture this was very, very strange. The evening finished abruptly and the players were keen to go on to a club. A derogatory remark by one of our players, Steve Pilgrim, led to a mass brawl between the Namibians and us. This was disrespectful to our hosts after they had entertained us so royally. We had spent the evening waltzing the night away and now were fighting them. This was a full-scale brawl and probably the only time I have thrown a punch, which was in defense of one of my teammates, Rob McNaughton.

After our brawl, we ended up in a club called Namib Nights. We were taken there by Andre Stoop, one of the best full backs ever to play the game, who had been let out of prison that morning to play the game. We were told that he had been put away for diamond smuggling, but I will never know if this was true or whether it was just a local rumour. He was a perfect host that night as we entered a club where we as whites were in the minority. It was the presence and respect that Andre had in the club that ensured we were in safe hands. Needless to say there was no waltzing going on in this club, just a sea of Africans partying. Imagine the scene in an Ibizan nightclub and there you have Namib Nights. This trip gave me a taste for Africa. Namibia felt geographically and politically isolated. I had loved visiting this beautiful country and experiencing the dramatic landscapes and cultural differences. However, I was a callow youth of twenty-one and the prospect of going to Canada with Northampton Saints seemed more appealing.

Ian Hunter and I landed at Heathrow on 7th August at 10:00 a.m. local time and then, two hours later, after a shower in the airport, boarded the plane to St Johns, Newfoundland. I joined a Saints team that had just won the league and consisted of many of the players I had known when I made my debut in 1987. Ian and I were not treated any differently because we had just come from Namibia, that wasn't the Saints way. In fact for much of the trip I roomed with Lenny Newman and Paul Alston, who took advantage of the fact that I was an inexperienced tourist. They operated a fairly ruthless policy of allocation of beds and duties whilst in the room. The net result was that I performed all the duties they gave me. It was like the old fagging system in public schools, which was thankfully on its way out when I went to Wellingborough. Lenny and Paul were long standing members of the Saints Squad and so there was a certain amount of respect shown to them. On this tour they hadn't brought their wives, unlike most of the other players, so they took advantage of my reassuringly naïve qualities and I became a happily obliging stand-in wife.

Canada was a casual tour and very different to Namibia. I think the opposition of the first match gave it away, Swilers RFC. The tour was organised on a budget, so we found ourselves being "billeted" by local rugby players at the different places we visited. It was potluck who you got; your name was picked out by the opposition and they would be waiting for you at the airport. This was a rugby tradition and it was strange to stay with the player who you might be facing the following day on the field. The quality of your trip depended on your host and how motivated he was to show you the local sights. I loved it because as soon as you arrived, you had a friend who had local knowledge and wanted to take you to places and introduce you to people that you would never have met if you had gone to a faceless hotel.

I got lucky in Newfoundland and was taken to a superb house with my own bedroom with en suite bathroom. Some players had shockers, staying in locations that resembled a fraternity house in National Lampoon's *Animal House* movie. The fun was always meeting up with the other players to hear the horror stories of where they had been billeted. I was staying with a local family in an open-plan Canadian house and the vivid memory I have is not of the beautiful soft furnishings, décor and size of the house, but the fact that each room had speakers and a separate volume control knob. This is common place now but not in any house I knew in 1990.

We played Swilers RFC with a side that included Barry Corless, the ex England and Moseley centre, who had joined Northampton Saints as the the country's first paid club administrator. This was a very important stage in rugby's development, know one in rugby at this time was being paid to coach a team. Barry wasn't able to coach the first team because this would have breached the amateur rules, however he became now what have been called a coaching director, responsible for the overall direction of rugby at the club. This was big decision by the newly appointed Saints committee to get someone of his stature within the game. This job was left to Paul Bryant and Terry Burwell. The match included Paddy Johns, known in rugby as "The Quiet Enforcer" he eventually won 59 caps for Ireland, but found himself in St Johns playing rugby and eventually got married to a local girl. The other member of the opposition was Rod Snow, who played 62 times for Canada. He was a bull of man.

Paddy and his teammates were perfect hosts and made sure we had a true Newfoundland welcome, which meant good food, drink and partying. We also had someone on our tour who, like Paddy, had attended The Royal School Dungannon, a town in County Tyrone in Northern Ireland. His name was Alan Clarke. It was his first Saints Tour. He was studying in Northampton's Nene College, to become a teacher and had played for my local junior club, The Men's Own.

I got to know Alan very well, when we saved his bacon on a section of the Ottawa River on a whitewater rafting experience. The Rocher Fendu section of the Ottawa River, located downriver of Pembroke, Ontario, is one of the world's best, most constant whitewater runs of about eight kilometres, and took the best part of the day to complete. The runs had great names like Butcher Knife, Angel's Kiss and Hell's Half Mile. On one run we were told in advance that if we capsized, we should swim to the right to avoid the rapids and being dragged down the riverbed because its stones would cut us to bits. We went over the edge of a rapid and Alan Clarke was thrown into the water. He emerged in what seemed like minutes later, but I am sure was only a few seconds, shouting "I am f***ing drowning!" We managed to get the Irishman back on board and he thanked us for our help. The only odd thing about it was he kept calling me Tony. I later found out that it was because he had heard my name on rugby special but thought it was "Tony Croft" instead of Thorneycroft. Allen Clarke is now the Head Coach for Ireland Under 21s. I wonder if he still thinks my name is Tony.

We travelled across Canada taking in Montreal, Ottawa and Toronto. Rugby in Canada was very popular with both men and women. The Saints were still very traditional and at after-match receptions we would wear what we called "number ones", when the opposition would be in jeans and a T-shirt. Our dress consisted of a club blazer, grey chinos, white shirts and club 1st XV ties. We were given blazer badges to embroider on the blazer which made specific reference to the tour. I still have this badge and was very proud to wear number ones. It was a uniform that differentiated you; however, this sartorial elegance soon got phased out as my rugby career progressed.

Geoff Allen, our club president, encouraged us to leave an after-match reception, after witnessing a slightly unusual riposte to our after-match entertainment. Northampton Saints had a series of songs that they sang, known as "The Northampton Medley", which included old school songs like, *You Are My Sunshine, Shine On, Harvest Moon* and generally finished with a rendition of *Running Bear*. It included Indian chanting of "UGO UGO" during the three verses, as well as the Indian war cries. This medley had been passed down by players who would sing it travelling back from rugby games. It was very traditional and very well received. The Canadian response to our singing was rather alternative. One of the players demonstrated to the aghast audience his skill of being able to get an astounding amount of dollar coins up his foreskin and a lady rugby player, or so she said, showed us how years of cocaine abuse had enabled her to perfect the skill of snorting a raw egg through her nose and out of her mouth, onto a barbeque, which she then proceeded to cook. It was at this point that Geoff, who still remains the clubs announcer at Franklin Gardens, thought it would be a good time for players and their partners to leave.

It isn't often that I travel somewhere and leave feeling disappointed; however, Niagara Falls was one such place. Our approach to the Canadian Horseshoe Falls was by coach on the Ontario side. Niagara Falls is the second largest on earth, next to Victoria Falls in Southern Africa. It was a big tourist attraction, both at daytime and in the evening. It was like going to Blackpool, with hoards of people flocking to see this natural phenomenon. We did the tourist boat trip, known as the Maid of the Mist, and ate in the Skylon Tower which has a revolving restaurant with perfect views over the falls. Niagara Falls was beautiful, but the area in front of it was full of hotels, casinos, theme parks and ferris wheels. It was a wonder of the world, destroyed by over commercialisation. This, along with a visit to the Toronto Blue Jays stadium to see major league baseball, were deemed to be the highlights of the trip. I preferred the wildness and beauty of Newfoundland and Namibia to these seedy tourist traps.

This tour marked a major turning point in the Saints history. The players that were lucky enough to be in the touring squad had restored the club back to top-flight rugby and for some this would be the last time they would get the chance to wear the black, green and gold. The club was changing and becoming more professional, and I was lucky to enjoy this trip with them before returning to Northampton to start the 1990/91 season. It was the last of the tours of this kind for Northampton Saints. It was the end of the era where the club represented a hobby for its players. The players were oblivious to what was about to happen to them and Northampton was at the cutting edge of this change in the sporting mentality. Change is inevitable and for some players this would be the last time that they would represent the Saints 1st XV. Many players stepped up in the new era and welcomed the arrival of Nick Beal, Matt Dawson, John Olver and Martin Bayfield, players who would help to restore the club to its former glory.

Nothing could have prepared me for the highs and lows of the 1990/91 season. I moved to London to do a year in industry for a firm of property consultants called Fuller Peiser in Hanover Square and moved into a house with some mates from university, John Sisman and Phil Morris, in Prebend Street, Islington.

The club that had languished at the bottom of the second division in 1988 was now an altogether different place. It had made real progress since that historic AGM and the end of the old guard. Saints were setting the pace in the UK from both the playing and non-playing perspectives. Having won promotion they had reached the semi finals of the Pilkington Cup. The players had gained recognition at national, divisional and county level. They had rallied the support of the business community who started taking advertising space, sponsoring games and leasing the eight hospitality boxes that had been built. The public started to come and watch us. We had always had a hard core of loyal supporters, but people who had never even watched rugby were drawn to the club.

Barrie Corless was responsible for orchestrating a playing revival. He was receiving a salary from the club to put a structure in place that would attract quality players to Franklin Gardens from the youth section, right through to the senior playing squad. He wanted to restore the club to one of the top five clubs in the country. We had a great group of players, which included our captain, Gary Pearce, who was our only England legend. Gary was the most unassuming individual you could meet and the only captain that the club could have appointed to lead the revival. He had joined the club in 1977 and went on to make 421 appearances, and won 36 caps for England. Not even this legend could have imagined who was about to turn up at Franklin Gardens in October 1990. The club was ambitious, but when Wayne Shelford, the All Blacks captain, pitched up in October, we all realised it meant business. To put this into perspective, no English club had overseas players or even players from outside England. I played against David Kirk when he was at Oxford, but he was a Rhodes Scholar, studying Philosophy, Politics and Economics, after he captained New Zealand's All Blacks Rugby team to victory in the inaugural Rugby World Cup in 1987.

Wayne Shelford, also known as Buck, had come to play rugby for very different reasons. This man was a rugby legend it was like having Muhammad Ali walk through the gates of your club. I saw him take off his shirt in our changing rooms for the first time just forty-eight hours after his plane had touched down at Heathrow. His back was like a road map from all the scars that he had received from rucking, which was legal at this time. He had a huge reputation and was a legend in the game. One Buck story that does not fade on the retelling was the tale of the second test of the New Zealand Tour of France in 1986, when he had his scrotum torn open during one of the most brutal games ever witnessed (dubbed "the battle of Nantes" by the media). This would leave most men screaming in agony and heading for the nearest hospital, but not Shelford. He calmly instructed the physio to stitch him up. The French public were bewildered as an over-eager pitch side cameraman filmed the stomach-turning surgery, and even more so when Shelford returned to the field and carried on playing.

Buck brought prestige back into the *haka*, taking it from a mere flailing of limbs, to a challenge that brought emotion from opponents and opposing fans around the world. He was only defeated once on the international field, that day at Nantes, and let's face it he had been severely injured. He captained the All Blacks fourteen times for fourteen victories. He was a world cup winner, joining our playing squad when Northampton had only won one trophy since 1880 (the Courage League second division). Buck wasn't able to play for the club in the league until the start of the new year; however, I played with him in his first run out at Franklin's Gardens against touring side Manley on the 17th October 1990. The *Chronicle and Echo* records two scorers that night: Shelford and Thorneycroft. When Buck first played for the All Blacks, I was running out at Chiltern School for the football team.

Buck had pulled in the crowds and doubled the normal attendance. Buck played that night against Willie Ofahengaue, a Tongan who was widely known as Willie O, and who went on to earn 41 caps for Australia from 1990 to 1998 and played in the World Cups of 1991 and 1995 and the World Cup Sevens in 1993. It was Buck that people had come to see, and our boys lifted their game because of his presence on the team.

The first league game that Buck saw was ten days later, which I am pleased to say I wasn't picked for. The match was Orrell v Northampton, when the Saints crumbled to an astonishing 60–0 defeat. I had been picked to play for England Students three days after this defeat and came across Willie O again at Peacecroft Ground, Stratford Upon Avon RFC.

England (Students Division) v Australian Emerging Players was the first of a four match international series for the students, which included Wales, Scotland and France, and a tour to Canada to play against the national side. England Students was a fantastic addition to playing Club Rugby and we were aware that after the tour to Canada, there would be an opportunity to play against England as one of their World Cup warm-up games. The Australian team that night with Willie O (41 caps) included Jason Little (75 caps), Richard Tombs (5), Garrick Morgan (10), Warrick Waugh (8) and David Wilson (79). The bench had John Eales (84), Peter Slattery (17) and Matthew Pini (8). This group of players would eventually go on to win 327 caps. John Eales went on to be arguably the most successful captain in the history of Australian Rugby, winning the world cup in 1991 and then as captain in 1999.

Student Rugby was quality rugby. The England manager, Geoff Cooke, would come and watch games. The greatest handicap during this match against Australia was that the floodlights at this ground were very poor and when the high ball went up, you would have to estimate where it would land because you had no way of seeing it. You would have thought that the RFU would have staged this game at a more prestigious ground with better facilities. However, I believe their policy was to allow less traditional rugby heartlands to see international matches, albeit at England Student level. We used this to our favour and as a result the game remained very close.

As well as club rugby and international duties, the club encouraged players to take invitations to foreign countries to improve their rugby pedigree. The league games in those days amounted to only eleven in total, therefore there was less pressure on the coach or player to produce top-level performance week in week out. All the other games we played were friendly and so if you missed the odd game then it didn't matter. Paul Bryant, my coach, was a teacher and he actively encouraged the prospect of touring with other teams. He felt that it took you out of your comfort zone and placed you in more challenging environments. Paul handled me very well when I went back to Northampton Saints; I was probably slightly arrogant and thought I should get straight into the team given the fact that I had played First Division Rugby for Nottingham. He dropped me from the first game of the season and this resulted in me running off to the corner of the pitch and crying my eyes out. This wouldn't have been normal for most players, but I was so desperate to play. He found a way of getting the best out of me and for that I was very grateful.

I was invited by Millfield Old Boys to the 21st Dubai Exiles International Sevens Tournament. The tournament had been growing year by year and the 1990 event boasted forty sides from across the Gulf, with eleven invited international sides. The matches were played on sand and this added to the mystique of the tournament. Dubai City is located on the shores of the Persian Gulf, and in the early 1990s Dubai had taken a strategic decision to emerge as a major international-quality tourist destination.

When I went to Dubai there was relatively little development and the only major hotel was the Hilton Hotel, which was a business hotel, most of the year, apart from when the Sevens were on. This was the first time I had experienced a subtropical climate, with blue skies and hot sunshine in December. Swimming in the Persian Gulf was like swimming in a warm bath and made Dubai a welcome place to visit before returning back to Northampton for the rest of the league season. The Hilton Hotel had a beach club some distance from the hotel, which I accessed via a shuttle bus. All the teams made their way there when the tournament wasn't being played. Everything we ate and drank whilst we were there was picked up by the hotel. I had to pinch myself whilst I was being pampered in this oasis in the middle of the desert. England was heading into winter and yet here I was on a rugby holiday without a care in the world basking in glorious sunshine. All the top teams in sevens were at this event, not representing their countries but for invitation teams like the Bahrain Warblers, Crawshays, or Queensland. It was Queensland who eventually knocked us out. They had six current or former Wallabies in their line up including Michael Lynagh, who at the time was the world's leading test points scorer. Millfield Old Boys v Queensland would appear to be a bit of a mismatch, but it was the sand and the heat that made it more of an even contest. The main pitch was a better surface than the outlying pitches; however, they were all sand, and we saw some horrific injuries and burns. It was all worth it just to be out in the heat and have everything taken care of by our generous hosts. It was extremely difficult to come home and resume the season.

Chapter 7

From the ultimate high to the ultimate low

Although I didn't realise it at the time, this would be the last traditional Thorneycroft and Allen family Christmas. Christmas was a huge occasion for the Thorneycrofts and Allens, and it was never to be the same again. For twenty-one years I had been part of a close knit family where my parents, grandparents, uncles, aunts and cousins would all come together to celebrate. The person who was the responsible for keeping the family together would never again be part of this festive period. I often reminisce about these Christmases and, although I will never be able to relive them, I'm very lucky to have been part of such great fun.

At the beginning of the New Year on 12th January 1991, I played in Buck's first league game for the Saints against Leicester and witnessed the clash of the Titans starring Buck Shelford and Dean Richards, the incumbent England number eight. We lost that day, but it was Buck who raised the standards of Northampton Saints. He was not used to losing and wasn't prepared to even consider it now, at the twilight of his career. Buck was thirty-four years old and I was fast approaching my twenty-first birthday. To say that I was influenced by him is an understatement. This was a man who carried the respect of a nation.

Rugby is popular across all sections of New Zealand society and many New Zealanders associate it with their national identity. We were privileged to have Buck at Northampton, and it was his standards that set the bench mark for the future of our club. The two matches I will remember most of that season were both at home and played within a week of each other. Don't forget that this was Buck's off season. He still had ambitions of gaining his All Blacks place back.

Having witnessed the Saints being trounced at Orrell some months earlier, he was able to affect the most remarkable turn-around when we were defeated Orrell to win a place in the Pilkington Cup. Wayne was in the twilight of his rugby career, but that afternoon at Franklin Gardens you would have never known this. He single handedly controlled the game, both at the base of the scrum and tactically. As a winger, it wasn't the most open of games. It was one for the purist. He knew what it was like to be a winner and what he needed to do to ensure we were at Twickenham for the final. There were very few opportunities in 1991 to play at the national stadium in front of a packed crowd, and the level of expectation from the crowd that day was remarkable. To get to the last four of the RFU Club Competition was an historic achievement. Orrell were tipped to win the match and came to the club as if the result was a forgone conclusion. This was the biggest game of most of the players' careers but for Wayne it must have felt like just another day at the office. I have watched the footage of the final whistle of this match and you would have thought we had won the cup. Players hugged each other in relief and spectators ran onto the pitch to congratulate their local heroes. The disappointment for Orrell was on their faces for all to see, and on no-one more so than on Dewi Morris who played scrum-half that day. The changing rooms were equally as boisterous. In those days our sponsor was Carlsberg and there would always be forty-eight cans of Carlsberg available to drink directly after the game. That night, we had to send for reinforcements and the lager never tasted so sweet.

The second game where Wayne showed his influence was when he scored two tries against Nottingham the following week, to secure our first division status. This was the first victory in eleven years for the club against Nottingham and it was very satisfying for me to beat the club I had left just a year before. It felt like complete vindication. I had made the right decision and picked the club that was hellbent on going places. Having completed a very thorough job for Northampton,

Buck went back to New Zealand to regain his All Black spot. He left Northampton to play in the biggest final in their history.

I am sure that every child who grows up aspiring to play sport dreams of playing on a big stage, and I was no exception. As a child, I used to watch the build up to the FA Cup Final on television. The build up before this football match was often the highlight of the day as the match could very often be an anticlimax. I would sit at home watching every minute leading up to a 3:00 p.m. kick-off. Bob Wilson was the person who would build the expectation. He was a former Arsenal and Scotland goalkeeper, and the television presenter of *Football Focus*. I always wanted to see the players on the bus with their FA Cup suits, which would have been made to commemorate the day. I thought this was very special. I met Bob some years later at a charity event for the Willow Foundation, which was founded by him and his wife as a lasting memorial to their daughter, Anna, who died of cancer. During the event I shared with him the vivid memories I had of him from when I was a child growing up idolising the players that played in the FA Cup Final.

The anticipation in Northampton before the Pilkington Cup Final, rugby's equivalent of the FA Cup final, at Twickenham on 4th May 1991 was extraordinary. This was the biggest sporting day out that any team could produce for the people of Northampton and the players were fully aware of their responsibilities. It is worth putting this into context: we were about to take on a Harlequins side that had eleven internationals compared to our three. The Harlequins side included Peter Winterbottom, who went on to be the second Englishman to gain 50 caps after Rory Underwood; Jason Leonard who was then at the start of a magnificent fourteen-year Test career that brought him 114 caps; and Will Carling, the captain of England from 1988 to 1996, who went on to win 72 caps. The Harlequins team at the time was full of talent and today we would not have stood a chance of competing against them. However, rugby was still amateur and many of our opposition had day jobs including high-pressure jobs in the city, which meant that the gulf between the two sides was slightly less pronounced by the time Saturday came and the players had got through the working week.

Peter Winterbottom, who became a great friend of mine, was a money broker in the city and would be at his desk at 7:00 a.m. in the morning, regardless of whether he had played for Harlequins or England on the Saturday. Harlequins had a reputation as being a team full of rich city boys, who would stroll around like prima donnas. The club was located in South West London with great clubs such as London Scottish, London Welsh, Rosslyn Park and Richmond all within a few miles of each other. In 1991, the supporters of Harlequins were very different to our supporters. Their supporters were very affluent who were probably debenture holders at Twickenham which is where Harlequins played some of their home games at the start of each season.

When you look back at both teams that ended up playing in the Pilkington Cup final in 1991, they were probably some of the most industrious individuals in terms of the way they managed their "three-lane highway". This analogy is something that Frank Dick uses to describe the way that people manage their careers in the outside lane, their family friends and environment in the middle lane and themselves in the inside lane. If any of these lanes cross then they affect the way you perform, and with rugby players in 1991 their achievements on the rugby pitch whilst holding down demanding full-time jobs and busy family lives still staggers me. It is difficult to imagine how any player who had a family found time to strike the right balance. I would not have been able to be the father I am to my children today if I was playing full-time rugby and trying to hold down a career. The simple fact was that something would have to give, and I am sure very often it would have been the family.

Our team consisted of players from very different backgrounds. When I look back at the team that took the field that day, we boasted a carpet fitter, two teachers, two policeman, a farmer, an army officer, a quantity surveyor, a construction manager and four undergraduates.

I was one of the undergraduates, living in London on my placement year with Fuller Peiser in the Investment Department, in St George Street, Hanover Square. This year opened my mind in terms of the affluence of London, at a time when I was paid £10,000 and living in Islington. Islington was becoming very fashionable. I would walk to the tube station at Highbury and Islington through Canonbury Square. I fell in love with this attractive square. Our house was a four storey fully-furnished Victorian terrace that was full of antiques. There were three of us living there at the time and the house was extraordinarily grand compared to the houses we had come from in Nottingham. I will never know why the landlords didn't remove the antiques from the house, they were probably worth as much as the house. Prebend Street was a short walk from Highbury and Islington tube which, via the Victoria line, took me to a different world. My office was in one of the few eighteenth-century houses still remaining in Hanover Square in the heart of Mayfair.

I would travel back to Northampton at least three times a week for playing and training, and this kept my feet firmly on the ground. However, London was expensive and I needed a way of enjoying the capital properly. I stumbled upon an opportunity to fund my new lifestyle in London when one day I was walking down Burlington Arcade in Mayfair and came across the shop run by the shoemaker Crockett & Jones, who made hand-welted shoes, a traditional method of shoemaking. I was astonished by the cost of the shoes in the window. My dad would always buy me good-quality shoes for school and would often say that you can tell a man by the shoes he was wearing. For many centuries, Northampton's staple industry was shoe manufacturing. The factories which still survive are all over 100 years old. Founded in 1879, Crockett & Jones was one of the big names, along with firms such as Churches, John Lobb, Joseph Cheaney & Sons, Barkers and Trickers, I saw an opportunity to supply contacts that I met in London with "slight seconds" that were sold in the factory shop in Northampton at a fraction of the cost of those in Burlington Arcade. I obtained permission from one of the directors of Crockett & Jones, who was a great rugby fan, and before a game I would go in and often by up to ten pairs of shoes. My clients would have their size and width measured in Burlington Arcade and supply me with their details. I got to a point when I would be able to look at someone's shoes and tell them whether they were a Churches, Crockett & Jones, Loakes, Barkers or John Lobb man. Everyone wanted a bargain and my business venture began to bear fruit. I would often get multiple orders from individuals and had three or four rugby boys selling these shoes into their own firms, whether that was surveying, broking or insurance. Two of these guys were established rugby internationals in their own right, Victor Ubogu and Simon Geoghegan. The sale was made between 8:00 a.m. and 9:00 a.m. on a Monday morning in the equity partners flat above the office in 18 St George Street. This was an amazing flat with its own private dinning facility and bedroom which could only be used by the partners who owned Fuller Peiser. The equity partners, including my boss Keith Blake, who actively encouraged this act of entrepreneurism and very often would be with me trying on shoes at 8am.

The money I made allowed me to go to see West End plays, concerts at Wembley and eat meals at quality restaurants. The only inconvenience to me was having to collect the shoes on a Saturday morning when I should have been preparing for the game. The only other way of making money at the time was through travel expenses, which I claimed, because of the bizarre journey I did each week from work to training. I never once thought that I would ever get paid to play rugby. It is odd looking back now that we were so loyal to our clubs and had no expectation that we should be paid.

I was about to play the biggest game of my career at Twickenham and the week before the match I was still working in London, and travelling up by train from Euston to Northampton for Tuesday and Thursday night training. I had done this for a whole year and it was hard work. I had to be organised to even get to training. The journey was very simple – leave work at 5:15 p.m. to catch the tube from Oxford Circus to Euston Station. The Northampton commuter train left the station at 5:45 p.m., so it meant changing in the toilet of the office and sprinting to the tube to stand a chance of getting on the train. I would sleep until Milton Keynes, which was fifteen minutes on the train from Northampton. I used this time to stretch before the train arrived in Northampton at 6:45 p.m. To save money, I would run or catch a bus to the ground. Training started at 7:00 p.m. sharp. If this was not enough to contend with, I was then dealt a really cruel blow leading up to the game. My mum who had been very ill for some years had taken a turn for the worse and was hospitalised.

I had always lived with the fear of my mum's health deteriorating. The fear of losing her was buried in my subconscious and was something that I had always refused to accept. I had spent much of my life knowing that she was very fragile, my dad had been nursing her for sometime. He was our rock and he loved my mum unequivocally. She had lost the sight of her left eye when she was younger because of a very severe migraine. Her migraines were disabling and cruelly impinged on her quality of life, often resulting in long periods in bed when my sister and I had to be quiet. We had been told years before that my mum's heart was only working at twenty-five per cent of its capacity, following a heart attack when we nearly lost her in intensive care in Bournemouth. I could not accept my mother's mortality. I was in complete denial, failing to accept that she was anything other than indestructible and would be around forever. It was a shock to get a call from Dad to say that she may not last the day in intensive care in Bournemouth. This had been a happy place, holding great memories of Easter holidays staying in old Victorian hotels in Boscombe. I travelled down in the car with my cousin Steve on the August bank holiday of 1987. The image that it holds in my mind is now very different, with my mum lying in intensive care fighting for her life. We lost her a few times and, remarkably, she pulled through. What had been intended to be a weekend of relaxation had gone badly wrong. I never thought she would die, but I knew that she was dangerously close to it. If it had not been for the staff in intensive care that cared for her she would not have survived. I don't know who they were, but I want to thank them now for keeping her alive. It still hurts me to think of how frail she looked when we eventually got her home; but at least she was home. She knew she was lucky to be alive and told us a little of what she had experienced during one of her brushes with death. She had seen her father, who had long since passed away, at the end of a tunnel of light. She asked him whether he had come for her and he replied, "Not yet."

My mum was a remarkable and unselfish woman who understood people and brought the best out of them. It was Dad who wanted to send me to a private school to give me greater opportunities, but it was Mum who made sure that I had the personal tools to equip me to succeed. She had no idea what O- or A-levels I took at Wellingborough. We used to joke that at least with a degree she should be able to remember it as there was only one thing to remember, but she wasn't interested in my studies. What she cared about was not what I achieved academically but what kind of person I was. She had a look that would bring me to my knees if she thought I had done anything that might be remotely immoral or wrong. Her values were very old fashioned and she subtly instilled these into me. I will always get up on a packed tube and let a lady have a seat, or say good morning to everyone I pass on my morning run. There was no substitute for manners in her world. She lived by the old adage, manners maketh the man, and I hope I will always meet her expectations.

The moment of my mum's illness before the Pilkington Cup was the moment that I realised I was going to do something with my life. I couldn't bear to think how poorly she was inside, when she looked so beautiful on the outside. She enjoyed a certain quality of life, but was very restricted in terms of what she could do. I would have given anything to give her my strength and energy, but it wasn't possible. I always made light of her physical disabilities, but it hurt me to the core. I lived in fear of the call telling me that she had once again been taken in to hospital. I remember the nights as a child, when an ambulance would arrive in the middle of the night to take her to hospital. Even when she was being carried out on a stretcher she never once gave us the impression she was scared or that we were in danger of losing her. She tried to protect us from feeling the fear that she inevitably must have felt. She gave us a very secure childhood. I suppose that's what you do for the children you love.

I overcompensated for her lack of opportunity by taking advantage of every opportunity myself. I still do this; it goes back to my deep-rooted fear of losing the most important person in my life, who I loved with all my heart. My fear of failure is not becoming the person she would have wanted to me to be – this is what motivates me, even now. Sport had been my liberator after her heart attack. In some strange way, I think I realised how short a time I was going to spend with her and was trying to do everything in my power to make her happy. I knew that rugby gave her pleasure. She loved the game and despite having Raynaud's disease, which turns fingers and toes blue in the cold, she would watch the Saints games even during the coldest winter snap, wearing heated socks and gloves. I remember her positive and selfless attitude vividly and I wanted to try and emulate them in my life.

The day the squad was announced for selection for England Colts at Loughborough in 1988, Mum had been rushed into hospital. Dad came to the game and there is no surprise that I had a stormer. I visited her that night after the game in hospital and she was so pleased that I had achieved this unbelievable accolade, that none of us had thought was possible. My mum was incredibly proud of my rugby achievements, her father, Sid Allen, had played for Kettering town and my games became something to look forward to whilst she was contending with failing health. It was my way of channelling the fear of the unknown into something positive that we could all enjoy as a family. I think that we were all living our lives vicariously through my rugby achievements.

Mum was taken into hospital on the Thursday before the Pilkington Cup Final and was told by the doctors that she wasn't fit enough to make the journey that Saturday to the game. This was a great sadness because she had been at Rosslyn Park in London the week before, when we had been beaten 48–0 and the selection had been made. Dad had taken her down to watch the game and she spent part of it in the car at one end of the pitch, and the other part in the stand. This was the last time I saw her beautiful face at a game. I can remember her joy at hearing my selection for the team. Life was good; Dad and Nicola were all at the game to mark one of my biggest achievements and the culmination of all their hard work. We were a very happy family – this was to cataclysmically change just two weeks later.

I visited Mum in hospital the day before the final, knowing that the only incentive I needed was to give her something to be proud of. Sport does this – it took me away from the monotony of life and the unending sadness and struggle. It gave me an escape, a way out of sadness and a way to express myself. The final for many of us in Northampton was one of the greatest days we had experienced. The sleeping giant that had been the Saints was now awakening and realising its potential. The expectations of the town, and the 18,200 people who bought tickets, was overwhelming. I had been kept informed of the anticipation that had been building in my home town since 4th April, when we had beaten Orrell, by reports from Mum and Dad, who were really looking forward to the game. Sadly, the circumstances surrounding my mum's ill health had taken the gleam off the occasion for me. However, my mum's selfless attitude soon changed all this when I visited her in hospital. She refused to feel sorry for herself and made sure that I was aware of my responsibilities. She said the things that I wanted and needed to hear and encouraged my passion to succeed. It's impossible to know what happened in her mind during that time in Bournemouth, when she was on the brink of death, or what mental state she must have been in seeing her body deteriorate before her very eyes. She was a beautiful lady and had only just turned forty-seven, she had a husband and two children who needed her. Dad managed to persuade the hospital to give her a room with its own television so she could watch the match. I can't imagine how she must have felt watching the footage of the final as her son ran out in front of a crowd of 53,000 people. You couldn't record the game in those days, it was live on terrestrial television. It is only as I look back now that I realise how lonely she must have felt as her husband and two children spent the afternoon at Twickenham along with half the town who supported us that day.

The final was just as I imagined an FA Cup Final would be when I was a kid growing up. The difference was that I was actually participating in it and not a spectator. My most vivid memory of the build up is very bizarre. Brian Winkworth, the club steward, and his wife cooked a full English breakfast in advance of our journey down to the capital. The importance of nutrition had not really entered the game in 1991, and the prospect of a greasy fry up was very appealing – none more so than for Gary Pearce, our club skipper, who was interviewed whilst he tucked into his breakfast. There was no hotel in Twickenham the night before. Instead, we joined the town in the pilgrimage down to Twickenham on the morning of the game. There wasn't a coach to be had in Northamptonshire and surrounding counties. The M1 that day was a mass of green, black and gold. Our first stop was the London Irish Rugby Club at Sunbury, to do a team walk-through, before getting a police escort to the game. This was one of my highlights of the day. We came down the A316, watching vehicles parting as we weaved through the traffic. I live very close to the ground now and whenever I get stuck in traffic coming off the M3, I think how nice it would be to be able to have the same treatment as the traffic police gave us that day. The distance was only about six miles, but the police ensured that we got there on time. When we eventually got to the stadium, the reality of the occasion had started to sink in. This was the first time the club had reached a national final and we were representing the hopes of all our supporters.

This was a good place to be as a twenty-two-year-old playing in front of a full house at Twickenham. We had to undertake our warm-up inside the changing area because we were not allowed to warm up on the pitch. This seems madness in today's game, but then we accepted it and got on with it. The warm-up consisted of some basic stretches and a great deal of nervous energy confined to one area. You would often see forwards bashing their chests against each other like two gorillas in the jungle. The backs on the other hand would read the programme notes, before coming together in a group huddle, which you were lucky to get out of without any broken arms or ribs, such was the force that the forwards put through you. The floors were concrete, so this gave you a great opportunity to sharpen your studs, despite the fact that the referee checked them before you ran out. The referee would always get the front row together and stamp his mark on what he was expecting from them, which of course would be ignored in the first scrum. It was a relief to get out on to the pitch. Paul Bryant did the team talk but there was no need to motivate us we could do that for ourselves. We had a team photograph on the pitch before the game, which seems odd now but this was the tradition and who were we to break it. I stood at the end of the lineup, looking up at a sea of spectators and singing the national anthem, feeling very proud. This was the calm before the storm. The game was brutal – we tackled our hearts out, but didn't really get a chance to express ourselves in attack.

That day I played against "The Prince", Andy Harriman, the quickest man in World Rugby at the time having run 200 metres in 20.9 seconds, and probably the richest. He was a real character, whose background lay in wealthy Nigeria. He was the eldest son of a Nigerian tribal chieftain, Chief Hope Harriman. His tribal name was Tuoyo and he was heir to the chiefdom of the Itsekiri tribe. He had been educated at Radley and Cambridge and was one of rugby's greatest characters. The tales surrounding Harriman were legendary. Harlequins were playing away and the team bus was due to leave the car park at their ground at a certain time. In rugby, you are frowned upon if you arrive late for anything, but on this day they couldn't leave on time because Andy hadn't shown up. When he eventually did appear it was sitting in the back of a Bentley driven by a uniformed chauffeur, who handed him his kit bag after opening the door for him. Andy apologised to coach Dick Best, informing him that the Ferrari wasn't behaving itself and he had had to borrow his father's Bentley. The Prince saved the day for Harlequins that afternoon by rounding me six minutes from full time. It was one of the only tackles that I missed that day and showed me how fortunes can change quickly in sport. His try levelled the scores 13–13 at full-time and we entered a period of extra time where we were well beaten.

The vanquished Northampton team went off to the Runnymede Hotel for a subdued celebration of the club's achievements that season. This mood was short-lived. Win or lose on the booze! It is worth noting that the following morning I was up to play for Fuller Peiser in the Surveyors Sevens at Richmond and for Northampton on bank holiday Monday in the Heart Foundation Sevens at Moseley. Two weeks after the final of the Pilkington Cup, my mother passed away from a heart attack and I had played for the charity that could have helped her. I look back at losing my Mum not with sadness but with a great deal of pride. I spoke to Mum the night before she passed away, telling her that I had been selected to play for the Penguins in the Sicily Sevens and for the Saltires in the Lisbon Sevens. Her response was incredibly impactful and the last words she ever said to me were, "take advantage of every opportunity Harvey, because I won't get them in my lifetime", and these have stayed with me forever. Everything I have ever done since that conversation has been about trying to live life to full. I resented the fact that she had been taken away from me and my family, but I wasn't going to let this stop me living my life.

I can't tell you that she knew she was going to die, but I am sure she was aware that her time was coming to an end. Her words have reverberated throughout my life. Her spiritual presence is always with me and I often think that although her life was cut short, she passed her passion for life into me so we could both enjoy it together. During the short twenty-two and a bit years that we spent together, she shaped my moral code. This will remain with me for the rest of my life and for that I am eternally grateful.

The loss of my mother was a terrible turning point in my life. I had gone from the ultimate high to the ultimate low in the space of two weeks. For twenty-two years I had experienced the most unbelievable upbringing, loved by both my parents and afforded every opportunity. My dad, who still remains a rock in my life, had just lost the woman he adored and had nursed until her death. He was there by her side until the end and now had to live life on his own. The magnitude of the task ahead was too much for him to contemplate and I knew I had to be strong for the family's sake. My grandma came to live with us in the early days after my mum's death and everyone rallied around. My sister was more vulnerable than we knew at this time and she reacted completely differently to the way that I did to my mum's death. I was very close to my sister and, whilst we tried to console her, her grief resulted in a gradual decline in her spirit from which she was never to recover. Nicola was only twenty years old and she and mum were very close. My Nan would probably have said on hearing of the death of her beloved Patricia that a little piece of her died that day as well. I hope I never have to experience what it's like to lose a child. It must be the most painful bereavement a person can experience. The death of her daughter brought great pain to my Nan. She found it impossible to come to terms with it, and with the lynchpin that had been my mother gone the very fabric of our family was destroyed. I was thankful that I had rugby to channel my emotions.

Rugby was my saviour and Dad insisted that I play the week after Mum's death in the Sicily Sevens. He urged me to "take advantage of every opportunity", it was what Mum would have wanted. The funeral was unable to take place until a post mortem had been conducted. Dad and Grandma drove me down to the hotel, which was on the Bath Road adjacent to the runway at Heathrow, the night before our flight, and this journey will always live in my memory. Dad drove to Heathrow by the longest route he could ever have taken, but it gave us a chance to chat about what had happened. We were three generations grieving their loss together. We really didn't know what to say to each other. The loss was so fresh that it seemed odd to be going off on a trip like this. However, Dad was resolute in his desire to make sure that I took advantage of every opportunity, as Mum had said the night before she passed away. We all took some sort of solace from the fact that we were fulfilling her last wishes. I boarded the plane bound for Catania full of emotion and feeling very vunerable. It was the best thing I ever did and two characters, Neil Back and Andy Harriman, helped me get through that weekend. I will never forget the empathy they showed me, and rugby players are not famous for their compassion.

I had been invited by Tony Mason who founded the Penguins in 1959 with Alan Wright. The club is still the best travelled club, having played in fifty-seven countries. The objective of the Club was to foster the development, goodwill and fellowship of Rugby Union worldwide. Tony had picked a great squad to play in the Italian RU International Sevens in Catania. It included three international rugby players, Andy Harriman (1 cap, England), Sean Lineen (29 caps, Scotland) and Owen Williams (Wales), who became known as the "three asterisks" – the asterisk alongside a name in a rugby programme denoting an international cap. It also included Neil Back who would go on to be one of England's greatest internationals. He was my roommate on tour and along with the rest of the squad knew that I had just lost my mum. They got me through a difficult time.

The three asterisks were responsible for setting tour rules. On the first evening we were all assembled in the hotel for a meal in a private dinning area set off from the main restaurant. The restaurant was full and was typical of the area that we were staying, serving superb fish and homemade pasta. The tone of the tour was set at this meal. The rules had been set that if you mentioned "and", "it" or "of" in any sentence whilst you were in conversation, then you were duty bound to finish your drink, which was a very heavy Sicilian red wine. You were not allowed to eat your meal with a knife and fork, and upon completion of the meal you had to present your plate back to the waiters as if nothing had been served upon it. This was very difficult to do when the fish dish served was a firm and bony swordfish steak. These rules proved very difficult as you might imagine. This was the quickest I had ever got drunk in my life and was the first time that I had ever eaten a swordfish steak without any cutlery. Casualties were disappearing to the toilets for what was affectionately described as a tactical chunder. Neil Back was the only person who didn't succumb, mainly because he ate bread and didn't say a word through out dinner. This wasn't the best way to prepare for a Sevens tournament. The Sicilian reds were heavy and alcohol-laden, and we were knocking it back like cordial. It took me a long time after this trip before I could appreciate red wine again.

You may have thought the next day that I would have woken with a hangover, instead Backie woke me looking as white as a sheet. He had heard an English female voice shouting for me.I recognised my mother's voice and immediately ran to the door to open it. Outside, I could feel her spiritual presence. It gave me a feeling of great elation and was supremely emotional. Downstairs in the lobby I telephoned Dad in tears and together we worked out that the disturbance was exactly one week since she had passed away. Dad reassured me that it was just Mum coming to say goodbye. Many things like this happened in those early days and weeks after Mum passed away.

This first night in Catania had been a great way of getting to know the team, but after this brief chance to let our hair down we began to take it seriously. However, not as seriously as Fiji who we eventually played in the final, who were then and still are regarded as the greatest exponents of the seven-aside game of rugby. Before each match, Fiji would perform a lovely ritual and drink *kava*, which is made from a plant that is entrenched in the traditions of Fijian life. It was seen as a way of easing the anxieties of the match. It was the first time that I played against Serevi, the player widely considered to be the greatest rugby Sevens player of all time. We were convincingly beaten by Fiji, however, which is not surprising as our attitude to Sevens was very different to our opposition. We were part of an invitation side made of players from all over the UK, and to be selected to be at this tournament was a big deal. This was well before the International Rugby Board Sevens Series, which was created in 1999. In the northern hemisphere, Sevens was regarded as secondary to the fifteen-man game. I enjoyed going on these trips, because they were great fun and the tournaments were in superb parts of the world. It was a chance to play with other players from different clubs and countries. The Penguins was similar to the Barbarians in spirit, but didn't have the same standing with the RFU. This didn't prevent them getting great players, but they didn't have much money to fund the trips.

The after-match reception was a major affair and as beaten finalists we were expected to show some sort of decorum. Sadly, the pre-reception tour court put paid to this. It was a tradition, when rugby clubs like the Penguins go on a tour, to institute a "Tour Court" to deal with any transgressions that may be committed by members of the tour party. These touring tribunals were kangaroo courts, providing little opportunity for the accused to be found anything but guilty. It was Andy Harriman who came off worse from the punishments that were meted out by the judge, "Justice Owen Williams". Andy was fined for talking to the fairer sex too much and his punishment took the form of eating a raw clove of garlic. I am told that for two weeks after the event, he could still taste garlic and it was growing in his hair. I had confessed my love of tomatoes and had to hold a rotting beef tomato throughout the function, and be prepared to confess my love of the fruit at regular half hour intervals. Sean Lineen had a penchant for sunbathing, so, as I was confessing my love of tomatoes every half hour, Mr Lineen had to strip down to his boxer shorts and imagine he was sunbathing on the floor in front of our banqueting table. The function was memorable not because of us but because Fiji sang some traditional songs from their Islands which included the *cibi* – Fiji's version of the *haka*.

The night before we were due to fly back to England we were faced with a major problem. The hotel was not prepared to release Andy Harriman's passport unless he paid his phone bill, which amounted to hundreds of pounds. We were party to a conversation that "The Prince" had with Tony Mason. Andy explained to Tony that he must pay his phone bill, and the reason he gave was legendary: "Look, Tony, if you invite champagne, then you expect to pay champagne prices." I never knew who paid the phone bill that trip, but we all got home eventually and my friendship with Andy Harriman and Neil Back became very strong because they helped me take my mind off the funeral that was to come. They were both strong family men from very different backgrounds and their no nonsense approach to me was exactly what I needed.

Backie drove me home to Northampton to prepare for my mum's funeral. I felt strong enough to help Nicola and Dad through the ceremony. Dad had a profound desire to fulfil Mum's last wishes. Mum was very modest and she wanted this reflected in her funeral: she didn't want to have an expensive coffin, just a basic box that could be put in the back of the Volvo and taken to the crematorium. This was not as easy to accomplish as it sounds. However, he found a way of collecting the coffin from the mortuary at Northampton General Hospital and took it home to our house in Old Duston. Dad wanted Mum's last journey to be from home to the crematorium and my sister and I accompanied Mum and Dad, listening to Carpenter songs all the way. I have deep respect for my Dad for making this happen exactly the way she would have wanted it and I was honoured to be part of this intimate funeral. This day marked a major change in my life and I refused to let myself be dragged down by the enormity of what had just happened to my family. Rugby was my lifeline, through which I channeled my loss. I made a pact with myself on the day of Mum's funeral: I would never settle for mediocrity and would take of advantage of every opportunity I came across. It was also the first time that I realised that as a rugby player in Northampton I was susceptible to the press, because the team was high-profile now. "Saints Star Mother dies at 47" was in the local paper, and I realised then that there was a price to pay for the fame that I had gained whilst playing for the Saints. I wasn't allowed to mourn in private. It didn't matter how strong I was, it wasn't nice reading this in the paper.

I took my Mum's advice and seized every opportunity. Rugby was a part of a balanced approach, which involved finishing my degree, seeing my family and friends, the occasional relationship and, of course, travel, which had become my passion. It was very difficult to keep all of these areas of my life engaged. However, in 1991, when rugby wasn't professional I had no choice. At twenty-two I couldn't have imagined being a professional rugby player. I think if my only desire had been to play rugby for England then I may have thought differently.

I was passionate about my sport, because of the doors it opened, the countries I visited and the people I met. On the day of my mother's funeral, the 18th May 1991, I vowed that I would jump on any train, plane or automobile to play rugby. There seemed no better way of seeing the world than through eyes of the different cultures that played rugby. The great part about rugby is the code that goes with it. This is the same in every respect to the moral code I had been taught by Mum and Dad, and it allowed me to bounce my way around the world without getting into too much trouble. I had been described on more than one occasion as "reassuringly naïve." However, losing Mum made me grow up and realise that the cocoon that she had created for me wasn't how everyone else lived. I like the world according to Harvey, I think it's important to have an acceptance of other people and to believe that good things can and do happen. Mum had given me the roots to grow and the wings to fly, and whilst she continued to inspire me with her spiritual presence I knew I was in safe hands.

Chapter 8

The travels of an
impoverished student

The first trip that I went on was to Lisbon with an invitation side called the Saltires, whose roots, as the name would suggest, were in Scotland. In those days you would get a call out of the blue and board a plane, not even knowing the team you were going to play with. The Saltires were similar in every respect to the Penguins. Other sides that regularly attended this event were the White Heart Marauders, the Bahrain Warblers, the French Froggies and the Crawshays.

The White Hart Marauders were founded in 1982, specialised in seven-a-side rugby and were based at the White Hart pub in Eversley, Berkshire. Outstanding International players such as Will Carling, Peter Winterbottom, Jeremy Guscott, Lawrence Dallaglio, Mark Titley, Colin Hillman, Jon Sleightholme and Dewi Morris played for the team. The tournaments they played in attracted tourists dressed up in various costumes.

The in-team at this event were the Bahrain Warblers, who played in pink shirts. They were established in 1981 on the principal of being able to attend a multitude of social events and play good rugby. David Campese, Micheal Lynagh, Dallas Seymour and Eric Rush are just a few of the illustrious names who went on to play for the Warblers over the years. However, for this tournament The Prince, Andrew Harriman, was the key danger man. Rugby was seen as a secondary part of the weekend in Lisbon. The main activity was the social scene and you were expected to indulge in copius amounts of beer and local wines and spirits. Performing on the pitch was, of course, a prerequisite. Our hotel was in central Lisbon and we spent very little time in it, preferring instead to catch the train at the waterfront Cais do Sodré Station in Lisbon up the coast for about thirty kilometers, west of Lisbon to the beach resorts of Cascais and Estoril. Rupert Moon was on this trip with me and it was on these train journeys that we got to bond with the team, playing touch rugby and beach cricket on magnificent beaches, and eating out in the evening at some fine restaurants. All the teams headed out to the coast; no-one stayed in Lisbon. We were more intent on getting a suntan rather than playing rugby.

Whilst we lost in the final to the Warblers the most memorable part of the whole event was the after-match banquet. It was The Prince Harriman who started one of the biggest food fights that I can ever remember being part of. The banquet was held on one of the seven hills that make up the geography of the city of Lisbon. The organisers of the event had gone to considerable expense to feed the teams in such a unique location.

There were hundreds of guests including the players. Andrew Harriman had got up during the starter to go to the toilet. His return seemed to provoke an avalanche of bread rolls thrown in his general direction. Some hit him but some strayed from the target. This provoked retaliation from the people who were randomly hit resulting in a twenty-five minute food fight, where tables were turned over in an attempt to shield the guests from the food that was being thrown. The top table remained stalwart, only protecting their faces by covering them with the plates that they had been given for the starters. The evening soon came to an end with horrified officials claiming that rugby players were like savages. The evening resumed when we returned to the hotel for even more drinks. I was at the bar when Andrew Harriman ordered champagne. The barman replied, "Yes, sir. French or Portuguese?" and in disgust The Prince replied, "French, of course. Is there any other?"

The next phase of my voyage of discovery was a summer with England Students. It was a great time to be involved with this set-up from a rugby and a touring point of view. The prospect of going on another tour of Canada from east to west was something to look forward to. It also meant the opportunity to play against Canada, the first full international side I had faced. The other opportunity was the chance to play against the full England side in one of their world cup warm up games, prior to the 1991 World Cup, which was going to be held in France and England.

The manager of the tour party of Canada was Jack Rowell, the Bath coach who led Bath during the golden era when they won eight John Player/Pilkington Cups and five League Championships. Jack conducted a parallel life as a successful business man, holding down very senior roles with a number of companies in the public and private sectors, mainly in the food industry. Jack was unique in rugby and knew how to produce top quality performances from the sides he led. On reflection, it is difficult to understand why he would find himself looking after England Students. Rugby was amateur and so he probably had no contractual obligations with Bath. It is peculiar to think that someone so senior in business would get the time off from the board of Dalgety plc, where his responsibilities were for the consumer foods division. I can only imagine that he had been given the nod, that he was being groomed for the coach of the England Rugby Team, so he was just cutting his teeth. In fact, between 1995 and 1997, Rowell became the coach and won twenty-one of their twenty-nine matches, including the 1995 World Cup quarter-final against Australia. In percentage terms of games won, Jack Rowell was England's most successful rugby union coach.

Our backs coach on this trip was Les Cusworth, the Leicester and England fly-half. I had first come across Les when I was picked for a Midlands v North game at Otley at the tender age of nineteen. We trained at Birmingham Rugby Club prior to the game and were asked before we went out onto the field to introduce ourselves. I have never been so nervous standing up in front of some huge names of the game, including Dean Richards, Gary Pearce, Gary Rees and Les Cusworth. Everyone knew each other and I was the new boy in the squad. I announced my name and Dean Richards said, "Who?" It was Les who reassured me and put me at ease. Les had won 12 caps for England as a mercurial fly-half between 1979 and 1988 and 365 times for the Tigers, scoring 947 points. He was without doubt one of the best ball players you could ever meet and when we played touch rugby with him, you could never get near him even at the age of thirty-seven.

We were very privileged to have these two coaches for the matches against Canada and England. The England Students side was very strong and was lead by Rupert Henry St John Barker Moon, who I toured with in Lisbon. Rupert was one of England's top scrum halves and whilst his name sounds like he had stepped out of Brideshead Revisited, he was actually born in Birmingham and spoke with a slight brummie accent. Rupert and I had played at England Under 21 level and had a mutual understanding. Rupert was very ambitious and eventually went on to play for England at B level, before qualifying for Wales by playing his club rugby for Abertillery RFC and Llanelli RFC, and earned many caps for Wales in the national rugby team. After retirement from international rugby, he played for Newport Gwent Dragons, became a television presenter on BBC Wales and became Head of Group Commercial & Business Development for the Welsh Rugby Union and the Millennium Stadium in January 2006 before leaving in 2007.

Jack, Les and Rupert led this touring party with great aptitude. Canada is a great place to tour, it has such a diverse landscape. In the east in Fortune Bay, Newfoundland, we encountered whales, dolphins and porpoises that migrate into the waters adjacent to the Newfoundland coast every year. We saw Humpbacks arriving off Eastern Newfoundland in late spring from their Caribbean winter breeding grounds. They were reputed to be over fifty-three feet in length.

We stayed in Jaspar, in the heart of the largest park in the Rocky Mountains and the gateway to some of the most majestic, pristine and accessible wilderness of Canada and a UNESCO World Heritage site. Nothing quite prepares you for the unearthly beauty of Lake Louise, its bright blue waters mirroring the surrounding mountains and glaciers, and having lunch in Chateau Lake Louise.

One of the highlights for us on this tour was whitewater rafting on the Athabasca River and visiting the Athabasca Glacier, one of the six principal toes of the Columbia Icefield, which is the most visited glacier in North America. I think if someone had taken me to this region when I was studying glaciers for my geography A level, I would have paid more attention.

In complete contrast, we visited the cities of Toronto, Montreal, Edmonton and Vancouver. Canada had everything from the wilderness to superb cities. We visited a Blue Jays baseball match in the SkyDome. We stayed in chic Montreal, the largest city in Quebec and after Paris the largest French speaking city in the world. Edmonton was interesting because it was an opportunity to get in touch with some of my relatives that lived in Canada. Vancouver was by far the best city I had visited at that point in my life. It is a city that I would want to go and live in, one of the only places in the world where it is possible to ski, snowboard, hike and golf – all on the same day. This city really opened my eyes to a side of life that I had never previously witnessed.

We played the match in Stanley Park and were told to visit Richard on Richards in the evening for beers. Richards on Richards was one of the largest and best-known nightclubs and on a Saturday night became one of the biggest party nights in the city. I will never forget leaving the club and being approached by prostitutes, who were openly selling themselves along Richards Street in Vancouver. Being "reassuringly naïve", I found this very disturbing! Many of the women who lined the street that night were dressed in the same style as Julia Roberts in *Pretty Women*, before she transformed from a working girl. It still amazes me that in a city like Vancouver the seedy side of life is so blatantly on display.

We won all of our games in Canada by huge margins, but narrowly lost to the full Canadian side in the very unmemorable Sarnia in Ontario. The town was located where the Great Lakes empty into the St Clair River. It didn't really have a heart like many of the other Canadian cities we had visited. The most memorable part of this leg of our tour was the invite that was extended by the Canadian team to come and party with them after the international. The two players who were the most hospitable and who went on to become legends of Canadian rugby were Norman Hadley and Gareth Reece.

"Stormin' Norman" was a massive six-foot-seven-inch, twenty-one stone (150 kilograms) lock. He was one of rugby's true characters and was completing his MBA from the University of British Columbia when we were in Canada. He eventually came over to play professional rugby for London Wasps and then Bedford Blues. While working in London and playing for Wasps, he gained perhaps his greatest notoriety for beating up two hooligans on the London Underground, an act which not only earned him praiseworthy column inches in the British broadsheets and tabloids, but even gained him a mention in the House of Commons by the Prime Minister John Major.

Gareth Reece is probably the greatest Canadian rugby player ever. During his international career, he played for Canada fifty-five times, captaining them on twenty-three occasions and scored 487 test points. He also played for Wasps playing a first XV game, when he was at Harrow School as a schoolboy. Gareth had also played in the 1987 World Cup for Canada.

The Canadian side we played that day were at full strength and we only narrowly lost. In fact, Canada went on to become quarter-finalist in the 1991 Rugby Union World Cup, being narrowly defeated by the All Blacks. This match was widely regarded as Canada's finest hour, where Hadley and a big, tough forward pack clearly had the upper hand over New Zealand and Gareth Reece skillfully led the backs. Gareth became one of a small group of players to appear in four World Cups. That night in Sarnia was one of the greatest ever post match nights out. Stormin' Norman and Gareth Reece were perfect hosts, leading us into battle with their ties around their heads and blazers turned inside out.

So this was the first taste of playing in an International, albeit it against Canada who were at that time regarded as one of the lesser nations of World Rugby. Quite ironic when you think they ran New Zealand ragged in the World Cup. I think when you get a taste of this type of rugby, it becomes addictive and I wanted to make sure I could sample more of it. It was the sense of anticipation before the international that I loved so much. A group of guys with a common purpose, just about to go into battle but what ever the outcome they would generally mingle with the opposition over a beer after the game.

Chapter 9

Life after the bright lights

The next challenge in the rugby hurdle was to ensure I got picked to play against England in the World Cup warm-up match in September 1991. It is very odd to think that the full England side would have played England Students as a curtain raiser before the biggest tournament in the sport.

The last World Cup was in 2007; England played two of her oldest rivals in warm-up games, Wales and France, as they prepared for the tournament in September. These warm-up games were played as full tests, two in front of full houses at Twickenham and one test this time in Marseilles, one of the French heartlands of Rugby Union and boasting some of the most fervent rugby fans.

This wasn't the case in 1991. The venue on this occasion was Grange Road, Cambridge University. It was great to visit the second oldest university in the English-speaking world to play against the full English side. However, it really gives some indication of how uncommercial rugby union was at this stage. The other strange thing to consider is a player's dream of playing for England one day; however, you don't expect to play against England and certainly not in an All Blacks shirt, with an English Red rose emblazoned on your chest. Grange Road was full to capacity, but probably only had 5,000 people watching. In 2008, to go and see England v Pacific Islanders, which would be one of England's lesser fixtures at Twickenham Stadium in the West Stand, would cost you up to £60.00. In 1991, the entry cost was £5.00 to see the National side (the side that would eventually lose in the final at Twickenham against Australia in the RWC 1991).

The field and The Club pavilion stand at Grange Road hark back to the glories of an amateur era in sports. As I entered the pavilion, I was taken aback by the tradition that you would expect from a University Club founded in 1872. A full oak-panelled foyer area led to antiquated changing rooms which had an open fire and yellowing photographs of varsity teams adorned the oak panels. It was like some of the pavilions I had visited whilst playing for Wellingborough against Repton or Charterhouse.

I turned up to the match as an England Student and our opposition, the full England side, were relaxing casually outside the Comber Stand as if they were going to play touch rugby in the park. The crowd was slowly filling the ground, yet there was no sense of urgency to get into the changing rooms. You couldn't have had a more laid back group of players. I can understand the reason for this casual attitude. In their eyes they were only playing England Students, but to us this was the biggest game of our lives and only the second full international side that I had ever played against. I don't blame the England boys for thinking that this fixture wasn't going to be hard, and this worked in our favour as they weren't truly prepared for us that day. It took them a long time to get into their stride before going on to beat us by a narrow margin.

My opponent was Rory Underwood, who I had faced for Northampton against Leicester once before. At the time he was a Royal Air Force pilot and he became one of the greatest wings in Rugby Union, winning 85 England and 6 Lions caps between 1984 and 1996. His brother Tony, who was five days older than me, was someone I had shared a house with in Prebend Street, Islington, in 1990. I had played against Tony at Cambridge University for Northampton in 1991, so it was funny to then be playing against his brother who was England's greatest finisher a few months afterwards. Ironically, it is Tony who is now the pilot flying long haul for Virgin Atlantic. Rory Underwood was the benchmark for any aspiring wing and his brother probably the number two in England. They were both deadly finishers and these were the brothers that I would need to try and get the better of if I was ever going to play for the full national side. Rory was the perfect winger. He was astoundingly quick and had superb balance with the ball in hand. In 1991 he had everything you needed to play the game. I am sure he would still be able to play the game today, but I don't think he would enjoy it as much. The power house wing had less subtle touches than Rory possessed and he was the person I looked up to as an example of how to play the game.

I played well that day and had a try disallowed. Geoff Cooke, the England Manager, and Jack Rowell, the future England Manager, were both there to witness my performance and I am sure that much of the success that I had in the coming years was a result of that performance. I was aware that the full England side played the game with a pace that we couldn't live with. However, I never felt that I was exposed and showed that I could handle the pace.

I walked with Jack to the after-match reception in one of the great old dining halls and he commented that I should set my sights on playing for the England team and consider joining his team – Bath, who in 1990/91 had become Courage League Champions. This conversation is one that you can reflect on after your career has ended, but no-one has the benefit of hindsight.

I met Jack some years later and reminded him of this conversation and discussed with him the reason why I didn't follow him to one of the most successful clubs in the country. It was partly because of the experience I had had at Nottingham but also because I loved being a Northamptonian. If I had just been committed to playing rugby then I would have gone to Bath. I loved the city and also enjoyed playing there. However, the death of my mother and the family that I had left were stronger ties to my town than rugby could ever have been. I don't regret this decision, I wholeheartedly embrace it. I was regularly chastised by Tim Rodber and Ian Hunter for leaving the Saints to go to Nottingham and I wasn't going to make the same mistake again.

In the same dinning hall, I had a conversation with Tony Rodgers, the Cambridge Coach, about the possibility of applying to join Cambridge University after my final year at Nottingham Trent. During the summer of 1987, I had understood the attraction of going to Cambridge when I worked for a hospitality company based in Northampton, which was run by Christopher Palmer-Jeffery who is now the Chief Executive of the European Group. I had seen how opulent the End of Term Balls were at Peterhouse and Trinity when I worked as a wine waiter. I would have loved the chance to have been a student at this seat of learning. There were only two things that I had to contemplate. The first being that my degree, Urban Estate Surveying, is a similar course to Land Economy, so in effect I would be repeating the same degree. This was the degree that many rugby players took to get into Cambridge as postgraduates. If I took up the course I would have been following in the footsteps of Chris Oti, Rob Andrew, Gavin Hastings, Tony Underwood and The Prince Harriman. The second consideration was to play varsity rugby, regardless of the prestige, would have been a downward step in terms of rugby. I did get the application forms, which I filled in and still have to this day. I never sent them back on the recommendations of my rugby coaches at the time. I regret this because I would have loved to have played in the varsity match, and Tony Rodgers and his team at Cambridge were always so accommodating when ever I visited on the numerous occasions I played in the Steele-Bodger's XV.

I knew the fun that the Blues had at Cambridge when we went out with them after these games. Richard Elliott, who I played with many times, was for me the epitome of everything that was good about being a postgraduate at Cambridge. He had attended Lougborough during his undergraduate degree before studying Ecomomics at Cambridge. He acquired a group of friends during those two years that would stay by his side for years, the likes of Adam Bidwell, Mark Denney and Adrian Davies, the former Welsh fly-half.

Looking back I had come a long way from my time at Wellingborough. The whole ethos of the school was underpinned by obtaining an academic background and, for the very best, the opportunity to go to Oxbridge. In just over three years after leaving school, I found myself having conversations with Jack Rowell about playing rugby for England and Tony Rodgers about attending one of the leading academic institutions in the world. The latter option, I can assure you, was because of the ability to play rugby – I had no other illusions. I was fortunate to be in a position where I had this incredible choice because of the sport I played and my academic background to date. The sport was interdependent of the degree and I felt proud that I could pursue both careers.

Sadly, with choice something had to give in my life and this is what happened in the next year. I returned to Nottingham to complete my finals, but I also needed to fit in a Premiership Rugby career, representative rugby, and a lot of travel and probably too much fun. Throw into the mix that I had lived a year in London, and the experiences I gained there didn't motivate me to want to go back to Nottingham to study valuation, law, land economics, management, planning and international studies as part of my degree course. I didn't go off the rails after I lost my mum, but something had gone from me and I never really felt the same about Nottingham again. If the truth be known, I think I would have rather stayed at home.

In professional rugby today, I am told that the tutors are a little more flexible. At Nottingham this was not the case; the tutors were not interested in my sporting career or the fact that I had lost my mum, with two exceptions: Brian Wetton and David Richmond. Brian was my tutor and David was my valuation lecturer but also a huge Derby County supporter.

The course that I was doing gave full exemption from the Royal Institution of Chartered Surveyors exams, which is what I thought I wanted to become when I left university. The only reason I had taken the course was because my mate, Andy Collier, worked for a firm of chartered surveyors and had a company car with an Allstar petrol card. This seemed to be a logical decision at the time! He used to pull his Escort up outside the Café Kilkea in Northampton and treat me to a toasted sandwich and a piece of carrot cake. He would always be dressed in a superb suit and hand-welted leather English shoes, and I thought he was the business and that his profession as a surveyor was the one for me. He still is a surveyor, heading up the out of town retail team for Cushman & Wakefield. He still looks the business in his suits, too, but has graduated to Cafes in the West End now.

The course was strict and was full of gregarious people who did just enough to pass their A-levels whilst actively pursuing a social life at school. This gave them just enough grades to get on a degree that might eventually allow them to seek a profession that their parents would have wanted for them at the end of the four years. The difference between me and some of my great raucous mates was that in their final year they decided to concentrate on their degree, with a view to completing their course on the 22nd June 1992. Only after that time would they would return to their boisterous lifestyles. However, for me the year I had ahead of me was to be very different and resulted in something having to give. This meant I was unable to sit my first exam. Instead I was on another continent, attempting to further my other career, the amateur sport of Rugby Union.

The other career started in terms of games on September 1st 1991 and finished on 2nd May 1992. In reality I had just over a month to concentrate solely on my degree. The average week was very full. I attended lectures during the day and trained every lunch time apart from on Tuesday and Thursday nights when I would get in my car and travel down the M1 for training. I will never forget those long journeys, listening to Steve Wright in the afternoon on Radio One. Steve Wright had his own brand of personality radio, with huge audiences – the highest shares on the station at the time. He was hilarious, inventive and like a breath of fresh air on the eighty miles I had to do twice week. He lead the way in the UK for what has been termed "Zoo" broadcasting, the technique in which the presenter surrounds himself with a crowd of people who contribute to the on-air gossip. He had the "Afternoon Boys" Posse, provided by Impressionist Phil Cornwell, whose cast of characters included John Cole, Mick Jagger and David Bowie ("Tell us what the time is! Tell us what the temperature is!").

On Friday or Saturday, dependent upon games, I would travel to Northampton to pick up the team coach or play in Courage League Division One. This obviously didn't include divisional rugby or England Students. There was a lot of expectation from Northampton Saints, because of our Pilkington Cup success and the return of Wayne Shelford and a new coach called Glen Ross from New Zealand. Glen Ross, a former teacher in the early 1980s, on the staff of Hamilton Boys' High School, in Waikato, went on to coach the provincial team. Glen was a lateral thinking coach who made sure we had an understanding of the basics, and that success was based on hard graft, a committed effort and considerable work ethics. He coached players at Waikato in the late 1980s who went on to become great coaches, like John Mitchell (who became All Blacks' coach), Warren Gatland (now coaching the Wales team), Stu Foster and Kevin Putt, who coached a Super 12 side in South Africa.

I lived my final year at university in Mapperley Park, a suburb north of Nottingham bounded by the triangle formed by Mansfield Road, Woodborough Road and Private Road. Mapperley Park was a conservation area with many distinguished Victorian houses and plenty of trees. I lived in one of these converted houses, and at the time it seemed very upmarket in comparison with my accommodation during the first two years of college. However, this location wasn't particularly conducive to training to become an international rugby player. There were no local gyms to join and the nearest athletics track was at Nottingham University which was about twenty-five minutes drive from where I lived.

Many of my mates who I was at university with were into rugby, but not really into a huge training regime. Phil Morris, who was on the same course at college, was the son of Bill Morris, the former Wales

International. The closest centre of excellence for rugby training was Lougborough University and many of my mates were studying there, so I visited regularly. The RFU had started to make sure that the players who were being fast-tracked for the 1995 World Cup Squad were monitored away from their clubs. We had to keep paper diaries of what we ate and how much training we undertook. I was regularly physically tested by the university's department of physical education, sports science and recreation department. The project director was Rex Hazeldine, who wrote the *RFU Handbook of Rugby Fitness* and whose name was synonymous with high level performance at the RFU in the early 1990s.

This was the first time that performance had been tested. The researchers looked at body composition, endurance, flexibility, strength, leg power, speed and speed endurance in the tests that they undertook on behalf of the RFU, and there was no way of getting around not doing the work. The difficulty was maintaining this elite performance whilst at college. I had barely enough money in that final year to pay for the calorie intake I was expected to take on board to maintain my power and pace. Tuna bake, spag bol and chicken with rice were very economical dishes washed down with a bottle of £1.99 Liebfraumilch from the local shop. This was as good as it got and I thought I was highly sophisticated. On a Friday night before a game, I would be back before midnight and this was an early night. I would be joined two hours later by my diligent housemates, who only went out at the weekends in the final year. I would still hear them come in, despite stuffing ear plugs in my ears fashioned from chewed-up tissue paper.

The introduction of a New Zealand Coach to Northampton raised the standards to a level never seen before. New Zealand was regarded as being where some of the best technical coaches of the game came from and Glenn Ross was one of their great exports. He brought coaching methods and training drills never seen before in the UK, and we felt very privileged to have him as our coach. He brought dynamism never seen before in an English Club. Glen and Wayne Shelford made a formidable partnership.

However, rugby was still amateur and I was on a student grant and finding it quite difficult to keep my finances in the black. Fortunately, I was playing well for the Saints and had won the Player of the Month for November. This was a very important award, not because of the prestige, but because the sponsor of the award was Houghton Hams. The presentation was a hamper full of meats, which, as you can imagine, came in handy as a student. I got to know Nigel Wagstaff, who ran the company, and he was personally responsible for feeding me in that last year of university.

By 4th January 1992, I had played in nineteen of the twenty-four first team games that were on offer and which had taken me all over the UK on bus trips. One of the really memorable trips was an away fixture at Portadown. I had no idea before I arrived in Portadown that it was the ancestral home of the Orange Order and, along with Lurgan and Craigavon, made up part of what was known then as the "murder triangle" during a period of history known as The Troubles. The rugby club, on the other hand, was as old as the Irish RFU who listed it as an affiliated club in 1879. It was a year older than Northampton and had strong links with the Saints. Throughout the years Portadown had remained the mainstay of normality and civility, through all the trying social and political circumstances, which had been a blemish on Portadown society.

Regardless of colour, race or creed, Portadown had promoted friendship, fair play and competition to its players, local community and peers. This is exactly what we experienced when we were there and was in total contrast to the reception that I expected from watching all the television coverage of the troubles. Shocking images of the atrocities such as car bombings by the Provisional IRA were commonplace. Everyone knew a soldier who was serving a term of duty in Northern Ireland and I later got to know someone whose father died whilst passing a car belonging to Conservative MP Hugh Fraser. A bomb had been primed to detonate, but exploded prematurely in Campden Hill Square, Kensington, London.

Rugby had the ability to bring people together like no other sport. This wasn't the first time that I had visited Northern Ireland and had been able to displace any previous image that I may have had of it. I was at college at the time with Stephen Deymond who had attended Methodist College Belfast, one of Northern Ireland's leading grammar schools and over many beers he had put me straight on what was actually reality in this part of the world.

I ended up playing in the game that was organised at Ravenhill, Belfast, for the Midlands against Ulster. One of my teammates was Dean Richards, and I will never forget the dinner we had the night before the game. We were staying at the Europa Hotel, a four-star hotel in Belfast that had a reputation as the most bombed hotel in Europe. Whilst making a speech over dinner, Dean Richards remarked on the pavement outside our window by saying, "Lads, have a good look at that – because in the morning you will be laying on it."

In fact, the Europa was damaged thirty-three times by Provisional IRA bombs, between 1972 and 1994. After the match, our coach was escorted back to the airport by an armoured vehicle. The reason for this was because some of our team were in the armed forces and the police, including Dean Richards who was a police constable in the Leicestershire force, serving most of that time on the beat in Hinckley. Dean, forever the joker, asked permission to travel in the armoured vehicle, because he thought that would be the best place for his protection. The police were very jovial with him and duly obliged. He travelled in the front of the coach and wasn't really protected because his head was always out of the vehicle, looking back at the coach in amusement.

I never saw any problems during my time in Northern Ireland, and this was another experience that shifted any impressions that I may have had because of newspapers or television. Travel was broadening my horizons and giving me a deeper education than I could ever have had if I had stayed at university.

On 17th January 1992, still on the honours trail, I was selected to play for England Students against the Scots at Watsonians. At the same time, another club mate, Tim Rodber, was being selected to play for England in the Calcutta Cup Match against Scotland. Tim and I had played England Under 21s together in Romania in 1989, so his rise to stardom was meteoric. This was largely due to his raw athletic ability and uncompromising nature, but also in part to the tutorage that Wayne Shelford had given him during his time at Northampton. There could have been no better mentor than Buck, and Tim was a willing recipient of his wisdom.

This selection had been a bold move by the England selectors who included our England Under 21s coach, Dick Best. Displacing Dean Richards from the 1st XV to the bench for this match amazed many rugby commentators. Tim decided to do away with one of the time honoured traditions of Rugby Union, which was to abstain from playing for your club the week before his first cap. I remember admiring him greatly for the stance that he took in playing for Northampton v Harlequins.

Calcutta cup weekend in Edinburgh was one of the best weekends of the sporting calendar. The city came alive for this occasion and it was great to be part of it. It was also another opportunity to impress the England management who would be watching the England Students game against Scotland Students.

I returned to college on 13th January and left again two days later to join the England Students to travel to Edinburgh. We played the game in front of the full England management, and after the game Geoff Cooke and I had a conversation. It was brief, but gave me the motivation that I needed to keep my dream of playing rugby for England alive, as long as I could fit all the other things I needed to do around it!

Our game was on Friday afternoon, which was a double bonus because you got to go out on Friday night after the game and then were given a ticket from the RFU to watch the international on Saturday. I will never forget my first experience of Murrayfield and the flower of Scotland. I stood on the old terraces of the stadium before it was redeveloped with a huge number of passionate rugby supporters who had travelled far and wide to see their beloved Scotland play.

Today, Murrayfield is recognised as one of the top stadia in Europe, but I preferred it when it was less corporate. I was so proud to be watching Tim Rodber play his first game, with my England Under 21s roommate Jason "The Fun Bus" Leonard. In fact, it was "The Fun Bus" who knocked Tim out during the game, entering a ruck which led to him being replaced by Dean Richards.

These weekends were superb, and by and large paid for by the RFU. It never occurred to me at the time how lucky we were to be travelling to the locations of the five nations and experiencing all the perks that were afforded to anyone representing England. I knew no different, because I was being fast tracked through the ranks and 1992 should have been the year that I concentrated on my finals. A degree in property had seemed interesting when I started it, but my rugby education was giving me far more than the chance to complete a dissertation on the cyclical nature of property investment. The only joy that this assignment gave me was a harsh realisation that I would be leaving college at a time when the UK was in a recession. I thought that if I concentrated on rugby at least I would have something to fall back on. This shouldn't have been the mindset of an aspiring international sportsman, but it was the reality.

Chapter 10

The Barbarian Football Club

The next England Students game was against France Students at Toulose University. As an impoverished student, the experiences of this weekend were remarkable. Imagine a weekend where you stay overnight in a top hotel in London, before flying to Toulouse to play a student international; you have a night out and then board a plane to go to see France v England in the Parc de Prince in the afternoon, sample the Parisian underworld in the evening, before boarding another plane to fly back to London to play in a Saints XV against a New Zealand XV at Franklins Gardens. I may not have been paid to play rugby back then, but I would pay good money to do this now.

Before the student international we stayed in Ramonville, in the southern part of Toulouse, in the Hotel Le Relais. It is traditional for the opposition to stay in a different hotel, but not for this match. I love France and particularly the food, but sadly we were not extended the same eating privileges as our student counterparts. Whilst we sat down with the team to eat a set menu, the main course of which was chicken that looked like it had been cooked with a hair dryer, we were able to glimpse, in an adjacent room, the sumptuous banquet that had been prepared for our opponents. It was like being in prison looking out from the foyer of the hotel to a private glass banqueting facility. Our set menu was very different to that of the French Students, which included fish soup and mussels in a white wine and cream sauce to start, and char-grilled pork cutlets with roasted peppers and sautéed potatoes, peppered beef steaks with red onion salsa for the main and a deluge of desserts. It is quite sad that I kept the menu just to prove the difference between how the teams were treated. I think they call this reverse psychology.

We played the game on the main pitch at Toulouse on Friday 14th February 1992 in front of a packed crowd of students who were passionate about their rugby. The star of the show that day was Thierry Lacroix, who had played in the 1991 World Cup and went on to win 43 caps playing at fly-half. The after-match reception was held in our hotel and was memorable because at various points during the course of the banquet, the French team would stand up and applaud their teammates who one by one would leave in the direction of the hotel bedrooms. I was intrigued by this and followed one of the opposition. Inside a closely guarded room were some girls, who were providing some "massages" courtesy of the French management. I couldn't have imagined the RFU ever being so generous with their expenses.

We boarded the plane on Saturday morning with heavy heads to fly to Paris to watch a double header, France B v England B in the Stade Jean-Bouin at a pitch adjacent to the Parc de Prince, where many of my mates including Neil Back, were playing in this fixture. England B was the next level for me to reach from the students' platform and this was a significant step. It was the 2nd XV of England and it was a big deal to be picked for it.

I had arranged to watch the main game with Backy. As we entered the stadium, I witnessed for the very first time what was to come for Neil Back. Even in 1992 Neil Back was known in the rugby community in France. They likened him to a cult figure – Jean-Pierre Rives, a fearless open-side flanker, whose mane of blond hair earned him the nickname "Casque d'Or" (Golden Helmet). Backy possessed the same blond hair. Jean-Pierre was more than a than a blond bombshell of a forward; like Backy, he was everywhere on the field and became his country's most capped flanker. He was by no means the biggest of flankers, standing barely five-feet-ten-inches, but he was admired for courage, commitment and an aptitude for winning, all the qualities that Backy also possessed.

This was the first time that I had been to Le Parc des Princes, which was in the 16th arrondissement of Paris on the right bank of the River Seine. Le Parc des Princes was the national stadium until the Stade de France was built in 1998. The atmosphere was unbelievable when you entered the stadium, like no other in the world. A mixture of up-market Parisians, passionate supporters from the South of France playing musical instruments, tribal English supporters and, of course, a live cockerel, which was placed on the pitch – a recognised symbol of French sovereignty. I witnessed one of the best ever matches played by England against France. Barely four months after the acrimonious 1991 World Cup quarter-final between the two, England beat France and I saw my old house mate, Tony Underwood, score a try. The game was most notable for France's spectacular implosion, with both Gregoire Lascube and Vincent Moscato being sent off.

Two nights out "on the raz" in France, one in Toulouse and one in Paris wasn't the best preparation for a match against a New Zealand XV at Franklins Gardens. Ian Hunter, who had been playing for the B Team in the Stade Jean-Bouin, and I flew back to Heathrow from Paris and made our way up the M1 for the match. I don't know why we were asked to play, but we took the field in mind rather than body.

Wayne Shelford had assembled a mighty side made up of many of the All Blacks he had played with, who were now either playing or coaching in Europe. They were so far ahead at halftime that Wayne asked his team to take their foot off the gas and allow us to get back into the game. It was at this point, hungover from the night before, that I realised the gulf between the All Black mentality and that of the Northern Hemisphere. Whilst the game was a friendly and organised with the intention of compensating Wayne Shelford in an amateur era, through the proceeds of the gate, his side played a style and pace of rugby that we could not live with. I was invited that night to join Wayne and his mates back at their hotel. I thought very hard about it, but declined in preference of my degree course.

The next international that I played in was against Wales Students at Newbury RFC on the 6th March 1992. The team met two days before the game at the Hilton Hotel and was informed that we would each be given a ticket to watch the international at Twickenham on the Saturday. I had been given the nod by one of the England Squad that he was very interested in purchasing all the student tickets to sell for corporate hospitality. I had to be discrete, but some of the players were keen to sell their tickets and I was tasked with the responsibility of delivering the tickets to him.

The England Team were staying in the Petersham Hotel in Richmond and it was decided that we would meet at a midway point down the M4. We had been offered a sum of money per ticket that had been agreed in advance by the players which was probably twice the face value. I watched as my Northampton teammate counted it out on his walnut dashboard in crisp "pink salmons". He then turned to me and said, "Well done. Now what can I give you for your trouble?" I immediately thought of a figure and to my amazement he paid it. As I travelled back that night I felt a bizarre sense of achievement. I paid the players, who were very happy indeed even though it was only a small amount of money in the general scheme of things. I was very happy, too, until I found out the mark up that he had placed on them – no wonder I got paid what I had requested. This is one of the ways that amateur players were able to fund themselves through college. The other was through travelling expenses.

I have always regarded myself as an honest person; that was, until I was found out for trying to claim too much on expenses. On one occasion I received a letter back from JR Simpson, a past president of the RFU, who was charged with the responsibility of looking after student expenses. The match was England Students v Irish Students, this was being played at Waterloo Rugby Club in Liverpool. The letter read: "I duly received via Twickenham your expenses claim form in respect of the match against Ireland. I was however rather surprised when I read your claim. Apart from the fact that the AA distance for the return trip form Northampton to Liverpool is 312 miles and not 415 you in fact never drove your car to Liverpool. Les Cusworth drove you from Leicester to Liverpool and you told me that Craig Barrow was driving you back to Leicester." The letter came on official Rugby Football Union paper with the red rose emblazoned on it. This was a stark reminder to me that you cannot buck the system, there is always some one there to catch you out.

I should have concentrated on my degree, but it was so difficult to turn down putting on an England shirt whatever the level. This was a valid excuse when applied to representing your country; however, could the same logic be applied when out of the blue I got a phone call to play for the White Heart Marauders in the Hong Kong Tens from Fred Smith, on the 23rd March 1992?

This is the kind of invitation you cannot turn down and I am so glad I didn't. I was able to travel to the Far East, on my first ever long-haul flight to this part of the world. The odd thing looking back was that Northampton Rugby Club actively encouraged players to go off around the world as they felt it added to a player's rugby education. I had to be back for a mid-week fixture against Leicester, but that was my only commitment. This would never happen now.

Taking place on Wednesday and Thursday night before the Hong Kong Sevens weekend, the Hong Kong Tens attracted social sides from around the globe to the Hong Kong Football Club. The Tens was first conceived in 1986 and was an integral part of the week-long Hong Kong Rugby Festival.

My first long-haul flight was not a problem to me, but to get to Hong Kong at that time you had to land at Kai Tak Airport. The players who had visited Hong Kong before had informed me about the runway, which jutted out into Victoria Harbour, it was very difficult to land there because of the numerous skyscrapers and mountains located to the north. They weren't wrong: the approach to the airport was bizarre and not for the faint hearted. In fact, a crash did occur on the 4th November 1993 when a 747 couldn't be stopped and skidded off the 9,100-foot-long wet runway, ending up in the shallow water of Hung Hom Bay.

We stayed in the twenty-two-storey Lee Gardens Hotel, which was close to Happy Valley, a mostly residential suburb of Hong Kong located in the north of Hong Kong Island. The Hong Kong Football Club was adjacent to Happy Valley Racecourse, which was regarded as the most expensive real estate anywhere in the world. It was first built in 1845 to provide horse racing for the British people in Hong Kong, but over the years became more and more popular among the Chinese residents. The matches were played on the main pitch at the HKFC, but also within the Happy Valley stadium. This was a unique location in the world to play rugby, surrounded by skyscrapers. It was similar to the HAC Club in the city of London, but on a grander scale.

One of our teammates in the Marauders was Mark Thomas, the son of Richard Clem Thomas, a Wales and British and Irish Lions international who wrote a history of the Lions, which was published just after his death in 1996. Mark Thomas was at Cambridge with the likes of Gavin Hastings and Rob Wainwright, who I would end up meeting on this trip. He was a similar rugby character to Andy Harriman, in as much as he knew everyone. He also came from the same village as Catherine Zeta-Jones, and was great friends with her brother. Mark Thomas eventually moved to Hollywood to become an actor. Within a few days of getting to LA, he landed a role in Friends as a former boyfriend of Ross's then-current English girlfriend. Mark played a rugby player!

As soon as we arrived in Hong Kong, Mark was on the phone in the hotel to a friend of his who worked in one of the island's big banks. He organised a driver to pick us up and take us on a tour of the island, which took in Stanley Market. Stanley Market was one of the must-go places for tourists when visiting Hong Kong. It was an array of little shops selling everything. I bought myself some silk boxer shorts and some branded sportswear that was so cheap compared with the UK.

I of course needed silk boxer shorts at that time of my life. Sadly, the average extra large Chinese man didn't have the thighs of an average rugby player from Northampton, and I found that they just about came up to my knees. Stanley Market is located in the southern part of Hong Kong Island and with a driver it took a good hour to reach. We were able to discover the contrast of the Island from leaving the congested Sky Scrapers, to the less densely populated areas where the market was located.

The Marauders were a very social rugby side, so drinks were compulsory and the tour court was in full swing even on the first night. The first person to be fined was Dewi Morris, the then England scrum half. His crime was not turning up to the bar for pre-dinner drinks on time. Dewi had been set up by some of the players. He was told that the Barbarians' honorary secretary Geoffrey Windsor-Lewis wanted to meet him in the hotel reception to draft him to the Hong Kong Sevens.

The Barbarians, who were representing the Home Nations, had picked a very strong squad of players that included the scrum half Andy Nicol, who had only just been capped for Scotland and had played against Dewi at Murrayfield. There was obviously a lot of rivalry and there was no reason why Dewi Morris shouldn't have believed that the Barbarians would want him in their squad which included Gavin Hastings, Ivan Tukalo, Rob Wainwright, Andre Joubert, Ian Hunter, Derek Stark and Justin Cassell. Sadly, the meeting was bogus, Dewi had been set up; they knew he was pissed off having not been picked for the main event and they wanted to make it worse by making him think that his luck had changed. The net result was him being late for the pre-dinner drinks, which resulted in his drinking forfeit.

The Court session was held in a little bar just a short distance from the hotel by foot. The last thing I wanted to do was drink after an eleven-hour-forty-minute flight, but it was expected of you and a large part of building the team spirit. We were told the plan for the next few days, which basically consisted of drinks parties on board junks and some rugby. Junks were a way of life in Hong Kong among the expatriate community. The junk is an engine-powered, wooden-bodied fishing vessel converted into a comfortable boat. The only caveat to this fun was that we needed to get into the final of the Tens tournament, so we could enjoy the last few days on junks and watch the Hong Kong Sevens.

There were some very good sides that entered this event; however, there were also some veteran sides who were quick in mind but not body. Jon Raphael was one of these players. He was our club doctor and had been involved with my club, Northampton Saints, as a seven-year-old when he watched his first ever 1st XV game and went on to play and captain the club, as well as become its president and medical director. Jon was one of the most unlucky England players to have never got a cap. He sat on the bench many times behind Peter Wheeler, going on two England Tours in 1975 and 1977. He was out there with his mates, which included a small red-headed extrovert scrum-half, Steve Smith, the ex-England captain and founder with Fran Cotton of Cotton Traders, the clothing brand. Their brand was very strong in rugby playing communities even in 1992, just five years after they had set it up. I can remember speaking to Steve in the stands of the Hong Kong Tens about why they had decided to set it up.

Cotton Traders was formed after much deliberation and research and originally was a mail-order sports clothing company. They had been impressed by the fact that the biggest sales of rugby shirts in the world was by an American company in the United States – so they thought that if the Americans could sell rugby shirts, so could they. Today, Cotton Traders is a highly successful company. It was a conversation with Steve Smith that made me realise that at some point in my life I wanted to run my own business and the extent of what was possible with the brand of rugby.

Another of the players that was on this trip was Tony Bond, who had played for England from 1978–82, making his debut at Twickenham with a side that contained some great names – Hare, Squires, Dodge,

Bond, Slemen, J Horton, Young, Cowling, Wheeler, Nelmes, Beaumont (captain), Scott, Dixon, Rafter, Uttley. This was the era of rugby that I watched as I was growing up. I watched Bill Beaumont who was the captain and probably the most recognisable rugby player at the time. You could see from the Tens team that they entered, that there was still a great spirit and they were truly amateur.

We eventually got to the final and were narrowly beaten by a side that included the big North Walean, Arthur Emyr, who played thirteen times on the wing for Wales in the late 1980s and early 1990s. This was a tremendous effort from our team, considering the amount of alcohol that had been drunk in Banana Joe's on the nights before and during the tournament, but sadly we were lightweights compared with Jon Raphael side.

The Hong Kong Tens dinner was held at the twenty-six-storey Hilton Hotel which was one of the most prestigious in the colony. I sat next to Dewi Morris during the dinner. You can imagine my surprise when Ian Hunter, my teammate from Northampton, who was staying in the hotel with the Barbarians, came up to me and suggested that I go to the bar. He informed me that I was picked in the squad and that Micky Steele-Bodger, the President of the Baa-Baas and Gavin Hastings, the captain, wanted to meet me. I quickly dismissed the invitation out of hand, assuming that it was another team wind up but Dewi told me it was true and I should go straight away. The players were aware of why I had been summoned but I was oblivious.

I was met at the bar by Micky Steele-Bodger who turned to Gavin Hastings, who had his back to me. I was introduced in a very formal way as the new Barbarian joining his squad. I can safely say that was probably one of the greatest moments of my life. As a kid I had always gone down to Franklins Gardens with Wellingborough School to see the East Midlands v Barbarians play in Mobbs Memorial Match, and had recently played against the Barbarians for the East Midlands. I had never dreamt as a kid of playing for England, as I had never watched an international. However, I had seen the free flowing play of the Barbarians and aspired to pull on a shirt one day, which arrived earlier than I thought possible. To be picked for the squad to play in the Hong Kong Sevens was life changing.

Gavin Hastings bought me a beer and introduced me to the rest of the squad. The reason I had been called in was because Derek Stark, the Scotland Wing, was injured and they needed a replacement. I was told to check myself out of the Lee Gardens Hotel and check into the Hilton Hotel. I finished my beer and a driver was arranged to help me collect my kit and that was it. The Hilton Hotels back in 1992 had a really prestigious brand, I would have never imagined that I would ever stay in one.

I was no longer in the Tens that had finished, I was now in the Sevens coached by my old England Under 21s coach Dick Best, who was also the newly appointed coach of England. As I entered the lift to go to my room that night, a certain David Campese entered the lift with me. Campese is considered one of the greatest wingers in Rugby. His brilliance during some of Australian rugby's vital moments led him to be called Australia's greatest rugby player and possibly one of the greatest rugby wingers in the history of the game. He was capped by the Wallabies 101 times and held the world record for the most tries in test matches (64) until Daisuke Ohata scored his 65th try playing for Japan on 14th May 2006. It was surreal. This was a man who I had admired from watching on the television, and now here I was having a conversation about my amazing good fortune. "Campo" congratulated me and wished me good luck, and before I knew it he had gone to his room.

We trained the next morning before going off to discover Hong Kong and visit a tailor to have some shirts, a pair of trousers and a jacket made. I was still an impoverished student, but I could not resist treating myself. Hong Kong was so different to anything I had ever seen. It was the first time I had seen people on mobile phones. They didn't exist in the same quantity in the UK. Technology was everywhere you looked, yet in the same instance you would see a butcher delivering freshly slaughtered animals to a restaurant with blood dripping across the floor as diners looked on. There was no such thing as health and safety at the markets I visited. Dogs, cats, palm civets, chickens, turtles, frogs and snakes were stacked in crates, cages and buckets ready for sale. Customers would look in the cages at the animals before choosing what would be their day's meal. They would then watch as the butcher cut up the animal with knives and machetes, spreading blood, guts, faeces and urine all over the market floor. The markets were full of people and if you were not surrounded by sky scrapers then you could almost imagine that nothing had changed since medieval times. It was primitive and brutal.

The people I spoke to believed that eating *ye wei* (wild game) was beneficial to their health. Indeed, there is a saying in Hong Kong that "anything with four legs, except a chair, and anything that flies, except an aeroplane, can be eaten". A particularly famous dish is the dragon, tiger, phoenix soup, the ingredients of which include snake, cat and chicken. Animals arrived at these markets stressed, diseased, dying and dead. This was the side of Hong Kong that I didn't enjoy but accepted as part of the culture.

My evening was in complete contrast to the afternoon. I had an invitation to dine with one of Gavin Hastings' Scottish friends in the Hong Kong Club, a private business and dining club in the heart of Central, which was close to our hotel. This was the night before the opening matches of the tournament and I wasn't going to jeopardise this opportunity by drinking. The squad was being entertained by the great and good of Hong Kong. "The Club", as it was referred to, had members who were among the most influential people in the colony, including government officials and the heads of the major trading firms. I have never seen so much silverware laid on a table for dinner, which included fine crystal glasses. After the meal was finished, Gavin toasted our hosts and thanked them for the meal. The liquid he used for the toast was reputed to be some of the best single malt whiskey he had ever been given.

The old Hong Kong Club was also the venue where the Hong Kong Sevens was conceived in 1975. The original home was where we played the tens competition however, the tournament moved to the Hong Kong Government Stadium which is where we played.

I woke on the morning of the tournament and saw my name in the headlines of the *South China Morning Post* as the latest recruit to the Barbarians team. I will never forget pulling on the Barbarians jersey for the very first time. The Barbarians were very popular amongst the British ex pat community in Hong Kong and of course the team that they supported. The tradition was that the Barbarians were allowed to warm up at the other end of the pitch to the changing rooms. This resulted in a standing ovation from the crowd before each match as the team needed to pass in front of the main stand to get up to the warm up area. I was told off by Piggy Powel, who was in the stands that day and was a former Northampton and England Player. It was traditional when playing for the Barbarians to wear our club socks with our kit. I hadn't expected to be picked for the squad so I hadn't packed any Northampton kit. Remarkably, socks were found for me before I ran out; I had to respect the tradition.

The experience of playing for the Barbarians and having international teammates alongside me made me want to keeping striving to play international rugby. The team that started the first match was Wainwright, Hunter and Hastings in the scrum, Nicol at scrum-half and Joubert, Tukalo and Thorneycroft in the backs. A very proud moment for an impoverished student from Northampton!

The after-tournament dinner at the Hilton Hotel was as memorable as the tournament because every team had to perform an act on stage. We were dressed in full number ones, Barbarian bow ties and, of course, sheep masks! We sang our hearts out on stage, before being joined by teams dressed in black wigs, grass skirts and coconut bras from Hawaii performing hula and traditional songs. The French team, which included Philippe Sella, Laurent Cabannes and Sébastien Viars, also included Thierry Janeczek, who became the French Sevens coach. He, for some reason, dressed in a blonde wig and a G-string, with nothing more than a white apron, and proceeded to sing French songs which they found very amusing but we didn't understand. Fiji won the event, beating New Zealand 22–6, and then sang beautifully, as did the Tongans and the Western Samoans. The only things we won were the drinking games.

Chapter 11

From Mumbles to a Maori

My relationship with the Barbarians was to continue for many years. There was a saying that if you were invited to play for the Barbarians and you turned it down then you would never get the chance to play for them again. A white invitation similar to one for a drinks reception would be posted to you and you were expected to reply in writing. The invitation read, "The Barbarian Football Club, the president and committee have pleasure in inviting H Thorneycroft to play for the Barbarians on the Easter Tour 1992", and the initials GWL (Geoffrey Windsor-Lewis) together with the club badge were included on it. This was the first time that I had received an invitation, and when it arrived in the post I felt very special. The squad would then very often be published in the national broadsheets, which was an honour. At Wellingborough School, a pupil called Michael Ellis, who is now a practising barrister in Northampton, always used to pay for his birthday to be published in the *Times* and whenever I had my name in a broadsheet I thought of him.

The only qualifications considered when The Barbarian's issued an invitation were first that the player's rugby was of a high enough standard, and secondly that he should behave himself on and off the field. The club philosophy was based on attack with flowing running rugby with lots of tries, and this was the style of rugby I loved playing. It was an honour to be invited on the Easter Tour, and the itinerary in 1992 was a lot less congested than previous Easter Tours that would have had fixtures on Good Friday against Penarth and Newport on the Tuesday. Instead we played Cardiff RFC on the Saturday 18th April and Swansea RFC on Easter Monday.

The non-match day of Easter Sunday would always be left for the Barbarians golf day at the Glamorganshire Golf Club, in Penarth. I had seen a Rugby Special programme the year before when the tour was featured and couldn't believe I was getting a chance to experience it. We played against Cardiff on the Saturday in front of a capacity crowd and narrowly won. My opponent that day was Steve Ford, who still holds the record as the club's top try scorer with 187 tries. We then ventured out into Cardiff in the evening to sample the delights. The hotel we stayed at had a room that was dedicated to the Barbarians and contained some fantastic memorabilia which had been collected over the many years of touring. This is where we met for team meetings and for dinner. The Barbarians had no formal clubhouse to display items, so it looked very incongruous in this hotel.

The Barbarians Golf Day was unusual for a number of reasons. My two teammates were Martin Johnson and Neil Back and none of us could play golf at the time, but were expected to play anyway. "A good walk spoiled" was the expression that we used at the time. You couldn't have got three worse hackers than us on such a beautiful golf course. The golf day was taken very seriously by the committee and included one member in particular, the late Major Fergusson, who was the treasurer. He had been with the Barbarians for years and the expression "all the gear no idea" comes to mind. His knees were "playing him up" so he had the assistance of a buggy. He had Ping golf clubs and the latest Pringle golf clothes. Sadly, as we all waited to watch him tee off in front of the main clubhouse, we saw him hook his first shot straight back into it. Needless to say, he bought the first round of drinks after the tournament. This was a very traditional day in the Barbarians Clubhouse and each player would be asked to sing a song from his country, then the day would finish with the club song *The Way We Are in the Baa-Baas*. The Baa-Baas were selected from different countries, and on that tour England were well represented. The English contingent consisted of Neil Back, Brian Barley, Martin Johnson, Martin Bayfield and me. The English lack passion when it comes to these sorts of moments and we ended up singing *Sloop John B*.

In our tour party we had Toshiyuki Hayashi, who eventually went on to gain 38 Japan caps and at the time was a member of Oxford University. He sang the Japanese National anthem, which was followed by Nigel Meek, the Welsh Hooker, who had sung in a male voice choir and did the most perfect rendition of *Unchained Melody*. However, it was a Canadian Number 8, who brought the house down. Glen Ennis must have changed this traditional after-match sing-a-long forever, when he got the whole team, including the ageing committee, to do a rendition of Queen's *We will Rock You.*

The drive back from Swansea on Easter Monday was memorable. We had won the game and I felt very satisfied that I had been part of Barbarians' history. Many of the best rugby players in the world have represented the Barbarians and still talk about the fun they had wearing the black and white hoops. In terms of appearances Tony O'Reilly of Old Belvedere and Ireland made thirty appearances for the club between 1955 and 1962, and scored thirty-eight tries, the most by any Barbarian. I have never had the chance to meet him but read his biography, *The Player: The Life of Tony O'Reilly*. This book had a profound effect on me. I was particularly struck by how Tony as a rugby player could converse with people from all walks of life and enjoyed his rugby career and the fun that it afforded him. He is without doubt the most successful rugby player in terms of the transition he made from the sport to business. I subconsciously took on board some of the lessons that were in his autobiography. The closest I ever got to him was in 2003 at Lansdowne Road in Dublin; we were part of the same crowd that earned a place in the Guinness Book of World Records for singing in the world's largest karaoke session. At halftime, lyrics were displayed karaoke-style on the stadium's big screen and we sang along to *The Fields Of Athenry*, a favourite anthem of mine and Irish Rugby. Tony O'Reilly sat very close to us and he looked just like Albus Dumbledore from the JK Rowling's *Harry Potter* series, with his white hair and worldly allure. I felt that it was significant to be part of an elite Club that Tony O'Reilly had graced. Little did I know that within a couple of weeks I would be selected to Tour New Zealand with England B at the same time as I was supposed to be taking my finals in Urban Estate Surveying.

Before the tour we attended a training weekend at Bisham Abbey on the 16th and 17th May 1992. England Rugby had their training base at Bisham Abbey, an 800-year-old Abbey, situated in 43 acres on the banks of the River Thames, close to Marlow. This weekend gave me a perspective on life. I was 23 years old, with no real idea of how the world worked, but I was learning fast.

It was a big deal in Northampton to be selected on this tour and I took advantage of the new-found interest that was being shown in me. Arlington Motors, the local Mercedes garage in Northampton, who sponsored some of our players with cars, lent Gavin Baldwin and me a car to travel down to Bisham Abbey. Northampton was ahead of its time in terms of the commercial arrangements that it had with the business community, and it was therefore quite unusual for two students to arrive at the National Sports Centre in a brand new Mercedes. Sadly, we didn't have the best car in the squad. We were upstaged by Andrew Harriman, who arrived for training in a red Ferrari. There were very few cars that could have competed with this. However, I soon realised the gulf between the two sports I was playing when the England Football team arrived for training.

We were on level playing fields in terms of where we were training at Bisham Abbey, but in 1992 the gulf between the income they received for playing football and the life of an amateur ruby player was vast. The attention that the England Football team received was huge, as it is today with the England Rugby Team. The England team trained at Bisham, but unlike us didn't have to stay in the purpose-built accommodation facilities within the grounds. Mentioned in the *Doomsday Book*, Bisham Abbey played host to Henry VIII and Elizabeth I. Sadly when the architects designed the accommodation blocks in the grounds they must have been off their heads. They were purpose built in the 1960s for accommodating sports teams and were simple, functional and more importantly value for money. I don't know how planning permission was ever granted as Bisham Abbey is a Grade I listed manor house originally built in the thirteenth century as a community house for two Knights Templar.

Whilst we were staying at Bisham Abbey we were given a stark reminder of how amateur our sport was compared with other sports. A bus arrived, whilst we were training. The bus was full of press who had been shipped in to interview the England Football Team. The occasion was a friendly with Brazil on Sunday 17th May 1992, which was being played at Wembley. I was fascinated by this media frenzy and the relative importance played by the agents in terms of negotiating deals on the spot for England players to give exclusive interviews with the press. The press were not just UK based, they were from all over the world, and this provided the players with even more lucrative opportunities.

It was great to meet the players that I watched on television week in week out, but I couldn't help thinking that the players and the people associated with professional soccer lacked an integrity which rugby had managed to maintain. The assembled squad of rugby players that was about to embark on a tour to New Zealand were doing it because they wanted to play for their country and placing a red rose on their chest was enough to keep them highly motivated. In 1992 there was nothing else on offer. I didn't get the same feeling from the England football team. There was one exception and his name was Gary Lineker. He worked the media with great ease. Gary seemed very comfortable with himself and those surrounding him. I don't think this was because he was the genuine star of the team, which would have been a very good reason, but because he appeared to be very humble and extremely articulate. It is no surprise to me that he was able to carve out a career in media after his England career ended. Gary Lineker eventually retired from international football with 80 caps and 48 goals, one fewer goals than Bobby Charlton's England record of 49 goals. He missed a penalty that would have brought him level in this friendly against Brazil.

The main purpose of this weekend at Bisham Abbey was to test the squad to check that they were fit enough to get on the plane for a brutal winter in New Zealand. Rex Hazeldine and his team from Loughborough University were on hand to administer the official fitness tests, which were endurance, flexibility, strength, leg power, speed and speed endurance. We had completed these tests many times before but the stakes were much higher at this session. They may seem primitive compared to the tests that players undertake now, but then they were ahead of their time. The report that was presented to me after Bisham Abbey was entitled, "A physical and physiological assessment of Harvey Thorneycroft."

The bleep test was at the time the test that every rugby player hated completing. This multi-stage fitness shuttle run test, was used to estimate an athlete's VO2 max (maximum oxygen uptake) or cardiovascular fitness, one of the all-important "Components of Fitness". If you weren't fit in a cardiovascular sense then you would be badly exposed on this test. In 1992 there was only one player who enjoyed the bleep test and that was Neil Back. On many occasions, when the players had got to their maximum levels, Backy would be running in isolation against the bleeps, always trying to beat the record he had set in the test before and continuing to uphold his reputation as the fittest player in England. For me, as a sprinter, the bleep test was not my favorite. There was always a minimum level set that a player was expected to achieve and I would dig in mentally until that level and then bow out a few runs later. I recorded 56 (ml/kg/min) or 12/8 (level/shuttle.) The mean for the bleep test that day was 57.3, so I was just below average, but the range was 64.6–46.5 for the backs.

The tests that I enjoyed the most were the sprint tests, and as a winger you were expected to do well. On the England B Tour of New Zealand 1992, the management had selected three other wingers, who were the quickest in England. Andrew Harriman, Tony Underwood and his teammate at Leicester, Steve Hackney. The Nigerian-born Prince from Harlequins was greased lightning, and had clocked up 20.9 seconds for 200 metres, which was Olympic qualifying standard. I ran 15 metres in 2.27 seconds and 30 metres in 3.99 seconds, so I wasn't too disappointed. Andrew Harriman on the other hand ran 2.24 and 3.85 seconds, respectively. There was nothing on him, with 8% body fat compared to my 16% and at the time 96.9 kilograms of weight. Players were given positional fitness priorities. For wings, it was power and speed over 60 metres.

We boarded the plane for New Zealand. The domestic season had finished in England and my club mates were preparing for a summer break before getting back into pre-season. At Nottingham everyone was locked into finals mode and I had been informed that I could take my finals at the end of the summer when I returned from New Zealand. I accepted this as I had no choice because once again the tutors that ran the Urban Estate Surveying Course at Nottingham Trent had never had a student selected for his country at any level so there was no precedent set. The tutors were very good to me, but probably didn't realise the significance of this tour at that stage of my career. New Zealand was the testing ground for any player and to be selected to tour was a massive honour.

However, the New Zealand Authorities had not really given us an itinerary that justified the quality of players that were included in the squad. New Zealand couldn't really get their head around England B, the name was indistinct, which led to it being changed in 1993 to England A. The RFU didn't really fund it in the way that an international tour should have been. This was reflected in the flight over to New Zealand, which wasn't direct because it was too expensive. Instead we flew from London to Singapore, from Singapore to Sydney, Sydney to Melbourne and Melbourne to Christchurch. This took 36 hours and you might argue was not the best preparation for an International Tour. We were asked to train as soon as we got to Christchurch having just got off 36 hours of flights. This was the best thing we could have done to get rid of the jet lag, but it didn't seem it at the time. We trained that night in Lancaster Park, the Canterbury Stadium – it was like a baptism of fire, travelling from the start of an English Summer into a New Zealand Winter. Any excitement that I had before I left was completely gone when I arrived in New Zealand. The itinerary that had been selected for us was tough not because it was an eight-match tour but because it took us all over South Island and North Island.

One of the first locations we played at was a sleepy town called Oamaru in North Otago, North of Dunedin on the South Island. There was not too much to Oamaru's compact nineteenth-century streetscape, it was like visiting a set out of a Western, yet this town claimed New Zealand's largest number of heritage buildings. Oamaru is made up of a Victorian precinct and harbour, with neoclassical buildings built from Oamaru limestone and designed by the finest architects of their time. We were staying in Kingsgate Hotel Brydone, Oamaru's oldest and largest hotel built in 1881. It was a fine example of Victorian architecture by New Zealand's standards, but its interior was dated and was in need of refurbishment. My mum always said that if a hotel was clean then that was all that mattered; however, we were in the middle of a New Zealand winter and the hotel felt dark and uninspiring. Oamaru was in the heart of the Waitaki District, which is a beautiful part of New Zealand. The locals made sure that we were kept occupied and took us jet boating on the Waitaki River.

The first match we played saw us beat North Otago by 68 points to 4; however, the final result was no reflection of how difficult the game was. A schoolboy curtain-raiser had cut up the soggy pitch and by half time the gold jerseys of North Otago and the white of England were indistinguishable. The match was kept going only by the skill of David Bishop, the top New Zealand referee, who was on his way to Australia to referee the Scotland tour match. We scored 14 tries and I got a hat trick. If you factor in the mud and the ferocious rucking then you would have felt that the game would have been a lot closer. I had seen the results of rucking on the back of Wayne Shelford and now knew why he was so scared. It was the first time that we had worn studs from New Zealand. The UK studs were kite marked with the British Standards logo on them and a lot safer and smaller in length. These studs were lethal and very often the referees were oblivious to them being worn because when boots were inspected the players would show a different set of boots to the ones that they were actually going to wear. It was like going into a food blender when you took the ball into contact. You lay on the ground waiting to be shredded.

Our next match was in a place called Invercargill, the southernmost and westernmost city in New Zealand, and one of the southernmost cities in the world. It is the commercial centre of the Southland region, the name of the next side we would play. It lies 18 kilometres north of Bluff, the southernmost town in the South Island. In fact, when we were there people described the Bluff as, "The arse hole of New Zealand with Invercargill being 18 kilometres up it. "

It was home to Jeff Wilson, a so-called "Double All Black", because he represented New Zealand in both rugby union and cricket, an increasingly rare achievement in the professional era. The match was a success against a very strong Southland side that included All Black Paul Henderson who played in the game. The next match was at Athletic Park in Wellington on the 17th June against New Zealand Universities. Wellington was a vibrant and beautiful city, the capital of New Zealand and the seat of Government since 1865. It was full of history and art and culture. It is fair to say that Wellington is in fact the windy city. We went up to the botanical gardens in a cable car to see some of the best views of Wellington. The gardens are a unique landscape including protected native forest, conifers, specialised plant collections. It is now classified as a Garden of National Significance by the Royal New Zealand Institute of Horticulture. Another victory took our journey to the more rural locations of Masterton and Wanganui on the west coast of the North Island.

New Zealand was certainly a beautiful country; however, in the rain in winter we didn't see the best of it. Within 15 minutes north of Wellington we were in some of the most breath taking scenery. The bus trip from Wellington to Masterton took in the Rimutakas, one of several mountain ranges in the North Island of New Zealand which form a ridge running parallel with the east coast of the island between East Cape and Wellington. The Rimutakas seemed never ending as we travelled from the Hutt Valley to Featherston on a narrow, winding road that forms part of State Highway 2.

The major difference to me between Europe and New Zealand was the lack of historical buildings. I had spent most of my childhood holidays travelling through France and discovering the most beautiful countryside peppered with historical towns and villages. New Zealand had the most breathtaking views, but none of the quirky buildings that you would expect to find in Europe, which became an issue when you were on long bus trips to sleepy towns like Masterton and Wanganui. We were travelling to quiet towns in the middle of winter on long bus trips. There was no video on the bus and nothing to see other than fantastic scenery. There were only so many games that we could play and we only had one tape with us, Van Morrison's greatest hits, which played for hours and hours. The players kept themselves amused, but after a while it would have been good to have stopped at a quirky town with the facilities that we were used to in UK but this didn't exist. It felt that all there was were sheep farms.

It reminded me of the long bus trips we had in Namibia where we had to amuse ourselves playing cards, there was always a poker school going on. It was on these long bus trips that I encountered the phenomenon of the rugby player's insatiable appetite. We would stop for lunch at pre-arranged venues where magnificent banquets of food were waiting for us that must have taken ages to prepare. We stopped en route to Wairarapa Bush and as I walked to the toilet I saw an incredible buffet of locally prepared food. Just a few minutes later it was consumed by this ravenous group, leaving only pickings for those stupid enough to go to the toilet. It wasn't just the quantity they ate it was the speed it which it was digested. There was an expression on this trip, "if you snooze you lose", which I had to remember if I was going to eat.

At Masterton we played The Wairarapa Bush team at Memorial Park, which included Marty Berry. Another victory took us to Wanganui, The area around the mouth of the Whanganui was a major site of a pre-European Māori settlement. We visited a Maori village and experienced a Powhiri, the formal Maori welcome of peaceful entry. We were told that we should not show any emotion when we got off the coach because this was disrespectful. This visit was the first time that we were treated to the *haka*. The *haka* that we were familiar with was the one performed by the All Blacks; however, the *haka* is not always a war dance. Hakas are performed for various reasons: for amusement or as a hearty welcome to distinguished guests. We were seen as distinguished visitors entering their village and so were extended this tradition. Unfortunately, Mike Slemen's retort to the villagers was for us to sing *Sloop John B*, which is not really a song that represents English Culture. I cannot say why this was always sung at times of pressure but it was a song that everyone knew the words to and was always sung on the back of the bus on the way back from away fixtures. We all had to sing it and we felt very inadequate. We ate a rich feast of Maori and New Zealand foods, steam cooked Hangi style, and enjoyed the warmth and hospitality granted to dignitaries entering a Maori village.

The first test of the tour was at Hamilton, and Wayne Shelford came to watch the game and I experienced first hand his demi-god status. Everyone recognised Wayne and it was like standing with the equivalent of Maradona in this rugby-mad country. However, he never showed anything other than humility. I remember inviting him back to the after-match reception to have a beer with our team and he was reluctant to come. This was because he had not been formally invited and didn't have a tie to enter the clubhouse. At the time I said, "You are Wayne Shelford, they are going to know who you are". He looked at me with such disdain, as if to say that is not the point, it is a rugby tradition and it doesn't matter who you are, you don't break with that tradition.

We narrowly lost the first test and this presented me with an opportunity to win a test place if I performed well in a tough match against North Auckland. Prior to the game everyone was talking about a player called Norman Rangi Berryman, a seventeen-stone winger who was in the same mould as Jonah Lomu. I was a big winger, but when this monster came out on the field I felt inconsequential. I had a good game but Stormin' Norman was so powerful and so difficult to tackle that any desire I had of getting a test place was taken away. I realised that I had a lot to learn about the game if I wasn't able to deal with the beast. Berryman played one Test for the All Blacks, as a replacement against the Springboks in 1998. He deserved more but he was probably the most laidback rugby player, born with so much natural talent. This was one of the biggest tests of my rugby career.

The biggest non-rugby test that I came across during my time in New Zealand was being asked by Stuart Barnes, the tour captain and fly-half, to act as the prosecution in the tour courts after each match. Tour courts were a time honoured tradition and regulated some of the antics that went on off the field of play and, in rare cases, on it. They were part of the after-match drinking culture, and in New Zealand in particular a chance to break up the boredom.

The only qualification to act as an official was that I was articulate. The tour judge was Andy Mullins, Martin Bayfield was the court sneak and the defense was Stuart Barnes. Defense was a thankless task, because if your name came to court then you were guilty as charged. I therefore never lost a case. I just had to come up with a semi-witty reason for the judge to issue a fine. One particular case included some video footage which had been presented to the court by the hotel receptionists. The footage was very innocent in terms of what was often played to the court. It involved one of the players taking a midnight jacuzzi. As he sat there naked and very well endowed, the hotel receptionists watched on and were entertained by his antics. The accused was being charged for being in possession of a weapon on camera. Needless to say when the video evidence was presented by the hotel reception, there was little room for defense. The final decision on his punishment was not given by the judge but by the president of the RFU.

You needed a quality set of boys to get through this tour. The team was highly motivated and won every game leading up to the two tests against New Zealand XV's. However, on such a long trip it was inevitable that from time to time players would show their frustrations.

This was dealt with and if you ever stepped out of line and had a "wobble" then you were presented with the "wobble wig". This was a pink wig that didn't look good on anyone, not least Graham Dawe, the farmer from Devon. This man was one of rugby's great characters and became a good friend on tour. We bonded on one of the only days off and went to a cattle sale in one of New Zealand's cattle markets. I was keen to see a bit of the countryside and wasn't particularly interested in the scrotum size of a prize Aberdeen Angus, who seemed to be the star attraction at the show. I took a picture of the beast, which I still have today.

Dawsy hated the wobble wig so much that if he if ever got it he would do anything to get rid of it. On one occasion he placed a boiling hot teaspoon on my hand. You can imagine the pain of having a hot spoon placed on your hand when you were not expecting it. I reacted badly and this was enough to warrant the "wobble wig". Graham wasn't bothered by the pain he inflicted he was just keen to off-load the wig. Graham Dawe was one of the unsung heroes of Bath's "Golden Era" during the 1980s and 1990s. It would be hard to meet a fiercer competitor. He would undertake the 300-mile round trip from his farm in Devon to train at Bath and play for the club, he was one of the game's true hard men, playing hooker behind Brian Moore in the England team, winning only 5 caps between 1987 and 1995. He played at a time when replacements were not permitted unless a player came off injured. He ended up sitting on the bench more than thirty times for his country. He was the modern day equivalent of Jon Raphael. He is now the head coach of National League One side Plymouth Albion and still playing late into his forties.

The last test was in Auckland and neither I nor my roommate, Andrew Harriman, were selected along. He deserved a place and was unimpressed with the selection policy of the management. He decided to name the "dirt-trackers" which was the mid week side, that didn't play in the final test the "bitter brothers." I think we were Brenda and Barry Bitter respectively.

The only consolation for not playing the test was that we were able to party in Auckland and on Andrew's Gold card. In 1992 Gold credit cards were rare in rugby circles and Andrew Harriman was the only person I knew who had one. The ringleader of the "bitter brothers" was intent on having a good time. The night before the test Andrew Harriman, Steve Ojomoh, Victor Ubugo and I went out into Auckland.

I wore jeans and our regulation England "PK" Tops. The Prince refused to wear these clothes and instead sported black leather trousers and a Chanel leather jacket. This was regulation dress for Norfolk Crescent, London, and on a night out with the Prince the regulation drink was pink Dom Perignon champagne. Champagne up until this night was a drink that I had only used to toast a special occasion. That night Andy and the "bitter brothers" were raising their glasses to the fact that they had got through a winter tour of New Zealand and returned to civilization in Auckland. This meant that we needed to party hard.

Auckland may not be New York or Paris, but it has its share of night entertainment. Licensing laws were not strict and some bars remained open until the early hours. We hadn't got a clue where to go so we headed down by the waterfront. The combination of rugby players and Dom Perignon was an interesting attraction to the fairer sex. We had a great night. I met a girl who agreed to give me the local's guide to New Zealand the following day and took me for breakfast in Devonport. This charming seaside village was at the very southern point of North Shore and one of the earliest settled areas of Auckland. The three small volcanic mountains of Takapuna, Takarunga and Takaroro were where the Maori's originally settled. A ferry crossing between Auckland and Devonport took about ten minutes, and we had great views from Mount Victoria of Ngataringa Bay, Devonport, the Harbour Bridge, Rangitoto Island and downtown Auckland. This was a magical island and the views were superb.

The final test was a pretty lack lustre affair with England B narrowly losing to a strong New Zealand team that contained players like Eric

Rush. Eric became the New Zealand Rugby Sevens legend, he was arguably one of the greatest Sevens players to grace the game. In a distinguished New Zealand Sevens career he played in more than sixty tournaments, with the highlights being two Commonwealth Games gold medals and the World Cup Sevens victory in 2001.

I enjoyed New Zealand and touring with an international side, but in retrospect I wish I had completed my finals. I had no choice. I had to go on this international tour to further any chances I had of playing for England. However, the experience of going to a Southern Hemisphere Country in the middle of winter was not one that I would have liked to repeat. I was relieved to get back from New Zealand and go on my annual pilgrimage to Puerto Banus in Spain to stay in my friend's Steve Oakenfull townhouse at the Los Naranjos Country Club.

I spent the rest of the summer studying for my finals, which started on the 7th September. This proved to be a tough ordeal given the fact that the new season started on the 29th August with a trip to the Selkirk Sevens playing alongside John Steele and Phil Pask, the current CEO of the RFU and England Physiotherapist respectively . I took the exams and passed all of them except one. The rule was that you had to pass every exam to get an exemption from the Royal Institute of Chartered Surveyors. The result of a 3% failure meant that I had to repeat the whole year and produce a new dissertation.

Chapter 12

Unrivalled landscapes

1992 had been a great year, but 1993 was the most disciplined year that I have ever had. I returned to university and accepted that if I wanted to become a chartered surveyor then I had to put my degree first. Ironically, I also played some of my best rugby and discovered a side to me that would prove invaluable in my future business career.

I had been picked for my country at England B level and lost my mother in the space of two years, yet my tutors gave me no dispensation. The rules were the rules and you had to abide by them. Returning to university to attend the lectures that I should have been at the year before was a valuable life lesson. I had never taken my studies lightly and even in that final year I thought I had done enough to pass the degree and start my job at a firm of chartered surveyors called Connell Wilson in Northampton. My mentor and boss at Connell Wilson, Tony Hewitt, attempted in vain to explain my circumstances to my course leader Paul Collins, but with no luck. He thought that I had mitigating circumstances; however, the university wasn't willing to set a precedent. Life was very easy for me during 1992, everything I had wanted I had got, and I was having a rude awakening.

I moved into the third bedroom of a 1930s house in Nottingham with three mates courtesy of Richard Oldham, the honary dad of the house. The house was a typical student house and I had the smallest room you could imagine. It was big enough to fit a single bed and a desk. I had come back to Nottingham to study and that was that. I needed no luxuries and I couldn't have afforded them. I was a very odd final year student in as much as very few people repeated their final year. None of my fellow students had sponsored cars with their name on the side. The local Rover dealer in Northampton had given me a car to travel up and down the M1 motorway and few students had a brand new Omega Seamaster watch donated by Burlington Jewellers. I enjoyed the benefits of playing rugby and I found the contrast in lifestyles very pronounced.

It took a lot of discipline to complete this year and I knew that I had to restrict the amount of travel I did if I stood any chance of completing my degree. This was the year that I taught myself time management. I also allied myself with one of the most able students on my course, Paul Denis-Jones, who originated from Northamptonshire and helped me a great deal. I remember a great man who also originated from Northamptonshire, Lyn Wilson, once told me, "Whatever you do in life surround yourself with people better than you". Paul was one of those people.

I now started to enjoy the degree course. My new dissertation was something that really interested me: "The property management of rugby stadia". The dissertation I produced looked at the way that all the leading clubs in the Courage Leagues managed their assets and where they derived their income. It included a look at the national stadium at Twickenham. I was in a very fortunate position because I was able to get unprecedented access to the inner sanctum that ran English rugby. My dissertation was an accurate reflection of how amateur committees were running rugby clubs on a part time basis. There was little or no money being paid to players despite the fact that large crowds were coming to watch league games, divisional, England A and International matches.

The key to the dissertation was the changes that had occurred to sports stadia as a result of the Hillsborough disaster. This was a tragedy that occurred on 15th April 1989, at Hillsborough, the home of Sheffield Wednesday, resulting in the deaths of ninety-six people from Liverpool FC. It was the deadliest stadium-related disaster in British history. The inquiry into the disaster, the Taylor Report, named the cause as "a failure of police control", and recommended that all top division stadiums in England and Scotland phase out their concrete terraces and become all-seaters. This report single handedly changed the face of rugby stadiums in the UK.

The odd thing that occurred as a result of putting my degree first and improving my time management was that my rugby improved. The 1992/93 season was the season for stepping up to senior rugby. The next challenge was to play regularly in the Saints 1st XV, which in turn would lead to being selected to play for the Midlands and then England A. This is exactly the route that I was able to follow. A televised game which saw Northampton beat Bath 11–8 at Franklin Gardens, led to a call up into the first ever England A squad. The squad that appeared in the sports section of the Daily Telegraph included some great names, Simon Hodgkinson, Chris Oti, Richard Hill, Nigel Redman, Andy Robinson and Mike Teague, all of whom had been part of the England World Cup Squad in 1991.

The first training session of this squad was at The Bank of England Sports Ground on Sunday, 18th October. The hotel that was used to accommodate the players was the Richmond Hill Hotel, on Richmond Hill. It had views across the Thames valley and was close to the gates of Richmond Park, home to herds of red and fallow deer. The hotel was part of an impressive Georgian building and was very different to the hotels I had been used to staying in with England Under 21s, Students and on the B Tour to New Zealand.

Queen Victoria wrote: "The view from Richmond Hill is, by universal consent, the finest within a few miles of London. Indeed, of its kind, it is difficult to surpass anywhere." It is the only view in England to be protected by an Act of Parliament. The Richmond, Ham and Petersham Open Spaces Act passed in 1902 protect the land on and below the hill and preserve the view from the hill. Immortalised in paintings by Sir Joshua Reynolds and JMW Turner, it was described by Sir Walter Scott as "an unrivalled landscape".

In 1992 England training was on a Sunday, and it didn't matter where you had played the day before you were expected to train on each Sunday. We met at the hotel on a Saturday night, to join the squad session. I felt very nervous with other young players including Damian Hopley, Adel Kardooni, Graham Rowntree, Richard Cockerill, Neil Back, Steve Ojomoh and Ben Clarke.

As soon as you had checked in, you assembled in the bar before dinner for an open tab provided by the RFU. This was England training and yet there was a big drinking culture. There was no limit on how much you could order on account, and very often the players would see this as a perk of playing for England as they weren't being paid.

After dinner I think I went to bed, but very often on other sessions we would go to the Roebuck. This was the nearest pub to the hotel and the England team pub, before they would go down the Hill into Richmond to the Orange Tree and then on to Park Avenue, the local nightclub. You can imagine after a hard game and beers you were often not in the best state to train on a Sunday morning.

I didn't think that I would ever go to a squad session where both the A and full England sides would be training alongside each other. This was at the Bank of England Sports Club, famous as the place where the England 1966 squad trained before they won the World Cup in 1966. This gave me a desire to keep playing for England and my next tough match outside club rugby was for the Midlands v South Africa, 4th November 1992, at Welford Road, less than half an hour from Nottingham and the home of Leicester Tigers. Bill Beaumont did the commentary that day. These were great fixtures in front of a packed Welford Road crowd and televised by the BBC. The side that ran out that day was made up of players predominantly from Northampton and Leicester, including Martin Bayfield, John Olver, Gary Pearce, Dean Richards and Martin Johnson, some of the all time greats of English Rugby.

This was the first Springboks tour of England since apartheid had been abolished and sanctions lifted. The side included two legends of the game that people had not seen on the world rugby stage, but had heard of even though South Africa had been in isolation. Both players had won their first caps together against South America in 1980 and played in their last tests together on the 14th November 1992. They were both the same age and retired when they were thirty-four. The first player was Danie Gerber, who would have been a strong contender for a centre spot in most experts' Legends XV's. The second was Naas Botha, one of the greatest Springboks of all time. Naas Botha was South African rugby's first media superstar. He was the greatest points scoring phenomenon South African rugby had ever known. In 2005 he was inducted into the International Rugby Board Hall of Fame, cementing his status as one of rugby's all-time greats.

I was lucky enough to play against them both for the Midlands that afternoon and would later get to work with them on a rugby project in Africa. Welford Road became my second home in 1992. Outside Twickenham it was the largest purpose-built club rugby union ground and held over 16,000 spectators. For rugby men, Leicester v the Baa-Baas, two days after Christmas, was a traditional fixture and as far as the Tigers players were concerned remained the prestige match of the year.

On Monday 28th December 1992, I received the call up to play for the Barbarians in a televised game against the Tigers. In these days, the Barbarians would carry an uncapped player and I was that player for this match. The Baa-Baas side that day included Gavin Hastings, Craig Chalmers, Jean-Baptiste Lafond, Tim Rodber, Damian Cronin and Laurent Cabannes. These players were legends of the game. Before the game we ate lunch at the Holiday Inn whilst awaiting the arrival of the French players. Imagine our surprise, when they eventually arrived with little time to spare before the game, and they ordered rare steak with chips and red wine. Mickey Steele-Bodger was happy for them to eat despite the delay to the team and when we eventually arrived at the ground we had forty-five minutes to prepare against a Tigers side that included Tony Underwood, Rory Underwood, Graham Rowntree,

Richard Cockerill, Darren Garforth, Martin Johnson, John Wells, Neil Back and Dean Richards.

This was not a side to take lightly and our preparation had been just a little too laid-back. The result was a 41–23 defeat, but some of the best rugby I have ever played in front of a passionate and faithful Tigers crowd. As is traditional after this game, the players all went back to the Holiday Inn for a Christmas drink. I re-acquainted myself with Gavin Hastings that night and Craig Chalmers who invited me up for Hogmanay in Edinburgh. Craig Chalmers was a big star in Scotland and had travelled to Australia in 1989 with the British and Irish Lions at the age of twenty-one. I had always wanted to go to Scotland for Hogmany. I travelled up with Dave Gowler, Julie and Nicola Izzard to Melrose for the night, in the Borders, before travelling further North to Edinburgh. We stayed with Craig in his flat and ended up going to Watsonians RFC for a party. The following day the Scottish Rugby Trial at Murrayfield was taking place and I can promise you, Gavin and Craig did not have a quiet night. It seems odd that the SRU would think that a trial on New Years day would be the best way of finding out the form of their players for the Five Nations Competition.

Leicester Tigers ground at Welford Road became my second home for representative rugby over the next few years, and this began after my selection to play for England A v France A on Friday January 15th 1992. The RFU had run a B international programme from 1978, but only with regularity from 1988 when league rugby came into existence. For many, the term B international meant second class and this was highlighted in New Zealand in 1992 when the New Zealand Rugby Union didn't do a great deal to market the B tour. The England management who returned from that tour convinced the RFU to call the second string team England A. I was chosen to play in the first match in the A programme. The principle of the A team was the production of the next tier of full international players. We genuinely believed that the B (or rather, A) was a launching pad to the full side. Players like Ian Hunter, Tony Underwood, Philip de Glanville, Victor Ubogu and Ben Clarke had all made the transition.

I travelled up to the ground with Matt Dawson, who had been selected on the bench to cover Richard Hill, the Bath scrum-half. I was living with Matt in Collyweston House in Pitsford, Northampton. As Northampton players we were thrilled to be included in this match. Matt was twenty years old and working as a security guard for the club sponsor, Firm Security. He had broken into the team at Northampton as a centre, not as a scrum half, but it wasn't long before he resumed his rightful position. There are very few players that you meet who come to a club and you can tell straight away that they are destined for great things. He was one of them. It was a tradition at Northampton that when you play your first XV game, a senior player walks you onto the pitch and describes what the feeling of playing in front of a crowd is going to be like. I had performed this rite of passage with the young Matt Dawson as Paul Larkin had with me.

By the time we had got to England A, Matt Dawson had played for England Under 21s and was on the fast track to the senior team. He was a very confident young man and on the journey up to Welford Road he asked me when he was going to get his sponsored car. I had worked very hard to get picked for the A team, through Under 19s, Under 21s, Students and the Midlands; for Daws, his talents were not in question and I told him it wouldn't be long before all the trappings of success would follow. I couldn't have imagined how true this was to be. Neil Back, Tony Underwood and Martin Johnson were also picked for this side. For them this was a home game, and for Martin Johnson it proved to be the launch pad for a full England Cap. Martin trained with us all week and didn't appear in the team meeting before the game. This is because he had got a call from the England management to go down to Twickenham to train with the full squad because Wade Dooley had injured himself. Martin nearly didn't get to Twickenham that day because Keith Bonser, a Midlands selector who was involved with the A squad, had offered to drive Martin down to London and nearly killed him when he drove through a red light. When he eventually got to Twickenham it was Kevin Murphy, the team physio, who told him that he would be starting. Martin Johnson won his first full England cap on 16th January against France when they squeezed home to a 16–15 victory over Les Bleus.

You would have never believed that Martin Johnson would go on to achieve all there was to achieve in rugby with that England debut in 1993. He went on to captain his club, Leicester, to all the major honours, winning four successive league titles (1999–2002) and two European Cups (2001 and 2002); he led England with huge success, including the 2003 Grand Slam and the 2003 World Cup, winning 84 caps by the end of 2003 and captained the British Lions on two tours. Martin was the most down-to-earth person you could ever meet. He had an astonishing knowledge of sport for a man that worked for the Midland Bank. The term "statto" should be used to describe Martin Johnson. I can remember attending the team meeting just before we were due to play France A to find out that Martin had left us and that Matt Dawson was to come in for the injured Richard Hill. From this moment, Matt Dawson and Martin Johnson never took a step back from A or full team level.

We beat a very strong French side that included Alan Penaud, Laurent Benezech and my opponent and right wing Philippe Bernat-Salles who had played for the French national team on 14th November 1992, against Argentina. He eventually won 41 caps for France.

Martin Johnson was picked alongside Matt Dawson in the second of the A games we played at Bath against an experimental Italian reserve team on the 3rd February. It was great to talk to him about his experiences with England and the fact that, despite not knowing the line outs calls before a gentle run through in the car park of the Petersham, he was able to run out at HQ the following day. This could never happen in the modern game, but in 1993 it did.

There is a Scottish expression that I learnt from Frank Dick, which is, "having a good conceit of yourself", which describes someone who has a natural arrogance but the ability to deliver at the right moment. Arrogance is not a quality that I admire in anyone but there were very few international players that I had encountered up until this point who didn't have a good conceit of themselves, none more so than a player called John Kirwan, who I played against on the 21st February 1992. From the time he first appeared in representative rugby as an eighteen-year-old in the Auckland union's centenary fixture against a President's XV in 1983, there was a special romance to his career. At nearly 1.90 metres and strongly built, he was unusually tall for a wing and had considerable pace and determination. From 1985 through to 1992, apart from when he was injured, Kirwan was pretty well an automatic All Black selection with his golden years being the three seasons between 1986 and 1988. I played against Kirwan the year after he became the first All Black back to reach the 50-test milestone. At his peak, in the seasons between 1986 and 1988, Kirwan was magnificent, exceeding even his great Australian rival, David Campese.

I met him in the clubhouse at Franklins Gardens before the match. I could remember the performances that he had put in as the star of the 1987 World Cup and his length of the field run for a try against Italy, which is often shown as one of the best tries of any world cup. He had agreed to play in a New Zealand XV against Northampton for Wayne Shelford. The side that we played against that day included Zinzan Brooke, Walter Little and Robin Brooke but John Kirwan was the star of the show. This was probably the first time in my life, apart from meeting Phil Bennett, that I had been given the chance to talk to a living legend and he just happened to be in my position. I felt quite confident in my ability, but that weekend he taught me a lesson in mentality that you need to play international sport and what it would take to reach the heights that someone like him had reached in his career.

I naively explained to John Kirwan that I was aspiring to play rugby for England but was finding it difficult to mix my degree and rugby. He looked at me with complete bewilderment. In his mind, if you had any chance of playing rugby for your country then you needed to put that first, whatever the sacrifice. A degree to him was not equal to playing rugby for the All Blacks and he was shocked that I thought you could mix both. In hindsight, the true legends of sport, business or life only see it one way – the Kirwan way. They have purpose, not just goals and ambitions. They are obsessed by their career and very few look at any other aspect of their life until they have achieved their purpose.

This moment in the clubhouse was a defining moment for me as I still believed I could keep a number of things going at the same time.

That day we lost to a New Zealand XV 71–27 and John Kirwan showed me what a true international winger was made of. I had made the mistake of telling him after ten minutes that he wasn't as good as people had said. This was a red rag to a bull and he proceeded to give me a lesson in wing play whilst I tried in vain to stop him. Kirwan remained a world-class player for the rest of his career and when he finished with the All Blacks in 1994 his 63 tests had brought him 35 tries, which was then the New Zealand record. In his first class career, which ended in 1994, he had finished with 199 tries, only being denied 200 because his swansong match for New Zealand Barbarians was not granted official status. He was a legend beyond any doubt, ranking with Jonah Lomu and Jeff Wilson as the greatest wings of All Black rugby, certainly in the modern era.

Another man who had a good conceit of himself, who I had played with for the Midlands but never in an England shirt, was Dean Richards. On the 5th March 1993 at Richmond, I got the chance. This wouldn't be a game that Dean would remember with great joy. That day Dean Richards was the captain of a very strong England A side that included Martin Johnson. In those days, if you were dropped from England to the A team you would have to go up Richmond Hill from the Petersham Hotel to the Richmond Gate; this was a short distance, but not one that established internationals enjoyed travelling. To play against Spain for Dean Richards was a bit of an insult. Spain was not a strong force in World Rugby and therefore Dean had nothing to prove to anyone. However, the England A side was regarded as the second best side in England at the time, so his inclusion in this side was not an outlandish selection and we felt boosted by having him in the team.

We were again given tickets to watch England v Scotland at Twickenham on 6th March 1993. Some of the players were not interested in going and decided to sell their single ticket to make some extra cash. Our match was on the Friday before the international and

I delivered the tickets. This time my journey to the buyer was a short walk down the hill to the Petersham, the England Hotel. I remember entering the player's room that day, to see him lying in a bed full of cash. I had never seen so much money.

An expected victory against Spain was followed by the last of the A games and one of my first away trips that season due to my degree studies. This time it was a trip to Dublin to experience an Irish international weekend. I left my 1930s house in a run down part of Nottingham and flew to Dublin with the full England side in number ones. Upon arrival at the airport we boarded a bus which, along with the England team bus, was escorted by police outriders through the busy Dublin traffic to our hotel via the England team hotel. The England team were staying in the Castle Hotel in Killiney and we were much further out in a town called Bray about twenty kilometres south of Dublin on the east coast.

Our match was going to be played at Donnybrook, a ground that held 7,500 people in the heart of Dublin. The A game was normally packed out by English supporters who had travelled to Dublin to see the international, and the atmosphere in the ground reflected that of Dublin itself with plenty of Guinness being consumed. We won the game against a strong Irish side and paved the way for an English victory the following day at Lansdowne Road. This stadium was unique. It had an Irish charm and was a mixture of old stands and terraces, and mock-tudor tearooms that used to be the home of Lansdowne FC.

On one side of the ground the DART train passed under the stadium and thousands of supporters were stopped in mid flow in front of the level crossing outside the ground whilst an old lady got off the train at the station. Only in Ireland could something like this happen. We were given tickets to the ground and stood on the terraces in our England A tracksuits expecting an England victory. We were very proud to be English at the start of the game; however, you can imagine the banter that we received from the Irish supporters when we were beaten 17–3.

If that was a football stadium then we may not have got out alive, but I can remember shaking the hand of the Irishman I stood next to on the terraces after the game, congratulating them on their victory. This is the spirit of rugby.

That evening I returned to England and that was the start of the build up to my finals. The irony was that I had played in an unbeaten England A team that were due to fly out to Canada on a summer tour. The Lions were touring New Zealand that summer and so this would have been a great opportunity to stake my claim for higher honours. Sadly, I had no choice. I had to do my final exam and forgo an international tour. The only saving grace was that the fixtures were not full caps against Canada and so I didn't feel too aggrieved that I had missed out. I passed the degree and decided that it was time to follow my passion. My passion should have been to play rugby for England, but this wasn't my primary driver. It was the vehicle that I used to allow me to follow my true passion for travel and meeting people. I think that when I played that match against John Kirwan I realised that I didn't have the right mental attitude to become an established rugby international. He had an edge about him that I have seen in many super performers, and that steely desire to follow their purpose and their reason for being.

I had played in a very successful Northampton and England A team and obtained a BSc (honours) all in the same season/academic year. At the time this would have been enough for any ambitious person, but I realised that this was just the start of my desire to have as many different life experiences as possible. The last thing I wanted was mediocrity. 1993 brought me self-discipline. I never had a more difficult year than this and yet it was probably my most consistent as a rugby player.

It is easy in hindsight to say that by not touring that summer with England to Canada I missed my chance of playing for England. I missed an opportunity to impress in an England shirt, and that summer Clive Woodward took an England Under 21s side to Australia with many players who would later go on to win the 2003 World Cup including Will Greenwood, Lawrence Dallaglio, Richard Hill, Simon Shaw and Kieran Bracken. Selection is fickle and the selectors probably would have expected me to tour that summer, but I made a choice and my future career was surveying and rugby was a hobby.

I joined a firm of surveyors in Wellingborough called Connell Wilson courtesy of my rugby mentor and chairman of the company, Tony Hewitt. I was paid £12,000 as a graduate surveyor, with an All Star petrol card. This salary enabled me to buy my first house in Abington, Northampton, for £45,000 – a three bedroom terraced house in a great part of Northampton's Victorian back streets. I got my first mortgage, which was set up by the club through one of the club sponsors, the Nationwide Building Society. Strictly speaking, I shouldn't have been able to get a 100% mortgage on a house, I was high risk, straight out of university on a low wage, but this was one of the hidden perks of playing for the Saints. This wasn't payment, but it was a leg up onto the property ladder. I was told to call a contact called Jeremy Wood and he would arrange my mortgage. I was also given the contact of a firm of lawyers. Everything was arranged and discounted. I went to the head office of the Nationwide to get my mortgage offer. You may think this was a little odd given the fact that Nationwide had an extensive branch system that included a Northampton town centre location. I thought nothing of it and just felt very grateful for their help and a 100% mortgage.

If I ever had a bad game my dad would say that I looked like I was carrying my mortgage behind me. At the time, a £45,000 mortgage seemed like a huge amount of money and the only way I could pay this was to take in tenants who were often rugby players from the Saints, players like Richard Reece and Andy Beales. It was probably one of the best opportunities that I had been given because I sold that house two years later for £80,000. Not a bad return.

The year started well from a rugby point of view when I was announced in a forty-six-man England squad, along with seven Saints players that included Paul Grayson, who had recently joined from Waterloo. I had played England A rugby with Paul and he was the first player that I can remember openly wanting rugby to become a professional game. I chatted to him in Dublin before we played Ireland A and he explained that wanted to be paid to play the sport. I was shocked that he was so open about his hopes at a time when "shamateurism" was the order of the day in our sport. I was happy to play the game and accept the intrinsic benefits that it afforded me. I didn't think that we would ever get paid to play and yet Paul expected that this is what would result from his single-minded ambition to become the best person in his position in the world. He had the same determined edge as other great players I have described. I am very proud of what he went on to achieve. He played 32 times for England and scored 400 points in an international career that spanned nine years. He was second on the English all-time list behind Jonny Wilkinson.

Paul had moved to Northampton Saints to improve his chances of playing for England and joined a group of players who would eventually go on and play rugby at the highest level. These players all lived in a house together in the village of Yardley Hastings provided by John Smith, a local supporter of the club. It was occupied by Matt Dawson, Tim Rodber, Paul Grayson, Brett Taylor and Ian Hunter. All of the players who lived at the house lived for playing rugby. They put Northampton Saints on the map and I am sure that many of the plans for the successes that were to follow for the club were hatched in this house in Yardley Hastings.

This was a great time to be a rugby player, particularly at the Saints. We were professional in attitude and fitness but strictly amateur in terms of not receiving payment to play. We set high standards, not because we were told to do so, but because running out at Franklin's Gardens with your mates against Leicester in front of 10,000 people was the biggest endorphin kick that you could ever imagine.

Our matches were televised from time to time on *Rugby Special*, as rugby became a greater spectator sport. You could sense the anticipation of the game in the town before a big match. They used to say the productivity of Churches shoe factory in Northampton would reduce by one-third on a Friday as people looked forward to the games. Northampton was a rugby town and the Saints influenced every facet of society. The Yardley Hastings boys and I were in our twenties playing sport, which was our first love, in a place that appreciated us. We had jobs, but they didn't really amount to much. Tim Rodber was an army officer, Matt Dawson worked as a security guard for Firm Security, Paul Grayson was an insurance broker and Ian Hunter a graphic designer running his own company.

I had chosen to become a surveyor, but, like the boys, didn't put it at the top of my priorities. It was difficult to keep everything in balance. The average week was work 9:00 a.m. to 6:00 p.m. I got an hour for lunch and very often I would train on the track at a newly built facility called Kettering Leisure Village. We were expected to train during the evenings when we were not club training on a Tuesday and Thursday night with the club. Every moment was filled during the week. The weekends were taken up with a game on the Saturday. If I was included in the England Squad, I would travel down to Richmond on a Saturday night to train on the Sunday. There was no time to yourself or for family or friends. It was full-on. The 1993/94 season was the first time that the leagues went to a home-and-away format. This meant eighteen competitive league games during the season, as well as a Divisional Championship and International Fixtures. If you were in the England Squad, which I was in 1993, you were expected to play a lot of games.

The England Squad that was picked on the 20th September was in anticipation of the thirteen-match New Zealand Tour of England and Scotland. I was lucky enough to play in two great representative fixtures before Christmas. The Barbarians match against Newport on the 5th October 1993, and for the Midlands Division against New Zealand on the 26th October 1993 at Leicester. The Barbarians match was yet another chance to play as the non capped player in a side full of internationals at Rodney Parade. It was the first time that I was able to reacquaint myself with Norman Hadley, who was playing for London

Wasps, since the England Students tour of Canada and Rupert Moon who had opted to play for Wales instead of England and was playing for Llanelli.

The Midlands Division match against the Kiwi's was a perfect opportunity to be measured against one of the most consistent international teams. The divisions presented players like me with a different framework from our clubs. At the time, to play against New Zealand or indeed a Southern Hemisphere side was rare. New Zealand had not played against the divisions for ten years when they lost 13–19. Matt Dawson and I were the only players from Northampton in the back line. The pack was mainly made up of the formidable Leicester side, which included Dean Richards, John Wells, Neil Back in the back row and, of course, Martin Johnson in the second row. That day the New Zealand team was captained by Zinzan Brooke, but included Ian Jones, Mark "The Bull" Allen and Eric Rush. The match was televised and played in front of a full house of 16,000 people. This was a great experience for a twenty-four-year-old.

My target that year had been to play New Zealand at Gateshead for England A. However, this wasn't to be. I played in all the divisional games that season and there were some superb wingers on show including Adebayo Abedayo, Chris Oti and, of course, my housemate Tony Underwood. Places were competitive and my form wasn't worthy at the time of being in the best four wingers in England. By the time we reached Christmas I couldn't have imagined the opportunities to travel that would present themselves in 1994.

To say that chartered surveying wasn't all it was cracked up to be would be an understatement. I worked in an office in Wellingbrough, the place that I had gone to school. Whilst I had great affection for the school, the town wasn't where I wanted to start my working career. It almost felt like I had taken a backward step and life became thoroughly depressing. I answered a question during one of the degree exams which was: "Surveying: a static profession in a changing universe?" This was exactly what it was like in the provinces and in the offices of Connell Wilson. Progress had passed it by, and many of the professional people I worked with were very diligent and exacting in their jobs but reticent to change. They had standard procedures that they would follow and there was a lack of team work and dynamism. You could feel the lethargy when you walked into the office and this was an environment that I didn't understand, coming from a team where everyone pulled together to meet one common objective. The atmosphere was "cloak and dagger". I quickly found myself demotivated and de-energised. There have not been many times in my life where I didn't have autonomy or felt that there was no correlation between the effort I put in and the reward that I got back. The work was complex and I was on a steep learning curve. There was only one computer for the office. This was the age when a surveyor had a secretary who would type letters that had been dictated in to a dictaphone, This was before the internet and email, when the average work-load was probably one-tenth of what it is today, a time when you had your own office and a car parking space with your name on it. I was working in the East Northants commercial property market that included towns like Corby, Rusden, Finedon. Irthlingborough and Rothwell. I assisted the other surveyors in the office acquire, dispose and let the properties within their portfolio. Naturally, if you are the last into an office, then you get the properties that no-one else wanted to touch. The bonus structure within the office was based on individual fee generation. There was no real incentive to help fellow surveyors out, so the structure was as far removed from a team environment as I could ever have imagined.

The person who kept the office together was Graham Stanton, a great boss who became a great friend. If it wasn't for Graham, then I would have lasted about the same time as I did at the Natwest Bank back in 1988. I knew that surveying was the wrong profession for me, but had no choice but to try and get qualified. The APC (Assessment of Professional Competence) was the practical training and experience that combined with my degree would eventually lead to RICS membership. The Royal Institution of Chartered Surveyors sets and maintains standards for the property profession. My aim was to become a member so I could offer clients advice on a diverse range of land, property, construction and related environmental issues. This was the plan and, as a consequence, I couldn't just bail out of my job. I had a mortgage and this was the profession I had chosen. It was Graham Stanton who released me from the monotony of surveying.

Graham loved rugby and knew that I was playing at the highest level and gave me every chance to take advantage of the opportunities it afforded me. The first opportunity was acceptable as I was selected to play for England Emerging Players against Spain in Elche on the 4th February 1994. This was another first for England that I was lucky enough to be involved with. England had been searching for a springboard for players to enter into the England A side and had formed this level to allow the selectors to study a wider group of players at representative level. For me, you could have seen this selection as a demotion from A team rugby, but I was glad to be able to keep on wearing an England shirt at any level, and the fact that the match was in Spain was a bonus. Sadly the match was a bit one sided, with us running out winners 86–17 in the Stadium of Elche CF which held 39,000 people. We stayed on the coast about 15 kilometres from the city and I remember with great affection the after-match reception, singing around a piano with the players and our coach, Richard Hill, the ex England scrum-half who Matt Dawson had replaced in the A team the year before. Lawrence Dallaglio was on the trip with his father, Vincenzo. He accompanied us as the official translator. His son was embarking on the start of a very long and illustrious rugby career. At the time, Lawrence had studied urban estate management at Kingston University and was about to embark on a surveying career with property consultancy Lambert Smith Hampton.

I returned to work from Spain and no-one even acknowledged the fact that I had just represented an England side in Spain. I never understood that mentality. If anyone I knew ever had success then I would be the first to congratulate them. It was this apathy in the office that turned me against surveying and made me determined to find a way out once I had taken my qualifications.

Later that month, I got a call from Peter Winterbottom, who at the time was England's most capped openside. Peter was a man of little words but he commanded respect. He had an international reputation like no other player. Peter had been invited to get together a squad of players to play in a provincial Sevens competition and he was inviting me to play in his squad. The call was short as Peter was a man of few words. I accepted his invitation to play in the Peter Winterbottom Select Sevens without asking permission from my boss and without knowing where the tournament was. Peter refused to tell me where the tournament was being held. I just had to be at Heathrow with my passport the following day and would be away for six days. I entered Graham's office to ask his permission to get time of work and I remember him looking at me with astonishment, when I said that I had had a call from Wints to play Sevens abroad but that I had no idea where I was going. I also had to take that afternoon off work to travel to Peterborough to get a new passport. He never refused me my trips away; in fact he actively encouraged it.

I cleared the snow off my car in February and met Peter Winterbottom, Kent Bray, Richard Langhorn, Richard Moon, Nick Chesworth and Jon Sleightholme at Heathrow where we boarded a club class flight to Cape Town to play in the provincial South African Sevens in 36-degree heat. I had never travelled in club class before and Wints had got the whole team upgraded. We drank from the moment we got on the plane, and were the worse for wear when we landed and were greeted by television cameras at the airport in Cape Town. This was not the best preparation for Natal, the provincial champions, in the opening game that afternoon live on South African television.

This was the nature of Wints, not to tell you anything and to expect you to perform dehydrated in 36 degrees. The opulence of the club class flight was in complete contrast to the journey that I experienced from the airport to the hotel. I saw the townships of Manenberg, Langa and Khayelitsha, just near Cape Town's airport – a sea of squalid, rusted, corrugated-iron shacks with little sanitation or electricity, which were homes to less fortunate people than me. We were driven to a hotel located on the Indian Ocean side of Cape Town where all the other players were staying. Unfortunately, the hotel was not up to the standard that Peter expected and he made sure that we were moved to the Clifton Heights Hotel on the Atlantic Ocean, just south of Cape Town, after the first afternoon of play.

We were badly beaten by Natal in the opening match of the tournament, in one of the most beautiful stadium settings in world. The Danie Craven Stadium at Coetzenburg in Stellenbosch was part of Stellenbosch University's sport facilities. Stellenbosch is the second oldest town in South Africa and is undoubtedly the most scenic and historically preserved, with its oak-lined streets and fine examples of Victorian, Georgian, Regency and Cape Dutch Revival architecture. The journey out of the city to the ground was breathtaking and the start of the oldest southern hemisphere wine regions just thirty-five kilometres from Cape Town. The Cape Winelands is extraordinarily beautiful with some of the most dramatic scenery that I have ever travelled through. Vineyards and Cape Dutch homesteads flank the road.

Wints couldn't have given us a worst preparation for this Sevens event. A twelve-hour flight with a lot of alcohol and the opening match against the provincial champions Natal that included my Barbarians teammate Andre Joubert in temperatures of 36 degrees. This didn't stop him laying into to us after the match. He was a winner and he expected us to win the plate competition. We returned to our five-star hotel in Clifton that evening and had an early night.

We woke the next day and went on to win the plate competition as Wints had insisted. The star of the show was Jon Sleightholme, who went on to win 12 caps and play rugby with me at Northampton Saints. Jon was one of the wingers that emerged from the summer England Under 21s tour that Clive Woodward had taken to Australia. The night after the tournament Wints said that we should go into Cape Town for a meal and some beers. I couldn't believe how cheap everything was in comparison with England. We were soon to find out what spending-power we had actually been given. Wints was given a sum of money for entering and winning the plate. He insisted that no player "on his watch" would be paid to play the game and that the £200 per person should be put in a central pool and placed on red in a casino of his choice. I think he was being bloody minded. He didn't have any passionate reason for not giving us the money, but he had a masterplan which we were about discover.

The nonchalant figure of Wints walked up to the cashier with our £2,000 in his hand in this smoke-ridden casino in Cape Town. He purchased a single chip and returned to the roulette table that we had all assembled around. He showed no emotion when he placed the chip on red on the table. You can imagine the emotion that erupted when less than a few seconds after he placed the chip on red we had doubled our money and now had a kitty of £4,000. We were not allowed to consider taking this money back to the UK. Wints insisted that the whole kitty should be placed behind the bar in a pub called The George and we couldn't go home until it was drunk. The spending power of this money in 1994 was about five times that figure today, maybe even more. We ended up dragging people off the streets to come in and drink with us. The bar manager must have thought his Christmas had come early. We attracted some attention and we got more fun from that night than we could have ever have got just from the money. Try as we could we couldn't spend £4,000 and this became one of the best nights I have ever had on any tour. Can you imagine being asked to come into a pub and then being treated to any drink you wanted and as much you could drink without knowing the people that were buying them?

The following day was spent sightseeing in Cape Town. Table Mountain and sunbathing on the beach in Camps Bay were superb. Cape Town boasts one of the most fantastic scenic bars in the world and a place where the "beautiful people" go to drink. La Med is the place to be if you want to chill out and relax about fifty metres from the breaking Atlantic Ocean.

Going back to Wellingborough from Cape Town was difficult and it wouldn't be too long before I would be back in Graham's office requesting time off for yet another amazing trip away. I cannot imagine what must have gone through his head when I pleaded with him to give me another week off work to travel to Bermuda on one of the finest rugby trips that I had ever been on.

Chapter 13

You go to heaven if you want, I would rather stay here

This time the call to go on the trip was from Tim Rodber, our club captain. It was complete fortune that I had been invited to go on this trip. The original invite to play in the Easter Rugby Classic in Bermuda had been extended to Rob Andrew, the England and Wasps fly-half. The match was to be played on Monday 4th April 2004 and Rob was unable to go because Wasps had beaten London Irish 29–14 in the quarter-finals of The Pilkington Cup and were due to play the Semi Finals on Saturday 2nd April 1994, preventing them going to Bermuda. Their loss was my good fortune and Tim Rodber was kind enough to ask me along with Matt Dawson from Northampton. The other players who were invited from England included Damian Hopley (who stopped in on his way back from Hong Kong) and Gareth Reece (the Canadian fly-half) who both played at Wasps. Three other Irish internationals were invited, Jim Staples, Simon Geoghegan and Neil Francis. The only other player that was invited was a Frenchman, Philippe Daubas.

Before I went to Bermuda I thought that it was part of the Caribbean. In fact, the islands are hundreds of miles north of the Bahamas in a staggeringly stunning stretch of the Atlantic east of North Carolina. Tim and I flew direct with British Airways from London to Bermuda and I will never forget the view from the plane as we approached the airport.

If I had to describe an Island Paradise then Bermuda would be it. As I approached the airport I could see the coral reefs, pink sandy beaches and crystal blue waters. The over whelming image was how green the Island was. Mark Twain remarked of Bermuda, "You go to heaven if you want, I'd rather stay here", and these words spoke to me. Bermuda was the island paradise I had always dreamed about. A Caribbean-style band welcomed me as I entered the most laid-back airport in the world. The trip from the airport to our billet was very different to the journey through the townships of Manenberg, Langa and Khayelitsha near Cape Town's airport. Instead of a sea of squalid shacks I saw opulent square buildings with white roofs and pastel-painted walls. Bermuda is not just one Island, it is made up of about one hundred and thirty-eight islands, linked by bridges and divided into nine picturesque parishes. As Britain's oldest colony, rugby was a sport played on the Island.

The Easter Classic sounded like a big event; however, it was just a rugby match where players from the UK were mixed with a Bermuda Invitational XV and an Irish International XV. I was asked to play eighty minutes of rugby and for that was given a free week's holiday with all my food, accommodation and flights taken care of by local families. The principle contact and one of Rugby's great gentlemen was Hugo Macneill. I had played against him in my very first game for Northampton Saints and he played in 37 tests for Ireland. He had been to Bermuda many times and arranged for all the players to be billeted in local people's houses on the Island.

Tim and I were taken to Oleander Cycles in Valley Road, Paget to collect our scooters which would provide us with our only means of transport for the week. Tim was six-foot-six-inches tall and found a 49 cc scooter quite restricting. We arrived on a day when it was raining in Bermuda. This wasn't the cold, grey rain of England that I was used to. It was a warm, tropical rainstorm. We followed South Shore, one of the few main roads in Bermuda, to my idea of heaven. Tim was staying with George and Carol Hammond in Tuckers Town at Cable End, the house where it was reputed the underwater cable landed from Portcurno in Cornwall. Our journey probably took about twenty-five minutes but took in some of the most amazing scenery. Spittal Pond

Nature Reserve hugged the south shore coast and John Smith's Bay, named after Captain John Smith who produced a map of Bermuda in 1624, had a coral reef lying about 200 meters from the beach. The narrow, winding South Shore Road was flanked by colourful hedges of hibiscus, oleander, bougainvillea, poinsettia, morning glory, passion flower and Bermudiana. Bermuda used to be rural and I could see evidence of little farms with crops of potatoes, onions and carrots. The trees were amazing – the Bermuda cedar, olivewood bark, Bermuda palmetto, Casuarina trees, the loquat, royal poinciana, screw pine, paw-paw, cassava and banana all worked together to weave a magic on me that would never wear off.

Tucker's Town is a small settlement in St George's Parish close to the shore of Castle Harbour. Tucker's Town is still one of the most exclusive parts of Bermuda and favoured by American and European billionaires including Silvio Berlusconi, Michael Bloomberg and the Doyle family who made their initial fortune rum-running during prohibition. The only way to access Cable End was by passing by a guardhouse. People who do not live in Tucker's Town are not generally allowed onto the Tucker's Town Peninsula. This is sadly ironic because in the early years of the twentieth century the area was a predominantly black, thriving, independent community. However, in the early 1920s, the all-white Government of the day uprooted the black inhabitants – by way of eminent domain – "in the name of tourism." By the time I visited it, Tucker's Town Peninsula was an enclave of only the most wealthy. Whilst Bermuda didn't have the townships of South Africa, segregation was still at work.

George and Carol Hammond were Tim's hosts, and billeted him for the week he was there. They were the most normal couple that you could imagine despite the fact that they lived in one of the most exclusive parts of the world. Carol was a local doctor and George ran an automotive parts business called Weir Enterprises. George had come to Bermuda from Ireland to join the Bermuda Police and met his Irish wife there. He discovered a gap in the market for providing Bermuda with automotive parts, which proved very lucrative. They made us incredibly welcome in their house, which had its own private beach where Tim and I spent most of the week. The concept of being on this island for a week and experiencing the lifestyle of our hosts was hard to come to terms with. John Kane, a host from that magical week, and I met some years later in Bermuda and he told me that that was the last Easter Classic that they ran because they were not able to get hold of the right cailbre of players at Easter with a congested fixture list in UK and Ireland. He was the man behind the World Rugby Classic, which takes place in Bermuda every year in November. The Classic was just an excuse to get drunk. I played in a game whose score was 95–61 in our favour, came off the pitch and drank champagne.

It didn't seem possible that in return for one game of a very average standard we could be allowed to roam paradise with our mates. One beautiful morning we were invited by Ashley Redmond, a local Bermudian rugby player, for a day on his boat. Ashley was a few years younger than me and Tim, and was the perfect host after the match. He took us around the Island by boat to all the best sites, which you would never have got to see as a normal tourist. Ashley would fill his boat up with fuel like we would fill up our cars. He made sure that the boat was equipped with bottles of human fuel, which was Bermuda's national drink – Rum Swizzle. The recipe is eight fluid ounces of Gosling's Black Seal rum, six dashes of Angostura bitters, the juice of two lemons, crushed ice, five ounces of pineapple juice, five ounces of orange juice and two ounces of grenadine syrup. The combination of the sun and this drink were enough to blow my head off. However, this didn't prevent Tim Rodber challenging the boys to jump off a cliff face that had previously been used by the American high diving team. I scrabbled up the cliff face, following Tim to jump off a platform, closely followed by Matt Dawson, Damian Hopley and Gareth Reece. It seemed to be the right thing to do at the time. We were filled with Rum Swizzle and were fearless. That was until reaching the top of the cliff and looking over the edge. We had to clear a small ledge, before being able to jump into the clear water. Ashley had informed me that our momentum would easily allow this, however, there was still that buttock clenching moment when I took a run up and jumped and was then suspended in mid air for what seem like a lifetime. I knew it was OK because Rodber led from the front and I was very relieved to see his very large swede of a head submerge with a beaming smile.

That week I decided to try and revisit Bermuda as often as I could. I have managed to do this ten more times, but no other trip could ever be more pleasurable than my first visit to the island and seeing the pink sands of Horseshoe Beach. Horseshoe Bay is the most popular and arguably the most beautiful of Bermuda's beaches. If ever there was a reason to play rugby it was because it took me to places like Bermuda and introduced me to a rugby community that were as passionate about the sport as we were back in the UK.

Returning to the commercial world of Connell Wilson was difficult. How could I explain this experience to someone who resented me being afforded the time off, when they were working hard through out the year to get their two-week break? I found this working environment extremely tough. I was caught between two stools – playing rugby and trying to build a professional career. My heart wasn't in the latter; it did not evoke the same passion that rugby did and even in 1994, less than a year after graduating, I was looking for something else to do. If you aren't happy at work then all other aspects of your life are affected. I saw no progression within the company. The people who worked their patches were very protective of their clients, which produced an atmosphere of distrust and lack of teamwork. Graham Stanton kept me going through this time and would eventually give me the opportunity to take a risk that would change my life for ever.

The players who I had met back in Cape Town had also shown me a side of life that I wasn't getting in Northamptonshire. I kept in regular contact with Peter Winterbottom, Richard Langhorn and Kent Bray. This involved jumping in a car and heading down to Parsons Green where all these boys lived. Parsons Green was a relatively expensive area to buy property and a great place to live if you wanted access to the stylish shops and restaurants on the New Kings Road and Fulham Road. If you were a Harlequins player in 1994 you could visit all the best spots, and the boys had disposable income to die for from their jobs in the city. They were money brokers during the week and rugby players at the weekend. I would stay with Richard Langhorn in his flat on Wandsworth Bridge Road and we quickly became very good friends.

It was Richard who invited me to come on the Kent Bray Rugby Legends Trip to the Neuchâtel Sevens in Switzerland in May 1994. Kent Bray was celebrating his thirtieth Birthday and invited all his mates to fly to Geneva and then catch a train to a village tournament in Neuchatel. Kent was an Australian rugby player who had come to play rugby for Oxford University and was one of rugby's true characters. He was a great friend of Richard Langhorn and was very Australian. He had played for Oxford University in the varsity match in 1989 and claimed that he had Scottish Ancestry. I watched a *Rugby Special*, when Kent was featured getting measured up for a kilt. This was the most ridiculous use of ancestry. This was the start of home nations' sides like Scotland, Ireland and Wales casting their net in southern hemisphere waters in the hope of catching something substantial. I don't think Kent played for Scotland, but probably would have done if he had the chance.

The trip was not sold on its rugby, but on the fact that it was a great place to visit and the nightlife was better than London. Neuchâtel is on the northwestern shore of lake Neuchâtel, and the atmospheric old town is extremely attractive when you approach it on the train from Geneva. This is one of the great train journeys of the world. I was billeted in a superb town house overlooking the lake. I had never had a Swiss fondue before and was invited by the family to sit and have a Fondue Neuchâteloise using forks to dip bits of bread into a warm cheesy sauce. We all stirred the mixture continuously, as it heated up in the *caquelon*. This was a great way to sample local traditions and get to know people who lived here.

We had far too good a squad for this event and were always going to win the final on the Sunday. We took about twenty players to the tournament, including Peter Winterbottom and Troy Coker, who played against each other in the 1991 World Cup Final that Australia won. The reason why the squad was so big was because directly after the tournament, ten of us were going to board a sleeper train to Toulon in France to play in a Sevens tournament, which was arranged by Richard Langhorn.

It was on this trip to France that I was to get to know Richard Langhorn very well and invited him to join me in the second week of my holiday in Bermuda. Ashley Redmond and I had stayed in touch and I called him during a bleak day working for Connell Wilson to see whether I could come for a summer holiday. Ashley was always very good in these situations; to him, life was for living, and he never refused me a trip to Bermuda and always provided me with a bed in his parents' house. So at the end of July 1994, I boarded a plane bound again for Bermuda, to sample the delights of Cup Match. I arrived at Hamilton Airport where Ashley was waiting for me not in his car but on board his boat. I threw my suitcase into the back and we went straight to a beach party. This was probably my favourite airport transfer. The whole island was preparing for Cup Match, which was a two day national holiday in Bermuda. The first day was Emancipation Day, marking an end to slavery, and the second, Somers Day, honours Admiral Sir George Somers whose shipwreck in 1609 led to the English settlement of Bermuda.

My memories of the first night are hazy, but I do remember dancing to *Hot Hot Hot* at a Soca concert in Royal Naval Dockyard in Sandys Parish at the far end of Bermuda. Soca music is a cross between soul and calypso and there were hundreds of people at this party preparing for one of the biggest weekends of the Bermudian calendar. I woke the next day in a cabin of the Paradox, which was owned by Dan Farris, one of Ashley's mates, with two young ladies either side of me, to the sound of Counting Crows, The band were big in 1994 and their hit single *Mr Jones* was played time and time again on this fifty-foot motor cruiser.

Waking up in paradise and diving into the blue ocean from the Paradox was a dream come true. I had fallen in love with the island during my first visit and I couldn't believe I was back in my idea of paradise with Ashley "Redballs" Redmond. He was the son of an English couple, Gill and Doug, who had a great house in Gilberts Hill, Smith Parish, where you could see both sides of the Island. The house was like a little oasis of Englishness. Doug loved model trains and had a track running through the basement of the house into the garden. Ashley's parents were away for Cup Match and so we had use of the whole house. However, for two of these nights, Ashley informed me that we would be staying on one of the many Islands of Bermuda, camping out under the stars and visiting Cup Match.

They say that more alcohol is drunk by the inhabitants of Bermuda, which totals about 66,000 souls over the weekend of cup match, than on one night in Chicago, which has more than 2.8 million residents. I went with Ashley to the local liquor store in Hamilton to fill up for the weekend and could not believe how much they intended to consume. We filled his boat up with liquor and fuel and headed out to an island where his mates were setting up camp for two days of drinking and no eating. His brother Jeffery was an engineer and had constructed a floating picnic table that could be towed behind their boat, whilst eight people sat drinking in the water.

The term "hot" in Bermuda meant drunk and for two days these very wealthy, very nice kids were exactly that, manoeuvring their parents' boats, which cost hundreds of thousand of dollars, around the coral reefs of Bermuda. Drunk in charge of a boat seemed to be normal and these kids were adept at navigating the water during the day and at night. I will never forget seeing flying fish at night. These deep blue fish with very long fins were beautiful to watch in mid air.

We eventually went to see what Cup Match was all about and saw a hotly contested match between East (St George's) and West (Somerset) cricket clubs, an occasion that had been taking place since

1901. But there was much more to Cup Match than cricket. This is the only time on the island that you were allowed to gamble on "Crown and Anchor" gambling tables in big tents adjacent to the ground. The Crown and Anchor game board consists of six sections, each with a symbol: crown, anchor, diamond, club, heart and spade. These symbols correspond to those on the dice. The board is controlled by a "banker" and assistants. Players bet on which symbol they think the banker will roll. Bettors can win as much as three times the amount of their stake, depending on how many selected symbols turn up. If no selection appears, you lose your stake. This was the first time that I had eaten since I had gone out to the island and I devoured mouth watering traditional Bermudian fare, from food booths at the match serving conch stew, fish chowder, and mussel and beef pies. The booths were located all around the boundary of the cricket square and people paraded in their Sunday best sampling the food and enjoying the music that was being pumped out of a huge sound system every time a four or six was hit. It was a carnival atmosphere.

I ditched the idea of spending another night on a volcanic off-shoot of Bermuda and went back to Ashley's family house which was empty, or so I thought. I found out late at night that Ashley had a mad Auntie Chrisse, who tried quite innocently to get into my room during the night as I slept presumably to have a chat. I am sure she had something on her mind that she wanted to discuss but I wasn't going to take the risk. It was quite unnerving so I pushed a large wardrobe behind the door to prevent her entering and slept like a baby.

It wasn't until a week into the trip that Richard Langhorn arrived to join me and Ashley. Richard was the most laid-back person you could ever meet. Ashley and Richard got on like a house on fire. Richard was six-foot-six-inches tall and could drink for England, and so could Ashley. He had found his soulmate on this trip. It was on the last day of yet another week of parties that we bumped into an English sailor who would be responsible for fulfilling one of Richard's dreams to cross the Atlantic Ocean to North Carolina. He had a passion for all sport, but particularly rugby, skiing and sailing. He had longed to go on a proper sailing trip and on the last day of our holiday he fulfilled his dream. We had taken a trip down to St George and were admiring the yachts, when we struck up a conversation with a man who had played rugby with Ian McGeechan during his time at Headingly. He agreed to take us out for an afternoon's sailing. The boat we sailed on was a forty-two-foot wooden Scandinavian sea vessel that had been lovingly cared for. He kindly took us twenty-two miles off the coast into the deepest ocean waters on the most perfect day. Just three of us on a boat – there couldn't have been anything more magical. Malcolm, the sailor, had a broad Yorkshire accent and it felt quite surreal to be in the hands of an accomplished rugby playing sailor from North Yorkshire in the ocean off Bermuda.

The highlight was being able to swim in crystal clear water without any sight of land. I was enjoying this experience, until I caught sight of a barracuda, which is a ray-finned fish known for its large size (up to six feet in length and a foot in width) and fearsome appearance. Like sharks, barracudas have a reputation as being dangerous to humans and should be respected. I wasn't about to take any chances and I got out of the water quicker than I had got in. It is one of the only times in my life, when I have been physically scared. I am sure I wasn't in danger, but I felt incredibly vulnerable in a strange environment that was another creature's habitat.

On the way back to port, Richard decided to take the next week off work and sail back to North Carolina with Malcolm the sailor and his wife. I made the call to Richard's boss in London to tell him what was happening. I am so glad I played some part in his dream. He ended up staying with Malcolm and his wife in Maryland before flying back to the UK. He sent me the pictures, which I still have, of that last sailing trip that he took. These pictures included pictures of submarines surfacing in front of the channel they were sailing in and pictures of dolphins playing in front of the yacht's bow. He took many shots and posted them to me when he returned to the UK. This was one of the best spontaneous decisions he had made and he couldn't stop talking about it when he returned.

Tragically later that same year, in November, Richard Langhorn died at the age of twenty-nine as a result of a routine back operation. I had spoken with him every week on the phone after we'd returned from Bermuda and he'd become part of the social scene in Northampton at the local jazz club, The Black Bottom Club. The weekend before he died he invited me, and many of his close friends, to a white spirit party in his flat on the Wandsworth Bridge Road. That night he introduced me to Monica Kelleher, one of his friends. People came from all over Europe to this party because of his enormous popularity. I felt very privileged to have known him even for such a short time. He had a major impact on me during those bleak days at Connell Wilson. I can remember the last time I saw him, the morning after the party, dressed in a rugby top, shorts and flip flops on a cold November day. He was very happy that he had introduced Monica to me and was very relaxed about his operation. I asked him why he was having it done. He said that his back felt OK but needed sorting if ever he was going to play rugby again.

The last time I spoke to him was whilst I was preparing to play the North for the Midlands at Otley. I rang him from my hotel room in Harrogate to find out how the operation had gone only to discover that he was in intensive care. I didn't realise just how serious this was. Later Peter Winterbottom called me to say that Richard was in a bad way and Andy Beales, my flatmate, kindly drove me down to London to pay my last respects. The news of his illness spread far and wide amongst his vast network of friends; Ashley Redmond was in a boat off Bermuda and received the news of Richard's death, which shook him to the core. No-one knows to this day what happened. Monica tried to find out, but there was no reason to kick up a fuss. We could never bring him back. He was a sad loss to many people. Immediately after his death Peter Winterbottom set up The Langhorn Trust in his memory. Richard had served the Harlequins Club for over ten years, and was selected for England A. Richard loved sports, so the mission of The Langhorn Trust was to provide sporting opportunities for young people regardless of their age, gender, race, ability or background. The trust has since supported and encouraged hundreds of children around the world. The Richard Langhorn Trust has touched people's lives from coaching rugby and providing a home for poverty stricken children in Calcutta, to funding wheelchair basket ball in the UK. In 1995 the organisers of the Sevens tournament in Neuchâtel introduced the Richard Langhorn Memorial Cup, which is presented yearly to the best player of the tournament by Richard's father, Stephen. In honour of Richard's association, the tournament is now called The Richard Langhorn Neuchâtel Sevens. There is also a road named after him at the Stoop called Langhorn Way. The loss of such a dear friend made me even more determined to follow my passions. Richard lived life to the full and used to say, "This is not a dress rehearsal"; how right he was.

The next representative game that I played was Emerging England Players v Canada on Tuesday 6th December 1994. The CIS Divisional Championship had been won for the first time by the Midlands at Wasps, on Saturday 3rd December 1994. By then the championship had attracted a degree of cynical criticism from the press. The price, the press argued, was too high, with busy, well-established internationals being asked to prove themselves unnecessarily. I had played in the divisional championship for the past five years and it was part of Geoff Cooke's long-term plans to revitalise English Rugby. I always enjoyed it because it was an opportunity to meet players from different clubs and to play against international sides like the Springboks and the touring All Blacks. I had never won the championship until our game against London and then I was able to "bag" two tries.

The ridiculous thing about winning the championship was that there was no time to celebrate because I then had to travel down to Bath to play against Canada. I arrived in Bath on Saturday to find that the Hilton hotel had been double booked, and was told to go to the Bath Spa Hotel. This was the most welcome cock up that the RFU could have ever made. The Bath Spa Hotel was a Georgian mansion with a long sweeping driveway leading to a classically colonnaded front. It was formerly an elegant private house dating back to the 1830s, secluded within beautiful grounds. We each had our own bedrooms with wonderful views over the city. This was unique, normally you had to share with another player. The hotel was luxurious and we took advantage of the fact that the RFU had made a mistake in booking us into one of the best hotels in the country. I can remember lying on my bed, watching the Midlands beat London on the Sunday on Rugby Special, in a dressing gown provided by the hotel, eating afternoon tea. It was this hotel that made me want to sample many more like it around the world. I just needed to find a way of doing it.

We beat Canada that night at Bath with a side that included two of the players that would be selected in the starting XV for the World Cup in 2003, Richard Hill and Will Greenwood. It was an opportunity to enjoy another beer with Jon Sleightholme, who played on the other wing to me that night. I still have the crystal glasses that we acquired from the bar at the Bath Spa Hotel. Jon and I fancied a port late after the game. As residents you could drink until the early hours, so at 1:30 a.m. we decided to sample the port. We were oblivious to the cost of the port we ordered, but it was Dow's Port 1983, one of the best of the vintage. We decided to keep the glasses as a memento of this great night. I had no idea about port at the time, but some years later, as a guest of the Orient Express Group, I got to sample the same vintage in the Lapa Palace. This is a nineteenth-century palace located on a hilltop overlooking the Tagus River in Lisbon's diplomatic quarter. The general manager loved port and I told him about that port in Bath. He found the exact vintage for me to drink again, as well as some other great ports. Sadly it didn't taste as good as that night in Bath having just beaten Canada.

I returned to the club after representative duty knowing that the Saints were at the bottom of the Courage League. Ian McGeechan had become our club coach and came with a huge reputation. He had won 32 caps, playing at fly-half and centre for Scotland with 9 as captain. He had toured with the British and Irish Lions in both 1974 and 1977. He had coached Scotland in 1988 and in 1990 he coached the team with Jim Telfer that won a Grand Slam victory in the Five Nations Championship. Ian was the British and Irish Lions coach in

1989 and 1993. He inherited a side without many of its established internationals. We had some great players but they were all injured like Pete Walton, Ian Hunter, Matt Dawson and Paul Grayson. We had only managed to win two out of the nine courage league matches. However, it wasn't all bleak; Christmas was coming and Christmas was always superb in Northampton. My traditional Christmas was midnight mass, followed by Christmas day at home in Old Duston and a double header on Boxing Day with the hunt at Harlestone Firs in the morning, before running out in front of a full house in the afternoon at Franklins Gardens.

Harlestone Firs was a large wood outside the village of Harlestone. Boxing Day was one of the biggest days in the Pytchley hunting calendar and it started at Harlestone Firs. Many people followed the hunt in the morning and then went to the club to see the Saints in the afternoon. Many of my mates, who were scattered all over the country, would come back for Christmas and we would all meet at Franklins Gardens for a beer after the game. The abuse that I got from these boys on Boxing Day was highly amusing. I was very protective of my sister and many of the boys were aware of this. One of my great friends Andy Collier had dated Nicola and was a perfect gentleman. I am sure no brother wants his mates anywhere near their sister and one of the best ways to get to me was to hurl derogatory remarks about my sister from the crowd. I loved finishing the game and going back with some of the players to our house for the left overs of Christmas dinner, cold turkey and a fantastic spread of food which my Dad and Joy always laid on. My Dad had recently met Joy, who along with Emma and Becky, her two daughters had moved in to our house in Old Duston and we enjoyed a superb Christmas.

Despite the bad results at the club, I did manage to play my way back into the A squad. I made the bench for the matches against Ireland A on the 20th Jan 1995 and France A on 3rd February 1995. I started on the 19th February 1995 against Italy A at Gloucester. England A was still a very strong side in 1995, the year of the World Cup in South Africa. There were only five places up for grabs in the squad that would visit South Africa in the summer and many of the players wanted to be on that trip. England A in 1995 contained players like Richard Hill, Lawrence Dallaglio, Simon Shaw, Mark Regan, Neil Back and Paul Grayson. All of them would represent England in the World Cup in 2003. These players were some of the best that ever played for England.

England A had an unbeaten record which they enjoyed defending. It is not surprising that these players were not losers. They used the A team as a stepping-stone to full honours. Neil Back, Lawrence Dallaglio and Richard Hill went on to become the most formidable back row of history, and this was no accident.

Nothing had changed in Backy's mind. He was driven towards one single goal to play number 7 for England. Richard Hill was a quiet, mild character from Salisbury. He had represented his country at every level, spanning Schools 16 and 18 Groups, Colts, Students, Under 21s and Emerging Players. He was one of the new breed of players that were destined for the big time. I shared a room with him during the 1995 A games and he said that if he didn't get picked for England in the next two years then he would give the sport up and try something else. He made his debut in 1997 against Scotland and scored against both Ireland and Wales in his first four internationals. Lawrence Bruno Nero Dallaglio was very different to both Backy and Richard. Lawrence was born in Shepherd's Bush and educated at King's House School in Richmond, Ampleforth College, one of the leading Catholic boarding schools in England, and at Kingston University. In 1985, as a thirteen-year-old chorister in the King's House School choir, he had sung backing vocals with twenty other choristers on the song *We Don't Need Another Hero* by Tina Turner and, as part of the same choir, at the wedding of composer Andrew Lloyd Webber. Dallaglio's father, Vincenzo, was Italian, and his mother, Eileen, was half Irish, so he was eligible to play for both Italy and Ireland, as well as England. He was destined to play rugby for England and the death of his nineteen-year-old sister Francesca in 1989 became one of his drivers to achieve greatness. Lawrence had been a member of the inaugural World Cup Sevens-winning squad with England in 1993 with Andy Harriman and eventually made his debut for England in November 1995 as a substitute against the Springboks. He went on to win 85 caps for England and will be regarded as one of the greatest players of all time. I have got to know him very well and he is one of the strongest personalities that I have ever met.

By 1995 I had been given every chance to step up to become part of the full England Squad, but players like Jon Sleightholme and Adebayo Adebayo were playing great rugby. They were also playing for Bath under Jack Rowell, the England coach. Damian Hopley who played for Wasps was knocking on the door and could play both wing and centre. If you add Rory and Tony Underwood into the equation then this was a very competitive environment. I felt very fortunate to be in the top five best wings in the country at the time, but this was not the mindset that the top players would have taken. Back, Hill and Dallaglio wanted to play for England at any cost. It was their purpose. They were the mountain people that Frank Dick had described.

What is the price of obsession? I maintain that rugby was my first love, but it wasn't my only love, which it should have been if I wanted to get capped. I am not saying that I would have been good enough, but I wasn't prepared to sacrifice everything in pursuit of my goal, which other players were prepared to do. I was playing in a Northampton side that eventually got relegated that season, which didn't help my chances of making the World Cup Squad. Instead, I made non-travelling reserve. This didn't stop me finding some way of going to South Africa. I obtained the blessing of Ian McGeechan and went to Durban Harlequins that summer. This trip enriched my outlook on life and and the experiences I had there directly resulted in me changing my career.

Ian McGeechan had come to Northampton Saints amidst much expectation in an amateur era as the coach of the British Lions. This was a big coup for Northampton Saints and as players we should have done better in our first year under his stewardship. Even up until the

1994/95 season the club still encouraged its players to go and seek rugby experiences beyond the club. Ian McGeechan, who had taught sport and geography at Moor Grange County Secondary School in Leeds, realised that going out seeking new adventures was good for a player's education.

Chapter 14

Nkosi Sikelel'i Afrika
(God Bless Africa)

I had manufactured an opportunity to go and play rugby in Durban during the off season. This was conceived on one of those bleak afternoons sitting at my desk in Wellingborough, working for Connell Wilson. Andre Joubert had given me his number from the Hong Kong Sevens, and I called and asked him whether there was an opportunity to play for his club during the summer. At the time Andre was a Springbok, playing provincial rugby in Natal, but affiliated to The Harlequins Rugby Club. He gave me a number to call Mike Gedye, the chief executive of Froggie/Michelle Footwear, the main sponsors of the club. Mike and Sarah, his wife, said they would be happy for me to play rugby for them and invited me to stay at their house until I found my feet. Geech gave his blessing and I left after the last game of the season against West Hartlepool. This was a match that we won, but because Harlequins won at Gloucester we ended up going down.

I thought of Durban as a small fishing village on the East Coast of South Africa; I must have based this on my perception of Africa from my visits to Cape Town and Namibia. It was a huge shock when I arrived in Durban. It had a population of almost 3.5 million, the third biggest city in South Africa and the largest city in KwaZulu-Natal. It was famous as the busiest port in Africa. The contrast between the industrial areas and the city's warm subtropical climate and beaches was bizarre. The club was based on the The Bluff, just south of Durban, with the Indian Ocean on one side and Durban Harbour on the other.

The first weekend that I had in KwaZulu-Natal still remains one of my most vivid memories. Mike and Sarah's house was on Marine Drive, with views over the Indian Ocean and within walking distance of the two main beaches, Brighton Beach and Anstey's surf beach. After arriving on the first day I went straight to the beach, which was populated with die-hard surfers even at the start of an African winter. I made a mental note that I was going to learn to surf on this trip. As luck would have it, I was on one of the best surf beaches in South Africa. I returned to the house to be informed that I was starting that evening for the 1st XV, who were playing Glenwood, on one of the back pitches adjacent to the main rugby stadium in Durban, called Kings Park. This was the second time that I had flown on a long haul flight to South Africa and been asked to play on the day I arrived. Fortunately this time I hadn't been asked by Peter Winterbottom to drink the plane dry before I arrived.

The match in Durban was a club match and nowhere near the standard that we played in Cape Town against the provincial champions. However, one of the odd coincidences was that one of the players I had played against in 1994 in The Danie Craven Stadium at Coetzenburg in Stellenbosch was Cabous van der Westhuizen, the Natal Sharks and Springbok wing. He started that night on the wing for the Harlequins side and I ended up on the other wing. Rugby was still very amateur in Durban and when the players were not playing for Natal they played for their clubs in Durban. Harlequins therefore had Andre Joubert and Cabous van der Westhuizen, to call upon from time to time. The gulf between playing club rugby and provincial rugby in front of a packed 55,000 crowd was vast. Cabous was part of the Natal Sharks teams of the 1990s, which included great players like Dick Muir, John Allan, Steve Atherton, Gary Teichmann, Henry Honiball, Kevin Putt and John Plumtree. They were legends of Natal Rugby and close mates who partied hard. They also played hard and forged the famous Natal spirit that saw them win time and time again. It was a privilege to play with Cabous who was known for his long hair and huge fan base at King's Park, where his try-scoring triumphs became legendary. You could tell his class. He had the ability to ghost his way through for tries in an almost effortless manner. Cabous is still the record holder for the most tries scored in a career season for Natal (1992 to 1998), most tries in a season (1993) and most tries in a Currie Cup season (1996).

It was Cabous who introduced me to the nightlife of Durban, but not before I encountered a very odd tradition in the changing rooms after the game. I had a shower as usual, but slightly less usually was then given eight slaps on the arse from the forwards of my team before I could go into the clubhouse for something to eat. I was quite concerned before this ritual was performed. I had flown to South Africa, played for a team that I had never trained with and then suddenly I am in a clubhouse having my arse slapped, all in the name of rugby tradition. I agreed to go out with Cabous to sample the nightlife, but had nothing planned for the weekend. This changed when I entered the clubhouse and bumped into Billy Davidson, who I had toured with in 1990 to Namibia with England Students. Bill was also playing club rugby in Natal for Glenwood and was going out with Mags, a South African girl. Her parents lived in Melmoth, a little town in Zululand, just 200 kilometres northeast of Durban. They invited me to spend the weekend with them and said they would pick me up the following morning from my house in The Bluff.

I had a big night with Cabous and was picked up the following morning by Mags and Bill, and travelled to the gateway of the Zulu Highlands. Melmoth was a "gold rush" town, founded in 1888 and named after Sir Melmoth Osborn, the resident commissioner of Zululand. One of the main reasons for coming to South Africa was to immerse myself in its cultures and traditions, but I couldn't have expected what was in store on my first weekend. We went for dinner on the first night to Shakaland, which was between Eshowe and Melmoth, nestling on the top of the Entombeni Hills and overlooking the Phobane Lake. This was an example of a traditional Zulu *umuzi* or homestead. This was a chance to sample Zulu food, before entering the world of Shaka, King of the Zulu, at his Great Kraal. We saw *assegai*-wielding warriors and witnessed traditional customs such as tribal dancing, spear making and a beer drinking ceremony. The village of "Shakaland" was a film set, but still gave me an insight into Zulu Culture.

Waking up in Zululand the following morning felt alien to me, but I was enjoying every moment of it. The day was spent quad biking in sugar cane fields with one of Mag's girlfriends. The quad bike trails meandered through the rolling sugar fields around Melmoth. There were no set trails, just tracks along cane breaks, over hill climbs, through muddy patches, over water crossings, across bridges and along narrow bush paths. The bonus was having a South African beauty to share the experience with. We went far north of Melmoth to Wintershoek Farm, which straddles the high and low veld and overlooks Emakhosini, the "Valley of the Kings". I wasn't a great lover of birds but it was impossible to not be inspired by the Wahlberg's eagles soaring overhead. We returned to Durban from Zululand on Sunday evening whilst witnessing electrical storms churning over the countryside. The lightning was magical and lit up Zululand. I have this image of a burning mass of fires scattered in the fields along the roadside.

The weekend was extended when I was invited to the leaving party of my quad bike companion at a restaurant in Durban on the Monday night. I was introduced to a very interesting custom that I am sure was brought on by too much alcohol. This was the custom of taking a run up and hurling yourself into a hedge. My companion appeared to have no regard for her safety or looks. This moment of madness resulted in her resurfacing covered in cuts and bruises. After she had recovered from suspected concussion and stopped bleeding, she kindly gave me a bed for the night and I awoke the next morning in the house of her brother-in-law Craig Jamieson, the former Natal captain. Not a bad weekend, and ending up in the house of the general manager of the World Cup was a bonus. This weekend cemented my decision to take a risk and put my career on hold. I risked it all for the experience that Africa could give me. Playing rugby in a foreign country was superb, but the bi-product was the opportunity to experience the cultures, people and landscapes of KwaZulu-Natal. I wasn't running away from what I had in England because all of this was secure. I went to Africa to seek new opportunities. Failure would have been coming back from that trip and resuming the life that I had before. I had reached a point in my life where I needed a change, and I got it.

I was joined at Marine Drive, a few days after my arrival, by David Weatherly from Swansea rugby club who had come for the same reasons as me. David lived close to Llangennith, on the Gower, one of the best places to surf in the UK, and he taught me to surf on Ansteys international Blue Flag beach. There were always a bunch of hard local surfers that were happy to help us. Surfing and rugby went hand in hand in Durban.

I lay on my surfboard with David alongside me at 8am on a Monday morning. I asked him, "What would you be doing in the UK right now?" David replied, "Sitting in traffic waiting to go to work." We didn't need to say any more. We realised that we were very lucky to be doing this at a time in our lives when people were busy building careers and contemplating starting families. David and I made a pact, to make sure that we lived every moment of our time in KwaZulu-Natal to the full. This was the first time in my adult life where I had had no responsibilities. David and I had a simple routine, surfing in the morning on Ansteys Beach, followed by brunch at the beachside café. This was followed by a trip to the centre of Durban to use the track at The Kings Park Athletics stadium; we'd then have lunch and head off to Kingspark Stadium to our job coaching in a scheme called Rugby for Africa, run by the Natal Rugby Union. This took us to underprivileged areas of Natal to help youngsters learn the game of rugby. On one occasion, we were assigned to Hubhushe Senior Primary School in the K section of Umlazi. Umlazi was a township on the east coast of Durban. At the time it was very run down, but the school we visited was surprisingly full of hope.

I visited the school just before they broke for the afternoon of activities and was startled by how smart all the children looked in their school uniforms. In South African schools, school uniforms were compulsory. The uniform instilled a sense of belonging and pride in the school. This was evident when you saw the kids come out of their classrooms into the playground. When we came to do the rugby coaching the kids didn't have a change of kit. I then remembered that I was in one of the most impoverished parts of South Africa. Their parents couldn't afford a change of kit so they trained in their school uniforms. They may have been penniless but there was richness in their voices as I crept into the school hall to listen to the school choir singing *Abide with Me*. This choir had the voices of angels. I listened, out of sight, under the stairs leading to the stage. I had learnt a few Zulu words so I could at least greet the people in their own language. The local people were all keen to talk to me and the other coaches.

I had little in common with the people who lived in this township and felt an over whelming feeling of despair for them. My feelings were unfounded; most people were very positive. Apartheid had been abolished and with the election of Mandela there was a feeling of hope that their lives would get better. At no point did I ever feel under threat, despite witnessing a gunman close to the play ground firing his gun into the air. The children didn't even flinch. This was obviously a normal occurrence. It only takes an isolated incidence like this to realise that not everyone I met was glad to see me in their patch. It was a shame because the other coaches and I reported what had happened when we got back and they never sent us to Umlazi again. I had good memories of Umlazi and I was pleased that some years later that the BBC Radio 5 Live's Umlazi project was a success. Football kit and equipment from all over the UK was collected and distributed in this area, and it always made me smile when they reported from a school that I had visited.

It was important for me to get to know this side of South Africa during my stay so I understood the country's rich diversity. We would coach rugby for Africa each afternoon and were paid 50 rand, which at the time was the equivalent of £10.00. This allowed us to go out for dinner every night and drink a few beers in the best restaurants in

Durban. I suspect many of the children we coached had never been to a restaurant.

During the week we would train with the club on Tuesday and Thursday nights and at the weekend play matches around Natal. Club training was our only major commitment; everything else was up to us. Just before the start of the rugby world cup we played in Empangeni. This town was located approximately 160 kilometres north of Durban. Empangeni Rugby Football Club was a great ground in the centre of the town. The match was being covered by ITV who were trying to get some footage of club rugby. This was in preparation for England's arrival to play their pool matches in Durban. I was interviewed after the game, as an England A player playing club rugby. I couldn't stop extolling the virtues of KwaZulu-Natal and the hospitality that I had received. This sense of the hospitality and the land was enhanced on the next leg of the trip that David and I went on.

Empangeni was captained by another Natal player, who Cabous van der Westhuizen knew very well. Kevin Putt was a New Zealander who had settled in Empangeni. He first played for Natal in 1992 and played 128 matches for Natal and the Sharks. Kevin Putt was one of the liveliest and most competitive scrum-halfs that I had met. Cabous introduced us to Kevin, and David and I enjoyed many beers with him in the clubhouse. It was Kevin and Cabous who introduced us to Alexis Steenkamp, the founder of Zululand Baconry. They explained that we were keen to see Zululand and Alexis insisted that we stayed at his house. It was a great place to go back to for an impromptu *braai* directly after the clubhouse. We were made very welcome and he arranged for us to see Zululand from a local's point of view over the next few days. Rugby is one of those sports where the people who play it or support it are kindred spirits the world over.

We entered the club house on Saturday night knowing only our teammates, and by the end of four days with Alexis had been treated to the most memorable experience. Alexis was part of a family who, since 1949, had made consistent contributions, through experience and passion, to the success of the South African meat and catering industry. They had access to people and places in Zululand only afforded to the very wealthy. Alexis had promised over a few beers to give us an experience we would never forget and my God did he deliver. He planned an itinery for us that you couldn't have paid for.

The trip started out at a Kentucky Fried Chicken Restaurant. Alexis had arranged for two of his friends to pick us up and take us deep sea fishing in Richards Bay. Kokkie Crous was one of the men and he worked with Alexis and had grown up in Empangeni and spoke fluent Zulu. Both these men had been part of The South African Special Forces Brigade. Alexis made some calls and a motor cruiser, equipped with shark-catching equipment, was made available for us to go out into the choppy waters of Richards Bay. These two men jumped the boat off the waves as David and I tried to cope with the seasickness. A tip for anyone with seasickness: eat Kentucky Fried Chicken – it does the trick. Deep-sea fishing is one of those experiences I wouldn't choose to repeat.

The next leg of the trip took us to one of the farms owned by the Steenkamp family close to the Mozambique border. Kokkie Crous informed us that we were about to take one of the most scenic journeys known to man and one which it is impossible do today. We travelled to St Lucia Estuary, a town which is the southern-most entrance to the world-renowned Wetlands Park, and rode in our 4X4 to Sodwana Bay before going inland to the farm. We undertook this journey in 1995 and in 1999 the coastal area between Maphelana in the south and Kosi Bay near the border to Mozambique in the north, including the wetlands around Lake St Lucia, were declared a World Cultural Heritage Site by the UNESCO. The reserve was called St Lucia Wetland Park and is now the iSimangaliso Wetland Park. Lake St Lucia is sixty kilometres long and we drove parallel to it along the beach. We were joined for most of our journey by a fish eagle soaring high above us. There is now a ban preventing 4X4s from taking this journey, something that has caused much local controversy.

We arrived at Sodwana Bay, on the coast within the Greater St Lucia Wetland Park. The reserve lies next to Africa's southern-most coral reefs and is regarded as the scuba diving capital of South Africa. We then headed west on dirt track roads to Jozini Dam, located in North Eastern KwaZulu-Natal on the main route to Mozambique.

Alexis had arranged for us to stay on his farm and for us to shoot an impala, which he needed to have back in Empangeni the following morning. The impala is the most common antelope found in Southern Africa. It is a beautiful reddish-brown animal, with a lighter belly and two black stripes down the back of the rump. The Impala on his farm were bred to be eaten. However, the concept of shooting one didn't sit very well with me. David, on the other hand, was keen to be the marksman that evening. As night fell we picked up Zulu who worked on the farm and, with Kokkie, headed into the bush. The vehicle was armed with a spotlight and it was superb to see the wildlife roaming late at night. Kokkie provided David with a rifle and instructed him on how to use it. The vehicle came to a stop and Kokkie told David which animal he wanted him to shoot. David shot a single round without any hesitation and we were then told to fetch the animal and bring it back to the pick up with Zulu.

This was my second hunting trip in Africa and was surprised when we went to retrieve the animal, which weighed about forty-five kilograms, that all we could hear was the sound of gunfire. We had spent the day with these guys and didn't think that they would take us into the bush to shoot at us. I didn't know at the time whether I should hit the deck with the snakes or take my chances with the bullets. We later found out that it is traditional to shoot in the air, when some one has killed their first buck. We took the animal back and watched Zulu skin the impala and then butcher the animal ready for its journey back in the morning. At the time I thought that if Mr Beales, my biology teacher at Wellingborough, had brought me out to witness an impala being butchered then I would have learnt more biology than he could have ever taught with a textbook. Zulu was given the offal or the entrails of the butchered animal for his family, which is regarded as a delicacy.

We were given the Impala's testicles to eat whilst we sat around an open fire and reflected on the day.

David and I had been given a local's insight into the physical environment of KwaZulu-Natal. This area is never talked about in the travel books about South Africa. It was wondrous to get a first hand perspective on South Africa and the changes that were occurring in this country since Mandela had been let out of prison. It had undergone many changes and I was visiting it in a significant period in its history.

Kokkie recounted how he had grown up in Empangeni in a God-fearing and law-abiding family. His passion was rugby, the exclusive domain of the country's minority white population at the time. This was exactly the type of person that the South African Special Forces Brigade were keen to recruit. The recces, which is the nickname given to the Special Forces, had to be very fit indeed. Kokkie explained that as an eighteen-year-old he was recruited to be part of this group. The training took place in the Ngoye Mountains in South Africa and was a mixture of physical, mental and emotional training. It was designed to spot any weakness of his character and whether he was a team player. He had no understanding of what he was being groomed for and just wanted to outperform his peers. I don't know what Kokkie was asked to carry out during his time in the army, but it was a period of his life which he looked back on with great sadness.

His innocence had been taken away at a time when he was about to embark on his adult life. He recalled the memories of his army career that still haunted him and often kept him awake at night. He explained that he regretted this period of his life and some of the actions that he took part in materially altered him as a person and removed his wholesomeness. South Africa had little international influence at this time of his life. The country's first television broadcast took place in the major cities in 1975. The government had resisted the introduction of television, fearing that it would dilute the state's control over the press and radio.

In April 1994 South Africa had only just had its first democratic elections. Nelson Mandela and the ANC had been elected by the people of South Africa, who wanted change. Nelson Mandela planned to create jobs, promote peace and reconciliation and to guarantee freedom for all South Africans. In May 1995 when I arrived in Durban, the Rugby World Cup was to be held in South Africa and was the first to be hosted by any single nation. Perhaps no-one despised the racial divisiveness of rugby more than Mandela himself. While imprisoned at Robben Island, where he was held for eighteen of his twenty-seven years as a political prisoner, he goaded white guards by rooting for whoever opposed the Springboks. However, just a few weeks before the World Cup, Mandela realised that a symbolic act could resonate in the world of sport, a highly symbolic environment.

A few days before the opening match, which I watched on television in a bar in Kingspark Stadium, Mandela met with the team, put on a Springboks cap and told the players, "The whole nation is behind you." He went on television and urged the people to "back our boys." Standing next to him, team captain François Pienaar, pledged to win the championship "for our president." Mandela took his message to the streets, telling a black crowd in Ezakheni township, "This cap does honour to our boys. I ask you to stand by them because they are our kind." A speech in a white neighborhood left the crowd chanting, "Nelson! Nelson! Nelson!" Mandela's call for unity was heard loudly and clearly. The Sowetan newspaper explained the rules of the game to its black readership. A headline blared, "Our Springboks". Team members learned the new national anthem, *Nkosi Sikelel'i Afrika* (God Bless Africa). The Springboks even adopted *Shosholoza*, a ballad sung by black workers, as their theme song. On the eve of opening day, the team requested a tour of Robben Island. More than 60,000 people at Ellis Park, including a rugby jersey-clad Mandela, watched the Springboks beat Australia, winners of the previous World Cup in 1991. In the neighbouring black township of Soweto, residents watched the game on television, even though the Springboks' first and only black player, Chester Williams, was sidelined with an injury.

To be in South Africa during this period of time was unbelievable. It was odd to see the convergence of the rugby world and the good values that the sport was associated with in the UK with a country emerging from a terrible history and finding its feet. I hadn't planned to be in South Africa during this time, it was amazing good fortune. I had no idea of the effect that it would have on my future life.

Durban was the location for all England's pool games, England v Argentina on Saturday 27th May, England v Italy on Wednesday 31st May and England v Western Samoa on Sunday 4th June. We went to all the games, as tickets were easy to come by in Durban. It was strange watching these fixtures with a degree of envy. I had been in the A team that season and played with a number of players that got capped for the first time on this tour. However, when I visited Ian Hunter and Tim Rodber in their hotel, who were in the England Squad, I soon realised that their experience of South Africa was mostly confined to their hotel on Durban seafront.

So many friends, including Andrew Langley, Kirsty Richards, Sheena Mackness, Giles Wilson and Andrew Beales, came to visit me and we spent the time travelling to the best locations in Natal, as the rugby club games were often cancelled. One of the locations we visited was a hotel called Cathedral Peak Hotel in the Drakensberg Mountains. The journey was about 250 kilometres from Durban and was an incredibly scenic journey. The Valley of a Thousand Hills is about a half hour's drive from the centre of Durban. The area is named after the thousands of hills that tumble down to the Umgeni River, which flows from the Drakensberg Mountains to the Indian Ocean. On through Pietermaritzburg, the Capital of KwaZulu-Nataland, then on to the Howick Falls waterfall on the Umgeni River. Eventually you get to the winding road leading to the Cathedral Peak Hotel, hidden away in the mountains under the the Drakensberg.

The hotel was opened in 1939 by the van der Riet family and remains one of the most popular resorts in this area, which became a World Heritage Site. As I approached the hotel I got a real sense that

I was in a remote area, which was very different to other parts of Natal. Imagine an alpine landscape with scattered villages where the local people lived in much the same way as they had for thousands of years. The only anomaly was the school children dressed in uniforms. I got a real sense of happiness. People waved at us as we passed; they knew we were going to the only property in this area.

This region was originally inhabited by the San people, also known as Bushmen. They lived in caves and overhangs in the sandstone cliffs of the little berg, leaving a legacy of their paintings on the sandstone cliffs and cave walls, depicting their way of life and the various animals and people they encountered. The Drakensberg is one of the richest rock painting areas in the world. Over the last forty years, 30,000 individually painted images different rock shelters have been recorded.

Giles Wilson, Andrew Langley and I arrived at the hotel, which felt like returning to colonial days. I sat on the hotel patio watching the sunset, looking out on the mountain peaks, enjoying the last rays of sunshine in the late afternoon. It was a place where you could put the world to rights, a place where time forgot. Harry's Bar, the late night drinking spot, even had a roaring fire. The hotel was in easy reach of the mountain walks, which took us to places like Doreen Falls and Rainbow Gorge, and the summit of Cathedral Peak. It was the last place that you would think you would bump into English rugby supporters. As we sat down for a beer, we looked across and at the table next to us was the Sky commentator Jamie Salmon, who was leading a tour. Jamie Salmon has a special place in international rugby as the only man who has played for both the All Blacks and England.

The other place we often visited was Hluhluwe-Imfolozi Game Reserve, which is the oldest game park in Africa founded in 1895, to see the Big Five game animals – lion, rhino (black and white), elephant, buffalo and leopard. Everyone who visited wanted to go to a game reserve and I was happy to take them there. It had an abundance of wildlife including Nile crocodile, hippo, white and black rhino, leopard, lion, cheetah, hyena and elephant. The Memorial Gate entrance to the reserve was inconspicuous and it took about forty-five minutes to travel the fifteen kilometres to get to Hilltop Camp, in the Hluhluwe Game Reserve. The camp had been rebuilt and enlarged in the early nineties and we stayed in thatched rondavels and ate in the restaurant. On my first visit, I signed my name in the guest book to find that the last person to sign in was from a village in Northamptonshire called Grendon. The menu at dinner included ostrich, kudu and springbok meat, sourced directly from the reserve. The camp was not cut off from the main reserve and often you would be woken up in the morning by zebra directly outside the patios of the rondavels. This was the first time that I saw a pride of lions as they brushed against our car as we went out on one of the game drives. We were told not to panic as they were used to the vehicles, but never to get up or attempt to get out because there was every chance that we could disturb them.

This period of my life was probably as good as it could have got. I was staying in Marine Drive, in a great house overlooking the Indian Ocean on The Bluff, where I often saw schools of dolphins. I had no financial worries. I was playing club rugby and training with the Natal Squad. I was getting to see England play rugby in the World Cup and travelling extensively in one of the most beautiful parts of the world. Dave and I visited superb beaches, game reserves and the mountains.

Andy Beales came to visit me during my time in South Africa; he played with me at the Saints and was my housemate in Broadway, Abington. He announced that he had tickets for the World Cup final, which was taking place at Ellis Park, Johannesburg on the 24th June 1995. Tickets for any World Cup final are hard to come by. There was no way that we were going to turn down this opportunity, despite the fact that England were not in the final. I had listened on a radio going to the Hluhluwe Game Reserve as they had been beaten 45–29 at Newlands Stadium by New Zealand on the 18th June 1995. This was largely due to the efforts of Jonah Lomu, who shocked the 51,000 spectators when he ran in four tries, including a try in which he ran straight through England fullback Mike Catt.

We had decided that we would make the journey by car from Durban to Johannesburg, which was approximately 566 kilometres, with one of my teammates from Durban Harlequins in a VW Jetta. The journey wasn't possible to complete in a day, so we stayed overnight in a small town en route. This was a real opportunity to see more of South Africa including the Blue Mountains that Kokkie had talked about during his special forces training. It was a chance to learn first-hand the views of an Afrikaans person, who had originally been brought up in Bloemfontein.

There was so much positivity in South Africa at this time and people felt that the country was on the up. President Mandela was a revelation and the World Cup could not have gone any better for him in terms of providing him with a showcase for the outside world on how far South Africa had come since the dark days of apartheid. He used the 1995 Rugby World Cup to reconcile people of all colours in South Africa. Only five years earlier he had been released from prison and the country could have been on the brink of civil war. Rugby was a way of life for the average Afrikaner. To Mandela, it had been a symbol of apartheid. Brilliantly, he used this global tournament to persuade the country to come together around the national rugby team. I sat in the stadium at the final and heard Afrikaner fans singing the Xhosa words of the new national anthem, which had once been the symbol of black defiance.

I am proud to say that Andy and I had been part of these these historic sporting crowds. I watched as Afrikaners, who previously may have applauded Nelson Mandela's imprisonment, who may have wanted him dead, who had been planning to go to war against him, were now chanting his name. Sean Fitzpatrick who captained the Kiwis that day recalled what it was like to see Mandela wearing the number six jersey of 'Bok captain Francois Pienaar. He felt part of a historic moment that will live with him forever. On that day, Mandela removed the fear that some white South Africans may have had of him and other black South Africans and I witnessed a remarkable sporting occasion. The match was relatively disappointing but the build-up and post-match celebrations were something to savour for the rest of my life.

It didn't matter what colour you were that night in Johannesburg, people came together to celebrate a remarkable victory. We went to a shebeen, which was an illegal local township bar on the outskirts of Johannesberg. We were the only white faces in the club and everyone celebrated the victory that day. I went into a late-night food joint in a seedy part of Johannesburg and recognised someone from the UK. Neil Pearson, an actor who first shot to fame in the television comedy series Drop the Dead Donkey, was spending an interesting year in South Africa filming the BBC biopic of Cecil Rhodes.

This was an amazing moment for South Africa to win the world cup, but no-one could have predicted that after this game the sport would undergo the most radical changes in its history. I had not heard of the names of Rupert Murdoch and Kerry Packer before the final of the Rugby World Cup; however, these two men and their media corporations entered into a battle over rugby that changed the face of the sport forever. Shortly before the final match we read in the local press that Murdoch had acquired the broadcasting rights of all games between South Africa, New Zealand and Australia, now grouped together in an organisation called Sanzar. A price of $540 million was reputed to be the figure that he had paid for this privilege. Not to be outdone by his fiercest rival another Australian media magnate, Kerry Packer, formed Rugby World Corporation. Packer intended to buy the world's 900 best players to create a world series competition starring the greats of rugby, to be broadcast on his network. I had got wind of this whilst training in the Natal Squad and the person leading the discussions at the time was John Allan, the captain of the Natal team, who I was lucky enough to chat to again relatively recently about this period of time. Big contracts were being offered to all players in the Natal squad and all of the discussions were very discrete and behind closed doors. I called Tim Rodber, our captain back at the Saints, to discuss what I had seen going on in South Africa. He confirmed that he had been approached along with other leading players in England.

It was clear from the outset that the future of rugby was not big enough for both these media tycoons. Only one would be left standing and Rupert Murdoch prevailed. All the discussions concerning big money contracts soon dissolved but the threat that Kerry Packer brought to the Rugby Unions around the world was enough to propel rugby in a new direction. Where unions had always disguised the overt compensation of "amateur" players, lucrative contracts suddenly became available. With South Africa, New Zealand and Australia already paying players the last bastion of amateurism, the International Rugby Board (IRB) had no choice but to announce rugby a professional sport after over 150 years of amateurism. It was Vernon Pugh, the first elected chairman of the International Board, that persuaded the delegates that they had no choice but to vote for radical change at a three-day meeting in Paris. This decision rocked my world forever. I left England as an amateur player and returned to find out how my club and country would come to terms with a professional sport. My trip to South Africa had changed my perspective on life and my sport was entering a new dawn. This was the excuse I needed to get out of surveying.

In the stands at Ellis Park in Johannesburg on the day of the final, I saw a man who was wearing my club colours – the black, green and gold of Northampton. His name was Alistair McLennan. He had spent most of his professional career in Africa working for companies that installed mobile phone systems. I met him after he returned from Ghana, to set up a business in Northampton. I had come back from Africa looking for a number of opportunities which might allow me to get out of surveying. The thought of going back to Wellingborough to the offices of Connell Wilson filled me with dread. I decided to take a risk based on a conversation that Alistair and I had in his office in Hazelwood Road, Northampton. It was a big risk at the time because I had a mortgage to pay and only £2,000 to my name. The project that Alistair and I decided to embark on was probably the most enjoyable project that I have ever been involved with. It became known as The Discovery Tour of West Africa and took place in May and June 1996.

This tour was born out of looking at a map of Africa in his office. At the time, despite studying the cocoa growing plantations of West

Africa for Geography A-level, I had no idea where Ghana was and Alistair pointed out it was next to the Ivory Coast. The only knowledge I had of this country was through watching a tragic match at the rugby world cup. The game was between Ivory Coast and Tonga. With only three minutes of play Max Brito, a young winger, caught a ball and ran out of defence, to be tackled by Inoke Afeaki, the Tonga flanker. Several players fell on top of Max Brito, leaving him prone and motionless on the ground. Brito was taken to the intensive care unit of the Unitas Hospital in Pretoria where medical staff worked to treat damage to his vertebrae. Brito was left paralyzed below the neck. This moment shocked me to the bone. A simple moment like this, which I had been in a thousand times before in my rugby career, changed his life forever. I read reports in the paper that there was very little support for Max Brito from the Rugby World Cup and Alistair and I decided from our office in Northampton to see whether we could organise a tour to redress this. We set out our aims, which were to raise money for Max Brito, to play rugby in Ghana, a non-rugby playing country, and to have fun on what became the last amateur tour for players of the quality we hoped to recruit. This project became all encompassing; it was the vehicle I needed to get away from surveying and allowed me to travel, a passion that I had grown accustomed to. In principle the idea was superb, but in reality was extremely difficult to pull off.

The words of my grandma rang in my head when I returned from South Africa and I told her that I was not going back to the profession I had studied so hard for, "Harvey, when are you going to get a proper job." To her, being a surveyor was prestigious. I had a company car, letters after my name, a salary and prospects for the future. I felt differently, I felt like I was being shackled. I had little autonomy, the work wasn't complex and there was no reward in terms of the effort I put in and what I got back. It was at this point in my life that I wanted to take a risk and create something for myself. I had very little responsibility and I had a safety net on the horizon, which was professional rugby.

Chapter 15

The Discovery tour of West Africa

Up until now none of us had been paid to play the sport we loved, so you can imagine the surprise that ensued when the club I was playing at and the England A squad decided to pay players to play rugby. This didn't happen immediately but there was an understanding that we would get paid to play when the RFU and Club had come to terms with the huge changes that Vernon Pugh had brought about. These changes were meteoric for rugby. Can you imagine what JR Simpson, the past president of the RFU, must have thought about these changes? He had chastised me for claiming too much on my expenses form and now players like me would be on the RFU pay roll. The first time I got paid to play was after winning a Sevens competition in Newcastle. We had won the competition and there was a £10,000 prize. There were ten players in the squad including Paul Larkin the coach, Tim Rodber, Jonnie Bell, Gregor Townsend, Paul Grayson, Matt Dawson, Nick Beal, Simon Foale and me. We all travelled back from Newcastle on the train. The talk in the station was about how we would spend our money. There were no delusions of grandeur. The concept of being paid to play was enough. Nick Beal was going to treat himself and have a new patio laid in his house! The sad part about receiving this money was that when it came in a payslip, with its national insurance and income tax deducted, it just didn't feel the same as when Peter Winterbottom placed it on red in a casino, doubled it and then we all headed to the nearest pub to drink it. Our sport had changed and with it some of the fun had gone. We divided our pay into equal amounts; there was no hesitation in making sure the whole squad got the same amount including our coach, we were a team and that was that.

Northampton Rugby Club was one of those clubs in the country who were professional off the field and had enough businessmen as committee members to get their heads around the huge changes. However, Northampton were in a very precarious situation in 1995. They had been relegated to the 2nd Division and had one year to get back to the Premiership. They had Ian McGeechan, the British Lions coach, as their club coach. He would have been a big target for clubs aspiring to secure his services. The Northampton squad was made up of international players like Martin Bayfield, Gregor Townsend, Michael Dods, Jonnnie Bell, Tim Rodber and Ian Hunter. These were the guys whose services were important and they agreed to support Northampton despite the relegation to the 2nd Division. The club also had A internationals like me, Matt Dawson, Paul Grayson and Nick Beal, who remained loyal. Loyalty was a big part of the sport in 1995 and all those players, under the captaincy of Tim Rodber, agreed to stay at the club and make sure that promotion was achieved. Tim and Geech were the reasons we stayed. You couldn't have a more formidable partnership than this and we were keen to make sure the club regained its place in the elite of the sport in England.

Fortunately, no-one really knew what to expect from professionalism and very little changed for us in that first year. We were paid in a truly transparent way. Everyone knew what each other was going to get and it was based on past success. We still trained on Tuesday and Thursday nights as a club and our only real strategy was to make sure that we won every game by 30 points, which soon became revised to 50 points mid way through the season. We were unbeatable in this league and it was some of the best rugby I have ever played. Geech set a very ambitious mission statement to be the best club in Europe and his foresight and ambition were achievable.

Geech encouraged us to be adventurous and we were so fit that no side could live with us after twenty minutes. Geech was not a loser and he didn't intend to do anything other than regain the clubs rightful place in the higher echelons of English rugby. The demands on my time in that first season of professional rugby weren't huge, so there was ample time to work with Alistair MaclenNan in his office during the week. I had no intention of going back to become a chartered surveyor; there was only one firm to work for in Northampton and it was as far removed from the team environment I loved as you could ever get. I did not fit into its culture, despite retaining close friendships with people like John Burbage and Tony Hewitt. John Burbage regularly won the UKs top industrial agent and was at the top of his tree. There was no space for a graduate who was part-time because he was also playing professional rugby.

The Discovery Tour of West Africa, as it became known, was a superb distraction from rugby. Alistair was the first person that I had met who had spent most of his career abroad working in some oppressive regimes in Africa, like Angola and Uganda. I was fascinated by his stories and his passion for Africa. Most of his recent career had been spent in Ghana working for Mobitel, the first mobile telephone company in Ghana. Alistair was in a market that was about to explode and he knew all the great and good of the country. This became invaluable in terms of what we were hoping to achieve. It was a quirk of fate for us that England were not due to tour that summer; so we had a chance of getting a very strong squad to join us to go to Ghana and the Ivory Coast. At no point in recent rugby history have an England team not toured in the off season. This was serendipitous for me and as Dean Richards has mentioned there will never in the history of rugby be a tour like this to this part of the world with such high profile England squad players. This was billed as the last amateur tour and it certainly was just that – a fantastic, unpredictable, unprecedented, melting pot of fun in the sun.

The first people I told about my intentions were Matt Dawson and Paul Grayson, who I had played with for England A at Northampton. You can imagine the conversation. We were sitting on a bus on the way to a premiership match and I couldn't wait to tell them about the plan that I had hatched. I explained that I had this idea to tour West Africa with a view to raising money for Max Brito and because I was aware that England wouldn't be touring that summer. Every one of the players had seen Max playing against Tonga and were aware of the outcome of his injuries. Matt and Grays were aware that very little had been done to support him and his family, so the prospect of going on a fun trip and supporting a good cause was well received. I had no idea at the time what Ghana and the Ivory Coast looked like. I was just full of enthusiasm and "reassuringly naïve". They knew that I was ever so slightly mad and there was little likelihood of pulling this hair-brained scheme off. I have to say if someone presented this to me today, I would have probably thought that it was a bit far-fetched. In the modern game players don't get a chance to attempt projects like this because their contracts are so restrictive. I wasn't trying to be a maverick, it was just an opportunity that presented itself, but it was the closest that I have come to craziness in my life. I was willing to take the risk. I had nothing to lose.

I managed to get the boys to write and sign letters of intent promising that they would support me in my quest. These letters came from some of the leading players in the country. The vast majority were written when the Midlands played Western Samoa on the 2nd December 1995 at Welford Road Leicester. We were stuck in a hotel for a few days before this match and so I managed to sit down with some of that team and explain what I was trying to do and more importantly get them to commit to going if I could get if off the ground. I will never forget Darren Garforth sitting down with his huge meathook hands to write this letter: "I would be delighted to accept your invitation to Ghana and the Ivory Coast, should it go ahead, and you have my full support." This wasn't language that he would have used, but it looked great when we eventually took it to the sponsors.

Eight players that started the game against Western Samoa eventually went on the trip to Ghana in the summer. Neil Back, Tim Rodber, Darren Garforth, Richard Cockerill, Graham Rowntree, Matt Dawson, Paul Grayson and me. I also got letters from Martin Johnson, Peter Winterbottom, Nick Beal, Keiran Bracken, Will Greenwood, Dean Richards, Martin Hynes and John Steele. These names and their letters of intent were sufficiently strong to allow me to pick up the phone and speak to the legendary Naas Botha. In one call he agreed to bring a Springbok side to play us in Accra in the National Stadium. Naas had been quite vociferous in the press at the time about the way that the Rugby World Cup authorities had treated Max Brito and was keen to help. He questioned that if the same injury had occurred to one of the leading players of the game at the time, would the level of support been the same as that which Max Brito received? This was the strength of the rugby community: one phone call to a legend and he agreed to organise the South African part of this event.

This tour wouldn't and couldn't be repeated today. The clubs wouldn't release the players, the players wouldn't get insurance to travel. England have not had a summer off since that tour. The players would want too much of an appearance fee for travelling. But in 1996, we pulled it off from a small office in Northampton. It was at this point that Alistair introduced me to Herbert Mensah, who transformed our good ideas from a vision into a reality. The event became one of the biggest sporting events that West Africa has ever seen. Herbert Mensah was a huge man. He looked like a heavyweight boxer. He was erudite, having been educated in the UK at Sussex University, and a highly successful businessman. Alistair had worked with him in the early days in the mobile phone industry in Ghana.

Herbert was the biggest mobile handset distributor in sub-Saharan Africa outside South Africa, with distributorships for Motorola, Sony Ericsson and Nokia. Herbert was also the Country Manager for Ghana for M-Net, the South African digital satellite television network, into Africa. He was used to developing and producing some of the biggest and most memorable media extravaganzas in Ghana, and it was he who brought to life our pipe dream. I met him for the very first time in Harrods with Alistair. He was impressed that we had been able to get the players from England and South Africa to sign letters of intent, and the meeting was arranged to discuss other aspects of the tour. Herbert was a man you could trust and there is no way we would have ever pulled off this event without him. He loved sport, and in particular rugby and football. He knew the players that we had signed up and gave us a guarantee that if I could deliver the players then he would deal with executing all the ground arrangements, and assist us with getting the flights and hotels sponsored. If I had known then the background work that was needed to put on an event of this size in West Africa, I would have never have undertaken it. However, with Herbert I was in very safe hands and he was a man of considerable ambition. He had plans for this event that extended well beyond a rugby tour. He turned it into one of the biggest sporting occasions to ever take place in this country. He was a man you could trust and I put my future reputation in his hands.

Ghana had never hosted an international rugby match and was more interested in the round-ball game. Herbert had a plan that our rugby international should be a curtain raiser before a huge African football match between Ghana and an All Stars team made up of some of the leading African players who were plying their trade in Europe, which included the George Weah, the AC Milan player who won European Player of the Year 1995, and Tony Yeboah, one of the most prominent and prolific goal scorers in Ghanaian and African football who was playing for Leeds United. This format would attract the crowds, and of course television and sponsorship.

Herbert had contacts all over Ghana and explained that I should travel to his country and the Ivory Coast to meet these contacts and convince them that some of the best talent in world rugby would be arriving on their shores in May 1996. It was difficult to see how I could do as that the rugby season was in full swing and I needed to concentrate on my rugby because this was now my profession. Herbert travelled up to Northampton Saints to meet Ian McGeechan and Tim Rodber, who Alistair and I had asked to be the tour manger and team captain. Herbert gave such credibility to this project that, up until the point that he joined us, I don't think anyone thought we could have pulled it off. This was until they met him. This softly spoken Ghanaian articulated his plans whilst cutting a pineapple with a small machete that he had brought from Ghana. He said, "This is a taste of my country". It was all systems go from that point onwards. Ian

McGeechan gave me permission to take a week off rugby and travel to Ghana and the Ivory Coast. The familiarisation trip I was about to embark on required an entry visa, a yellow fever vaccination certificate and my passport.

In 1996 it was difficult to visit Ghana unless you had a reason for going and permission. Herbert hosted me during my stay in Ghana and I was accommodated in the Labadi Beach Hotel, which was run by an Englishman called Mark Edwards who became very influential in ensuring this event went well.

This trip was a voyage of discovery in many ways. I had never been to this part of the world and neither had any of my England rugby colleagues. It was important that I put an agenda together that truly reflected the country and an insight into its history, both good and bad. The first objective was to make sure that this trip was fun. We also wanted to raise much-needed funds for Max Brito and to play rugby in a non-rugby-playing country. I wanted to give the players an understanding of how fortunate they were and a glimpse of a culture that they would never usually get to see.

I did not know what to expect when I arrived in Ghana. I only knew what I had gleaned from travel books. It had once been a British colony known as "The Gold Coast", and on 6th March 1957 it had become independent and assumed the name Ghana. In 1995, when I arrived, the country was led by Jerry Rawlings, a Ghanaian former air force officer and politician. Herbert told me that we would need to get state permission to stage a match of this size in Accra and I would need to meet Jerry Rawlings to inform him of our plans. To say I was nervous was an understatement. After all, Jerry Rawlings, with support of both the military and civilians, had led a bloody coup some years before that ousted the Supreme Military Council from office and brought the AFRC (Armed Forces Revolutionary Council) to power.

Herbert accompanied me on all the visits when we were in Ghana and took me all over the country so I could get an idea of what would work for our tour. I came to see the country through his eyes. We visited Kumasi, the capital city of the Ashanti region, and the the Manhyia Palace, the seat of the King of Ashanti and its vast central market, which was as vibrant as any in Africa. The Ashantis were one of the few tribes in the country who protected and upheld their customs, traditions and beliefs, resisting all forms of outside influence. It was amazing to visit this place. Herbert Mensah explained the significance of the Golden Stool in Ashanti culture.

The Golden Stool represented the symbol of their nation, as it was reputed to hold the soul of Ashanti. The solid gold stool was considered to be so sacred that no person was allowed to sit upon it. It was kept under the strictest security and was taken outside only on exceptionally grand occasions. When Herbert and I visited Kumasi, the King was the Asantehene, Otumfuo Opoku, who was enstooled as the fifteenth occupant of the golden stool on 6th June 1970, at the age of fifty-one. He was an old king and Herbert was keen to make sure that relevant dignitaries in Kumasi informed him of our intention to stage this sporting event. We were informed that he was familiar with rugby from watching it whilst studying in the UK.

Herbert was keen to give me a true taste of his country and we visited the world famous village of Bonwire, near Kumasi, where Kente cloth was woven by hand in the colours that represent Africa. Red for life and blood, blue for innocence, green for mother Africa and mother earth, black for people and unity, and gold for strength and fortune. Kente cloth is worn at celebrations all over the world to show African heritage and is made from cotton, silk, rayon and lurex thread. I was informed that Kente was sold in Harrods, a far cry from the village that I walked through with Herbert, where all ages of the village worked to produce cloth. The distance from Kumasi to Accra was only seventy-four miles, but the roads were single track and it took around three hours. On this road trip I got a true understanding of Ghanaian culture and an insight into Herbert Mensah's personality. He was truly a remarkable man; he spoke with impeccable English but would then happily switch into the different languages of Ghana, of which there are reputed to be seventy-nine.

Herbert explained how things happen in Ghana. Herbert was equally at home in Europe and Africa, and this is what made him such a powerful man in this part of the world and a great advocate for the tour. I was pleased that I visited Ghana before I took the players there. It was important to meet the sponsors that Herbert had lined up. Ghana Airways were sponsoring the flights and the Labardi Beach Hotel was providing accommodation during our time in Accra. They could only provide a few nights as they were a business hotel and we had to look elsewhere for alternative nights during our ten-day trip. Herbert took me to visit Ada, a town in eastern Ghana, lying on the Atlantic Ocean coast east of Accra, on the estuary of the River Volta. The Paradise Beach Resort was well known for water sports such as jet skiing, sailing, swimming and deep-sea fishing, which we thought the boys would love. We visited a hotel close to the Akosombo Dam, a hydroelectric dam at the Akosombo gorge on the Volta River. Herbert thought a boat trip on Lake Volta, the world's largest man-made lake, would also work well on the tour.

The final leg of the inspection trip took us to Kakum National Park in Cape Coast to see the rope bridge walk, of which there were only four in the world. The walk was suspended above the rainforest canopy and only a two hour drive from Accra. It was made up of seven rope walks, which were as high as forty metres above the forest floor that bounced and swayed as you walked through the V-shaped side netting and onto six platforms. This location was magical. It was the first time I had ever seen a rainforest, with the call of birds and the rustle of monkeys scampering, among the limbs of ebony and mahogany trees. Kakum, became a national park in 1990, it was a 135-square-mile remnant of the vast forest that once stretched near the Atlantic Ocean shore of western Africa, from Guinea through Sierra Leone, Liberia, Ivory Coast and Ghana.

On the same day we visited Elmina along the southern Cape Coast region of Ghana, west of Accra. The town was a fishing port with a bustling commercial scene and lively atmosphere. It became famous on account of the colonial fort built here in 1482. Saint George's Castle in Elmina and Cape Coast Castle were the two places where it is believed more Africans passed through to slavery in Europe and the Americas or perished than from anywhere else. The physical beauty of Saint George's and Cape Coast Castles, both brilliantly whitewashed, immaculately clean and impressively perched on low rocky peninsulas that jutted into the Atlantic, concealed a dark past. They were among the places where some of the worst atrocities occurred, similar in many respects to other concentration camps in Europe.

Saint George's Castle was built by the Portuguese and captured by the Dutch in 1637. It came under British control with the rest of the Gold Coast in 1872. We went on a tour of the fort and saw the commandant's quarters, the church, a museum, and storage and trading rooms for goods, and the turret room where the British imprisoned the Ashanti king Prempeh I for four years. I couldn't reconcile seeing the empty slave dungeons, which were small, dark, underground chambers, where several hundred slaves were kept at a time in their own excrement and vomit for up to several months until being shipped out. This place of horror had a church perched on its roof. How could those who worked at the fort truly be God-fearing if they had allowed so many people to suffer in the dungeons under their feet? There were five dungeons for men and two dungeons for women at Saint George's Castle alone. Also shocking were the "death cells", punishment cells where "misbehaving" or rebellious slaves were packed tightly together and left until all were dead.

I used to watch *Roots* with Mum and Dad, a television show based on Alex Haley's best-selling novel about his African ancestors, shown in the 1980s. It followed several generations in the lives of a slave family. We watched every episode of this mini series and saw brutal whippings and many agonising moments including rapes, the forced separations of families and slave auctions. This had a lasting impression on me and I made sure that Saint George's Castle was included in our tour to Ghana. I will never understand how human beings can be so brutal to each other and I wanted the boys to come here to experience first-hand the accounts of the guides at the castle, who articulated the brutality that their ancestors suffered.

The popular misconception was that the slave trade was only about the whites shipping goods and slaves in the triangle of trade that was made up of three journeys. The Outward Passage from Europe to Africa carrying manufactured goods, the Middle Passage from Africa to the Americas or the Caribbean carrying African captives and other "commodities", and the Homeward Passage carrying sugar, tobacco, rum, rice, cotton and other goods back to Europe. This was true at the initial stage of the trading. Parties of Europeans captured Africans in raids on communities in the coastal areas like Elmina. But this soon gave way to buying slaves from African rulers and traders. The vast majority of slaves taken out of Africa were sold by African rulers, traders and a military aristocracy who all grew wealthy from the business. Most slaves were acquired through wars or by kidnapping. The fort at Saint George made a lasting impression on me, and I became even more determined to raise money for Max Brito and bring the players to Ghana and the Ivory Coast. Herbert gave me a fascinating insight into his country and then packed me off with a French translator on a plane to visit the Ivory Coast. This was to be the next leg of the tour and was the birthplace of Max Brito.

The Ivory Coast lies to the west of Ghana; to the east is the Gulf of Guinea and the Atlantic Ocean to the south. The country was very different to Ghana, much more developed and French speaking because it used to be a French colony. The country gained its independence in 1960, although continued to maintain close ties to the West, especially to France which helped its economic development and political stability. The country had been prosperous through the production of coffee and cocoa, and this was reflected in the buildings that I saw when I visited Abidjan.

I nearly didn't get into the country, as I forgot my yellow fever certificate and this is an entry requirement. I was taken, along with my French translator, to an office in the airport with the threat of an injection supposedly for yellow fever. I wasn't prepared for this and refused point blank to have the injection. The translator saw my anxiousness and nervousness of being led into an office to be presented with a needle and stepped in to sort the situation out. I don't quite know what he said but the officials beat a retreat. I was told later that it was customary to "grease the palm" of the officials and because I hadn't done this I was threatened with the needle.

We only had one night in Abidjan and drove straight to the Stade Félix Houphouët-Boigny where we were going to play the international against the Cote D'Ivoire. We were then shown the team hotel, the famous Hotel Ivoire. I thought I had entered the set of an Austin Powers movie. It was like taking a trip back to the 1960s; there had been no significant changes or modernisation to its interior or furniture since its construction. Geometric shapes, shagpile carpets, bold, brash colours and an excessive use of indoor plants. The casino roof was like a spiral ice cream cone. However, it did have a massive swimming pool. The Ivoire was once the place to stay in Abidjan. It had everything, including a casino, ice skating rink, bowling alley, cinema, shopping mall, supermarket, nightclub and tennis courts, but now looked a little neglected. In the evening we ate under the stars whilst listening to traditional Ivorian music, having just returned from the British Embassy where we discussed plans for the forthcoming visit. This leg of the trip was more political than anything else and a chance to play the Ivory Coast.

I returned home to the UK and back to the club to finish the season off. There was a fascination about the tour and it was a great distraction from a season that was relatively easy in the second division. We had originally started the season with desires to win every game by more than 30 points but this soon got revised to 50 points. It was such a great year to be playing rugby. We had a squad of players who would have graced most international sides let alone the premiership. We had, in Geech, a coach that was willing to try new things and attack from everywhere. The sides we played during this season could not compete with our power and pace and it became apparent that as long as we didn't become complacent then we would win the second division title and restore our premiership status. Rugby had become professional but we still maintained the same training schedule and not much changed in the 1995/96 season, apart from that we got paid. This gave me time to concentrate on a much more difficult task – that of funding and sponsorship for the tour of Ghana and the Ivory Coast.

We knew that the flights and accommodation would be paid for whilst we were in Ghana and the Ivory Coast, but we needed to find a sponsor who could pay the boys' expenses. At this stage in my career I knew no-one in the sponsorship world, and had no idea about how to raise funds and what benefits you should put in place for a potential sponsor. However, Lady Luck played her part and the project began to fall into place. Alistair and I met up with Stuart Jarrold, who was a passionate rugby supporter and presented the sport on regional television. Stuart Jarrold had been with Anglia since 1980 and was well known to all the players and respected. We met him in Banjo's Coffee House in Northampton and explained what we were trying to do, and he thought that he could get it covered by ITV as a documentary billed as one of the last amateur tours. The calibre of the players and the letters of intent that we had received were strong enough to warrant the idea being considered by the powers that be within ITV.

The final judgement was made by Malcolm Wall, who eventually went on to become the chief operating officer of United Business Media, the chief executive of Virgin Media's content business and now the Harlequins chairman. He agreed to sign off a budget, which would allow a one-hour television documentary to be produced for ITV. This was a huge bonus for our pipe dream, which had now becoming a reality. It was thanks to Stuart Jarrold and his persistency and desire to want to attend the tour that gave us television coverage.

We still needed a sponsor and I travelled down to London to meet Andrew Hampel at IMG to get some advice about the event and the benefits that we could offer a potential sponsor. His advice was invaluable, and armed with his experience we approached the only corporate company that we knew at the time, which was Land Rover. I was introduced to Land Rover by Trevor Key, who I had met whilst receiving sponsored cars through the Henley's Rover dealership in Northampton. Alistair and I put a presentation together, which looking back was so basic I am surprised we even got through the doors of Land Rover's head office at Birmingham. Time was not on our side, so we needed to nail the presentation and I took reinforcements with me, in the form of Martin Bayfield who was then the England lock and had pledged his support to go on the trip.

I thought the presentation needed impact, and what better way of achieving this than by taking all six-feet-ten-inches of Martin with me. Martin had been playing for England since 1991 and went on the 1993 British Lions tour to New Zealand, and was part of the 1995 World Cup squad. He gave me massive credibility in the meeting. This was the first presentation I had given to a corporate audience. We presented to Kim Withnall and his boss Mike Wright. Both these men were in the international division of Land Rover and had experience in working in Africa. We were seeking £30,000 of sponsorship and this was not an inconsequential amount of money, but if you think of what we were presenting to Land Rover, they must have thought their Christmasses had all come at once. All of our players had either played for England A, England or the Lions.

We had individual letters of intent from all of the English players and a letter from Naas Botha confirming that he would bring a former Springbok side to Ghana to play against us. We also had a letter from Anglia Television confirming that they would produce a one-hour documentary on ITV, signed by Malcolm Wall. Land Rover loved our idea and said that they would like to support us. It was at this point that we really saw the momentum of the project grow. Land Rover threw their considerable corporate weight behind the event, which later became known as The Discovery Tour of West Africa May/June 1996. I was on a steep learning curve from that point onwards as I was their principle link.

Herbert Mensah didn't want to be upstaged by our success in obtaining television coverage and convinced M-Net SuperSport, South Africa's first dedicated sports channel, to cover the match in a highlights program. He also contacted all the major African footballers playing in Europe to come back to play in an Allstars XI against a Ghana XI, which would be coached by Brian Kidd, then assistant coach to Alex Fergusson at Manchester United and a former member of the Manchester United team.

Land Rover didn't want to be upstaged by us either. They arranged for the match to be shown live in all the dealerships that subscribed to Land Rover TV. Land Rover had been presented with an amazing opportunity to be part of this unique event and intended to leverage this to the full. We could have probably asked for more sponsorship, but the figure we requested was the figure we needed to make it work. We felt fortunate that the idea that we had in a little office in Northampton had suddenly become global in terms of interest. However, looking back, we were very naïve. We had created a project that had received a huge interest both in the UK and Africa. Land Rover realised the value of what had been created.

Land Rover assigned budget to this project to leverage the opportunity. They had a commercial acumen that I lacked. Before the tour they invited us to Eastnor Castle, a nineteenth-century mock castle, two miles from Ledbury in Herefordshire, by the village of Eastnor. The grounds were used by Land Rover to test their vehicles. The off-road circuits at Eastnor Castle provided some of the most challenging all-terrain driving experiences in the UK. I had never had a Land Rover experience and gladly accepted the invitation to attend along with the other players. I thought this would be a great opportunity for us to get together and officially kick off the tour with our title sponsors. The players were similar to me, in as much as they perceived this as a great opportunity to do something different at the end of the season in preparation for our tour to West Africa. Alistair and I made two appointments prior to going to Eastnor Castle – Dean Richards as tour manager and Tim Rodber as the tour captain. These appointments would go on to be very wise decisions!

Eastnor Castle gave Alistair and I credibility. We arrived at the foot of the Malvern Hills to probably one of the most perfectly executed corporate events that I have ever attended. Land Rover made sure that all of their products were on display outside the Castle and we were made to feel like dignitaries. This was probably the first event that I had attended of this kind. Land Rover knew that Martin Johnson, Matt Dawson, Dean Richards, Peter Winterbottom, Will Greenwood, Tim Rodber, Paul Grayson, Keiran Bracken and Neil Back, to name but a few, would be attending this event. To get hold of this group of players for an event would be nigh on impossible to achieve if you tried to do it today because of the cost of their personal appearance fees. Land Rover knew they were on to a good thing and threw money at the day, and invited all of their top dealers and clients for off road driving and clay pigeon shooting, followed by a lunch in the dinning room. The commercial cost of getting these players to attend for Land Rover was zero.

I have a picture that was taken of the tour party that went to West Africa. It was taken in the Great Hall, a sixty-foot-high room in the castle, decorated with works of art and suits of armour. This picture shows the last ever truly amateur tour party made up of some of the best players in England. Every person in that picture had their lives changed forever as a consequence of rugby becoming professional. These players were some of the hottest stars of the game and yet none of them had any idea of their commercial value. This was a great time to be in the game; you were judged on your ability to play the sport and the contribution you made socially to the club. No-one got paid to play on tour, just travelling expenses, and they came out of choice. Martin Johnson joined us on the tour even though he was unable to play, as he had broken his arm. Neil Back came along, but couldn't play due to a controversial moment that arose in Leicester's Pilkington Cup final defeat against Bath in 1996. As the final whistle was blown, Neil pushed referee Steve Lander to the ground. Backie maintained that he had mistaken Lander for Bath back-row (and future England head coach) Andy Robinson. Neil was given a six-month ban from the game and so was unable to play on the tour.

I travelled back home with Matt Dawson from Eastnor Castle and we recalled the first time that I had mooted the idea of this event on the team bus going to a premiership match. Neither of us could believe the momentum that had been gathered in the ten months that Alistair and I had been working on the project. We were lucky that we had come so far.

The last two tasks that Alistair and I had to do were relatively simple compared with what we had achieved to date. But, if anyone had told us we what we would be doing ten months earlier then we would have told them they were mad. The first task was to get permission from 10 Downing Street to travel to West Africa for this tour. We had been told that an international tour in this region of Africa needed to be with the permission of the British High Commission, and by default a reporting line back to Number 10. We had been informed by The British High Commission in Accra and the British Embassy in Abidjan that this needed to happen before we could get on the plane.

Luck was on our side again; one of the players who attended the tour was John Steele, the newly appointed chief executive of the Rugby Football Union. His best man, Godric Smith (who I had met some years previously at John's wedding to Sophie), worked in the press office at 10 Downing Street and helped us draft the few words that the Prime Minister would need to see to give his approval. The Prime Minister at the time was John Major. Imagine our surprise when a letter from the Prime Minister arrived in the post confirming that we had his blessing to tour and his good wishes for such a worthy cause.

The last task was to secure funding to play for the players expenses and we did this by getting six business men to pay £5,000 each to attend the tour. Keith Barwell who paid £1 million to gain control of the Saints in 1995 as the game turned professional and still remains the club's owner and chairman today, was one the businessmen. The support that Keith showed me in this venture was characteristic of him. Keith was the first businessman to support the Saints, following the revolution in 1988, and he was one of the unofficial recruitment team that included my mentor Tony Hewitt. Keith had dedicated an awful lot of time and money to the Saints and had been responsible for putting the packages together that had helped bring over Buck Shelford and Glen Ross from New Zealand. In fact, Keith had been involved with the club behind the scenes for as long as I had been there, however, none of the players realised this at the time. He hadn't sought adulation and was extremely humble. I had come into contact with him after the England Under 21s trip to Holland in 1990 when Jonathan Howard, another member of the unofficial recruitment team, asked me and Gavin Balwin to go around to Keith's house to pick up a sponsored Rover 216 which was going to be provided by Keith's company. Gavin and I played "hic, haec, hoc" (the "paper, scissor, stone" game) to decide which colour we got. The choice was between maroon and white and my choice was the former. Needless to say, I drove away in that coloured car from Keith's house in Blisworth and a year later he sold it to me for a peppercorn! Keith was just an ordinary bloke who had made a lot of money. To have him and Tony Hewitt, two of the new directors of Northampton Rugby Football Club Ltd, as part of the tour with Colin Richardson and Brian Richards, was an honour. At this stage, with everything in place, we concentrated on ensuring that we delivered the players to Ghana. Little did we know the reception that would be waiting for us as we arrived in Ghana in May 1996.

We embarked on our tour of Ghana in May/June 1996, having had the most unbelievable year of rugby. The International Rugby Board's decision to make the game open in August 1995 meant that rugby was never out of the headlines. The RFU had appointed a commission to examine the implications of the open game. In true RFU style, no agreement was reached with the senior clubs until May. By this time, Ian McGeechan had led us through one of the most extraordinary seasons. Relegation the year before for Geech had been a bitter pill and he and the squad needed little motivation in knuckling down to secure our Premiership status.

The Saints in the 1995/96 season broke every record set in the courage league, setting new marks that are unlikely ever to be beaten. Records were made for the most points (867), tries (125) and conversions (88) scored in a season. Eighteen wins out of eighteen, with the highest match aggregate, when the Saints beat London Irish 65–32. We also had the highest attendance for a division two match, with 7,418 loyal supporters coming to Franklin Gardens to see us play London Scottish. It was in this season that I felt rejuvenated despite all that was going on. I became the focal point of the crowd's constant humour. Affectionate chants of "Harvey-Harvey" rang out to the tune of Portsmouth Football Club's famous *Pompey Chimes* every time I did something of note – and occasionally when I made the odd error. I enjoyed this affection that the Saints crowd showed me. I felt invincible when I ran out at Franklin Gardens, and because I knew that adulation is often short lived I wanted to make sure that I enjoyed it to the full. I wanted to entertain those people who had come to see the team play. Geech provided them with a style of rugby which no-one else was playing at the time which he wanted to take through to the premiership.

I was in a great place, physically, mentally and emotionally, and had purpose. I had signed a contract with the club that entitled me to receive a signing-on fee based on my England A status. This was the only fee that varied with each player. For the team that ran out, each would receive the same appearance money and a win bonus. The game was really semi-professional. Martin Bayfield was probably the only player who was into full-time professionalism. Geech had shown that he was still keen for us to have interests other than rugby. He felt that it kept our minds fresh. This was how it was in May 1996, prior to our departure to Ghana. This was probably the best season that I enjoyed at Franklins Gardens. We played bold, imaginative, outrageous rugby with a group of players who had sublime skills. The 1996/97 season brought Premiership Rugby, a European competition and an Anglo–Welsh competition, as well as the Pilkington Cup. With the increased competition came an inevitable change in attitude to the game. However, this would come after The Land Rover Discovery Tour of West Africa May/June 1996.

We landed at Kotoka International Airport in Accra and were taken to The Labadi Beach Hotel to be greeted by its general manager, Mark Edwards, his staff, and Max Brito and his family. If ever the players needed a reason to justify why they were here in West Africa, seeing Max in a wheelchair by the swimming pool was it. Set amidst tropical landscaped gardens, adjacent to one of Ghana's most popular beaches, the hotel was the only five-star hotel in the country. The players felt at home here despite the fact that less than half a mile from the entrance of the property, people were living in shacks with very limited amenities. The temperature when we arrived was in the nineties, tropical and humid. The rainy season was in full swing and they were expecting heavy rains whilst preparing for an after-match banquet around the swimming pool.

The day before the international the heavens opened whilst we trained on the pitch at the Accra Sports Stadium. The players arrived at the stadium to see a pitch that looked like any other they had ever played on. They were oblivious to the fact that Alistair and I had sent the pitch dimensions to Herbert Mensah before hand, because rugby had never been played in the stadium before. If you have never played rugby before, where do you think you would get posts that are 5.6 metres wide and three metres high at the crossbar? The answer is the Kakum National Park in Cape Coast, where the tall hardwood trees grow up to sixty-five metres high. We were used to rain in the UK, but a tropical rainstorm was very different and, rather than let this spoil our fun, Dean Richards incorporated body surfing as part of the pre-international training. The site of Dean Richards and Darren Garforth surfing on their bellies from the 22 to the half way line was a site to behold.

We were joined on the pitch by Naas Botha and a Springbok team that included many old internationals. The team included Frans Erasmus, a South African prop who was capped many times. I learnt after the tour that his story had a tragic ending. Frans' wife died tragically in an automobile accident. Frans never really recovered. A month or so later, Frans Erasmus died in an automobile accident on the same corner where his wife had died. The team also included Dannie Gerber, who I had played against for the Midlands v South Africa on the 4th November 1992 at Welford Road. I had only made one phone call to Naas Botha and yet here in front of my eyes was the legend himself. This is the power of rugby. If someone agrees to do something, then inevitably it happens. Naas Botha had connections with Land Rover and was a rugby commentator for the South African M-Net and Supersport television channels. He teamed up with Etienne Heyns, the M-Net marketing and development director, who was a close friend of Herbert, to make sure that this match got maximum coverage in Africa. Brian Kidd was on the same pitch coaching the Ghanaian team who were due to play an All Stars XI after our international. The scene was set for a bizarre sporting event conceived whilst looking at a map in Alistair's office. This is an example of what can be achieved by dreaming big.

The rains had cleared when we woke the next morning and the skies were perfectly blue. We ran out on to the pitch, into one of the hottest and most oppressive stadiums I have ever played in. The stadium was full with much more than the capacity of 40,000 people. People were swinging from the rafters and the atmosphere was electric. We waited in line to sing the national anthems, whilst listening to Jerry Rawlings make a political speech, despite the fact that Max Brito was alongside him with his family and this was the real reason for the sporting showcase. His speech was met with timely boos and interruptions from the many people in the stands, and he quickly finished. It was so hot standing there waiting to be received that I thought I was going to pass out, let alone play a game of rugby. Tim Rodber introduced the President to all the players as a plane flew directly over the stadium. In the UK, regulation forbids low air traffic above sporting events, but this didn't seem to apply in Ghana. There is an expression, "West Africa rules again", which means anything goes.

This was one of the most difficult things I have ever had to do. One minute I was part of Herbert's team organising the day, and the next I had to put on my boots and play an international. The match was over before it began and we departed victorious to the most amazing chants, as Ghana welcomed their national football team on to the field and we departed for the changing rooms. We changed as quickly as we could, so we could go and watch the football match which was the real reason why the stadium was full. I watched Tony Yeboah score a perfect volley and saw the crowd erupt before we departed back to the Labadi Beach Hotel.

It was only when I got back to my room and started to change for the evening banquet that the reality of the match started to sink in. We had played in front of the biggest black audience to watch a game of rugby. Max Brito was present with his wife and family, and the match was in his honour. The team that took the field would have never forgotten the images that they saw that day. Many of the players would later go on to represent England, the Lions and ultimately win the World Cup in 2003. However, they will never encounter a match like it again. Peter Mensah who played in the centre was born in Kumasi in 1966 and was the only Ghanaian that we knew who played rugby at the top level for Harlequins. For him, returning back to his place of birth was like a dream come true. The crowd got wind of his ancestry and whenever he touched the ball there was an air of expectation. He did not disappoint the crowd, scoring twice in a high scoring game. It was extremely hot and humid so we ended up playing the match in quarters. Dehydration was a huge problem, resulting in us having to replenish our bodies with electrolytes in our water, the taste of which was not particularly good. This grueling experience did not stop the team of elite professional athletes drinking themselves into oblivion until the early hours of the next morning.

The banquet took place around the swimming pool and Max Brito gave an amazing speech, a large sum of money was raised at the auction on the night. Alistair conducted the proceedings and many of the players donated memorabilia, which was bought by the expatriate community who had paid a handsome price for the privilege of sitting with one of the South African or English players. The evening ran away with itself and the memory I have is of Damian Hopley playing the grand piano in the foyer of the hotel, surrounded by the boys. Damian was an Old Harrovian, and a former theology student who had attended St Andrews University and went on to Cambridge in 1992. He was a very accomplished pianist by rugby standards and led us into song. He was very different to the rest of the tour party, but the common bond of rugby held us all together. Damian was unable to play on this tour, but came as a tourist due to a knee operation. This knee forced him to retire soon after this tour, where upon he set up the Professional Rugby Association (now the RPA) and is now their chief executive.

To say that the tour went down hill from the moment we stepped off the pitch would have been an understatement. The day after the night before was not the best time to meet Dr David Walker CMG, CVO, MVO, the British High Commissioner of Ghana, at a hog-roast in the garden of his official residence off Gamel Abdul Nasser Avenue. The boys were hung over and stinking of beer; the bigwigs that were invited as David's guests were probably not expecting to see the players in shorts with naked torso's. It wouldn't have been so bad, but Darren Garforth had a skin complaint called psoriasis which I am sure may have put a few people off their roast pig.

After the formal speeches we boarded the bus to make our way to The Paradise Beach Resort at Ada, a small town 110 kilometres east of Accra at the mouth of the Volta River. You can imagine the state of the players at this stage of the tour. They had been dehydrated the day before in the humid Accra sun and then proceeded to drink until the early hours, and were now on a bus going to a location which was a far cry from the luxury of the Labadi Beach Hotel. It was mid-afternoon and one the players demanded a "piss stop" and we pulled into a roadside bar in the middle of nowhere. Beer was presented to the boys and they could not refuse its cooling effect in the hot African sun. Peter Winterbottom, who was only on tour for a few days, covering the Ghana leg, felt a little hungry and told me to go in search of food. Now this was a roadside bar in the middle of nowhere and not the White Horse Pub on Parsons Green where he was used to having a Sunday sherbet. There was certainly no chef at the back of the bar who could sort out a few club sandwiches. However, the locals did have a goat that was minding its own business until a busload of rugby players arrived. The Ghanaian people sensed a quick buck was potentially on the cards and before you knew it goat kebabs arrived. Some hours after our arrival we decided it was time to board the bus and the Leicester Tigers amongst our party decided that they would introduce us to a ritual that takes place after away games. The Tigers were renowned for being very physical players, but some of the best fights occurred off the field on board their own team bus. The four toughest players were Cockerill, Garforth, Rowntree and Martin Johnson, and they challenged the rest of the party to eject them from the back seat. This provoked mayhem after the players stripped down to their boxer shorts and fought in the quest for the back seat. It was like entering a food blender; you went in whole and came out in pieces. This challenge in the African heat went on for just under an hour. In the end, three players remained: Tim Rodber who held the heads of Garforth and Cokerill, in a lock between his considerable forearms. From time to time, they would attempt to gouge Tim's eyes out and he would then summon up the little strength that he had to bash their heads together in retaliation. Cockerill eventually bowed out leaving Rodber and Garforth to share the coveted prize of the back seat. I am told that Darren Garforth, who was part of the ABC club, with Graham Rowntree (A) and Richard Cockerill (B) never lost a back seat fight and he played over 300 appearances for his club wearing the (C) shirt.

We eventually arrived at The Paradise Beach Resort at Ada. The boys were tired and hung over and just wanted their beds, none more so than the team captain, Tim Rodber. You can imagine the surprise when we arrived at the reception to find that the hotel had been double booked and we ended up having to share double beds with fellow team players. We were obviously surprised to hear this, but all I could think of at the time was the bed scene in *Planes, Trains and Automobiles* when Steve Martin (Neal) and John Candy (Del) share a bed in a sleazy motel. Del unconsciously cuddles with Neal in his sleep. When they wake up, horrified, Neal asks Del where one of his hands is. He replies, "Between two pillows..." Neal exclaims, "Those aren't pillows!" I ended up sharing with Nick Beal, my club mate from Northampton.

Unfortunately, many of the players were not happy with the prospect of recreating this scene from 1987. Tim Rodber came to speak to me before dinner explaining that the boys wanted to go back to Accra to the Labadi Beach Hotel. Quite frankly, I didn't blame them. The Paradise Beach Resort was far from paradise. But, we had no alternative and I explained that to him with not a great deal of success. He was tired and hungover, and probably didn't think much of sharing the night with John Steele.

I had a potential mutiny on my hands and felt under considerable pressure. When they are not happy, rugby players are a hard bunch to appease. I also knew that the Labadi Beach hotel was a business hotel and they were fully booked during the week, so we had no chance of going back. It was at this point that I knew the appointment of Dean Richards as the tour manager was a good choice. I explained the situation to Deano and he told me not to worry, he would sort it. I will never forget his oratory as we sat down to eat that evening in a covered area that was being battered by a tropical rainstorm and a spectacular electrical storm, similar to those that I had seen in South Africa. Dean addressed the players before dinner and you could hardly hear him speak because of the sound of the rain. The first thing he said was that The Paradise Beach Resort was a shit hole, probably one of the worst hotels he had ever stayed in. He then went on to say that the tour to date was one of the best he had ever been on which had resulted in many of the players feeling slightly jaded. He acknowledged that there were some players in the tour party who had some grievances about Ada and wanted to return to Accra. At this point the players' heads went down. Dean informed the players that we were here to stay as we had no choice and we should just grin and bear it. At no point did anyone question his decision, not even Tim Rodber, and I was very relieved.

We made the best of The Paradise Beach Resort but were unable to do any water sports. A rumour, that spread like wild fire, had got out that bilharzia was present in the water that flowed into the Atlantic Ocean. The players knew nothing about bilharzia and a rumour spread that it could cause blindness if you went in to the water, and no-one wanted to risk it. I will never know whether that was true. We stayed two days in Ada before departing for a hotel close to the Akosombo Dam on the Volta River. One of the local businessmen that lived in Ghana put on a barbeque for the players with a local band.

Many of the players were still tired from the excesses of the weekend, but those who stayed were treated to a magical evening where the microphone was open to whoever wanted to sing. Our host had invited some of his friends, including some locals who had voices of angels. The memory I will always have of this part of the tour is of the bus driver's assistant who accompanied us where ever we went. We later found out that this was because he wasn't a driver, he was a mechanic, and we had the only "luxury" bus in Ghana at the time, and it certainly wasn't that luxurious after the back-seat fight. He approached me during this open-mic session and asked whether he could sing. I asked him what he would like to sing and he said Bob Marley. I was and still am a huge Bob Marley fan. He stood on the make shift stage, took of his hat, exposing his dreadlocks, and then proceeded to sing track after track of Bob Marley. It was as if Bob Marley had been reincarnated before our very eyes. He was a legend, and we rewarded him and the driver with the bucket load of Ghanaian cedi we had been carrying around with us. The currency was worthless to us, but for "Bob" and "Drives", as they became known, it was apparently the equivalent of three months salary.

The agenda for the tour ran as I had planned it: a boat trip on Lake Volta, Kakum National Park in Cape Coast to see the rope bridge walk and a very emotional visit to Saint George's Castle in Elmina, which was truly humbling for the players that visited. On the way to Kakum National Park the bus broke down and, bearing in mind there was only one bus in Ghana of this quality with air conditioning, we had a bit of a problem on our hands. This was until Bob stepped in to inform us that the accelerator cable on the bus had snapped and needed welding back on. In Africa, they are industrious out of necessity, and Drives and Bob informed us that they could get to the rope bridge walk by activating the accelerator at the back of the bus. They needed two volunteers to help them to do this and Cockerill (B) and Garforth (C) of the ABC Club stepped up. Cockers was then an antique restorer and Garfs was a scaffolder prior to rugby going professional so they were very practical. I will never forget the scene. The driver raised his arm at the front of the bus and when he wanted some speed he would drop it towards the floor, and the boys would push down the accelerator from the back of the bus where they sat in a little compartment under the floor, and miraculously we would get up the hills.

This was insignificant compared with the mechanical fault on board the plane from the Ivory Coast on the way back from the match. We were informed that there was no radar on the plane. Dave Simms hated planes and this news physically filled him with dread. The pilot had to estimate where he was in relation to Accra and he manoeuvred the plane in such a way that meant that he had to dip the tip of the plane under the cloud cover prior to our descent. Most of the players saw this as a great opportunity to pick fun at Simmsy and the one weakness of one of the hardest men I have ever met in rugby. This was until the pilot repeated the manoeure many times, leaving the whole squad and the rest of the passengers in complete silence. We all thought we were going to die that afternoon; it felt like the pilot was totally out of control. It was the worst plane journey that I have ever been on and many of the players swore that they would never go on a plane again. It wasn't funny – I had some of the best players of English Rugby at the time on that plane, Martin Johnson, Neil Back, Will Greenwood, Matt Dawson, Paul Grayson and Kyran Bracken to name but a few. I also had Keith Barwell, the owner of Northampton Rugby Club, on board. I was very relieved when we got back for our last night at the Labardi beach hotel. The players were silent that night. They had all felt the worse was going to happen. I could have single-handedly changed the face of English rugby union history if the plane went down that day, as five of the players did go on to play in the World Cup Squad in 2003. I am pleased that they got to experience this type of tour, but I would never want to put them through this experience again.

They boarded the plane to fly back to the UK the following day. I have to say that I was tremendously relieved when I got back from the UK with all the players and businessmen in one piece. It was a huge risk putting this event on, and when I travelled back up the motorway to Northampton I felt elated by what had been achieved.

This had been a gargantuan undertaking that Alastair and I had pulled off. Neither of us truly realised what we had accomplished. The sad part about the whole trip was the controversy that resulted with the takings from the stadium. The Sports Minister and certain accomplices misappropriated the takings from the sale of tickets on the day of the game, which later led to his imprisonment. The funds that we raised at the auction and at a charity ball, held after the tour at Birmingham Metropole, went directly to Max, and Herbert presented him with some money which he personally delivered to Max's house in France.

Max Brito is now mostly bedridden. He and his wife have sadly separated and he now lives with his parents in Bordeaux. Some people have been critical of the way that Max's plight has been allowed to fade into obscurity. This is a fine example of how cruel life is; in three minutes Max went from a dashing, twenty-four-year-old, dreadlocked winger playing in the Rugby World Cup to a tetraplegic. I cannot imagine how this must have felt and whether I would have wanted to live with this injury. I made a conscious decision when I arrived back in England that I was going to do something with my life. Not everyone gets choices in life and I have been presented with many. It is "choice not chance" that determines your destiny.

Alistair and I had been able to turn a pipe dream into a reality. I will always be indebted to him for taking a risk with me. He invested his time, but more importantly his money. At this point in my life, all I had was enthusiasm and an overwhelming desire to do something that made a difference and provided fun to the people that were involved with it. This tour was one of the biggest and most bizarre events that I have ever been associated with. Many of the players and sponsors will never do anything like that again. The contracts that are now with players of this quality have removed their autonomy to make a decision to go on this kind of tour. This was truly the last amateur tour of its kind, and I am very proud to have been able to facilitate it with Alistair.

Chapter 16

The birth of Rodber Thorneycroft

However bizarre The Discovery Tour of West Africa may have been, it came a very long second to the World Hairdressing Championships that I attended in Washington DC that summer. The world's best hairdressers converged every two years for seminars, exhibitions and hair performances, which in 1996 were in the Washington Convention Centre. Jake Richardson, a great friend of mine, had planned to take his girlfriend as a guest of Wella to Washington. There was a falling out and I happened to be the first person he saw to invite, and I was more than happy to go at a moments notice. The hairdressing world was one that I was not familiar with. However, an all-expenses long-weekend trip courtesy of Wella was not something that I was going to turn down. We were flown to Washington and treated to a suite in the Hyatt Regency on Capitol Hill. Jake and I were great mates, but this was the world hairdressing competition, so everybody assumed we were gay. We couldn't have both been more heterosexual if we tried, but we played along with the intrigue for the other guests. Jake's family ran a number of hair dressing salons alongside their other businesses and a property company in Northampton. They were an established distributer of Wella hair products, so each year they would be invited to attend an event like this. The trips were unique and this event, known as "Hair World", had no expense spared.

On the first evening we were invited to dinner in the Presidential Room of the famous Occidental Restaurant, which had been around since 1906. The walls of the restaurant were adorned with original oil paintings of past United States presidents, including Teddy Roosevelt,

J Edgar Hoover, who was the director of the FBI and an amazing collection of black-and-white photographs of politicians and other famous faces. The restaurant was famous for many important events, none more so than a clandestine meeting in 1962 between John Scali, an ABC-TV state department correspondent, and an unidentified KGB agent that led to the official negotiated settlement of the Cuban Missile Crisis.

Jake and I were on a table with Steve Lowe, the MD of Wella, and two male hairdressers who ran Vidal Sassoon Eastern and Western Seaboard, respectively. It became apparent during the course of the meal that I wasn't Jake's boyfriend and that I played professional rugby. Their reaction was superb. They said, "Tonight I am going to be Fergie and my friend is going to be Princess Diana, and, Harvey, you can be our Will Carling." Will Carling, the England rugby captain was rumoured to be having an affair with Princess Diana at the time. He had split up with his wife, Julia, in 1996, the same year as Charles and Diana. This was the only link that these hairdressers had with rugby and it made for an amusing night for Jake as he watched me being chatted up by two men. I, of course, played along with it up to a point.

Jake and I made the most of visiting Washington DC, which was known at the time as the "murder capital" of the United States. This was due to a crack epidemic that greatly affected the city and led to a massive increase in crime and homicides, despite it being the headquarters of multiple federal law enforcement agencies such as the FBI (Federal Bureau of Investigation) and United States DEA (Drug Enforcement Administration). We didn't see any crime whilst we were there and visited its monuments and memorials. I remember Arlington National Cemetery, a quiet, shaded oasis of 420 acres, in the midst of the city, held in respect by Americans for the dead of the Civil War, Medal of Honour recipients and high-ranking government officials. I remember the Washington Monument, which was built as a tribute to George Washington's military leadership from 1775–83 during the American Revolution. Another highlight was seeing the White House and visiting the Smithsonian Institution, the world's largest museum complex, and seeing a couple of the nineteen museums that it had to offer. But the real highlight for me was being a guest of the biggest banquet that I have ever seen, held by Wella, at Union Station. They closed the station for four hours whilst 2,000 guests were fed and entertained in the station's grand hall. Over $160 million had been spent in the 1980s restoring the station to its former glory and it was used for private special events, such as this and the Presidential Inaugural Ball. I have never seen so many people in one place and the attention to detail was unbelievable. There were no kitchens in the station, so the food had to be brought in on trucks. You can imagine the logistics of serving 2,000 people, it was like a military operation and it made the events that I had done pale into insignificance. However, it gave me an insight into what could be achieved and the sort of expenditure that companies like Wella are prepared to make promoting their brand to their clients.

There were people invited by Wella from all over the world, including staff competing in the championship. One person who was on our table was Patrick Cameron, a New Zealander who appeared at the time on BBC make over programmes like *Style Challenge*. He was also working for Wella as one of the leading hairdressing manufacturers, doing shows for them and demonstrating products. The Kiwis that I had met up until this were very different to Patrick, who had long black hair and was overtly feminine. You can imagine my surprise when he asked me to dance at this gala dinner. I am sure he had been set up, but I was genuinely shocked and headed straight over to the blonde beauties that were occupying the Wella Dutch table to ask one of them if they wanted to dance. I returned to Northampton to contemplate my future beyond rugby once again.

You could call the first encounter I had with Alistair in Ellis Park in 1995 serendipity. I am sure it was preordained. All of us get opportunities to do things with our lives, but few of us choose to take them forward. Many people sadly languish in mediocrity and don't want to take risks or cannot make choices because of personal circumstances beyond their control. This period of time from leaving the relative security of a job as a chartered surveyor and travelling to Africa had taught me many things, the most important of which was that life should be lived on the basis of intrinsic motivators rather than extrinsic ones. I had been fortunate enough to have some of the most amazing experiences and wanted to find a way of sharing these with other people. This heralded the birth of Rodber Thorneycroft Ltd (RTL). I went to see Tim Rodber after we returned from Ghana with an idea.

Rugby had gone professional and I was no longer practicing as a surveyor. Tim was still in the army, but only really in an ambassadorial role. Tim had seen first hand the event that Alistair and I had helped create, and I proposed that we set up a company which gave corporate clients access to people and places they don't normally have access to by using events. There was no risk associated with this business other than the time that we invested. We had no clients, no offices and no investment, but this didn't stop us agreeing to get together. We bought a company "off the shelf" called Rodgate Associates Limited and on the 5th September 1996, "having by special resolution changed its name" it was incorporated under the name Rodber Thorneycroft Limited with company number 3234300.

You always remember your first client, that one person willing to take a risk on you. This was a company called Design Bridge, which had been founded in 1986 by Sir William Goodenough and John Morris. My client acquisition strategy was quite strange. Soon after the Ghana tour I got yet another one of those calls from Peter Winterbottom, who informed me that the Richard Langhorn Trust was going to undertake a cycle ride from London to Paris over a period of three days and did I want to go? I spent the summer training with Geech and the Saints for our return to the premiership so I was in pretty good shape, but not cycling fit. The event was being sponsored by Eurostar. Peter Winterbottom and Lawrence Dallaglio were the two high profile names used to generate publicity for the Langhorn Trust. The start of the race was at Waterloo Station and the finish was the British ambassador's residence, in the rue du Faubourg Saint-Honoré close to the Champs-Elysées. I had never undertaken a cycle ride of this distance, but it was a superb experience and we were given everything we needed to achieve our objective of getting to Paris. We had top-of-the-range bikes and support vehicles to help us along our way and provide food and drink.

On the second day of this cycle ride I spent at least 60 kilometres of the 112 kilometre leg with Bill Goodenough, who turned out to be my first ever client, discussing life, and I mentioned that Tim and I ran an events management company. I told him about The Discovery Tour of West Africa and he invited me to go and see him for a meeting with Tim at 18 Clerkenwell Close in London. I will never forget completing that bike ride and cycling up the Champs-Elysées with outriders to attend a garden party with Michael Jay, the British Ambassador to France.

We stood in the Avenue Gabriel and positioned our bikes in two lines opposite each other, and held our bikes in the air. Peter Winterbottom then proceeded to ride through the middle of the bikes and we dropped the front wheel forty-five degrees, as if saluting him and as a mark of respect prior to us going into the embassy. I am sure the British Embassy hadn't realised what they had let themselves in for. I think we ate and drank them dry. Eurostar had booked us into a restaurant in Paris where we continued the fun late into the night. The night is memorable because it is the first time and last time I have ever been stabbed. Not by a hooligan, but by Headless Hunter, a winger from Rosslyn Park who I knew very well and who was one of my teammates on the trip. I don't know to this day why he decided to plunge a knife into my shoulder, but I have the scar to prove it. Rather like Odysseus, this is now one of the identifying marks that I have on my body. Sadly, I got mine whilst drinking in a bar in Paris rather than hunting on Mount Parnassus.

This was the first time that I had spent time with Lawrence Dallaglio and his then girlfriend and future wife, Alice. He was able to converse with people like no other player I have met. I remember chilling out in a flat with him and his friends in Paris thinking, "This man will go on to greatness". Fourteen years later I found myself cycling alongside him, after he had retired from rugby. On the 12th February 2010, Lawrence, alongside a bunch of celebrity mates and over 250 other people, started cycling to all of the Six Nations stadia, starting in Rome then onto Paris, Twickenham, Cardiff and Dublin, and finishing in Edinburgh on 13th March. He raised approximately £1 million for charity having spent twenty-four days in the saddle and cycled over 2,800 kilometres. In the middle of winter I did the London to Cardiff leg, which was superb fun.

Back in Northampton I was happy to be part of an elite group of players. I relished the opportunity of taking the adventurous style we had played the year before in division two into division one. Geech was determined for us to be the fittest in the league and that summer was spent achieving this. Pre-season training at Northampton after we returned from Paris was the most difficult that I can remember. As players we feared "two minute" runs, which were increased from six to an end-of-season record of twelve. The expression that was later used on the pitch, that there was nothing harder than the "two minute" runs, was something that gave us a mental edge. The fitter I became, the more energy I seemed to have to want to build Rodber Thorneycroft. I know now that physical, mental and emotional fitness are all linked.

I followed up our business's first lead and travelled down to London to understand the nature of the job. Sir William Goodenough had given us an opportunity and it was up to us to deliver. Joanna Bowers, the HR Director, knew that we were newly formed. She gave us the benefit of the doubt and persevered with us as we responded to her invitation to tender for the companies 10th Anniversary Celebration. Their budget was £35,000, which seemed like a huge amount of money to me at the time, bearing in mind what we had been able to achieve with a budget of less than this for the Discovery Tour of West Africa. It was important to establish our credibility, particularly with a client who was willing to allow us to grow into the role. I can remember our first meeting to discuss the proposal. Tim and I travelled down to

London. On the train he read the *Financial Times*, whilst I practiced a presentation that I put together on a computer that Tim had been given. There was nothing sophisticated about RTL in those days, just "sheer bloody-mindedness."

I was as nervous as I had ever been before a rugby match. We were presenting to a steering committee of very bright design-led brand consultants who worked for some of the biggest brands in the world. I thought we would be eaten alive and yet the presentation went very well. Tim was dressed in a tailored pinstripe suit. He had his suits made and looked the epitome of sartorial elegance. I was in a Marks and Spencer off-the-peg suit, looking slightly incongruous. Our potential clients were laid-back and casual and were only interested in our ideas, not our suits. There was one point in the meeting when a number of the designers were pontificating about what the theme of this event should be when it all seemed rather surreal. You can imagine the scene – two rugby players in suits in a boardroom with some of the most creative right-hand brains the design world had to offer. It wasn't a likely match.

Tim was getting frustrated with their dithering and sat back on his chair and said, "It's your tenth anniversary celebration, why don't you base the theme around decades?" The silence, seemed like an eternity and then the general consensus that it was a great idea and we had passed the test. To this day, I will always thank Bill and Joanna Bowers for their hand-holding and enthusiasm. I didn't know my arse from my elbow when it came to business, but learnt very quickly thanks to Design Bridge.

The event was a multi-activity team-building day in the grounds of Althorp House, followed by a gala dinner in the evening in the house. Built in 1508, Althorp was the home to the Spencer family for nearly 500 years and was three miles from my dad's house in Old Duston in the heart of rural Northamptonshire. I knew the house well and had biked there as a child to the tearooms. In those days there had been no security on the gates of the house and people were encouraged to visit. My sister had a boyfriend, Robert Eyton Jones, who had been a part-time butler at the house and lived above the stable block, so we used to regularly drop her off at the house. It is surprising that the house didn't have more security as it contained artwork by some of the world's greatest painters, Van Dyck, Reynolds, Gainsborough and Rubens. In fact, it had one of the finest private collections of portraiture anywhere, as well as some fascinating porcelain by Sevres, Bow and Chelsea.

Althorp was often used for corporate events in 1996 and I worked with its general manager, David Horton-Fawkes, to see whether Design Bridge could come and have their event in a house that I loved and was on our doorstep. The clients loved it because of the connection with Diana, Princess of Wales. The house was occupied by Charles Spencer, Diana's older brother, and one of the selling points at the time was that you could eat off of the family crockery and, in some rare cases, the Earl would welcome your guests for dinner when he was back from living in South Africa. Design Bridge really entered into the swing of the event, converting their lift into a mini stately home prior to the event and designing elaborate invitations with the Spencer crest adorned in full colour.

The interpretation of the decades theme in the evening for the banquet was a sight to behold. The guests were invited to wear fancy dress and you had people in full Elizabethan dress, right through to Harry Enfield's Scouser characters, equipped with curly black permed wigs. The house was rocking that night. Sadly, the princess's untimely death in August 1997 led to Althorp becoming the centre of world attention when she was buried on an island in an artificial lake and we never again saw it as it was in November 1996. The house changed out of all recognition. The tearooms, in the old stables, which we used to visit as kids and see Earl Spencer and Raine Spencer selling wine and various artifacts, were converted to hold an exhibition devoted to Diana, celebrating her life and charitable work. Change is inevitable, I suppose. Before the stables were tearooms, they had accommodated 100 horses and forty grooms. The exhibition that replaced the tearooms contained Diana's schoolgirl letters, her silk wedding dress, a range of her haute couture clothes, and poignant films of her as a carefree child dancing and as a mother riding with her sons, William and Harry. You could no longer get access to Althorp without entering by electric gates and I felt that it lost its charm.

Delivering our first job was important and the start of one of the most enjoyable periods of my life. Tim and I had no knowledge of how to build a business. It was a case of "suck it and see", with the luxury of having the income we were getting from rugby to fall back on. At this stage we had no costs associated with the business and were not restricted by who we could sell to, or what we could sell them. We didn't have a website or email – they didn't exist. The company didn't have a brand if you define a brand as a logo, but our brand was our ability to deliver. It didn't seem to matter that we had no stationary, business cards or computers. We just got by until we could afford to pay for what most people would consider essentials.

We were lucky enough to have a high-profile case-study in event management, from the Discovery Tour of West Africa, which provided us with a chance to grow Rodber Thorneycroft. We were a small business with two highly motivated founding partners who only cared about succeeding and growing something we were proud of. Tim and I had diametrically opposed views on most things apart from business. Our overriding desire was to make sure that we succeeded not only in business, but also in being part of one of the best rugby clubs in Europe.

Tim and I lacked business knowledge so our first pick to become non-executive chairman was Tony Hewitt, my mentor and fellow tourist from West Africa. Tony had over twenty years' experience in the commercial property market in Northamptonshire and had served on the boards of two public companies, and was a director of Northampton Saints. He gave us instant credibility and provided Tim and me with his business acumen and capital when we really needed it. Tony gave us our first office in the grounds of his Old Rectory. I took on board the words of Lynn Wilson, who once told me always work with people better than you, and in Tony and Tim I was surrounded by two great people.

We had attended many events as rugby players and felt that there was a gap in the market. This was to transform the way people entertained their clients or staff. We saw no barriers to entry into this market. We felt that we could put together the most cost effective and creative events, using an amazing network of personalities and suppliers. Tim gave us the "reflected glory" that we needed to create market awareness for our company. His name would very often get us to the top table within many companies and then it would be down to me to provide the creativity required to win these events. Tim wasn't that interested in the products that we sold, he was more interested in the strategic direction of the business and managing its growth, cash flow, expenditure and investment in people, with the help of Tony Hewitt. In the early days of the business we were restricted to local Northamptonshire clients and very often this meant running events in the UK and in the counties north of London. This wasn't a bad thing because ICI (*Imperial Chemical Industries*) used to say if a business succeeds in Northamptonshire, the cynical heart bed of the Midlands, then it will succeed anywhere. The Discovery Tour of West Africa had generated a lot of press and we were approached by four Oxford graduates to undertake a project with them. Stephen Sparrow, Elizabeth Brearley, James Elliot and Andre La Trobe were launching the Harry Birrell Trust, whose aim was to provide scholarships for under privileged children to St Andrew's College in Grahamstown, an innovative independent school founded in 1855. Harry Birrell, as a young man, was a first class sportsman playing cricket and rugby alongside Colin Cowdrey and MJK Smith. Harry was also responsible for Oxford University setting the trend of having a hooker rather than a winger throwing into the line-out, a trend that caught on. As a teacher at St Andrews, he coached children's sport at school and provincial level. Harry's greatest talent was his wonderful perception of those around him and his ability to give someone a chance, which is why they named the charity after him. Stephen Sparrow was a trainee lawyer in London at Cameron Markby Hewitt (now Cameron McKenna) and Liz Brierley worked for PriceWaterhouseCoopers in the corporate finance department at Plumtree Court. Tim and I saw this event as an opportunity of raising our profile within the Oxbridge community in London. However, one of other reasons we took this job was because of Liz Brierley, the niece of Mike Brierley, the former England Cricket Captain. Tim and I were so impressed with her that we didn't want to let her down. She was bright, good looking and sporty and we hadn't met many women like her. Liz and her friends were part of a network that was far ranging and it was a great opportunity for us to get visibility.

We embarked on an event that wasn't as big as the Discovery Tour, but was based on the same principles and very enjoyable to be part of. The principle this time was to reunite the victorious 1989 Lions that had been led by Finlay Calder in Austalia, against a combined Oxford and Cambridge side. The match would be played at Iffley Road, Oxford Universities sports ground, next to the track where Sir Roger Bannister ran the four-minute mile on 6th May 1954. After the match we would then retreat to the Randolph Hotel, a five-star Victorian gothic building in Oxford, built in 1864. This was a great event to be involved with and in the spirit of rugby some of the most high profile rugby players agreed to come out and play. They included Wade Dooley, Mike Teague, Peter Winterbottom, Brian Moore, Robert Jones, Finlay Calder, Dean Richards, the Hastings brothers, Rory Underwood and Derek White. We were able to get a record crowd at the game.

I ended up playing because Gavin and Scott were late arriving at the ground due to their plane being delayed from Edinburgh. Land Rover sponsored the event and for me it was an honour to run out with these players. I then got the opportunity of walking in with them into the ball in the evening led by Finlay Calder, who held a unique place in Lions history as the only twentieth-century captain to lead the team to a series victory after losing the opening test.

The match took place on the 17th May 1997. This was the day that Tim left to go to South Africa with the Lions. Finlay led the players into the Ballroom at the Randolph, carrying the toy lion that he had with him before all the tests in Australia. Needless to say, we raised funds for the Harry Birrell Trust but also enjoyed a great night dancing to the Ginger Pig Band from Northampton. Two things stand out about the evening, talking to Gavin Hastings about the fact that no-one had done a reunion of that kind since the tour, and secondly staying in the presidential suite of the Randolph Hotel with its view down St Giles, one of Oxford's prettiest streets. Bill Clinton had stayed in the room I stayed in when he received his honorary degree in 1994 and Val Kilmer had slept there whilst filming *Batman Forever* in Oxford's Bodleian Library. It was very important to me to have an interest outside rugby, but it became increasingly apparent that in the professional era of the game there would be less time to spend on building the business. This didn't stop us building RTL, and having Tim as the club captain was a help. He took the pressure off us both, because Geech knew that we would never let it interfere with our main passion, which was, of course, the rugby.

The 1996/97 season was the first taste of things to come in the professional era. There were four competitions to play in, but the most glamorous was the European Conference. This was another opportunity to travel to new places. This was also true of the Anglo–Welsh competition. It meant that we were spending a lot more time at the club with the players and as a consequence our rugby standards improved beyond all recognition. This was reflected in the match we played against Toulon on Sunday 13th October 1996, where we beat a French side who had not lost at home for four seasons. *L'Equipe*, a highly respected newspaper, reported after the match, "that Toulon could do nothing against the technical skill, the discipline and the depth of play of the Saints trained by the magnificent Scottish Coach Ian McGeechan." It was great for me going to European cities in the south of France to play in municipal stadiums like the Stade Mayol. Geech encouraged us to take our unique style of play into Europe and so this is what we did. Matt Dawson made sure that all penalties were played quickly by hand, and as a winger it was great to play. I can proudly say that I was the first Saints player to score a try in Europe against Toulon.

I had the opportunity of playing in Italy again during this first season in the European Conference in Padova, a city in the Veneto region in northern Italy, forty kilometres west of Venice. I never imagined Padova to be so beautiful, and so rich in art and architecture. Seeing the frescoes in the Arena Chapel, which are believed to be Giotto's first mature masterpiece, were truly awe-inspiring. The Basilica di sant'Antonio was as impressive as the Basilica di Santa Maria del Fiore in Florence where Neil Back had punched me to the ground in 1987.

On the evening before the game, Gregor Townsend, Jonnie Bell and I decided we needed to take in the nightlife of the town. We headed for Prato della Valle, which is the largest square in Italy and the second largest in the world just after Red Square in Moscow. We decided that we would watch the evening go by with coffee and ice cream. Gregor for some reason gorged himself with as much rich Italian ice cream as he could possibly eat. We thought nothing of this until the warm-up of the game when Gregor was seen at the other end of the pitch being sick, which prevented him taking part in the match.

On the Sunday after the game we visited Venice as a team. I can think of better people to visit this romantic city with than a squad of hairy-arsed rugby players. St Mark's Square in the heart of Venice is one the most photographed locations in the world, with arcades on three sides and St Mark's church on the eastern end. The square was full of people, pigeons and music, and I could have spent the whole day here. Sadly, the boys didn't want to feed the pigeons or look at the architecture and so we ended up in a pizza restaurant having bought Matt Dawson a very expensive leather jacket. Although I didn't get a chance to see much of Venice, the water taxi back to the airport was fun.

We had a great side in 1996/97 season and it saw the emergence of two young players who would eventually go on and play in the side that won the World Cup in 2003. They were a new breed of rugby player that only knew professional rugby and both were in the centre of excellence run by Brett Taylor and Martin Bayfield. The first time I saw Steve Walter (Thompson) was at Pitsford Grammar School, when a fresh faced Wallie was being watched by Geech and Tim, whilst playing in a curtain raiser for his school, Northampton School for Boys, against Pitsford. At that stage he was slightly overweight and not that mobile, but when he got the ball he stood out from the rest of his teammates. Wallie had an edge about him like his teammate at the Old Scouts Rugby Club, Ben Cohen. Ben was a winger and, like Wallie, had been brought up in Northampton.

The first time I met Ben was prior to a Sevens event at Henley, when we were preparing on the Thursday evening on the main pitch at Franklin's Gardens. We had put together a good squad of players for the Sevens, which included Tim Rodber, Nick Beal and Matt Dawson. Ben had been invited to come to the tournament and was keen to impress. So much so that whenever I got the ball he dumped me on my arse with some huge tackles. This wouldn't have been so bad but we were playing touch rugby. It was obvious from a very early stage that Ben would go on to greatness. He had everything he needed to play premiership rugby. He was over six feet tall and had superb skills and out-and-out raw pace.

He made his first appearance for the club on 10th September against Treorchy in the Anglo–Welsh league. I was on one wing and he was on the other. He was seventeen years old. He was instantly spotted as a player that would become a future international and the first seventeen-year-old to be paid for playing rugby in the country. He made his courage league debut against Orrell some time later in March 1997 and I remember it well. We both scored tries that day and I was left wing, which was important in the context of the conversation that I was about to have with Ben on the way back on the team bus. Ben and I had a few beers together on the back of the bus and, as the alcohol set in, he started to chat about what his ambitions were for the future. It had been ten years since I had made my debut against London Irish and here I was sitting in front of a player who very clearly wanted my place on the left wing for Northampton and was ten years my junior. I distinctly remember him saying that he would give me six months before he took my place. He was naturally arrogant, which I believe is a trait that you need to succeed at the top level. It was like speaking to a young Matt Dawson.

I wasn't quite ready to give up my place, so I listened intently as he then told me what his dear old dad, Pete Cohen, had told him. "My dad says that when Harvey Thorneycroft wakes up and looks in mirror in the morning, he will wish that Ben Cohen was never born." This was quite an odd thing to say to a senior squad member and if I had been Tim Rodber I would have probably knocked his block off. However, I admired his ambition although at this stage of his career it only extended to getting my place, which is funny given what he achieved with England and the Lions. We became great friends over the years and I went to his wedding. I bought him and Abbie an appropriate wedding present, which was a mirror with the words emblazoned on the back, "When Ben Cohen wakes up in the morning and looks in the mirror, he will wish that Harvey Thorneycroft was never born."

Ben Cohen later became a genuine hero of mine on the rugby field. It was superb to see him follow in the footsteps of his Uncle George, who had won the 1966 World Cup Final. I was proud of Ben when he lifted the trophy in 2003 with England and his fellow teammates Paul Grayson, Matt Dawson and Steve Thompson. I knew from the moment I met him that he was going to be good. He turned out to be one of the deadliest finishers in the game, second in the all time try scoring record for England, topped only by Rory Underwood.

Chapter 17

The dampening of the Corinthian Spirit

The great thing about the professional era was the amount of rugby on offer. I loved any opportunity to play, but the fixture list became congested. Leicester and the Saints joined forces in the 1996/97 to take on two touring sides, Western Samoa and Otago. This gave me another opportunity to play in front of a big crowd at Welford Road on 4th December 1996 and we then played each other four days later in the courage league. This would never happen in today's game. I was playing well and this afforded me two more opportunities to play for England A.

The first was at Bristol on the 31st January 1997 against Otago, and then again at Welford Road on the 28th February 1997 against France A. This was the first time that I had played for England A since the game went professional and was the first time I was able to meet other players from around the country to find out what other clubs were being paid. Matt Allen, Matt Volland and I were all in the England A side from Northampton that night and had conversations with Dorian West, who was from Leicester, and Martin Corry, who was then at Bristol. It soon became apparent that we weren't getting as much as other players in the premiership, but it didn't seem to matter. I would have played for nothing and putting on an England shirt was a huge honour. However, players' attitudes towards the RFU and their payment methods were become increasingly fractious.

Steve Ojomoh was our captain that night and he got us together in a meeting room to negotiate what fee we were prepared to accept for playing for England A. He wasn't happy with the figure that had been put forward and negotiated a better one, which we were all very grateful for. The mood of playing representative rugby had drastically changed from one of a Corinthian spirit to that of a bunch of mercenaries. This may be too strong, but the banter had turned from the nightclub antics that the team got up to two days before an England A international to how much money we were going to get from the RFU to play for our country. It felt more like a football mentality. This is the first time that I ran out in an England A shirt feeling that the pride in the jersey had gone. We were well beaten by an Otago side that included some great players. We weren't worth the fee we got paid that night and I think this marked a turning point in rugby. It wasn't that we were being paid; I think this was inevitable. It was the attitude that anyone who comes into money at an early age seems to have. To go from nothing to something fundamentally changed the players' and the RFU's attitudes. It was a voyage of discovery for all of us and suddenly I felt less free. The influx of money brought accountability and a sense that I was beholden to the club. I was no longer free to make choices about my time. The coaches felt that they had to justify the time that a player spent at the club. Squad sessions exacerbated the situation because you were exposed to other players and the deals that they were on. This was unnerving because any ambitious person wants to get the best possible deal and sadly the "playing field" was no longer level. Each club came to terms with what was happening and made judgment calls about individual players and, more importantly, the part they would play in the long-term future of the clubs they represented. I came back from this A game and actively sought a meeting with Geech to discuss what I had heard from other players. Fortunately, Geech had put a system in place so everyone knew where they stood. It maybe wasn't as good a deal as other clubs, but I would have played for nothing. I just wanted to run out at Franklin's Gardens. It was forsight and good judgement that kept the Saints on a sound financial footing and enabled them to build in the professional era. They were more frugal, but this stood them in good stead.

My call up for the England A match against France A on the 28th February was unexpected. I was at Oxford University undertaking some early preparations for the event we were organising on behalf of the Harry Birrell Trust when I got a call from the England A management the day before the A International at Welford Road. Much to my bewilderment and that of my teammates I was called in to start the game, having no idea of the back moves or other calls. The team was packed full of internationals including Gareth Archer, Neil Back, Keiran Bracken and Chris Sheasby, and aspiring internationals like Martin Corry, Dorian West, Will Greenwood and Richard Cockerill.

The France A was packed full of men who would go on to play many times for the full French side – Philippe Bernat-Salles, Stephane Ougier, Raphael Ibanez, Olivier Brouzet, Serge Betsen and Thomas Lievremount. I was twenty-eight years old and felt very lucky to be picked in this game as there were some incredible wings emerging in the country. Players like Austin Healey, Jim Naylor, Paul Sampson, Ben Johnson, Spencer Bromley, Jim Fallon, Dan Luger, Adebayo Adebayo and David Rees, to name but a few. They were all aspiring, like me, to pull on an England shirt. The only difference was that they were all younger than me. This was the third time I had played against France A at Welford Road over six years.

I think I knew that this was probably the last time that I would pull on an England shirt and sing the national anthem. The first time was at the Stadio Comunale di Prato on Saturday 19th March 1988 for England Colts, nine years earlier. I had no regrets about getting a full cap; some say that I was unlucky. I would say that I wasn't good enough and I probably didn't want it as much as my competitors. During the nine years that I played in England representative sides they contained some of the best players that will ever wear the red rose of England including Neil Back, Lawrence Dallaglio, Richard Hill, Martin Johnson, Jason Leonard, Matt Dawson and Will Greenwood. They all went on to win the World Cup in 2003. I was proud to have spent many happy times with them.

By playing for England A in 1996/97 I automatically received a letter asking for my availability for the British Lions tour to South Africa in 1997. I still have this letter and whilst I never really stood a chance of getting on the plane, four of my mates did – Tim Rodber, Matt Dawson, Paul Grayson and Nick Beal. The night before the squad was to be announced I sat at a table with Ian McGeechan, our coach, and Johnnie Bell, the Irish centre, and Matt Dawson and Gregor Townsend. We were in the Trinity Pavillion, which used to be the clubhouse for Trinity Rugby Club and was bought by the club as they were expanding the ground in the early 1990s. Geech was the height of discretion, not revealing anything about the squad that he was about to announce the following day. Gregor, Bellie and Daws were intrigued as to whether Geech would reveal anything that would give them some indication that they might be selected to tour South Africa. There was a great deal of anxiety in the room, but he just talked about the Lions and the reverence he had for this elite club as a former player and now as coach. We were misty-eyed, hanging on his every word. The following day, Tim, Bealer, Gregor, Grays and Daws were selected to tour. Johnnie Bell sadly didn't make the cut and I will never forget his disappointment.

I did tour in the summer of 1997 with the Barbarians to Italy, to play club sides Lupi in Rome and Zebres in Milan. These sides masqueraded as full Italian sides with some of the best players in the country playing in one of the two matches. Italy had not joined the Six Nations at this stage and to play a match against the Barbarians was regarded as an honour. This Barbarians tour, whilst still an honour to be selected for, sadly had not attracted the best players of the game. The Lions were touring South Africa and England played two tests in the Ferrocarrill Stadium in Buenos Aires, during the same time as the Barbarians were on their trip. There were still some big names like John Mitchell, the All Black, Scott Hastings, Graham Dawe and Brian Redpath, but like me these players were reaching the twilight of their careers. However, players like Leon Lloyd and Tom Beim were on that tour. Leon Lloyd gained two caps as a replacement against South Africa in 2000 and played in the England side during the 2001 tour to North America, where he played in three tests. Tom Beim won two caps on England's 1998 "Tour from Hell" to Australia.

This was the first time that I had visited Rome and I was overwhelmed by the beauty of its buildings. My favourite style of architecture was that of the Italian Andrea Palladio. I had seen fine examples of this style at the Circus in Bath, the stable block at Althorp House and Horse Guards Parade, Whitehall, but to see Palazzo Venezia, theTrevi Fountain and St Peter's Square was truly memorable. The Vatican and the Sistine Chapel were a sight to behold, particularly Michelangelo's frescoes in the Sistine Chapel. The Coliseum was evocative not because of the vastness of its structure, but for what it represented. I had the same feeling as the day that I visited Almina in Ghana. I will never understand the brutality of humans. The Coliseum made a spectacle of human and animal cruelties, slavery and human bondage. It is most remembered for the "blood sports" that took place behind its walls. Gladiators, slaves, criminals, Christians and wild animals were used in "battle to the death" contests held in the arena. Exotic animals were imported, mainly from Africa, and were concealed in cages and pens under the floor. Many gladiators who fought in the arena against other gladiators were not enemies. They fought as hard as they could in order to survive and to buy their freedom at the end. It is difficult to imagine why people would do this to each other, but this is sadly not confined to Roman history.

We played our first match in the Stadio Flamino, on the 11th June 1997. It was a night game and we were beaten by Lupi. The preparation for the game wasn't ideal. It was very hot and most of the boys took advantage of the swimming pool at the hotel and post-season beers. Mickey Steele-Bodger wasn't happy that we had lost to an Italian side and after a few beers he said to Scott Hastings, our captain, that night, "Hastings, you're finished, you will never play for the Barbarians again." The next time I played for the Barbarians, Scott was captain, so Mickey couldn't have remembered what he had said the morning after the night before.

The second game was at the Stadio Communale on the 14th June 1997 in Brescia, a town in the north of Italy in the region of Lombardy, between Milan and Verona. It had one of the most beautiful squares that I have ever seen and I discovered it on foot with John Mitchell. The most memorable moment was in the after-match reception held in a restaurant owned by an Italian International. For some reason, our second row Richard Kinsey decided that a good after-dinner game would be to rip the pockets off the Barbarian player's shirts. This was slightly amusing to us, but not to the general public who had come in for a nice meal. Leon Lloyd was approached by Richard Kinsey, a 109 kilogram, six-foot-five-inch second row, and to our astonishment refused to take part in this childish activity. Rather than verbally refusing, he dropped this very big man with a headbutt and followed it with a great left hook. This was a winger dropping a second row. The odd thing is that Leon came from the same club as Neil Back, the delightfully named Barkers Butts club near Coventry. Neil had been kind enough to knock me out in the The Basilica di Santa Maria del Fiore in Florence in 1988 and this was history repeating itself. I don't know what was in the water at Barkers Butts, but they did produce some hard players who went on to greatness, none more so than Danny Grewcock, who was regarded as one of the most aggressive players to have played the game.

Returning home form my tour of Italy enabled me to watch every test of the Lions in Auntie Ruth's bar in Northampton. Auntie Ruth's was the place we frequented after games and where we watched Rugby Internationals on the big screen. It was an institution in Northampton. Matt Dawson had developed a knee injury in the lead-up to the Lions and was very lucky to be selected by Geech to tour. He went out as a number two to Rob Howley, but in true Dawson style ended up getting into the side for the first test when Rob got injured. It was his try, an audacious dummy that led to a first test victory of 25–16. We watched the match from the bar and I called him twenty minutes after the final whistle, expecting to get an answer machine, and instead spoke to the man himself whilst he was trying to get some quiet time to reflect on what he had just done on the toilet in the changing rooms. We were ecstatic. One of our mates had achieved international recognition on a large scale. We just wanted to share in the moment with him. The Lions went on to clinch the series with an 18–15 win in the second test which transformed the careers of my four mates. This was great for me because Tim was even more in the public eye, which raised the awareness for Rodber Thorneycroft. The summer before we had all been in Ghana, and now here they were on the world stage playing for the Lions.

It had been a long season for us, but none more so than Nick Beal and Matt Dawson. After the Lions they flew to Sydney to play Australia in the inaugural Cook Cup. England lost 25–6 in a match that was a bridge too far for these players. This was the professional game and the rugby authorities had just agreed to play each other bi-annually for ten years, on a home-and-away basis. Grays and I watched Nick and Daws play in the Robin Hood Pub in Bermuda.

I had organised for Matt, Grays, Bealer and me to go to Bermuda for a holiday with our partners Natalie Pinkham, Emma Grayson, Jo Beal and Louise Lonsdale. Nick and Daws flew from Australia to London and then got on the first flight to Hamilton, Bermuda. Grays and I were there to meet them at the airport, to give them an official welcome. When they arrived they looked drained. We were slightly put out as we had gone to such an effort to welcome them from their travels, but they were just knackered. It took them a while to realise they were on holiday, which is not surprising, given what they had just accomplished. They soon settled down and let their hair down. Daws and Natalie were staying with George and Carol Hammond in Tucker's Town, where we spent days chilling out by the swimming pool and water skiing. This was like a scene from footballers wives; four rugby players, with four beautiful girls, in Tucker's Town, Bermuda.

George invited us to play golf at one of the best courses in the world, Mid Ocean Club, Tucker's Town and then for brunch in the clubhouse with our partners. Natalie was in her first year of Nottingham University, but the year before had been studying for her A-levels at

Rugby School. One of the subjects she was reading was politics, with an emphasis on American politics. She was extremely surprised to meet Ross Perot as she was waiting in the queue for her brunch.

Ross Perot was famous for being one the richest people in America and had unsuccessfully stood as an independent presidential candidate in 1992 and 1996. I knew him because he had a link to Northamptonshire and Deene Park where I had visited whilst I was at School. Our history teacher told us the story that a Texan billionaire had bought the last surviving thirteenth-century copy of the Magna Carta from the estate of the Earl of Cardigan and had put it in his family foundation. I never thought that I would be sitting in the same restaurant as this Texan billionaire having lunch. He was very gracious, but ever so slightly dismissive of us; after all, he was a billionaire who had run for president. I think this moment for me put into perspective the whole concept of fame. Matt had achieved international recognition on the world rugby stage, but it was all relative in comparison with the fame that Ross Perot had gained trying to become the president of the world's most powerful country.

I don't think he was particularly well liked on the Island. In 1985 he had bought two vacation homes in Tucker's Town, one for himself and one for his son. He hired a local firm to add swimming pools, verandas and air conditioning to both houses. Ross needed to find a way to dock his sixty-eight-foot cabin cruiser, the Chateau Margaux, at his doorstep. Unfortunately, his preferred anchorage in Castle Harbour was filled with species of marine life that were protected by environmental laws. Bermuda's Ministry of the Environment refused to allow him to build a dock and boathouse in front of one of his houses, because "substantial dredging" would be needed to bring his boat close to shore. Faced with this refusal, his builders realised that any similar request for permission to cut a channel in a nearby coral reef would probably be refused as well so, a week later, without permission, they blew up a section of the reef near his house. The story hit the *Royal Gazette*, and Ross Perot said he knew nothing about the damage to the reef and was quoted that, if this was going to become news, then he would sell his houses and leave. The threat seemed to scare the Bermuda officials, who quickly reported that there was no evidence to suggest that Ross Perot or anyone in his family had known about the "jackhammering" of the reef. As it turned out, records kept by Bermuda police, who strictly control access to explosives, show that 100 sticks of underwater dynamite and fifty detonators were issued on 10th June 1986 to Doug Mackie, a marine-construction expert hired by Ross Perot's builder. He was interviewed later and said that Ross Perot had put on snorkel gear and "dove the site with him and watched the drilling going on. He then watched from the shore as the charges were set off". None of this came to the attention of the Bermuda government.

Matt and I had spoken a great deal about our original tour to Bermuda in 1994 with Tim Rodber. Nick and Grays were very excited about going and it did not disappoint. Having three British Lions on the Island directly after the victorious series in South Africa was huge for the ex-pat business community. As a consequence, we got accommodation in local people's houses. The wealth in Bermuda is beyond anything that I have experienced in the UK. We were taken out by Scott and Andrew Correia, two local rugby players, on their motor cruiser for the afternoon. We were treated to food and drink. We were all very appreciative of the generosity that our sport afforded us. As a group we felt very privileged to be offered the opportunity to experience how the other half lived. We were still in the early throws of professionalism and therefore players like Matt Dawson, whilst well known, would never think of charging a commercial fee for their time; however, this was about to change. Agents were around, but there was no real money for non-rugby playing activities. Matt was the first to realise the commercial power of his fame. Some of his early experiences would have come from seeing fundraising dinners like the one we did in Ghana and the dinner that was held in his honour in Bermuda. The tables to attend an intimate dinner with the British Lions were sold at $5,000; this was $500 per person. Even more surprising was the fact that the shorts that Matt had worn on the British Lions Tour, signed by the whole tour party, had sold for $10,000.

This holiday was my first opportunity to go diving off the coral reefs and shipwrecks surrounding the islands. I did a beginners dive course off of the most magnificent yacht at Southampton Princess hotel with some of the boys. We explored the island on mopeds visiting some of the most beautiful beaches in the world, Horseshoe Bay, Tobacco Bay and Elbow Beach. Ashley Redmond took us out to the Royal Naval Dockyard, which was a fort that was originally built by slaves and convicts and was the setting-off point for British ships on their voyage to attack Washington DC during the Anglo–American War of 1812. It was difficult looking at the stores, restaurants, shops and museums that were now occupying this building to visualise the pain that would have gone into building these magnificent buildings. It felt a bit like a mirror image of Ghana.

My memories of Bermuda always make me smile. I think it is paradise, yet people who live on the Island sometimes suffer from something they call Island Fever. Living on a remote island twenty-two miles long and barely two miles wide can do strange things to your head, it is a kind of middle-of-the-ocean claustrophobia – some people just can't stand being on a tiny island chain that is far from a large mass of land. It is difficult to imagine how anyone living on the island of Bermuda could ever grow tired of it. There is a great man called Johnny Barnes, known locally as "Mr Feel Good" and "Happy Man," who has gained international fame for his friendliness. He became famous in Bermuda and around the world. The octogenarian retired bus driver would stand each weekday morning from 5:00 a.m. to 10:00 a.m. waving and blowing kisses at drivers and pedestrians. Rain or shine, he was always there with his radio, backpack and straw hat, providing a glimmer of hope that work won't be as bad as it normally is. In recognition of this, many Bermudians clubbed together and commissioned local sculptor Desmond Fountain to create a bronze statue of Johnny and that now stands near the Bermuda Underwater Exploration Institute. Island fever was what I got when I left the Island; I missed being there and I made a pact with myself – that I would try and get back to Bermuda each year come rain or shine. I managed to pull this off for over ten years.

Returning back to England after a summer holiday was always something I enjoyed. I started to get invitations to events that I hadn't known existed and I never turned down an opportunity to discover something new. Guards Polo Club was one of the largest polo clubs in Europe set within the Great Park at Windsor. I had been invited for lunch by Robert Thame, a professional polo player and the cousin of John Thame, who I played with at the Saints in the early 1990s. Prince Charles was playing alongside Adolfo Cambiaso, who was considered by many in 1997 to be the best polo player in the world, and one of the few players with a ten-goal handicap. I felt honoured to be invited to Robert's house before the match. This match was set up to raise money for Prince Charles's appointed charities. Robert Thame spent much of the year in Dubai, as the polo manager at Desert Palm Polo Club, working for Ali Albwardy. In 1993 Ali Albwardy, with the help of Robert, bought some land and built the first grass polo club in the United Arab Emirates. Robert had an idyllic life playing polo from October to May in Dubai and returning to Europe in the summer when it was too hot to continue playing. He was a perfect host and gave me a taste of a life that is only normally afforded to the super rich.

Robert was his own man and a very different personality to my preconceptions of someone who plays Polo. He was a country man through and through, and loved the outdoor life having been brought up in a farming community. Robert was a member of the Bicester and Whaddon Chase Hunt. It came as no surprise to me to read that Robert was part of the group that became known as The Commons Eight. They were a group of hunt supporters who dodged the security of the House of Commons to breach the chamber for the first time since the reign of Charles I. They walked unchallenged through a police cordon and into Westminster by pretending they were working on the Commons renovations, and on into the chamber, where they shouted and barracked ministers before they were moved. Robert Thame sat on the frontbench, wearing a T-shirt saying "Fcuk the Bill", in the Prime Minister's place alongside the rural affairs minister, Alun Michael, as MPs debated the hunting bill.

The following morning we travelled to Sir Richard Branson's country estate in Kidlington, Oxfordshire, as guests of Virgin. I couldn't believe how lucky we were to meet Prince Charles at the Polo and then Richard Branson the next day. Little did I know that the party was not going to be as intimate as the day before. Richard Branson held a big party every year for the staff, suppliers and clients of Virgin at his house Kidlington, Oxforshire. We arrived at the location thinking that we would be part of a small garden party instead to see the equivalent of Glastonbury Festival. We couldn't find our host as there were thousands of people there.

On Sunday 3rd August 1997 I was invited to The Double Print Horse Trials at Gatcombe Park, as a guest of Land Rover, and I took as my guest my ninety-two-year-old grandma, the year before she died. We were very close and she loved watching three-day events, in particular dressage. I saw her every other day when I was living in Northampton. She had been a rock to my Dad after Mum died, and provided a stability and a structure to our family during difficult times. It is unusual for ninety-two-year-old ladies to be taken to a corporate hospitality facility. After all, Land Rover were hardly going to sell her a car – she didn't drive; in fact, she caught the bus everywhere. She certainly wasn't going to supply them with a big order of fleet vehicles. However, that day, dressed in a beautiful suit with neck scarf, she indulged herself and me. Her knowledge of three-day eventing and its competitors was greater than anyone in that tent other than probably Mark Phillips, who was our guest speaker after lunch.

Gatcombe was the home of the Princess Royal and her family. Land Rover were the official suppliers of courtesy vehicles at this event and had been given a hospitality marquee, where we were treated to lunch and a presentation on the design of the cross-country course by Captain Mark Phillips. I had been invited to take part in the Land Rover Challenge, which was an obstacle course set up in the central arena, where a rugby team would take on a horse trial team as a bit of fun. Taking part in the challenge was a sixteen-year-old Zara Phillips, who went on to win the European Championship in 2005 and the

World Championship in 2006, becoming only the third rider to hold both titles at the same time. These achievements led to her becoming the BBC Sports Personality of the Year. It was great to be able to take my grandma to this event and fulfill one of her ambitions. I secretly found it very boring and both of us would have been just as happy with a picnic in the grounds.

The end of the month of August was marked by something that shook Britain. Diana, Princess of Wales, died after a car crash in Paris in the early hours of Sunday morning on 31st August. Scores of people, many in tears, made their way to Buckingham Palace and Kensington Palace to lay floral tributes. Radio and television abandoned normal Sunday schedules to broadcast news of the accident. Sporting events were postponed. The BBC played the national anthem and Buckingham Palace, Kensington Palace, Windsor Castle, Holyrood House and the grounds of Sandringham were all closed to the public. World leaders like Margaret Thatcher, Mother Teresa of Calcutta, Jacques Chirac, Nelson Mandela, Bill Clinton and Henry Kissinger paid tribute to her memory, and she became known as "the people's princess".

Something extraordinary happened in Britain the week after Diana's death, which produced intense national mourning. Silently weeping, millions lined the streets of London, breaking into spontaneous applause when the queen flew a flag at half-mast over Buckingham Palace. The funeral took place on Saturday 6th September 1997 at Westminster Abbey. I watched it on television in my house on Sunday morning. Elton John sang a special arrangement of his song *Candle In the Wind* and The Earl Spencer, the Princess's brother, delivered a very moving tribute. After a minute's silence, the cortège left Westminster Abbey for the journey from London to Althorp. The M1 motorway was brought to a standstill, from London to Northampton, for the funeral cortege, something that I don't think will ever be repeated again in history, a journey of seventy-six miles with people lined along the entire route.

We lined the road just outside the village of Harlestone, close to Althorp Estate and watched the cortège pass by. Althorp House had been our principal entertainment venue, prior to this untimely death. We had recently undertaken an event for Jon Drown, who was the finance director of a company called Inntrepreneur Pub Company, who owned 4,300 tenanted pubs in the UK. Jon ran a team-building day for the banks he worked with each year that provided his company with finance, as well as some of the professional advisers. We were given the task of running this day for them in the grounds of Althorp House and this was the last time we were able to use it. Althorp became the centre of world attention and they closed their doors to any corporate use. The simplicity of Althorp was lost forever.

Playing rugby and building Rodber Thorneycroft were my priorities at that time. However, I think I had realised that at some point my rugby career would come to an end and my ambition was to build a business with Tim that would allow us both to make the transition from sport into business. There was still a lot of rugby to play, but by the season of 1997/98 I was fast approaching ten years playing first class rugby. I had my first team debut for Northampton Saints at the tender age of eighteen. I was looking for a new challenge and aware that any international ambitions at this stage were just distant memories. Rodber Thorneycroft was a perfect vehicle to share some of the experiences that I had gained playing rugby with a corporate audience. Tim and I had attended corporate hospitality events as guests of clients and thought we could make them better or even create our own events.

Chapter 18

The grand European tour

The great thing about starting a business from scratch is that you have no points of reference. At first, we set it up as a way of improving our CV whilst playing rugby. The business was not restricted in terms of the products it could sell or the geographies that it operated in. The business sold ideas and we entered the market at exactly the right time. The UK economy had been enjoying an unprecedented period of economic growth since 1992, when the last recession had ended. Tony Blair had come into to power in 1997 at forty-three, becoming the youngest British prime minister this century, and under him the economy began to perform. Tim and I had complete autonomy and enjoyed the complexity that went with trying to work out how to grow a fledgling business. At that stage of the business I saw a correlation in terms of the effort I put in and the reward that I got out of it. It was exciting.

We invested in our first computer. The password for the computer was SA97 after the victorious Lions Tour that Tim had returned from. We accessed the internet through a dial-up/modem using a separate BT telephone line which connected to an internet service provider. This is now the slowest method of accessing the internet, but we were in the middle of the country and there was no broadband, just the telephone network. Looking back this is antiquated, yet in 1997 we felt we were ground-breaking. We only went on the internet to get emails, but it took so long we would only do this at certain times during day and if we got an email we were delighted. We had one computer and one email address. We had no website as it was too costly to build. Instead, we produced a very expensive corporate brochure that was beautifully put together, but as soon as it was produced it became obsolete. It contained many images of Tim and was designed by Ian Hunter, a club colleague who ran Jellyfish, a creative agency. We spent a lot of time on the design and photography of this brochure but the content left a lot to be desired. It could have been written by Bill and Ben, The Flower Pot Men.

Our selling angle was simple. If a hospitality product existed in the market place then we would add value to it. It was a blow not to be able to use Althorp House because it was a destination that every one knew that was on our doorstep. I went to visit David Horton-Fawkes at Althorp, to see whether he would consider asking Earl Spencer if he could recommend any other owners of stately homes within Warwickshire, Northamptonshire, Buckinghamshire and Oxfordshire who would be willing to allow us to run events in their beautiful houses. It came as a surprise when a whole list of the Earls contacts came back who had expressed an interest in talking to us.

One of these houses was Chicheley near Newport Pagnell. The house was owned by Sir John and Lady Nutting. I was asked to meet Lady Nutting at Chicheley Hall to see how we could make use of the house and grounds for one of our clients, Applied Floor and Wall Services, who originally wanted to go to Althorp. The house was set in twenty-five acres of beautiful gardens, lakes and woodland and was one the country's finest examples of early Georgian architecture. Lady Nutting was keen to promote it as a corporate venue because she spent much of her time in London, working with the Georgian Group, an organisation that existed to protect and preserve Georgian buildings, monuments and landscapes. The meeting at her house was like a scene from a classic period drama with her butler, who she brought up from London, serving afternoon tea and a freshly baked Victoria sponge cake. We did an event at Chicheley, as well as many stately homes in the counties surrounding Northamptonshire. A great location that we used many times was Arbury Hall, the seat of the Newdegate family for over 400 years. This beautiful Elizabethan house was the finest example of Gothic Revival architecture in the country. Northamptonshire had more stately Homes than any other county and we used locations like Castle Ashby, Rockingham Castle, Courteenhall and Lamport Hall. The sales pitch was easy: we would run a company event more cost effectively than our competitors, in the most unique locations in the Midlands. Our competitors didn't have the relationships with the owners of these houses, and we did. We used caterers like Sue Lonsdale Cordon Bleu, who produced the best food that was available at the time in our area. This was a time before celebrity chefs.

We built the business doing transactional events; team building, conferences, leadership events and client events. It was great fun working in a converted stable block and visiting the best locations that the Midlands had to offer. Our clients were big local employers, like Nationwide and Barclaycard. We met them because they were club sponsors. Our world was the Midlands and we established ourselves in one of the most difficult places to set up a business of this kind. It was Northampton Saints who I should thank for my ability to build relationships with companies. I liked people, so it wasn't a hardship to come off the field after a game and talk to the committee members who would join us in the changing rooms. They were generally successful businessmen and very interesting. It wasn't difficult either, upon leaving the changing rooms, to talk to children and adults waiting patiently for autographs. I had to learn to be able to talk to all types of people. The conversation with family and friends who we joined for drinks and food after the game was very different to that of the question and answer sessions I had to do as part of my contract in the corporate boxes. This is where Tim and I picked up business leads for Rodber Thorneycroft. There was no better way to do this than directly after the game when business leaders had seen you play. I didn't realise this at the time; if I had done, I would have probably handed out cards to the crowd as I was running down the wing.

The start of the 1997/98 Season saw the Saints play again in the European Conference. Our draw was superb because it took us to Galway in West Ireland to play against Connacht, Bordeaux to play against Begles Bordeaux and a match in Nice in the Cote D'Azur. I can't think of three better places in Europe to visit in September and October, and the fact that we were getting to play rugby in these locations as part of our job was amazing. The Galway Sportsground where Connacht played was unique for two reasons. Connacht shared their ground with the local greyhound racing club and running out to the game you had to cross the sand track around the edges of the pitch where the dogs raced. The other was that the local licensing laws only permitted liquor to be sold at the ground on race nights. So if the rugby team played on another day to the greyhound racing then the supporters weren't able to have a couple of pints, which went totally against the rugby ethos. Connacht overcame this law by releasing a greyhound to complete a lap of the 500-metre racetrack a short while before kick-off. This was deemed to be an official "trial" lap, which was condoned by the dog-racing association body, and constituted an official greyhound-racing event, which in turn appeased the licensing authorities, so beer could be drunk after all. Only in Ireland could this take place.

Galway was a real surprise. I expected a sleepy West Ireland town; instead, we ended up in a party town, with an abundance of pubs and clubs especially around Eyres Square. I will never forget being in a nightclub on the dance floor with the whole of the squad entwined with a local women's Irish football team who just happened to be staying in our hotel. Galway is one for the list for best party towns. I was lucky enough to return there again with RTL for the Galway Oyster Festival, set up to celebrate the opening of the oyster season which is now regarded as one of the most celebrated and longest running festivals in the world. The atmosphere I experienced in these three days in September was like nothing I have ever experienced before – Irish hospitality at its very best.

At the end of September we were treated to a ten-day trip to play Bordeaux-Begles at Stade André-Moga and Nice at Stade des Arboras. The second of the two games remains memorable for two reasons. Nice had a hooker called Jean-Francois Tordo, the former French captain. He suffered a horrific facial wound in the game against

Western Province at Newlands. He was a very impetuous person, which resulted in him being yellow-carded during the game for holding the ball up for our kicker prior to him kicking it, which apparently is illegal. Jean-Francois' father was so incensed with the referee's decision that he decided to come onto the pitch to remonstrate his son's innocence. This was the first time in my life that I have ever seen a father and son sent off in the same game. The second memory is visiting Monte Carlo for the first time and teaching Gregor Townsend to dive off the harbour wall without being aware that Andy Northey, our new recruit from rugby league, was having a number two in the sea. This is not the sort of image you have of Monaco and, as this was the first time we had met Andy, it wasn't necessarily the lasting impression you wanted to have of someone. Whenever I return to Monte Carlo, I can't get this image out of my head.

Andy Northey was the first rugby league player that the Saints signed. He played for St Helens in the European Super League as a second-row forward and came with a big reputation. He was a one-off in every sense, whose zany humour was infectious. You couldn't get two more unlikely characters than him and me, but it was Andy who kept me going in the professional era. He made out he was from a working class St Helens family, but this couldn't have been further from the truth. He teased anyone who had been to a public school, suggesting that they had a silver spoon in their mouth. Dom Malone was the butt of his jokes; he had attended Bedford School, a good public school. Andy constantly reminded him that his parents paid for the two most expensive GCSEs in the world. Underneath this larger-than-life rough façade was a very articulate character who was a disciple of the Greek philosophers Plato and Aristotle, their Chinese counterpart Confucius, and even Mao Tse Tung. He had a reputation for inspirational quotes, which he used in the dressing room at St Helens and the Saints.

He always talked of this mythical place, St Helens, and one day after a match at Sale I decided to go and see what all the fuss was about with another teammate, Colin Allan. Andy had a similar rugby background to me. He had previously played rugby union for Waterloo, but joined St Helens where his father, Keith, had played during the 1960s. He was the local boy done good and everyone knew him in St Helens. We went to a nightclub with the local legend and were afforded the treatment that Matt Dawson gets now when he goes out in London. Doors opened, tables were found and drinks were provided. Andy was very popular and by default, because we were with him, so were we. I was approached by a very attractive girl who had the voice of Ray French, the rugby league commentator. For those of you who don't know what this sounds like, it works wonders on the television for the rugby league pundit, but it isn't so attractive on a girl. This beauty opened her mouth and I couldn't believe what came out: "You're not from round here, are you? You look like Martin Clunes, with those lugs on the side of your head – do you fancy a shag?" It took me by surprise and I thanked her profusely, but told her where I was from we normally buy a girl a drink and indulge in a more formal dating process. To say this was a rough club would have been an understatement and kicking out time was exactly what it said on the tin.

We went with Andy and some of his mates to the obligatory local kebab shop and I asked, in a nice posh accent, whether they did chicken burgers, They said, "Of course, me ole mucker." I then got more than I bargained for when I asked was it real breast of chicken or reconstituted chicken made to look like real chicken breast. The lady behind the counter looked at me like I was a piece of shit and said, "It's a chicken burger, I haven't got a f***king clue whether its real or not, do you want it?" I left with a reconstituted chicken burger, back to Luko's (Luke, Andy's mate) house and I will never forget his immortal words, again in a Ray French accent: "Lads, we will go back to me flat for a few sups and we can watch some videos, I've got Leonard Rossiter in *Rising Damp*, Basil Fawlty in *Fawlty Towers*, some rugger or some porn."

It was an eye-opener going to St Helens. The open Northern sense of humour was fantastic and I could see where Andy got it from. However, Andy was not the working class boy he liked to portray. His mum and dad were teachers and they lived in a lovely 1930s house in a suburb of St Helens. We stayed the night at his house and the macho image that Andy exposed was broken in the morning when I heard Andy shout from his bedroom to his mother. "Mother, would it be possible...?" Before he could utter any other words, his mum said, "Don't worry Andy, it's on its way", and a tray of breakfast arrived on his lap in bed. I took great delight in going into to his room and asking him who had the silver spoon in his mouth now.

Andy Northey showed the respect that he had for Monte Carlo by placing a number two in the sea. A principality ten miles east of Nice did not impress our Mr Northey. it was a different world to our world in Northampton. It was considered a playground for the international jet set. Monaco provided tax concessions and discreet banking facilities, and attracted many extremely wealthy individuals as residents. We taught Gregor to dive in the main harbour with its expensive luxury yachts and boats. We visited Casino Square and had lunch at the Café de Paris, opposite the famous Monte Carlo Casino. One resident who kept his boat in the harbour was Ashley Levett. His boat was called The Richmond. The story of his involvement with this rugby club represented one of the very sad stories of the game going professional. He ran Winchester Commodities Group, a metal broking business that made spectacular profits in 1994, on the back of an inspired gamble in the copper market. Ashley was one of the entrepreneurs who bought into rugby after the game was thrown open in 1995. He was young, wealthy and saw in Richmond great potential to exploit the new professionalism in the game. He also saw twenty-seven acres of prime land, ripe for development. He bought 76%of the club and began funding it to the tune of £2.5 million a year. Some of the world's greatest players were bought, and the crowds grew from 600 for a game to 6,000, but things began to go wrong very quickly. Ashley Levett discovered that he could not build on his prime land and was forced to move the club to the Madejski Stadium in Reading. The club didn't make any money during this period and Ashley became very frustrated as the losses inevitably mounted. He knew he couldn't afford to carry on bankrolling Richmond and was only familiar with making money, not losing it. He eventually pulled the plug and stopped his monthly injections of cash. Richmond were not the first club to find themselves in a cash crisis. Bedford, London Scottish and Newcastle were in a similar position during this period of rugby uncertainty. As a result of his decision, the club was forced into administration and ejected out of the highest echelons of the sport at a crucial period in the game's history. They tumbled nine leagues into Herts/Middlesex One. The big names left and the fans seeped away. It took the club over ten years to reach National Division Three again in 2009. I ended up playing for Richmond in the twilight of my career and played a very small part in their resurgence, as did Bobby Skinstad, who played a few games before returning to play for the Springboks and winning the World Cup in 2007.

Monte Carlo was the first incentive trip that Rodber Thorneycroft ran. Our client Banctec, whose MD, Guy Harris, was a Saints rugby supporter, charged us with the task of reducing the cost on an annual trip that they ran for their internal staff. Guy felt it was too expensive and asked if we could do it cheaper. This was music to my ears. I spent a huge amount of time on this proposal. The company was spending tens of thousands of pounds on this event organised by an external company. Banctec outsourced the organisation to this company, who in turn would outsource it to a destination management company in Monaco. I couldn't understand why it cost so much to run so I jumped on a plane and went to see all the suppliers that were detailed in the proposal. I reduced the costs of the trip and presented these to Guy Harris. It was apparent that every supplier was marking their services up, but not doing a great deal for it. I was open to Guy about what I had discovered and he suggested that I run it. I was happy to do this, it was much easier than putting together the event we ran in Ghana and a lot more profitable. This was the first sales incentive that we won as a company. Tim and I went to see Guy Harris and his chairman Colin Jarman, in his office in Colnbrook, near Heathrow. The office was called Jarman House named after Colin, a huge Esher rugby supporter. All we needed to do to win that Incentive was to talk rugby. Tim was adamant that we should be judged on our ability to deliver the business not our prowess on the rugby field. I found out later when I got to know Guy as a friend that we nearly blew the job that day because Tim refused to talk about rugby.

The majority of work that we did in those early days didn't allow us to go on overseas incentive trips. The work was much closer to home. I got a call from Jill Husselby, an architectural historian married to William Husselby, the former High Sheriff of the County of West Midlands. Bill was a highly successful businessman who ran Cogent Elliott Advertising, one of the largest independent advertising agencies outside London. Their daughter was getting married and she had attended the ball we had run at the Randolph Hotel. I was invited to see how we could help them with their wedding plans. I travelled up to Fen End House, near Kenilworth – a quintessential English country house, set in formal gardens, with ponies in the paddock. The house wasn't quite as grand as Chicheley Hall, but not far off. The wedding was on the 7th March 1997. I remember the day distinctly because it was the day we played Leicester Tigers at Welford Road and, after losing the match, I travelled up to Fen End to take over from our PA, Becky Salmons, who looked after Tim and I, to run the evening. Francesca Husselby was marrying Rob Jardine-Brown, a Harlequins rugby player. Can you imagine their surprise when I turned up direct from a premiership match with a black eye? Our involvement in the wedding was minuscule. I think we provided the band and a takeaway van to provide bacon rolls for the revellers at midnight. I was on my last legs at this stage. I don't think there would have been too many other players from the two sides that played that day who would have gone and done this, but this is what we needed to do to get the momentum of the business going. We needed to take these early jobs to grow. It was London where we needed to be and these events gave us access to a different client base.

We couldn't move to London, so Tim decided that he would bring London to us. We recruited Paul Sherrell who worked at Twickenham managing hospitality and conferences. He had a wealth of experience and taught us a great deal. He brought us some key contacts from his time at Twickenham, which served us well. We felt that we should be offering hospitality at Twickenham and all major sporting events on the calendar, and Paul had the perfect experience to bolt this onto our offering. It was difficult to get into the hospitality market. It fell into two camps; official hospitality, which was sold through agents of the RFU, and unofficial hospitality, which took place on the outskirts of the stadium.

One of the first jobs we were asked to pitch for was with Sarah Rigby, who worked for a company called Dick Greenwood Corporate Leisure. Dick Greenwood was a former England flanker and the England coach between 1983 and 1985. He was also the father of my old teammate and Ghana tourist, Will Greenwood. Sarah Rigby was the wife of Wasps flanker Mark Rigby; she asked us to tender for supplying all the catering and a marquee facility at the Harlequins ground in Twickenham. She had an innovative idea to supply her clients with a hospitality package, which included a ticket plus a full English brunch including kippers, kedgeree and smoked salmon before the game and a hot curry afterwards. We supplied the food, the booze (including champagne), a jazz band and the marquee for £95 per person and still made profit. However, she added a ticket plus a player's appearance to the package and knocked it out at substantially more per person.

This was another lesson for me and Tim. Whilst the package was good and the profits were out of this world, it was still on the back pitch at Harlequins and did not sit nicely with us. Tim was playing rugby for England and when Paul came on board we decided to approach Twickenham to see whether we could become an official supplier. This was harder than you would have thought. Tim was very persuasive and Paul had great contacts having just worked at Twickenham. We ended up becoming an official rugby hospitality supplier at Twickenham selling packages in the River Suites or the Front Lawns, which do not exist now that Twickenham has been redeveloped.

We added value to our package by getting Tim to bring players, including him, directly after the game into our facility. It was a unique selling point that enabled us to grow the hospitality side of our business. The margins on the package sale were poor, 10% on a package that may have cost £600; however, Paul and I used this to build our London client base. We used to have competitions on who could get the most cards in one day and then would follow the leads up on a Monday morning. Tim didn't particularly like the hospitality environment, but recognised that this was a very cost effective way of building our business. It was great fun in those early days having our own branded facility well before Will Carling, Lawrence Dallaglio, Tigers Events or the RPA got their acts together. It was unique because no other member of the England Squad at that time had his own business, and so it became high profile. Tim's name was a big draw.

Our business model became clear. We added value to existing hospitality packages. However, for those companies who wanted an alternative option to hospitality then we would put together unique events all over Europe. I was twenty-eight years old and wanted to attend every event and travel to all the major cities in Europe. In those early days we worked out what we wanted to sell, and then Paul and I would find a client to buy it. Tim Rodber was a risk taker. He commissioned a firm of architects in Northamptonshire called Zielinski Baker, to help him restore a barn that he had bought on the edge of the village of Tifield in Northamptonshire. This was at a time when I was taking very small risks by buying my second house at 42 St Georges Avenue, Northampton. Tim was purchasing a barn that had no electricity or water but had huge potential. Tim had a belief that whatever he put his mind to he would eventually succeed in. Failure didn't come into Tim's head, despite the fact that this was a major purchase and the project would take significant funds to complete. Fear of failure to Tim was not completing the project and getting the house of his dreams. There were setbacks along the way, but they didn't seem to matter to him, and the result was a substantial property with land and stables in a picturesque setting. Tim was twenty-eight and there was no other man that I knew at that age who had property like this, which they had restored and paid for themselves. Before rugby became professional Tim had received the salary of an army officer, which was not substantial, but with the advent of professionalism he was able to derive income from Northampton Saints, England, the British Lions and, of course, endorsements like Reebok and Rockport. Completing his dream house relied on him getting picked for these teams. There would have been a lot of pressure on his shoulders, but they were very broad shoulders. It was this single-mindedness that he brought to Rodber Thorneycroft. It enabled us to grow our business. In the first two years of trading we had a turnover of £85,054 (1997) and £133,994 (1998), which seems very small compared to what it became.

Paul had taken a huge risk in joining us up in Northamptonshire from Richmond upon Thames, which is where he had been living. Paul taught us both a great deal in those early stages and wrote our first sales and marketing plan. He brought with him a database, which in the early days we "cold called". However, it soon became apparent that the only clients we were ever going to acquire were those where we had personal relationships. Our clients in the first two years of Rodber Thorneycroft included Land Rover UK, Golden Wonder, Reebok, Gemini Consulting, Coopers and Lybrand, Inntrepreneur Pub Company Ltd, Barclaycard, Nationwide Anglia and the Headlam Group.

All of the projects that we were doing for these clients were transactional and there were no long-term contracts. The fact that the job for Golden Wonder was a pub quiz hosted by Vinny Jones in Market Harborough and the job for the Headlam Group was a murder mystery evening at Lamport Hall didn't matter to us because having them on our corporate brochure gave us credibility, and the turnover was ticking along nicely whilst we still played rugby.

The 1997/98 season was the first season that I hadn't put on an England representative shirt at some level and, apart from the odd run out for the Barbarians, I ended up playing all my rugby for Northampton Saints. The competition for places became tough as Geech strengthened his squad. Jon Sleightholme joined the squad and I found myself in the position of being the oldest winger at twenty-eight. Ben Cohen was the baby at the tender age of eighteen, closely followed by Craig Moir and Sleights. It was a professional era so I expected competition. I soon realised that I could no longer mess around. If I was going to play any games then I needed to buckle down and adapt to professional rugby. It wasn't that difficult; it was a great lifestyle. I would get up and watch television over a leisurely breakfast and then train with the club from 10:00 a.m. until 12:30 p.m. Many of the boys would then go for lunch at Sorentino's or Gian Biaz before an afternoon sleep, before going to the gym to do weights in the late afternoon. I used to put on my suit and go to the office in Holcot after training. Geech trusted me enough to do my weights in the evening, and I spent the afternoon working with Paul who was the only member of Rodber Thorneycroft working full-time. It must have been frustrating for him seeing Tim and I wander in after training. However, he stuck at it for a few years. Life was easy, we were physically in great shape, playing in front of big crowds every weekend, and we were being stimulated mentally by Rodber Thorneycroft. It seemed like the perfect world and for the first time the profile of the sport increased so I enjoyed a degree of popularity in my town, which for a local boy growing up in Northampton wasn't a bad thing. It helped on a Saturday night when trying to meet girls.

It would have been easy to rest on my laurels and enjoy this period of my life. I had no issues to contend with, as long as I stayed fit, and I put myself in contention for the first XV. It was the start of the rugby squad system, which meant that coaches had to adapt to the demands of the modern game by rotating their players. This worked in my favour. I was being paid to play the sport I loved. I had a low mortgage on my house that was covered by the rent from my tenant. I had two rather nice perks. First, I had a contract with Reebok, which allowed me to select clothes, boots and trainers from their winter and summer catalogues up to the value of £1000 each year. I received no payment, just stash. Everyone loves stash. I had a boyhood dream to be sponsored by a clothing company and it had come true. The endorsement agreement that I signed read, "Thorneycroft hereby grants to Reebok the exclusive right to use his name, nickname, likeness, photograph, signature, voice, biographical material, statements and other Thorneycroft characteristics, for advertising, promotional, marketing and public relations". If I had an agent at the time there is no way they would have allowed me to sign this. I didn't care, I just wanted the stash. My other perk was a sponsored car through the local Rover dealership in Northamptonshire called Henley's. This, like Reebok, had been running prior to rugby going professional and saved me a lot of money. Northampton Saints provided many perks like free gym membership, free Churches shoes and cheap car insurance. If you added a salary on top of these perks, I felt quite affluent.

At that time of my life, I didn't want for much. Life was easy and I was in a comfort zone. There was competition for places in the 1st XV, but it didn't matter to me, I was sitting back and feeling lucky to be playing rugby and growing a business in my spare time. I think Tim realised this and played devil's advocate with me. He could see that we needed to push the business on if it was ever going to provide an income for us both after our rugby careers. His job was to strategically grow the business and my role was to generate clients to support that strategy. Tim wasn't that involved in the day-to-day operational side of the business; he didn't like events. He knew that we could grow a business and the fact that the core products were events meant that we were having more fun than if we were selling computers. Paul and I did like events and sold the business at every opportunity. We always found it easy to sell Rodber Thorneycroft. One such occasion was slightly odd. I was talking to Nigel Palmer, who was the MD of NRG, a local company, owned by Ricoh which produced photocopiers. Nigel lived in Surbiton but his company had its head office in Northampton, so he stayed over at a place called Overstone Golf Club. This is where we had free gym membership. At the end of each evening gym session I would use the pool, which also had a jacuzzi attached to it. It was in the jacuzzi that I sold my first ever ski trip to Villars in Switzerland. You can imagine the conversation.

"What do you do for a living?"

"I am a professional rugby player and I run a high-end events business."

Nigel was not a sports fan and didn't know anything about the Saints, but what he did enjoy was skiing and fine wine. He asked, "Do you organise skiing trips?" I said, "Of course". I had never been skiing.

Our contracts that had been brought in since the advent of professionalism prevented us from doing extreme sports or we would be in breach of contract. The contract stated in 7(vii), "the player promises to maintain a high standard of personal fitness and not participate in dangerous sport nor indulge in any dangerous activity without the written consent of the club". The sports that were deemed dangerous were winter sports, racing by horse, motor car or motorcycle, mountaineering or rock climbing, pot holing, parachuting, flying, association, Gaelic, Australian rules or American football, ice hockey, judo, karate and other martial arts. This didn't stop me selling Nigel a skiing trip. From that one conversation at Overstone Park, we ended up getting an opportunity to pitch for the annual NRG sales incentive worth around £80,000.

It is never the MD within these companies that organises these types of event. It therefore wasn't good enough to win his support; we needed to convince the marketing manager, Pat Percival. Tim and I went along to meet her and she wasn't that impressed with our rugby backgrounds. It was difficult to know how we won this piece of business having never been skiing before, but on the basis of a conversation that I had with Thierry Assaf, a former Olympic skier, I found myself going to Villars, in Switzerland three times that year and learning to ski for the first time. Thierry was someone Paul had met at an event that he had run at the Lausanne Palace and he acted as our local knowledge. He was a superb skier and knew that area of Europe like the back of his hand.

I can thank Nigel for my first skiing experience on a weekend when the Saints were playing. For the first time in my life I wasn't sad to not be playing rugby. This was when I knew I had made the transition from sport into business. This didn't stop me wanting to keep playing the sport. I just knew that times were changing and I had to learn to adapt. I did my second familiarisation trip to Villars with Pat Percival. This was superb because we went to visit all of the locations that the main party would visit. This included the eating locations for the three dinners, a vineyard in the Valais region owned by great friends of Thierry. We visited Chateau de Chillon, located between the shores of Lake Geneva and the Alps. Thierry Assaf told us about an American group that he had brought to this thousand-year-old architectural jewel and one of the group commented on how beautiful the Chateau was, but they couldn't understand why it had been built so close to the freeway.

It was too far from Villars to work for a venue for the Gala Dinner and we settled for Château d'Aigle, an impressive medieval castle close to Villars. We visited Chamonix to see a restaurant location for the non-skiers. This took us on the world's highest vertical-ascent cable car. This alpine scene was truly memorable. The Alps and Mont Blanc were on one side and the Aiguilles Rouges massif on the other. It was the first time I got to experience curling, which was an activity planned for the non-skiers in the ice rink in Chamonix village. I became close to Thierry Assaf on this trip. He was half Swiss and half Lebanese and spoke many languages.

The actual trip was organised for sales people who hit their target and was seen as part of their remuneration package for selling photocopiers. Like the law of diminishing marginal utility, the more you have of something, the less satisfaction you derive from it. This is what I sensed when I met the guests in the airport prior to flying out. Many of them had qualified on all of the last events that NRG had run as incentives to some of the best locations around the world. There didn't seem to be that level of anticipation that I would have expected. This was highlighted by one of the guests, called Nigel, who I sat with in the vineyard in the Valais region on the very first evening.

He was what Clive Woodward would call one of life's "energy sappers." He didn't drink alcohol, so the prospect of a night in a vineyard with his work colleagues necking wine probably didn't fill him with great deal of joy. He asked me whether I could get him some hot chocolate. The likelihood of them serving hot chocolate in a vineyard was remote and sadly I was unable to meet his request, which I thought nothing of, until the night after, at the Gala Dinner at the Château d'Aigle, when I was confronted by him. He mentioned that he was bitterly disappointed to see that there was no hot chocolate being served at the Gala Dinner and he thought I would have learnt my lesson from the night before. The audacity of the man was something to behold. We had enlisted the students from the International Hotel and Tourism Training Institute based in Neuchâtel to provide the catering that night. Their standards were regarded to be the best in the world and they delivered a superb banquet, but this was not good enough for Nigel. He didn't get his hot chocolate and nor was he ever going to. I was flabbergasted by his attitude and have never forgotten how rude he was, but at the time was polite because this was my job. The next evening at the restaurant, with the permission of the Managing Director, I served Nigel a hot chocolate every time we poured the other guests a glass of wine on his table. We served over twelve hot chocolates that night, and as word got out it became a bit of a joke. This transferred itself back to the office where he became known as "Hot Chocolate Nigel". I learnt later that he now drinks alcohol. I hope we didn't turn him to it. Nigel, if you are reading this, I tell this story at most dinner parties. You are infamous.

Chapter 19

We are not turning back

The 1997/98 season was finished off with an invitation to attend the South American Tour with the Barbarian Football Club. I had never been to Argentina and Uruguay and without hesitation jumped on a plane. This is the longest continuous flight that I have ever been on. It was 6,846 miles from London to Montevideo and the flying time was about fourteen hours. The first match on the 31st May 1998 was billed as one of the easier games, but we only just managed to win. It took place at the British School in Montevideo. It was odd to go all the way to South America and visit a school that was very similar to Wellingborough and had been founded in 1908 to give children an education based on principles of the best schools in Britain.

The South American Barbarians were founded thanks to one of Argentina's greatest players, Hugo Porta. I watched Hugo play against England in 1990 from the stands at Twickenham when he had been brought out of retirement to tour. It was his unique talents that lifted Argentina from their status as a minor nation to one of respect among the international rugby community. He was Argentina's Minister for Sport and we met him in a drinks reception in Buenos Aires at the offices of HSBC.

We had a strong tour party that included players like Martin Corry, Dorian West and Mike Brewer, the former All Black who was the player-coach of the trip. Another player on that trip was Paul Burns, a rugby league player from Barrow-in-Furness. Sadly, he got injured that day and was taken to hospital in Montevideo. In 1993 I had watched a film about the harrowing tale of a Uruguayan rugby team called *Alive*. This was my only connection with this country up until this point and it was probably the most popular rugby movie ever made. The film was based on a true story. On 13th October 1972 a plane carrying Uruguayan rugby players, their families and friends from the Old Christians Club in Montevideo on its way to Chile for a tour crashed in the Andes mountains. Only twenty-nine out of the forty-five people on the plane survived the crash. Several died later, including the captain Marcelo Perez who perished in an avalanche with seven others. By the time they were rescued only sixteen were still alive, including five rugby players, Nando Parrado, Roberto Canessa, Roy Harley, Antonio Vizintin and Gustavo Zerbino. Paul Burns had a conversation that day with Dr Roberto Canessa that day, a distinguished paediatric cardiologist in Uruguay and a former presidential candidate. He told us about the unimaginable ordeal that he had been through.

The South American Barbarians wanted to give us a taste of South America after the match in the form of a salsa show. We were treated to a thirteen-strong band with salsa dancers who produced a full-on unforgettable Latin American extravaganza. Rugby players are not great dancers, but when invited up by these scantily clad Latin dancers they had no option but to agree. This wasn't just for a few numbers; this was an evening full of dance and music and it was superb. At one point the whole squad was on stage dancing including Mickey Steele-Bodger. I used this idea for an event for my client Bantec at a Heathrow Hotel and it went down a storm.

The next leg of our tour took us to Tucumán a province located in the northwest of Argentina. We stayed at the Metropol, whose only redeeming feature was an outdoor swimming pool on the rooftop offering a great view of San Miguel de Tucumán the capital city of Tucumán Province. The city was seemed to have everything. It had archaeological interest, as well as varying topography and eleven micro-climates. We visited Obispo Colombres House, the historical House of the Independence Declaration, the stupendous Cathedral, Casa Padilla Museum and the El Cadillal dam. We were treated to a day out into the Sierra del Aconquija, the outlying ridges of the Andes, about an hours drive away from the city. The purpose of the trip was to go horse riding in the foothills of the Andes. When we got there we were given no tuition. I think they thought we could all ride. This wasn't true in my case. I was given a horse and assumed that it would be sedate, like the horses in UK riding stables that I had visited with my sister. Sadly, I was wrong and my horse had a will of its own, and took me away from the main group and out into the hills. I hadn't a clue how to control this horse and held on for dear life, and eventually it led me back to the stables, much to the amusement of all the other players.

Tucumán had a reputation for being a difficult place to play rugby. Jeff Probyn, the England prop who won 37 caps for England, always described what is was like playing a Tucumán Select XV on the1990 England Rugby tour. He recalled how England only just won the game against some of the biggest men that he had ever seen. They didn't disappoint and we struggled to beat Tucumán at Tucumán Lawn Tennis Club, where the game was staged in front of 8,000 spectators. One of their players, Omar Hasan, who was born in Tucumán and was of Lebanese origin, had just returned from playing Super 12 in Australia for this match and after the game he entertained us with his rich baritone voice and a mixture of opera, Argentine folksongs and the tango. Omar was a semi-professional opera singer with the bulk of Pavarotti and the voice of an angel. He played nine tests for Argentina in 1998 and went on to play in over fifty tests for the Pumas with an international career with Argentina spanning more than a decade. I have only ever come across one other player who had a voice like his: Matt Stevens, the England Prop who I heard singing at one of Matt Dawson's parties shortly after this.

That night Jon Philips, my teammate from Northampton, broke his arm during the game and carried on playing despite the pain, not realising the extent of his injury. This wouldn't have been so bad, but he was getting married two weeks later in Stamford and was under strict instructions not to get injured. Jon going down the aisle in a sling didn't impress his wife.

The last of the games on tour took us to the capital city of Buenos Aires and the most European of all Latin American cities. This is probably one my favourite cities. With its wide boulevards, leafy parks, grand buildings, and varied culture and nightlife, it reminded me of Paris or Madrid. The residents of Buenos Aires are very European – they descended from the first Spanish founders and Italian immigrants from the nineteenth century. Their culture and cuisine is obvious and could be seen in the countless art galleries, theatres and museums, as well as the fine restaurants that we visited. It was a true twenty-four-hour city. We stayed in the downtown area, which wasn't that great given the fact that we had to play rugby. The hotel was located on Nueve de Julio, which was nine lanes wide, the widest street in the world and within striking distance of the best luxury shops, restaurants and cafès. We were six storeys up in our room, but could still hear the buzz of the city despite the triple-glazed windows. The boys had decided that you don't get many opportunities to take advantage of a city like this, and from that point on it was damage limitations for Mike Brewer and the Barbarians.

The third and last match would be our strongest contest and was made up of the players that weren't selected by Alex "Grizz" Wiley, the Argentine Coach, (who used to coach the All Blacks) on the 13th June to play against France. We watched this game at the Estadio José Amalfitani, the national stadium for Argentina rugby. We saw France beat Argentina 35–18. Our game was on Sunday 14th June 1998 at a rugby club in the northern suburbs of Buenos Aires. We played the game and were treated to an exclusive banquet at one of the city's best restaurants. I sat next to Martin Corry and we got stuck into a beer or two. I had played with him at Bristol on the 31st January 1997 for England A v Otago and was interested to find out how the transition to the Tigers had been since he had made his debut in August 1997. The memory that I will always have is his single-minded desire to want to play rugby for England. That night, he talked about wanting to get into the 1999 World Cup squad and that rugby was all he was going to concentrate on. He was four years younger than me and had it all ahead of him. He had made his England debut against

Argentina on the 1997 tour. I watched his career after this conversation with great interest and it was illustrious. He won five Premiership titles, a Premiership Championship, two Heineken European Cups and an Anglo–Welsh Cup, 64 caps for England, including being a member of the World Cup-winning squad in 2003, runner-up in 2007 World Cup, and he toured Australia and New Zealand with the British and Irish Lions winning a remarkable 6 test caps. If there was an example of a player, other than Neil Back, who was dedicated to achieving his purpose then it was Martin. I think this is the difference between mediocre players and those like Neil and Martin. They don't just have goals and ambitions, they have purpose. This is what makes them super performers. This is something I later learned from a mind coach called Jamil Qureshi.

We stumbled out of the bar, on to a coach and were invited to go to a nightclub called Buenos Aires News. This was a rocking late-night club that played Latin and European songs. This club was like the Carlsberg advert. "Carlsberg don't do nightclubs, but if they did, they would probably be the best nightclubs in the world." It is significant that we played this match on Sunday 14th June 1998. Sunday is the biggest night out for Buenos Aires and we stayed out until 7:00 a.m. and ended up going for breakfast. It is also the day that the Falkland Islands commemorate liberation day, after they were invaded by Argentina in 1982. This was in the papers when we were there, so imagine how we looked when we got off the bus to get into the front of the queue for this nightclub, dressed in blazers and panama hats looking quintessentially British. We were sitting targets for abuse, but didn't see anything but good will. This tour was one of the best I have ever been on and I needed about a week to recover from the jet lag and partying before we got back into pre-season at the club.

Everyone should have the equivalent of pre-season in their lives. By this I mean that too often we don't get the opportunity to sit down with our team and examine how we can improve ourselves both individually and collectively to achieve sustained high-level performance. It is important to celebrate small victories and have a period of regeneration. In the late 1980s, we didn't look at this scientifically; we would meet at Franklin's Gardens and run to Harlestone Firs and back, which was about an eight-mile run. However, this was not the case in 1998 in a fully professional era. Geech had a vision for the club, which was to create a structure where everyone was pulling together for a common vision, from Keith Barwell to Brett Taylor and Martin Bayfield who ran the academy for youth players at the club. The vision was to win the Premiership that season and he assembled a squad of players who were capable for the first time of achieving this. The club was a million miles from where it was three years ago when it was relegated to Division Two. Without Geech's vision we would have been nowhere. There were no egos in the team. Every player pulled for one another and pre-season was where it started.

Geech and his coaching staff put in place a gruelling schedule from early July that tested the team's physical, mental, emotional and spiritual intelligences. To become top performers in the premiership we were given the tools to succeed, and then it was down to us.

I have been told by Caspar Berry, a friend of mine, that "the definition of hell is dying and the person you are meeting the person you could have been." For Northampton Saints, they needed to win something. We had a label of under achievers and this didn't sit well with Geech and Tim. That summer was the start of a journey that allowed us to achieve our vision to win the European Cup. I was part of this journey and it was probably one of the most exciting periods of the club's history. I played a very small part in the lead-up to the ultimate prize. I feel privileged to have been part of such a strong squad. The squad was full of internationals and players that had played representative rugby. It included Tim, Daws, Grays and Bealer who had been there for years and were the bedrock of the club, but other players of their calibre were also introduced like Federico Mendez, Garry Pagel and Pat Lam. Freddie, as he became known, had a reputation in England as the eighteen-year-old prop who knocked out Paul Ackford, playing for Argentina v England in 1990 at Twickenham. I remember the punch and Freddie leaving the pitch after being sent off with a look of bewilderment. He started his playing career with Mendoza, a town located on the eastern side of the Andes in Argentina. He had a great deal of experience to bring to the club, having played in the 1995 Rugby World Cup for Natal Sharks and for Bath where he won the Heineken Cup in 1998. He would become the first player to win the trophy twice.

Garry Pagel was regarded by many as one of the hardest men to ever play the game of rugby and had a reputation a bit like Freddie. He was brought up in King William's Town in the Eastern Cape of South Africa, where his parents kept a farm with sheep and dairy cattle, which is where he lives now. He had played for Eastern Province, prior to joining Western Province in 1993, where he played a touring France XV that was captained by our old friend and French skipper, Jean-Francois Tordo. Tordo sustained a horrific facial wound during this game, requiring fifty stitches. Sadly, Garry was found guilty of reckless use of the boot and, although the videotape evidence was not wholly conclusive, he was suspended for the rest of that season. A ban that was later halved on appeal. He returned to win a World Cup medal with South Africa in 1995 and came to Northampton because he was spotted by Geech on the Lions tour in 1997 when he played against Jason Leonard.

Pat Lam was probably one of the best signings for Northampton and we felt very fortunate to have him. He had been playing for Newcastle for two seasons and had helped them first to win promotion and then to the Premiership One Championship Title in the 1997/98 season. He had played in the 1991 and 1995 World Cup tournaments each time, helping Western Samoa to the quarter-finals. It was whilst he was on tour in that summer of 1998 in New Zealand with Western Samoa that he learned that Rob Andrew, Newcastle's director of rugby, had put him up for a transfer. Geech was surprised that Newcastle would be prepared to transfer him and wasted no time in securing his services. The squad had other internationals like David Dantiacq, John Sleightholme and Matt Stewart and players who would go on to represent their countries like Ben Cohen, Craig Moir, Richard Metcalfe, Steve Thompson and Budge Pountney.

We trained very hard that summer and got into great physical shape. Pre-season training took many guises including a two day trip to Sandhurst Army Officer Training Academy, which was unlike anything that I had ever experienced. We arrived on 3rd August 1998 with a considerable degree of apprehension. The last time I had visited the Royal Military Academy at Sandhurst was to attend the Commissioning Ball on the 7th August 1992 as a guest of Tim. Ian Hunter and I had gone to a shop called Scrooge Clothing on the Kettering Road that afternoon to purchase a second hand black tie suit and then travelled down to a hotel prior to the ball. I arrived at Sandhurst and saw Tim Rodber in his mess dress, looking the epitome of sartorial elegance, whilst Hunts and I looked like two tramps dressed in some old men's dinner suit that smelt of moth balls. Tim had, that afternoon, been commissioned as an officer in the Army. He had won the Sword of Honour, which was awarded to the officer cadet considered by the Commandant to be the best on the course and we were there to celebrate with him. He had gone through a course that had lasted forty-four weeks. We were at Sandhurst for our two days under the leadership of Major Adrian Geal and Captain Tony Wilby.

On the first day, we were split into teams and had to complete tasks in health, survival, bed-making in the wild, hygiene and how to make food if you really have to. The trainers brought us some white, fluffy pet rabbits. They were used to demonstrate how to skin a wild animal. The instructors asked if anyone would like to kill the rabbits and I felt physically sick. Martin Hynes and Garry Pagel stepped up and broke their necks. When we were presented with gutted rabbits, leeks and parsnips, we all thought that this was going to be our food for the night. Andy Northey demonstrated his survival techniques and stole some of the boys' vegetables with a view to making a fire and cooking his tea. About ten minutes after he had been found out, a truck arrived full of food and water and the team were happy again. That was until some Gurkha soldiers arrived in our camp and told us to take our backpacks and follow them into the night. The Gurkhas come from the Himalayan Kingdom of Nepal and form a unique unit in the Army with a reputation of being amongst the finest and most feared soldiers in the world. We were scared as we went off into the night. However, we soon realised that they were there to make sure we were dropped off in places away from each other, to spend the night under the stars and to put into practice the skills we had learnt during the day building a bivouac.

Our instructions prior to being dropped off were to build the bivouac shelter and stay there until sunlight. We were then told to use our compasses to walk due west until we hit a road where we would be picked up and taken for breakfast. This was the first time in years that I had roughed it. In fact, I had never slept on the floor of a forest with a plastic canopy over my head and gone to sleep at 9:00 p.m. You could hear the boys in the forest trying to communicate with each other through the night. It was hilarious. We all made it to breakfast at 5:00 AM apart from Grant Seely and our new French recruit David Dantiacq. The instructors were worried about him being late. He did not look like one of the soldiers from the French Foreign Legion. They eventually found him tucked up in his sleeping bag oblivious of his surroundings.

That day we ended up undertaking a set of command tasks designed to test our leadership skills and identify the qualities of our character.

At 1:00 a.m. Tim looked a bit apprehensive – it was time for less lateral thinking and the stretcher race, an assault course and a raft race on a raft that we had to build. The stretcher was an industrial grill grafted together with scaffolding poles and was very heavy to carry, especially when we reached a bog where we were waist high in mud. Up until that point I had been carrying the stretcher, and when we arrived at the bog I thought I would push ahead in front of the stretcher to see how deep the bog was. Sadly, this was being recorded on Anglia Television and I looked like I was not part of the team, which I wasn't at the time. I got some huge grief for this.

These two days at Sandhurst were amazing for team spirit. We had been despoiled, dispossessed of mobile phones and other material goods and yet there was no whinging from anyone. This set the scene for one of the most successful seasons in Northampton's history. We finished second in the Premiership that season. I played less rugby for the first team than any other season before because the competition was immense. This meant that I ran out three more times with the Barbarians. The first game was against the Combined Services at Portsmouth on the 10th November 1998 and the second was on the 29th December 1998 against Leicester at Welford Road, and the last game was at Franklin's Gardens against the East Midlands in March 1999, the side I had played in many times against the Barbarians.

In true Barbarians style on the morning prior to the game, we were treated to a ride in a CH-47 Chinook helicopter. Its role in the army was for troop movement and artillery emplacement so it could handle the weight of twenty-four rugby players. The ride was up to the Salisbury Plain training area to drive Challenger 2 tanks that entered service with the British Army in June 1998 and then for lunch in the officers' mess. I had played in the same fixture a year before and the Combined Services organised it so we could go up in an aircraft to see RAF Jaguars during mid-air refuelling. These were experiences that you could never do alone, but the respect that the armed forces had for the Barbarians meant that they made this happen. These experiences were very memorable and very well received. They may not have been the best pre-match preparation for a game, but this was the Barbarians.

The East Midlands game was memorable for two reasons. It was great to play a representative game on Franklin's Gardens in the black and white hoops. It was the Barbarians and the Mobbs Memorial Fixture that I had attended as a kid and watched in wonderment. These early experiences of rugby encouraged me to want to play the game. The second reason was due to a thief called Alan Phillips, who posed as an official in order to plunder cash and valuables from rugby and cricket clubs across England. Sadly, I was a victim of the scam. I took my bag into the away changing room at Franklin's Gardens before the game to be confronted by a man who didn't look like a Barbarian official. I remember thinking as soon as I saw him that he wasn't part of the Barbarians. I knew all the people involved with the club. He was putting the shirts up in the changing room. However, because this match was being played by two invitation sides I didn't really take any notice of Alan Phillips. This was the environment he needed to create the perfect scam. He was extremely helpful and even helped the physiotherapist with massages and strappings. You have to have some nerve to pose as an official and then just before kick off agree to collect valuables from the players. No-one suspected anything and I handed over my Seamaster Chronometer watch, which was a gift that I had received from a local jeweller in Northampton. The other players, like me, innocently handed over wallets, rings, watches and car keys. In all the time I have played rugby I can safely say that I have never distrusted the person that collected the valuables, even if I didn't know him. I should have trusted my instincts and to this day I still kick myself. This was the perfect scam and he performed it at over 239 clubs in the country before he got put away for two years. He apparently came out of prison and re-offended and was put back in prison. I went to the police station that night to report the crime and the officers were disbelieving. What a nerve.

A few months after this scam I was asked to attend an identity parade in London. Rugby players from all over the country were picked up and brought to a police station. We thought we would then get the opportunity to take our revenge on him and get him convicted. However, he refused to come out of his cell and the whole parade was cancelled. The police weren't allowed to bring him out under force and so they sent us all home. Even after he had been caught he didn't even have the character to admit his mistakes and come clean.

After one of the most successful seasons on record we each received a letter from Geech dated the 4th June 1999 entitled, "We are not turning Back!" He stated,

We must keep moving forward – be fitter and stronger to keep pace and intensity in our game, because I am convinced we have a game which can win us the European Cup. The style of the last seven games, in particular make us very difficult opponents for any side in Europe... But, as in everything we now do, it is down to your honesty and commitment. These are exciting times for us, lets make the most of them-we are definitely not turning back.

Chapter 20

Harvey Harvey

I was surprised when on the 10th June, at a press conference in Edinburgh, Geech announced that he would be quitting Northampton to work alongside Scotland coach Jim Telfer in preparation for the 1999 World Cup. Apparently, this was the only job that could have tempted him away a week after he had written his letter to us and he left without any compensation for the remaining four years of his contract. I spoke to him some years later and he told me that he had no intention of ever leaving Northampton. Sadly, his wife Judy was not well and he had to get away. It was sad to see him go, but he left a legacy at the club that set us up very well for the 1999/2000 season. I read his programme notes dated the 23rd January 1998 when we played against West Hartlepool. He wrote that the vision he had for the club was now taking shape and whether he was here or not in the future, the club should be able to run smoothly, and this is what he did.

Geech had predicted the season before that we had a game that could win the European Cup. Now that is visionary. I didn't always fit into his plans as a player, but I did seek his approval. He got us playing in a style that was unique and gave me many happy years at Northampton. He was influential in ensuring that my contract was extended and that I would be granted a testimonial. I met with Geech and Paul Larkin to discuss my future. At that stage many of the players had agents, but I represented myself. I presented a document entitled "Harvey Thorneycroft and Northampton Rugby Club" on the 11th June 1998. I had delusions of grandeur beyond my status even when I was coming towards the end of my career. I presented an impeccable "service history" and was keen to get more money and a testimonial/benefit season for 1999/2000. I kept a copy of this document as I was very proud of its contents. I indicated that I had no major injuries that would effect taking the field of play, and I continued to be the most durable of wingers. I mentioned that I had played in 90% of all league and cup games since 1987, and scored more tries and played in more 1st XV games than any other member of the 1997/98 first team squad. Did this get me any more salary? Of course it didn't. I knew in my heart of hearts that this would be the case, but I did get a testimonial/ benefit season for 1999/2000. I later found out, when speaking to Tim years later in the Salisbury Tavern Pub in Fulham, that the club would never have paid me more than they needed to because they knew if push came to shove that I would have played for nothing. I valued the intrinsic benefits of playing for Northampton more than the extrinsic benefits, which would have never stood me in good stead for contract negotiation.

I wrote to Keith Barwell on the 8th July 1998 requesting that he consider me for a testimonial/benefit season. The formal procedure is that members of the public write to Keith requesting that Harvey Thorneycroft should be awarded a testimonial for his services and loyalty to Northampton Rugby Club. I had asked a number of volunteers to sit on my committee, to help organise my testimonial, and Ian Kirkham had been appointed as chairman. He was the chief executive of Headlam plc, a floor coverings and furnishings distributor based in Northampton. Ian wrote to Keith Barwell and a benefit season for 1999/2000 was duly granted.

Historically, a benefit season was a method of financially rewarding professional cricketers to compensate long-serving players. The system originated in the nineteenth century to help cricketers who were paid low wages and couldn't play professional cricket much beyond the age of forty. I was the first individual to be granted a benefit season at Northampton Saints, although the town was familiar with cricket benefits at the County Cricket Club. The important part of a benefit, or testimonial, was that all the profits generated during the course of the year became exempt from tax. This was following the ruling of the House of Lords over the benefit for James Seymour, the Kent cricketer whose benefit in 1920 was the subject of protracted legal case, brought by the Inland Revenue, and was not fully resolved until 1926. Great care had to be taken by our committee not to breach the rules in any way, as this could provoke the Inland Revenue into challenging the tax exemption.

My committee was made up of local businessmen who had become mates. Ian was a great chairman despite the demands of running a plc business. Tony Miles, my solicitor, from Howes Percival, my old boss Graham Stanton, who ran Hampton Brook property developers, Jake, Colin and Jarvis Richardson, Giles Wilson, Andrew Langley, Wim van den Boogard, Paul Southworth and Gary McManus all played a part. However, it was Alison Hancock who brought an organisational edge to the year. They spent much of the early part of 1999 planning events that would start on the 11th September 1999 with a launch dinner at Althorp House and finish with a ball in the summer of 2000. The build up to this year involved a lot of planning. The committee had great fun planning this year and knowing that in some small way it was contributing to my future both professionally and financially. For that I will be internally grateful to them for all the hard work they put in.

We took some advice from two very well known sports men who had gone through a similar benefit year, Allan Lamb and Dean Richards. Allan had signed from Western Province as the Northamptonshire overseas player in 1978 and was a regular fixture in the middle order for England from 1982 to 1992, playing his last test against Pakistan at Lord's on 18th–21st June 1992. He had a great testimonial and provided us with some superb advice in his office in St Giles Street, Northampton. Dean Richards was the first rugby player who had been granted a testimonial for the Tigers and we followed a very similar format to him.

Probably, two of the most difficult parts of the year were compiling a testimonial video and brochure. I was very good friends with Gary Mabee, a former footballer for Tottenham Hotspur, who was a television news cameraman for Anglia Television, but also ran his own business producing live video recordings of the Saints and Cobblers games. We spent many long hours at his house going through the original tapes that he had in his library of games that he had recorded. The reason for the video was as a thank you to the Franklin's Garden's fans that had been so loyal over the years. I wanted to look back over the last ten years of Saints Rugby and include some of the most memorable tries, as well as moments and great characters of the Saints that I had played with. We included interviews with leading England players, which included Matt Dawson, Tim Rodber, Nick Beal, Martin Johnson, Dean Richards and Neil Back. Gary's son was a cameraman who worked freelance for Anglia Televsion. He helped me film the interviews that I did with the Northampton players at Daws' house. The edited version of the video was produced by Finlay Milne, the trumpet player in the Ginger Pig Band, who had worked on a variety of factual format programmes as Senior Editor at Molinare. His connections at Molinaire enabled us to get some time in one of their edit suites just off Carnaby Street in Fouberts Place, London. We were not charged for these edit suites, they donated this to the testimonial, which enabled us to produce a reasonable video at next to no cost. This was a huge undertaking – to take the footage from all the games and interviews and put it to music with a view to producing a one-hour video. He was passionate about rugby and I loved his music, so he gave up his time for my testimonial. The actual videos were produced by a company called AVTV and were sponsored by Jones Cash & Carry. This video took a lot of time to produce but was a great opportunity to look back and reflect on a journey from Wellingborough School to wearing the black, green and gold of Northampton Saints for over ten years. Most people in this day and age don't get to stay in one place or job for such a long period of time, and if they do their memories of time are not normally recorded like this. I am passionate about Northampton Saints and in particular its supporters. I enjoyed an extraordinary relationship with the crowd that supported the Saints from the terraces of the Gordon Stand, right the way through to the Corporate Boxes, who were not the "prawn cocktail brigade" once described by former Manchester United captain Roy Keane. They were just fervent Saints supporters that happened to do well in business.

Even to this day, I would trade the success that I have had since rugby to keep running out at Franklin's Gardens. It was the biggest "endorphin rush" and I am sure it was the passion that I exuded which caused the crowd to react in the way that they did. People used to say that it was because I was a "local boy done good", but I think I was living the dream of many of those supporters. Northampton was a rugby town and the supporters loved my physical style and desire to do everything to 100% of my ability. I was not the most gifted player at the club, but I was committed, and this manifested itself every time I went on a run. I got the same feeling when I watched Ben Cohen in a Saints shirt and I get it now when Paul Diggin makes an appearance on the wing. You sense something is going to happen, an air of anticipation that is like rocket fuel.

Before some games I would run onto the pitch with some of the most talented rugby players in the country. Before I had even touched the ball, the crowd would chant "Harvey-Harvey" to the tune of Portsmouth Football Club's famous *Pompey Chimes*. This gave me a huge boost and I felt that I couldn't let them down. The video we produced was an attempt to try and capture some of those moments. People still come up to me who bought one of those videos, and give me a hug to say how nice it is to look back down memory lane.

The other project that took a great deal of work was the production of a testimonial brochure. This was sixty-five pages of articles from people who had been influential in my rugby career and adverts. The articles were from people who I truly respected in the game: Tony and Rory Underwood, Mickey Steele Bodger, Will Greenwood, Gavin Hastings, Tim Rodber, Damien Hopley, Nick Beal, Victor Ubugo, Keith Barwell, Martin Bayfield and John Inverdale. John Inverdale is one of my favourite people in the world. I have so much respect for him. I had met him at various matches during my career and loved his coverage on Radio Five Live drivetime. It was John who I consulted about hosting my testimonial dinner in London. He agreed to meet me to discuss this at Esher RFC. I was quite nervous about going out to meet him. He was the face of BBC sport broadcasting. He had presented the investigative sports series *On The Line* and *Rugby Special, Grandstand, Sunday Grandstand* and *The World's Strongest Man* for BBC One.

I had no idea at the time where Esher was in relation to where I was staying in Pimlico. My knowledge of London was poor so I thought that it would take me about half an hour to travel the seventeen and a half miles from central London to Surrey. I rang John to say that I would be late, but forty minutes was unacceptable, given I was asking him to give me some advice. Invers was a perfect gentleman and informed me that he couldn't stay at Esher, but invited me to meet him off the A3 close to Guildford for lunch on route, to see the 1st XV play against Havant, Hampshire. I agreed that this was a great idea and it was only fourteen miles from Esher to Guildford. I was, of course, late for lunch, which he kindly bought. We had a great chat and he agreed to host my London dinner. He invited me to go down to Havant from Guildford a distance of about forty miles. You would have thought that I wouldn't have got this wrong, but I did. I followed him for a number of miles and then realised that I was going to run out of petrol and flashed him to pull over at the service station. I can't imagine what the now face of BBC sport broadcasting must have thought of this "muppet" from Northampton. This was a very odd day as I stood by him, watching Esher play Havant. He said, "One day you will be playing for Esher", and this was the club I joined for a year after Northampton Saints, when I first moved to London.

Invers wrote a great article in my programme about the "much under-rated Harvey Thorneycroft." He recalled how studio editors on *Rugby Special* were told that even if I had barely seen the ball during the course of a Northampton match, that some how my contribution to the game had to be recorded during the highlights from Franklin's Gardens. He said "that it became a rather pathetic litmus test to see how much influence *Rugby Special* had on then England coach Jack Rowell." He recalled that they were attempting to persuade Jack that I was indeed much wider rated and that he should include me in his side. Sadly, Jack did not pick me. The BBC lost the contract for rugby special and that great running gag became no more.

It is amazing how much preparation goes in to a testimonial year, and the committee soon realised that if they were going to hit their target then they had to split the group up and take responsibility for individual events within the seven-event programme. I was not able to be involved in any of the organisation as this would have breached the rules of the testimonial. This was difficult given the fact that I was going to be the beneficiary of the proceeds. I wrote and thanked everyone personally for their contribution during the back end of the 1998/99 season. The testimonial build up didn't stop me from having a mind-blowing summer trip. Unbelievably, I went to play in the Tusker Safari Sevens in Kenya, flew back to Heathrow to board a plane to Bermuda on the same day for a week and then caught a plane from Bermuda to New York.

Brigadier General Ralph James invited me to play for the Public School Wanderers in Nairobi at the Ligi Ndogo Grounds. I had never been to East Africa and was keen to go and play in the Tusker Safari Sevens. Nairobi the capital of Kenya was situated in the highlands of the southern part of the country at 5,450 feet above sea level. We flew into Jomo Kenyatta International Airport and the road that took us to our hotel in downtown Nairobi was an eye opener. I saw the slums where half of the city's population lives. The growth of these slums was apparently down to unplanned urbanisation. It reminded me of the landscape that I had seen in Cape Town and Durban in 1994 and 1995.

We had a great side made up of youth and experience, and this was the first time that I had ever been a captain. Justyn Cassell, the oldest of the players, had played for Saracens, Harlequins and with me at Northampton until 1998. He had also been part of the inaugural Rugby World Cup Sevens winning team at Murrayfield in 1993. In contrast, one of the youngest players was Richard Haughton. Ralph James had told me that he was one of the quickest wings in England and I was looking forward to seeing him in action. A very odd thing happened to Richard at this event. I think it was his first time at altitude and it is known now that this can lead to a progressive decline in VO2max, which compromised his performance. At the time he said that he felt out of breath when he ran, as if he didn't have enough oxygen. He was right – this is what happens. We all just thought he was mad, but it has been proven that altitude can affect your oxygen levels and performance. He went on to spend six years on the Sevens circuit scoring more than 100 tries for England and helping them to win the Hong Kong Sevens, and played in the Commonwealth Games. We completed the Tusker Safari 7's playing and beating Bristol 25–22 in the final.

The tournament was good, but the after-match reception was even better, at a place called The Carnivore on the Langata Road. This was an open-air meat specialty restaurant. Every type of meat imaginable was available roasted on traditional Maasai swords (skewers) over a huge charcoal pit. The waiters carried these swords around the restaurant ,carving unlimited amounts of meats onto sizzling cast-iron plates in front of us. This was the first time that I had ever seen crocodile, giraffe, waterbuck and zebra meat, which was slightly tough and gamey.

After the reception we went next door to the Simba Saloon, one of the biggest discos in Nairobi. The place was huge, with three separate bars, room outside and a large dance floor. This club was like something you expect to see in Ibiza. The disco was full of wealthy Kenyans, ex-pats and tourists. I had been given the kitty by Ralph James and you can imagine how popular we were as the winning side in this disco on a Sunday night in Nairobi. We had money to burn and partied hard after a great victory. We eventually got back to the hotel to find that the bar was full of rugby players, which you would expect and a few of the women we had seen in the club. It was only when the girls were refused entry to the hotels main area unless they paid $200 to the receptionist that I realised that they may have been ladies of the night in search of Western currency.

I returned home to the UK and within two hours of landing picked up a flight to Bermuda, via New York, with Yaser Martini. I had always undertaken some form of charity event each year since 1996 and this year I had planned with Ashley Redmond to take the Ginger Pig Jazz band to Bermuda in July 1999. Ashley Redmond had seen the Ginger Pig perform at The Black Bottom Club in Northampton and together we hatched a plan to get them to perform at the house of one of his friends, Kathy Herrero, who lived at La Paloma in Harbour Road Paget. The trip was organised primarliy to raise money for her charity Child's Wish. This charity was formed because one of her nephews had multiple sclerosis and the charity was raising money to help find out more about this illness. He was flying down from New York to see this concert in her garden.

The contrast from Jomo Kenyatta International Airport in Nairobi to that of LF Wade International Airport was astonishing. I had seen Kibera, the largest slum in Nairobi that was reputed to have 800,000 inhabitants, and then arrived in Bermuda, the third most densely populated place on earth, with a population of 68,500 in its 20.75 square miles. There were no slums in Bermuda; it was an oasis of wealth where the average price of a home was approximately $1.2 million dollars. I couldn't believe how lucky I was to see two extremes in such a short period of time.

In 1999 it was the New Orleans Style Jazz Band that provided the opportunity to return to Bermuda. I was friends with John and Colin Richardson and felt part of the band even though the only use I played was to help facilitate this trip to Bermuda with Ashley. It was Ashley who funded it with some local sponsors, and we remain indebted to him for taking this risk. The Ginger Pigs had become critically acclaimed for their spectacular performances and travelled to jazz and blues festivals throughout Europe including Ascona, Switzerland, and now they found themselves in Hamilton, Bermuda. I had grown up listening to their music and had told them about this magical Island over a pint in Aunty Ruth's. Never did I expect to see them playing here.

The Ginger Pig Band was full of musical backgrounds from the world of jazz and rock, but also celtic and African influences. One of the band members was Lee Jackson, the bass player and occasional singer, who had risen to prominence in the 1960s in The Nice with keyboardist Keith Emerson and drummer Brian Davison. The Nice recorded numerous albums and appeared in a notorious concert at London's Royal Albert Hall. We sat on this trip on the back of an open-sided truck, where he recalled to us that at one point in his career, he had travelled in a Silver Shadow Rolls Royce. The band played all over the island in private gigs as well as an open air concert in Barr's Bay Park, which is right on the Hamilton Harbour next to the Royal Bermuda Yacht Club. The gig on 4th July was at the official residence of the American consulate, a beautiful beachfront property. For Americans in Bermuda this was a day to celebrate freedom and an opportunity for them to give something back to Bermuda, in their adopted home-away-from-home. Corporate sponsors dined under the stars with families who brought picnics. The Ginger Pig Band stole the show and, as they finished their last number, we were treated to the biggest firework display I have ever seen.

Yaser and I were in our element. We were both single and spent the week sunbathing, talking, eating, meeting people and drinking Dark 'n' Stormy's, Bermuda's national drink, made up of dark Goslings rum and ginger beer with ice. In fact this was our official role – to supply the band members with drinks.

Yaser was one of the first people that I met at University and the person that I have remained in touch with throughout my life. He was a kindred spirit, the most positive person that I have ever met. He loved life and I loved sharing it with him.

Our livers were not prepared for the next leg of our trip, which was Ben Rodber's stag party in New York. I can remember, drinking cocktails on the 106th and 107th floors of the North Tower of the World Trade Centre. The view from Windows on the World was breathtaking. Tim toasted his brother whilst we looked over New York's skyline. We couldn't have imagined that on 11th September

2001 the tower we were standing in would be hit by an aircraft less than twenty-nine minutes after the South tower was hit. The hotel we were staying in was also badly damaged, as well as nearby buildings. I was in the swimming pool of the hotel, overlooking St. Paul's, a chapel built in 1766, on the northeast corner of the World Trade Centre. It was a beautiful old building and somehow survived the September 11th attacks. It was pummelled by shards of glass, smoke and debris; however, not even a single window broke. The only damage was a sycamore tree, which was knocked over in the corner of the graveyard. Over 2,753 people were killed, including all 157 passengers and crew aboard the two airplanes on September 11th. The chapel served as a place of rest and refuge for recovery workers at the World Trade Center site.

On one of the nights we were in New York, Tim took us to Sparks Steak House on 210 East 46th Street. It had a worldwide reputation for being the greatest steak house in Manhattan. It also had a fabulous wine cellar, with its wine list being awarded the *Wine Spectator* magazine's Grand Award every year since 1981. It was where Paul Castellano from the Gambino family of New York was gunned down in front of Sparks in 1985. We were aware of this story when we were sitting in the restaurant and needless to say we didn't do a runner.

I enjoyed New York and was surprised by how safe it appeared to be. We were in Manhattan and it seemed perfectly normal to walk around the streets late at night. We ended up in SoHo, a neighborhood originally associated with the arts. It rose to fame during the 1960s and 1970s when the cheap spaces vacated by departing factories were converted by artists into lofts and studios. It was Rudy Giuliani, the Mayor of New York City, who was credited with initiating improvements in the city's quality of life and with a reduction in crime, and this was really evident when we went.

I eventually got back to Northampton after this trip and focused on pre-season and the first testimonial event, which was the launch dinner at Althorp House on 11th September 1999. Pre-season was once again very demanding for us, but nothing in comparison to the regime that Tim, Bealer, Daws and Grays were going through. Playing for England had certainly changed from those days when the team met at the Petersham on a Saturday night and trained on the pitch at Twickenham on the Sunday morning. England were preparing for a world cup that was being hosted by Wales, although the majority of matches were played outside the country, shared between England, France, Scotland and Ireland.

In 1999 the standards of fitness and preparation of the England side were unsurpassed. They had attended a three-day exercise with the Royal Marines at the commando training centre in Lympstone, Devon, in July. Clive Woodward, who had succeeded Jack Rowell in 1997, wanted to give the team a sense of perspective and was implementing a very different regime to that of his predecessor. He was a modern coach who was happy to look outside his sport for best practice. He had visited the University of Colorado American football programme and introduced the concept of specialised coaching for offensive, defensive and kicking skills. He brought in Phil Larder from rugby league to strengthen defensive technique, as well as John Mitchell and Brian Ashton. He created a special environment for the players. The players moved from the Petersham Hotel to Pennyhill Park in Bagshot in Surrey, a five-star hotel with superb facilities.

I saw a complete change in the Northampton players that were in his England Squad. One particular memory springs to mind, attending Budge Pountney's wedding in Hampshire in the summer of 1999. The reception was held on his father's farm in Sparsholt, just outside Winchester. All the players came down from Northampton to the evening Barn Dance. However, it was the England players that stood out. I remember them weighing their food to assess the calorific and nutritional values. Something that Grays and Rodders hadn't done in New York, I hasten to add. This was part of the preparation for the World Cup and they took it very seriously, yet we thought it was comical when, having gone to all the trouble of doing this, they then got stuck into the beers. Gregor Townsend, Matt Stewart and

Budge Pountney were part of the Scotland Squad and rest assured they weren't weighing their food.

The launch dinner of my testimonial was at Althorp House on 11th September 1999 and was organised by Gary McManus. One of the highlights for me and him was a meeting with Althorp's general manager, David Horton-Fawkes. He showed Gary around the house before the event, which had not been used for any corporate functions since Princess Diana had died. A private tour of Althorp House and a visit to the island where Princess Diana was buried was something we would never forget. We had a private tour of the museum housing the wedding dress Diana wore for her 1981 marriage to Prince Charles. Diana's toys, her school reports and a film of her charity work with AIDS patients and landmine victims were also on show. One of the most moving exhibits was the collection of home videos showing Diana as a carefree child dancing and playing in the gardens of Althorp. Another section of the museum contained film footage and music from Diana's funeral, along with a copy of the oration given by Earl Spencer in which he attacked both the media and the royal family, which I watched live. We were then unexpectedly allowed to walk from the museum to the lake, where Diana's grave on the island was marked by a large urn carved in Portland stone. We weren't allowed on to the island itself, but we saw the temple and the plaque which read to "the unique, the complex, the extraordinary and irreplaceable Diana." It was at this point that I realised how lucky I was to have permission from Earl Spencer to host my event in his house.

I will never forget that evening. It was a black tie event in one of the most perfect settings that you could think of, just three miles from where I had grown up in Old Duston. As a youngster I had cycled to Althorp and had afternoon tea in the stable block. My sister had gone out with a butler at the house, and Dad and I had dropped her off in the car on many occasions, and here I was going back for an event that was being held in my honour. This was really very special. I loved Althorp. We had planned to have a drinks reception in the Picture Gallery, followed by dinner in the State Dining Room listening to the

Ginger Pig Jazz Band who I had been with that summer in Bermuda. The MC for the night was Martin Bayfield, and the great and good of Northampton were there to celebrate my testimonial launch.

The setting was breathtaking. When you first enter the Picture Gallery at Althorp House you are struck by its magnificence. It is 115 feet long with glorious views of the Deer Park. It has one of the greatest private art collections in the country, including paintings by Van Dyck, Rubens, Reynolds, Stubbs and Gainsborough hanging on the oak panelled walls. We had dinner in the State Dining Room, which is modelled on the State Dining Room at Buckingham Palace.

Ashley Redmond was the guest who had come the furthest, from Bermuda. He had travelled up from Bristol with one of his mates, Simon Tucker, who had a business selling scooters. Sadly, they had got to Coventry and their car broke down. Rather than catch a taxi or wait for the AA to tow them to Althorp House, they decided to take the two scooters on the back of a trailer and came the rest of the way on board scooter in black tie. They arrived late but had a very good excuse. Ashley was staying at my house that night and you can imagine my surprise when in the early hours he arrived in a Porsche 911 Carrera that he had stolen from Giles Wilson, one of the committee members. The next morning, I dropped the car off to its rightful owner who was oblivious that it had been taken and was still in bed fast asleep.

The next event in the testimonial year was a World XV v Harvey Thorneycroft Premiership XV at Franklin's Gardens on the 23rd October 1999. It seems odd that midway through the season we were able to put on a match like this. We had not been very diligent in our planning as it was the quarter-finals of the 1999 Rugby World Cup and Wales were playing Australia at the Millennium Stadium in Cardiff, which ruled out getting any players from Wales on the Saturday. England were playing South Africa the following day, at the Stade de France in Paris, and it is surprising how many players were in Paris working the media and hospitality circuit. There were no premiership fixtures. However, the rest of the English sides, Welsh, Irish, Italian and

French continued to play fixtures during the World Cup. This became the single most difficult event of the testimonial to organise. Rugby had entered a level of professionalism that meant that it was difficult to get players released to play in the game. I had written to all of the coaches at the Premiership Clubs to see whether they would consider releasing players and most were responsive, but they were under a huge amount of pressure and a benefit match was not really high on their list of priorities. John Steele, who had replaced Ian McGeechan as Director of Rugby, in the summer of 1999 wrote,

I would confirm that I am willing to release players for the match subject to league or Cup commitments and injury. You will understand that we cannot jeopardise our progress in any of the competitions by risking players in a non-competition match.

I understood this completely and the timing turned out to be perfect because if this had been at the end of the season then I would have not been able to get any players from the club because they were dropping like flies from injuries.

Despite the difficulty in putting this match together, Leon Barwell and I had great fun right up to the last minute working out who would actually turn up. I pooled from the great many contacts that I had made throughout my rugby career. This led me to speak to some of my childhood heroes, some of my old rivals and many of the up-and-coming modern stars of the future who might be willing to donate their time. We put together a truly representative World XV, which included Mike Teague, Peter Winterbottom, Rory Underwood, Paul Hull, Simon Geoghegan, Jim Staples, Martin Offiah, Gary Pearce and Neil Francis. The Premiership team wasn't bad either. It included three players that went on to win the World Cup with England, Andy Gomersall, Steve Thompson and Ben Cohen, who scored a hat-trick on the day. A few thousand supporters turned out to see the match, which was never very serious. Alan Lamb took all the conversions for both teams until the referee, Chris Rees, took over the kicking for the World XV and, in the closing minutes, snuck on a shirt and dived over the line for the final try thanks to a pass by Peter Winterbottom. I will never forget the linesman Chris Harris, parading up and down the touch line with his flag and an umbrella. The final score was Harvey XV 79, World XV 69.

The next event in our calendar was organised by Paul Southworth, who had been the longest-serving UK president of Avon Cosmetics, which was based in Northampton. The event was called a "World Cup Reprise" and was held at the Café Royal on the 11th November 1999. I went to the final of the Rugby World Cup final on the 6th November 1999 at the Millennium Stadium, Cardiff, where I saw Australia beat France. Philippe Bernat-Salles, Raphael Ibanez and Thomas Lievremount started that day for France, who I had played against for England A against France A on the 28th February 1997. In less than two years I had gone from playing against these players to struggling to get in Northampton Saints 1st XV. It is in moments of reflection that you realise how fickle the world of sport is.

The irony is that whilst I was watching the World Cup Final I had no idea that I would be running out to play against virtually the same Australian team on 27th October 2001. I found myself playing for an English National Division XV whilst at John Inverdale's club Esher, made up of English players from outside the Premiership. The match was being played at Welford Road my spiritual rugby home for non-club rugby. I had previously run out on that pitch against the All Blacks, South Africa and Western Samoa but never against Australia.

The match was being televised by Sky and this really was a game that I felt was a bridge too far. We ran out that day against nine of the players that I had watched win the World Cup Final in 1999: Daniel Herbert, Toutai Kefu, Joe Roff, Stephen Larkham, George Gregan, Michael Foley, David Giffin, Matt Cockbain and Ben Tune, who was my opponent that day. I was thirty-two and enjoying working in London and playing 2nd Division rugby. I had no right to be called into this game. I ran out onto that pitch with an assortment of part-time and semi-professional rugby players. Dave Sims was our captain and we were coached by Adrian Davies, the Welsh fly-half, and Richard Cockerill, the England and Leicester hooker.

There were some great players in the team but no superstars. On paper it looked like an appalling mismatch and ought not to have been played. However, we exceeded all expectations to produce a wonderfully vibrant and committed performance, which, though not quite good enough to defeat the world champions, certainly rattled them. Paul Stephens of *The Independent* wrote an article after the match and mentioned me: "Harvey Thorneycroft gave a barnstorming impression of his best days at Northampton." The final score was England National Divisions 22, Australia 34 – it was the last time that I was to play at Welford Road.

It is all about timing with events. Having a black tie dinner on the Thursday after the World Cup Final was not accidental. John Inverdale hosted the event and arrived on time, despite my earlier mishaps of trying to meet him. I was lucky to get a panel of speakers including Freddie Mendez, Pat Lam, Tim Rodber, Michael Lynagh, Martin Johnson and the fly-half who I had seen kick a drop goal to win the 1995 World Cup, Joel Stranksy, to attend. I found it amazing thinking, as I walked the short distance down Regent Street from Oxford Circus to the Café Royal, that 500 people would be attending a dinner in my honour. The event was supported by ING Barings. The link was Julian Bryant, the UK head of investment banking, who was a friend of Ian Kirkham. It was extraordinary walking into The Empire and Napoleon suite, given its history. Many people that I had grown up with over the years attended this event, together with many successful businessmen who worked in the city. My dad took a table that evening. He had lost his mother on the 21st December 1998, someone we had both loved so much. Marjorie Alice Thorneycroft had lived ninety-three years and three days and would have been so proud to have seen me and Dad dinning at the Café Royal. It was this extended team of people who were responsible for keeping me going through all of those years of rugby. Dad, Mum, Grandma, Nan and Joy were always there to support me, and it was as much a testimonial to them as it was to me.

The 1999/2000 season was a truly amazing year. It was a huge honour to be recognised by the Saints for the years that I had spent at the club with a testimonial, but the biggest honour for me came on Boxing Day 1999 when I was called into the team to play against Newcastle Falcons. In the professional era the Boxing Day game had virtually disappeared, but in 1999 it fell on a Sunday and this game was live on Sky television. It was a great game to be involved in regardless of the fact that it was my 250th appearance in the black, green and gold. Pat Lam was the captain on the day and he gave me the honour of leading the team out onto Franklin's Gardens. I ran out onto the pitch and looked around to see the crowd on their feet, clapping. It seemed like an eternity before Pat and the rest of the team joined me. That euphoric moment will stay with me forever. Sadly, the old expression you are only as good as your last game was also ringing in my ears. I can remember the words my Dad used to say to me after any bad game, "Harvey, you looked like you were carrying your mortgage behind you." I couldn't have a shocker on my 250th game, not after that standing ovation. I wasn't getting picked that often in the first team. I was fast approaching the end of my career at the Saints and so every time I ran out, I treated it like my last.

The endorphin rush was like no other on this day, so much so that I took on Epeli Taione, the Tongan nineteen-stone winger, who given his age and stature should have eaten me alive, but not at Franklin's Gardens. I glanced across at this giant of a man before the game began thinking, "This is going to be tough", but I had no fear of failure. At Franklin's Gardens I felt invincible. I went well that day. My confidence was so high and I was playing so well that Rob Andrew, the Newcastle Coach, decided to move Epeli to the other wing for the second half. Ordinarily, this would have been a good thing because clubs rarely kept an out and out winger on the bench, so who ever he replaced Epeli with should have been less of a player. Sadly, in his place and opposite me for the second half, stood Va'aiga Tuigamala, rugby's £1 million signing. "Inga the Winger" was my age and was known as one of the most powerful runners in the game. Inga was a physical wing that had played for the All Blacks before switching to rugby league with Wigan in 1993.

I had the audacity to think that I could drop my shoulder on Va'aiga, like I had done in the first half with Epeli. When I took the twenty-metre run at the big man he dropped me like a pack of cards in one of the biggest hits that I had ever received. Not only that, he picked me up off the floor in a heap and whispered in my ear, "Please don't try and do that to me, old man." After the game, he shook my hand and gave me a hug. I can safely say that he was one of the best rugby players that I had the pleasure of coming up against. He was known for his Christian faith, and was a perfect gentleman off the field.

Chapter 21

One sip of champagne from the Heineken Cup

Whilst I was worried about performing at Franklin's Gardens for the Saints, the rest of the world were worried about the Y2K bug, which experts thought could result in a world wide computer meltdown in the lead up to the millennium. The millennium bug was a failure for most computers to be able to recognise the last two digits of the year. IT companies around the world spent billions of pounds looking for the Y2K bug and working out how to fix it. Almost everybody raced around to make themselves Y2K-compliant before the fast-approaching deadline. Finally, when the big day came, many utilities and other companies switched off their main computers and put the backup computers to work. When the clock ticked 1st January 2000, no major problems were reported. Every bank worked, no major power outages were reported, airplanes still flew and the whole world went on with its normal life.

I was oblivious to all of this and celebrated the millennium at a superb party hosted by the Barwell family at their family home Bradden House. No expense was spared at this party, which was held in a huge marquee in their garden. The marquee was themed like the inside of a Bedouin tent, which for a little hamlet in the middle of Northamptonshire was quite exotic. There was a superb firework display put to music. But, like most New Year's Eve parties for the last ten years I couldn't let my hair down, because there was always the prospect of having to play rugby on New Year's Day or very soon after. One New Year's Eve when Tim Rodber hosted a New Year's Eve Party in his barn for the Club, we sang *Auld Lang Syne* then everyone left within five minutes in a mass exodus back to their beds in preparation for a New Year's Day match.

The next six months for the Saints were some of the most successful the club had ever seen, leading to the final of the European Cup at Twickenham on the 27th May 2000. This was the first year that the Saints had qualified for the Heineken European Cup and they found themselves in the final after the first attempt. The Club had been established for 119 years and they had never won anything. I watched the team defy all the critics when they ended up playing five games in two weeks prior to the match on the 27th May 2000. We had lost in the Tetley Bitter Cup Final at Twickenham against Wasps and having been in a commanding position in the league, cup and European Cup, found ourselves with one last chance to win any Silverware. I wasn't in the squad for this match and travelled down with the players, family and friends on a coach to Twickenham. I had been there two weeks before as part of the squad for the Tetley Bitter Cup and whilst I was excited for the team there was a huge feeling of nervousness. This was the biggest game for the club and we were going up against a Munster side that had lived and breathed the Heineken Cup Final, and had three weeks off to prepare for the game. This Saints side was probably the best ever to wear the black, green and gold, but injuries had taken their toll including Matt Dawson and Nick Beal, so no-one knew what to expect.

In front of a crowd of 68,441 spectators at Twickenham, the Saints won 9-8 in the final. It wasn't the prettiest of fixtures, a typical Cup Final, but no-one cared. I sat with the rest of the squad during the game and joined the team on the pitch after the final whistle. Ian McGeechan had instilled a squad ethos into the Saints and Pat Lam, who captained the side that day, was keen to make sure that everyone felt part of the big day regardless of whether they were on the pitch or not. I had joined the Saints in 1987 and had waited a long time to enjoy a day like this that turned into a long night and a very long extended weekend.

I walked around the pitch with the players whilst they presented the cup to the adoring fans that deserved this moment. They had waited long enough. The atmosphere was superb and was a fitting way to finish the season and reward the players for all the hard work they had put in over many years. We went into the changing rooms after the game and, like many matches of this magnitude, there was a whole group of people coming in to congratulate the team when the players are knackered and need time to reflect. Imagine our surprise when Peter O'Toole and Richard Harris walked into the changing rooms. This was a jaw dropping moment. We had all been to see *Gladiator* the night before the Tetley Bitter Cup Final and here was the actor that played Emperor Marcus Aurelius in that film standing before us. Richard Harris was a rugby fanatic and had played alongside Keith Wood's dad, Gordon, the Ireland and Lions prop. He was intensely proud of Munster and, more importantly, Limerick Rugby. He had been part of the 30,000 Munster fans who had travelled to see the game at Twickenham. These fans included Peter OT'oole, another huge fan of rugby, who attended Five Nations matches with him and Richard Burton.

Meeting these two men was a privilege. One of my favourite films of all time was *Lawrence of Arabia*, in which Peter O'Toole played TE Lawrence. They were both a little the worse for wear when they came into our changing rooms. They came to congratulate the boys on their victory and were kind enough to have photographs taken with the team. Richard Harris went on to take the role of Headmaster Albus Dumbledore in *Harry Potter and the Philosopher's Stone* in 2001 and *Chamber of Secrets* in 2002. Another Saints player appeared in both of these films, my old mate Martin Bayfield. A far cry from his renditions of the songs, he used to sing in the back of the bus. The one of which I remember with great affection is *Ernie (The Fastest Milkman In The West)*, which Martin knew word for word and would often be asked to sing it for the boys. It always had the boys in fits of laughter. Particularly the last verse,

Ernie was only fifty-two, he didn't want to die
Now he's gone to make deliveries
In that milkround in the sky
Where the customers are angels
And ferocious dogs are banned
And a milkman's life is full of fun
In that fairy dairy land
But a woman's needs are many fold
And Sue she married Ted
But strange things happened on their wedding night
As they lay in their bed
Was that the trees a rustling
Or the hinges of the gate
Or Ernies ghostly goldtop a rattling in their crate
They won't forget Ernie (Ernie)
And he drove the fastest milkcart in the west.

Sadly, Richard Harris died a few years later in October 2002 of Hodgkin's disease. At his funeral, the family printed the last letter ever written by Harris in his hospital bed where he said he would like to be reincarnated as three famous rugby players. It read: "I would like to come back as a compilation of Nelson [Jimmy], Galwey [Mick] and The Claw [Peter Clohessy] and terrorise the rugby world instead of terrorising the movie community." There is also a superb article which Richard Harris wrote on 24th May 2002 in the *Daily Telegraph*,

I would give up all the accolades – people have occasionally written and said nice things – of my showbiz career to play just once for the senior Munster team. I will never win an Oscar now, but even if I did I would swap it instantly for one sip of champagne from the Heineken Cup.

That night I was able to sip champagne from the Heineken Cup and immerse myself in the reflected glory of the players who I had grown up with who achieved Northampton's greatest accolade.

We travelled back to Franklin's Gardens with the cup in tow on the team bus. We knew that there would be a great reception. Pat Lam got all the players together and suggested that we should go and present the cup to the fans. The boys were dressed in suits provided by Gary Osbourne, a local retailer, with 1st team ties commemorating the European Cup match at Twickenham. Number ones were still very important even in 2000. In those days the 1st team bus would park at the South End of the ground, known as the Lakestand. As soon as you got off the bus you could hear the buzz from the supporters who were assembled at the North End or Sturtridge Pavilion part of the ground. As a squad, we linked arms on the try line with the European Cup and walked towards the supporters, who sang *When The Saints go Marching In* as we approached them.

There was no formal presentation; everything was impromptu and it was great. Pat Lam said a few words and it was so quiet you could hear a pin drop, even though there must have been a few thousand people on the pitch. Then, one by one, we all got the opportunity of taking hold of the cup and lifting it into the air whilst the crowd sang. I felt very proud to be a Northampton man that day.

We eventually got on the bus and it took us to Auntie Ruth's, which was the natural choice for the players to celebrate. Before we entered the main bar, we were taken down to the basement. That night we had it exclusively for a court session. The major fine that night was issued to Keith Barwell, who was penalised for the Sky television interview he gave prior to the Tetley Bitter Cup Final, predicting a thirty-point margin of victory. He was asked to drink a spoof pint made of some very horrible drinks. Once the court session was over, the boys lifted Keith onto their shoulders and marched him into the main bar with the European Cup in his hands. He then proceeded to stand on the bar and announced like the "Milkybar Kid" that the drinks were on him. This was a public bar and that night everyone who managed to get into Auntie Ruth's had their drinks paid for by Keith. There were people in the bar that night who knew nothing about rugby, who thought they had won the lottery and happily drank whatever was on the optic racks, including champagne, before it sold out.

Just two days later we repeated it all again on the 29th May 2000. I had planned as part of my testimonial year to hold an event for the Gordon Stand supporters, who over the years had given me a great reception. The event was held courtesy of Jake, Jarvis and Colin Richardson, at The Picturedrome. We had arranged for a very simple format with a comedian and live music from the Ginger Pig Jazz Band. This was going to be a great night to celebrate with the fans, which was planned well in advance of the final. I didn't anticipate that it would be on the night when Northampton Town treated us to an open top bus ride through the streets of Northampton, finishing at All Saints Church. It poured with rain that night, but it didn't matter. The only embarrassing moment was as the bus was leaving, Tom Sears, the press officer, had forgotten to pick up the European Cup and we nearly left without it. Thousands of people had braved the weather and came out to support the team. The bus came to halt opposite the town hall in Northampton. The reception the town gave us was superb.

I was not part of the team that won the European Cup and yet the players made me feel part of their victory. None more so than Matt Dawson, who at the end of the parade, with the consent of Pat Lam, walked me through a funnel of supporters who were assembled out side the town hall. He held me by the hand and in the other hand he held the European Cup. He said, "This is your moment", and gave me the silverware and walked back towards the bus, where the other players were. I stood in front of the crowd, whilst they chanted my name and lifted the European Cup in the air. It doesn't matter what I achieve in my life, nothing could give me a better feeling. This was an emotion that I couldn't share with anyone else; it is entirely different to getting married or having children. It was a euphoric moment as I stood in the town where I was born, sharing this moment with people who felt every bit the passion that I felt for our rugby club. I often remind Matt Dawson of this moment. I don't know whether he was conscious of what he did that night, but I will be forever indebted to him for his recognition. The open-top bus dropped us off at The Picturedrome and we piled in for an evening of beers and live music.

We finished the night off in a famous watering hole in Northampton called the Swan and Helmet.

The last of my testimonial events was on the 23rd June 2000. We wanted to finish the year with an event that was totally different. We contacted the people who ran The Royal Theatre in Northampton to see whether we could hire the venue for a party. The theatre was next door and linked to the more modern Derngate theatre. We planned the event so we could make best use of both locations. The Royal was relatively small, but an absolutely beautiful Victorian gem, and full of atmosphere. The Derngate was a superb concert venue known for its acoustics. We pulled off quite a coup. We persuaded the cast of the West End show *The Rise and Fall of Little Voice* to come up from London to give us a performance in the Royal and then finished the night off with dinner to the sound of the Ginger Pig band in the Derngate. The night worked very well and we had a guest appearance from Leo Sayer, who had come to see one of his friends in the show. We invited him to have dinner with us and he agreed to sing a song. He had a string of chart hits in the 1970s including *You Make Me Feel Like Dancing*, but his name is probably best known as Cockney rhyming slang for an "all dayer" (all day drinking session).

The summer was well and truly here and, like all the seasons before, presented a chance to go on an obscure trip. This time it was an opportunity to visit Dubai, to play in a Chairman's XV against the Dubai Exciles RFC, on Friday 30th June 2000 at 7:00 p.m.. This was a legendary trip to join Jim Lees for his annual dinner and the traditional end of season game. I was flown business class by Gulf Air to Abu Dhabi, part of the United Arab Emirates. I joined Scott Hastings and Derek Stark, who had been to this fixture the year before. Ollie Redman and Jim Hay were also part of the overseas players invited to strengthen the Chairman's XV. We were picked up in a luxury air-conditioned Mercedes and taken the 120 kilometres to Dubai. I looked at the outside temperature, 102 degrees Fahrenheit, and wondered how on earth we were going to play rugby in that heat. Linda Gordon looked after us during our stay and we were taken to private apartments donated by Arenco Real Estate, one of the game's sponsors.

We had cars at our disposal and spent most days before the game at the Jumeirah Beach Hotel, one of the most prestigious hotels of the world. I chatted to one of our drivers who was originally from a small village in India. He told me that as a driver in Dubai he earned approximately $200 a month. This wasn't a huge amount of money by our standards, but he told me that when he returned to his village in India his friends and family treated him differently because he was seen as a high roller working in Dubai. Living in Dubai he felt very isolated and outcast by the local community and it would appear that was also the case in his own region of India. He had gone to Dubai in search of a better life and more money and instead found himself more emotionally empoverished.

The Jumeirah Beach Hotel had only been completed in 1999 and represents a breaking ocean wave. It is awe-inspiring. We went each day for the most magnificent breakfast that you could feast your eyes and stomach on, with food from all over the world. The hotel was situated opposite the world's only seven-star hotel, the Burj al Arab (Tower of the Arabs), which is shaped like a billowing sail. You needed to have a booking to even get in the hotel, it was that exclusive. The hotel was on an artificial island, connected to the beach of the Jumeirah by a curving bridge. The hotel reception was covered with gold leaf, with a huge central fountain and a 321-metre atrium. We were shown the Al Mahara Restaurant, which had underwater views of the gulf, and taken to a room that had two floors and was adorned with Louis Vuitton bed linen and bathrobes. The bathroom was like something you might see on a film set, with a huge range of perfume and aftershave products provided free of charge for guests. We were offered afternoon tea. I was asked what type of tea I might like. I was feeling facetious and suggested, "PG Tips." To my surprise, the waiter typed this into his handheld computer and it came up with the nearest equivalent, English Breakfast. I enjoyed the visit but would never have wanted to stay in the hotel. It was too lavish. It was reputed to cost somewhere in the region of $1,000 per night for a standard room and the largest penthouse suite might cost $25,000 a night.

Our only commitments during this unbelievable few days in Dubai was to attend a black tie dinner in the clubhouse held the night before the game. This was one of the hottest dinners I have ever attended. We got stuck into the beers and wine at dinner and then played the next day at 7:00 p.m. to avoid the heat. The only saving grace was that the pitch was grass, which was a significant improvement on the pitch made of sand that I had played on in 1990. Dubai had changed much in the ten years since my last visit.

One memory that will stay with me from this trip was watching camel racing. Dubai had a racetrack located on the outskirts of the city. Camel racing was supported by the highest levels of UAE society, with former President Zayed owning a personal stable consisting of 14,000 camels and 9,000 workers devoted to their upkeep. Sheikh Mohammed, the former Defense Minister of the UAE, owned 2,000 camels and maintained a reputation of his own for high performance on the racetracks.

I returned from Dubai and indulged my passion for the island of Bermuda and the Ginger Pig Band once again. This was becoming an annual pilgrimage, but I never grew weary of this wonderful destination, particularly the view as you approach the island from the air and the sight of the coral reefs, pink sands and crystal clear water. The difference between this trip and the others I had been on was where I was staying. Paget Hall was one of the most impressive houses on the island. It was owned by Brian and Nancy Duperault who were involved in the charity event that the Ginger Pig Band were headlining. Brian was the founder of Ace, one of the largest reassurance companies on the Island. Brian had one of the best commutes anywhere in the world. You could see the Ace building across Hamilton Harbour from Paget Hall. He often commuted to work by boat, which was a more direct route than by road. Curtis was employed by the family to look after their boats, which included "Uncle Buck", on board which I explored the coral reefs with Nancy and some of the members of the band.

I was intrigued by what drove Brian. He had every material trapping you could think of, yet this wasn't his inspiration. Brian was like some of the sports men that I had met during my rugby career. He was driven by an individual purpose or a reason for being. Neil Back, Martin Johnson, Lawrence Dallaglio, Matt Dawson and Tim were similar in every respect. They all wanted to be the best players in their position in the world and failure to them was not achieving their purpose or long-term goal. It didn't matter how many setbacks they had to achieve their goal, these were part of the journey. It was inevitable therefore that when Tim informed me he was going to give up rugby at the end of the 2000/2001 season and concentrate on business that our lives were about to change.

At this point I realised that I needed to reinvent myself. Tim knew this well before I did, such was his insight. I resented him for wanting to cut short my career, but thank God I followed his advice. One of the attributes of those people I have worked with since my rugby career is that they have the ability to reinvent themselves to stay ahead of the game. Tim had achieved his own purpose for the club by lifting the European Cup and this was probably the pinnacle of his club rugby career. I didn't have the same purpose as Tim. I just felt very lucky to still be playing in the Saints team, which was filled with international superstars. I only played eleven games after my 250th appearance for Northampton. I wasn't training full-time with the club and got called in when required. My last game for Northampton was against Gloucester during which I achieved a milestone of a hundred tries for the 1st XV.

That season saw the retirement of three key players from the club, Pat Lam, Garry Pagel and Tim Rodber. The occasion was celebrated at an end of season dinner at Fawsley Hall Hotel. Keith Barwell thanked all of these players, but made a very special presentation to Tim.

He had purchased the spoke of a Roman chariot at Sotherby's and in his speech he felt that this gift was befitting of "the only true warrior that he had known". Tim was quite overcome by the presentation, but it was a fitting present for an extremely loyal Saints player who had had an illustrious career. Tim donated all his shirts to Northampton Rugby Club and the area under the West Stand is now known as The Rodber Suite. This shows the respect the club felt for his contribution over the years.

Tim had always looked at the strategic direction of our business and so we decided to join Paul Sherrell and David Spicer at the office in Richmond upon Thames that Paul had set up. This decision was influenced by the fee that we generated from helping the club with the marketing associated with the proposed stadium redevelopment proposals. We had been instructed by the club to do three things. The first was to canvas the support of the local community with a view to obtaining verbal pledges of financial support. This involved making presentations all over the county to interested parties. This took us to village halls, pubs and private houses, where we would answer any queries or concerns the fans had about the changes that were being proposed. It soon became very apparent that the community loved the idea of being able to buy shares in their club and we assembled a list of names that convinced the club that if they held a share issue, then they would raise the funds that they would need to complete stage one. We were then given another responsibility. To sell twenty new hospitality boxes to the local business community. We were able to sign contracts on the vast majority of these boxes, but instead of getting a fee for this work we agreed to have a half-share in a box for four years, which we shared with the KI Group.

I wasn't ready for the move to London; I was in my comfort zone, working out of a converted stable block in Holcot and playing the odd game for the first team. I had a five-bedroom house and a great lifestyle. My family was in Northamptonshire and life was good. However, I needed to reinvent myself under the stewardship of my former captain and great friend Tim Rodber. It was the right decision to move to London at the end of the 2000/2001 season. Tim, Paul and I had purchased a flat, 51 Kensington Hall Gardens, West Kensington, on the 19th January 2001, in preparation for the eventual move. The address seemed very grand although we were actually next to the A4 and West Kensington tube station. I purchased my third of the flat from the money that I received from my testimonial, which seemed the right investment to make at the time. It was a big change for Tim and me. It was like going back to being a student living in a bedsit or in the condemned house that Tim and Hunts had lived in in Collingtree. We spent all our time together, working during the day and returning to the flat in the evening. It was enough to make any of us stir crazy. The only thing that separated us were the walls between our bedrooms. This wasn't conducive to healthy living, but my God did we have a good time. The Best Magal, a local Turkish restaurant on the North End Road, is where we ate most nights. They did the best kebabs in London. They had a hot charcoal cooking area in the centre of the restaurant where you could watch your food cooking while you waited. We took our food back to the flat, before getting last orders at the famous Three Kings pub, which was once The Nashville Rooms, a pub that had been one of the high spots of the London new-wave circuit. Among the bands that played early gigs here were the Sex Pistols, The Jam, Siouxsie & The Banshees and Joy Division. Sadly, by the time we were going there the pub was reinvented as one of London's premier sports pubs. We had no idea about London. If we had, we wouldn't have bought a flat next to the A4 and West Kensington tube station.

It was a big risk, but my risks were insignificant compared to those that Tim took. He went from playing professional rugby with salaries from Northampton and England, endorsements from Rockport, Reebok and Land Rover, and a salary from the Army, to one single salary from Rodber Thorneycroft Ltd. He had moved from a converted barn in the country, indulging his passion for country sports to a flat on the North End Road. He was a risk taker and I admire his courage. Many of his England colleagues would not have even considered making this move at a time when he was still good enough to play in the Premiership. The result of this decision was that one day he was focused on rugby and the next, business. He wanted nothing more to do with the sport; he had mentally moved on and, by default, however much I wanted to hang on, so did I. I never quite understood his ability to switch from putting his passion into rugby into business. This was the mark of a super perfomer; his purpose was to achieve his long-term vision and I was taken along on that journey.

The growth of our business reflected a growing economy. You could say we were lucky, but we lived and breathed the business for two years. Paul, Tim and I learned to live with each other. It wasn't healthy, but it meant that no stone was left unturned in our pursuit of success. I knew a few people in London and when we first moved into Kensington Hall Gardens it was my role to bring in new business to the company either through existing clients or by acquiring new ones. Tim set targets on how many new business meetings he thought I should be doing. He plucked the figure of fifteen a week out of the air. He didn't know what was realistic and neither did I. This was quite a heavy target but I was none the wiser and just ploughed on. Before long we recruited two other directors to join the team, Lesley Russell and Ben Rodber. We had sufficient skills now in-house to offer our clients a fully integrated marketing proposition. In English this meant that we had event management, PR, conference planning and incentive travel and hospitality management skill-sets. This was a great time to be in London when we were building RTL. Our clients were looking for ways of differentiating their brands from those of their competitors and we were uniquely placed to help them spend their budgets wisely. Our client's placed no restrictions on us – the more unusual the event, the better. We were not constrained to who we sold our services to. We had unlimited products and a plethora of geographies to explore. This was a voyage of discovery for all of us. Rugby had presented some unbelievable opportunities, but I cannot believe what we achieved in such a short space of time in business. There was no way that Mr Burrell, my school's careers officer, could have prepared me for this part of my career.

Chapter 22

Streets are pathed with gold

We were growing a very significant business at the same time as having great fun. There was one person who was my rock throughout this period and that was Alice Bufton. I met Alice through Todd Williams, a former Australian hockey player who was a client of RT and was renting my house in Northampton. We had an arrangement that he would stay in the house in Northampton during the week and then join Tim at the weekends and use my room in the flat. On one weekend during the summer of 2001 I had been invited up to a polo match at Dallas Burlston's grounds at Stoneythorpe Hall. I invited Todd and his friend Alice Bufton to join me. Alice had never been to a polo match and turned down centre court tickets at Wimbledon to accompany Todd to Warwickshire.

I will never forget seeing Alice for the first time, wearing the Barbarian panama hat that she had borrowed from my house. Alice assumed you should wear a hat to go to the polo and grabbed my hat from my house to smarten up the rather shabby clothes that she had worn the night before. I am surprised I even noticed what she was wearing; she was beautiful and I became totally disinterested in watching the polo. This was just as well really because there was no polo to watch; instead, Dallas offered the guests an opportunity to eat and drink in his new clubhouse, whilst people raced around the pitch in his Ferrari. I knew within a few minutes of meeting Alice that she would eventually be my wife. It was as if it had been preordained. My gut feeling was then over-ridden by the conscious part of my brain, a process which most blokes experience. I tried to convince myself that she was too good for me and would never give me a chance. Sadly, she didn't give me a chance. But, she did tell her mum the following day that she had met someone who would be significant in her life. Alice became a great friend, offering me advice and counselling me when things got tough at work.

The flat at Kensington Hall Gardens had become a party flat by night as the boys let off steam after work. Jasper Burnham, a previous client of Paul Sherrell, who worked for East West records, was one of the main providers of the fun in London. Jaspar was a record plugger, and he and his boss had access to the inner sanctum of the music scene in London. Damian Christian was the first plugger to work with Take That. When we met him, he was head of promotions for East West Records. He had been responsible for introducing Nirvana, Guns N' Roses, Mary J Blige, The Corrs, David Gray and James Blunt to UK radio and television. Paul and Tim became very friendly with Jaspar and Damian, who loved their rugby, and by default I ended having some amazing experiences in London thanks to these guys.

The first of these experiences was Tim Rodber's testimonial, which was held at the London Marriott Hotel in Grosvenor Square. This event was held in the square in London that was the location of the American Embassy, on the 3rd October 2001, less than a month after the September 11th attacks. This was the first world event in my lifetime that I can remember exactly where I was when it happened. I entered the Eel Pie pub in Twickenham as a plane was hitting the second Tower. I had no understanding of the pictures I was seeing and the pub was in silence as we witnessed this moment in history together. As a result of what had happened, the US Embassy had erected large concrete barriers and bollards to ward off car or truck bombs, and had armed policemen patrolling day and night. There was a feeling of mistrust in London that I had never seen before. The Americans were paranoid that something was going to happen to them in London.

Tim had managed to secure the services of Jools Holland and the Rhythm and Blues Orchestra to play after dinner. Jools Holland's fee was huge, and this was before you took into account the rider in his contract. Each request was itemised down to the half-bottles of whiskey. Fortunately, Paul managed to negotiate not providing this before signing the contract.

On the 29th November 2001, we were invited by Jaspar to Studio 4 at Riverside Studios in Hammersmith, which is where they filmed TFI Friday, which was hosted until 2000 by Chris Evans. I had watched this religiously every Friday night for four years. The band we went to watch was The Corrs, who were releasing their first compilation album, *Best of The Corrs*, and performing with the BBC Concert Orchestra for a pre-recorded show that was going out on BBC Radio 2, on the 24th December 2001. I happened to be a huge fan of The Corrs and to be in a limited audience of 200 people was unbelievable. Not only that, we got to go to the backstage party for drinks directly after the concert. This was a great experience, but the following week got even better. Tim was still very well known at this time because of the notoriety he had gained as an England rugby player. He would often get invited to things that most people would have given their right arm to attend, but his response was always, "I would rather walk my dog."

Tim passed on an exclusive invitation to attend a fellowship reception at Buckingham Palace, in the presence of the Princess Royal, President of the Animal Health Trust. Drinks and canapés were served in the Chinese Room in the Palace. I turned up a quarter of an hour late, much to the disgust of the Palace authorities who were waiting for me. Tim gave me no briefing in advance and I didn't realise how small this event was and who the other guests were. They included Lord Kirkham the founder of DFS and Lesley Graham and her husband who had set up the Animal Health Trust. Lesley Graham presented *Channel 4 Racing* and was well known in the horse world. I turned up with a black eye, which I received from the Esher match the previous Saturday, and this caught the eye of The Princess Royal, who likes her rugby. It was quite surreal standing there in Buckingham Palace discussing rugby with the Queen's daughter. I explained to her how thankful I was to be invited to the event and it was by chance because Rodders was unable to attend. She was not greatly amused and replied, "Oh I am glad we have got a use."

The following day was even more surreal, I attended *Friday Night with Jonathan Ross* at BBC Television Centre. We had booked Jonathan Ross for the Unique Pub Company Awards an event that we ran at the Imperial War Museum. He sent us some audience passes and Paul Sherrell and I went to see the show. I arrived to see a huge queue for the ticket office and thought I would chance my arm and see whether I could blag my way into the show by making out that Jonathan had left me some passes on the main reception. I spoke to the receptionist and she said that they weren't behind the desk and telephoned Hilary Briegel, the floor manager, to see where they were. Whilst she was doing that a young lady dressed in a full length coat, took me aside and said to me, "You look like you can handle yourself", referring to my black eye. After a brief discussion, she ended up opening her coat, revealing a full bunny-girl outfit, complete with stockings and bows. She suggested that I escort her into the studio as her minder. "How very odd." I thought, "but anything to beat the queue."

I later found out that her services were required along with a bin Laden look-a-like and a midget to play a trick on a producer who was leaving the BBC to go to Channel 4. The bunny girl was shown to her changing room and I never saw her again. I was taken by associate producer to the Green Room for some food here, Otis Lee Crenshaw, Bruce Forsyth, Fay Ripley and The Stereophonics were all relaxing. The Stereophonics love their rugby and I discussed my black eye with lead singer Kelly Jones. I watched the show and then returned to the green room for post show drinks, where I met Mike Morgan, one of the writers, and Jonathan Ross's agent, Addison Cresswell. At this point I thought my forty-eight hours couldn't have got any better, Buckingham Palace and the BBC. I decided to go home, but my inquisitive nature made me have a look around television centre before I went. That night *Top of the Pops* was being filmed and the playlist was: Hear Say – *Everybody*, Ryan Adams – *New York New York*, Macy Gray – *Sexual Revolution*, Oxide & Neutrino – *Rap Dis*,

PPK – *Resurrection*, Basement Jaxx – *Where's Your Head At*, Daniel Bedingfield – *Gotta Get Thru This* and Geri Halliwell – *Calling*. I was minding my own business walking down a corridor, when Geri herself came walking towards me with her stage dancers. Gerri looked at my black eye and asked very politely if I would take a picture of her and the dancers. I duly obliged and was invited to have a drink. At this point I thought I had pushed my luck too far and decided to go home. I called Alice to tell her about the unbelievable two days that I had experienced. I couldn't have told Rodders because he was "walking the dog."

Alice was becoming increasingly important to me. She accompanied me to Bermuda in November 2001 to play in the Classic for the "Classic Lions." The invitation I made her was very casual. If I didn't have a girlfriend by the time this trip came around then I would invite her as a mate. I had no intention of ever inviting anyone else. I just wanted to spend a few days with Alice on the island of Bermuda. We ended winning the tournament that year and I presented my shirt to Brian and Nancy Duperault, who kindly put me and Alice up at Paget Hall. My shirt still hangs in his study, which is a great honor given all the beautiful possessions in his house. I met Lynn Davis, the first British athlete to win an Olympic gold medal in a field event since Timothy Ahearne's victory in the triple jump in 1908. He warmed us up before each match. I also met the great JPR Williams who was a regular attendee of the classic. These were iconic men in their countries and yet unless you knew who they were you wouldn't have noticed them. They were humble and self-effacing. These are great qualities of super perfomers.

This trip to Bermuda was like no other. It was the first time that I had been to the island when it was not beautiful weather and we had to work hard at rugby. There were three games in one week and the standard was very good, with teams from all over the world. I was still playing for Esher, so I was fit enough to deal with this excessive amount of rugby. We ended up playing the Springbok's in the final, which was not a festival of running rugby and was probably one of the few occasions when I ended up fighting with the opposition on the pitch. I threw a punch and promptly received six back for my one whilst huddled like a hedgehog on the floor. Fortunately, the referee intervened and I came away intact. On this trip I realised that I wanted more from Alice than just a friendship. She wasn't having any of it, but then something changed in the New Year.

In 2002, Alice came up with a plan that enabled us to spend some more time together. Esher was in Division Two and their matches were all over the country. Alice was fed up with being in London at the weekends and we ended up booking nights in various bed and breakfasts in close proximity to our away games with Esher. We remained friends throughout all of this period, until on one of these weekend trips to The Howard Arms in Ilmington, she said, "Harvey, you know how you can date Porsches? Why do you want to spend so much time with a Volvo?" This was a very odd way for her to describe herself, but I realised what she was saying and that day changed my life forever. There were very few days after this that I didn't spend with my beautiful new girlfriend. I eventually moved out of Kensington Hall Gardens into Alice's room in Tonsely Place, Wandsworth. I had now gone from a five-bedroom house in Northampton, to a bedsit in West Kensington, to a room in Wandsworth, but it didn't matter. I was in Alice's bedroom, which was infinitely better than the arrangement I had with Tim and Paul.

The business was growing quickly and was hitting the targets we had set. However, despite its growth we still managed to enjoy ourselves. In February 2002, I took Holley Blake, a property firm, to Courchevel 1850, one of the most stylish places to ski in France, with over 600 kilometres of pistes close to Meribel and Val Thorens valleys. Holley Blake was there to celebrate a great year of trading and no expense was spared on this trip. Their business was flying and this was reflected in terms of what they asked me to organise. We stayed at Hotel le Kilimandjaro, which was newly opened and regarded as one of the most sought after chalet hotels in Courchevel 1850. The hotel was made up of eleven chalets, linked with underground connections that all had direct access to the slopes at the foot of the Pralong ski runs.

The clients who attended this event were all gregarious property people who were enjoying a great year. This was highlighted when one client, John Cutts, nicknamed the "Godfather of sheds," rejected the offer of club class flights to Courchevel, instead opting for a private jet to take him to nearby Chambery Airport. It was my job along with Thierry Assaf, our former Olympic skier, to make sure that these guys had the most exclusive ski trip that money could buy. At the time, Corchevel 1850 was one of the only locations where you could undertake motorised activities, which took place adjacent to Courchevel Altiport at 2,000 feet above sea level. We hired ski-doos for the afternoon and raced them around a track that had been built for us on the Ferme de Pralong. The trip was hardcore. The clients skied all day and then drank heavily during dinner. I had first met Simon Holley as a young graduate surveyor. He loved his rugby, having played for Saracens and Richmond, and expected me to drink regardless of whether I had to be the first to rise in advance of the guests the next day. Although his roots were in rugby, business had been good to him and he had developed a passion for polo and fine wine. He said it was the closest sport to his love of rugby, now that his legs had gone. The horses provided the speed, and he used his guile and ingenuity to steer them in the right direction.

Thierry Assaf loved wine and whenever he drank a fine bottle of wine he would steam the label off the bottle and record it in a journal. That night he was horrified to see Simon Holley playing drinking games using some of the finest wine that the Hotel le Kilimandjaro could offer. The incident that tipped him over the edge was when Simon ordered Château d'Yquem, one of the very best desert wines from Sauternes. The 1982 was €500 a bottle, and the guests and I downed it as part of the game. I later found out that the winegrowers at this famous château go to exquisite care to produce this wine and we had had a total disregard for its quality. The grapes were picked one by one at exactly the right moment, when their sugar content is perfectly balanced to produce wine of this quality.

Simon Holley, Simon Blake and Keith Dowley had a huge reputation in the market for doing things well. I saw this on the last day, when I was due to fly back to the UK with Simon Blake and one of his colleagues. We had a transfer booked for the morning to catch an early afternoon flight. However, this was cancelled and in its place I was asked to book a helicopter from Courchevel Altiport. Simon was keen to ski for another morning with his clients and have lunch with them at one of the restaurants on the slopes. We booked the helicopter and organised for their bags to be taken directly to the helicopter, but it was my role to make sure the clients got there in time for their slot. The slot was weather dependent as it was at 2,000 feet and there was no margin for error. Simon was oblivious to all of this. We had twenty minutes before the helicopter was to take off for its journey across the Alps to Geneva. Simon was still at the restaurant pealing the wax off a five-litre bottle of Gran Cru wine and toasting his clients. To make the flight we had to down our wine and ski down to the bottom of the Pralong ski run via a black run. I was not an accomplished skier and they were, and I had never felt so much stress in my life before. We caught the ski lift to just above our hotel, boarded a minibus and only just made the helicopter. If I had been wearing a heart-rate monitor when the helicopter took off, I am sure I would have been at my maximum heart rate. It was worth it all just for the flight across the Alps. At the time I wondered if there were many jobs that would have given me experience like this. That trip was memorable and it was the start of many more. Holley Blake set the benchmark for the most extraordinary client entertainment and we built a strong reputation for providing these types of experiences within the property market, and then within other sectors. We took groups to Barbados, Las Vegas, Monte Carlo, Paris and Fiuggi in Italy during that year.

We would always undertake an inspection trip with the client, in advance of the event. This was often more enjoyable than the event itself. Fiuggi was a fascinating place to visit. It was a hill town, one hour southeast of Rome, 2,500 feet above sea level. It originally gained fame in the fourteenth century, when Pope Boniface VIII claimed his kidney stones had been healed by the mineral waters from the nearby Fiuggi spring. Two centuries later Michelangelo extolled the virtues of the same water that cured him of what he called "the only kind of stone he couldn't love." Acqua di Fiuggi was sent in bottles to all of Europe's royalty. We stayed at the Grand Hotel Palazzo della Fonte, one of Europe's best-known grand hotels built in 1912.

The highlight of this trip was the gala dinner, held in Fumone Castle. The Marquis Fabio de Paolis, like many aristocrats with properties like this, had to find a way of generating income for restoration works. We were therefore able to hire his house, which had been where Pope Celestino V was imprisoned between 1295 and 1296. In the eleventh century it was a fortress and had commanding views of the Albani hills and the Liri valley in Lazio. On all of the trips we always tried to find locations that people wouldn't ordinarily get access to for gala dinners. These trips were all about eating and drinking and we found the best places all over the world to do this. A salesman often sells things that he is passionate about and I was passionate about travel, food, drink and discovering new cultures. We were handsomely rewarded for managing these events, but on most of the trips, and like the rugby before, I would have done them for nothing. I tried to go on every trip I sold, much to the disgust of my colleagues.

We ran a trip for NRG to Monte Carlo in 2002 and for the Gala Dinner we hired a beautiful French Riviera property, the Ephrussi de Rothchilds Villa and Gardens at Saint-Jean-Cap-Ferrat, overlooking the bay of Villefranche on one side and the Bay of Beaulieu on the other. It is one of the finest listed buildings on the French Riviera and for that night we used the nine gardens for drinks, and the house for dinner and a live band. Cap Ferrat was the summer resort of Europe's most elegant and wealthy denizens. To be able to spend time in a house built in 1905 by Baroness Ephrussi de Rothschild as her personal folly was an extraordinary experience.

We were always looking for an angle and our weekend to see France play England in the Six Nations Championship at Stade de France, on 2nd March 2002 was one of those legendary weekends. We left from Church Street, Twickenham, to join our clients at the Eurostar terminus at Waterloo. We hired two first-class carriages for our seventy-six clients. I waited in the queue for the passports to be checked in and one of our clients saw Peter Stringfellow, the proprietor of the famous nightclub Stringfellow's in London's West End. The clients on these trips always think that you know everything that is going on and asked me what he was doing travelling to Paris on Eurostar. I had no idea but like any good salesman, I thought on my feet. I told the clients that he hires first class carriages and fills them with clients and beautiful girls, who dance for them from London to Paris. He then books people into a five-star hotel and the beautiful girls escort you to the game, before returning home from Paris to London, where they repeat the antics of the outward journey for you one more time. This would, of course, be illegal and the account was, of course, a complete cock-and-bull story, but none the less I was very convincing. The clients wanted to know the price and I came up with an exorbitant price of £10,000 per person and whilst they felt that was quite steep they thought that they could justify it for the right client. It was at this point that I knew I could sell almost anything.

I had to audit a client's expenditure on hospitality once. As part of a report, I was exploring how we could provide "more bang for their buck." There was a mysterious figure of over £50,000 that no-one could remember spending. It transpired that had been frittered away in The Spearmint Rhino Gentlemen's Club, a rival club to Stringfellow's. This was hugely popular entertainment for businessmen as part of client relationship management in 2000, a period of ridiculous excesses.

In Paris we stayed in the Hotel Gare de Nord, which was luckily the hotel where the French rugby team was staying which added to the occasion. We saw the players that would be competing the following day in the hotel lobby. We arrived on the Friday night and had organised Olivier Brouzet, who I had played with at Northampton, to come and say a few words in a drinks reception at the hotel before the clients went off into Paris. It was special to have a player talking to us the night before the game. Olivier came from a rich pedigree of French sport. His father, Yves, was holder of the oldest French national record for shot putting with a throw of 20.20 metres and had represented France at the 1972 and 1976 Olympic Games. The next day was amazing for our clients. The Stade de France was off the canal Saint Denis, and we hired a Grand Bateaux to leave from the centre of Paris in the morning to cruise up the Seine and join the canal system at the lock of Suresnes. This was a fantastic way to see Paris. We departed from the Musée d'Orsay, along the Seine, passing under the elaborately decorated Pont Alexandre III, with views of the Petit Palais, the Grand Palais, the Museum of Modern Art and the Eiffel Tower. It was traditional to have a pre-match question-and-answer session, which was hosted on board by Tim Rodber, Matt Dawson and the legendary Didier Camberabero, who represented France thirty-six times from 1982 to 1993. This was a great way to arrive at an international stadium. The clients sat back and indulged themselves before watching a match where England were seen as favourites to win, after impressing in their opening two matches, with an easy win over Scotland and a devastating victory over Ireland. Sadly, they lost that day and France won the Grand Slam.

In the evening after the international we went out for drinks with Matt and Tim and were joined by Nick Duncombe, the reserve scrum half that day. He was the youngest member of the England Squad. He was at the start of what should have been an illustrious career and was being mentored by Matt Dawson, having attended the same school, the Royal Grammar School, High Wycombe. Sadly less than a year after meeting Nick he died, aged twenty-one, of meningitis. This brought back memories of losing Richard Langhorn.

The 7th April 2002 provided another unique opportunity to go overseas and watch sport; this time with Holley Blake, who took their clients and partners to see England v Italy in Rome. I last played in the Stadio Flamino on the 11th June 1997 for the Barbarians and was now returning with clients who were staying at the The Hotel de Russie. This was a five-star hotel located in the heart of the city between the Spanish Steps and Piazza del Popolo on the Via del Babuino. It was within walking distance of the ground and places like The Vatican City, St Peter's, the Sistine Chapel, Piazza Navona and the Trevi Fountain.

Our business was going well, so we invited all the staff from RTL for a long weekend in Rome, to watch the rugby, and Alice joined me. The Hotel had only been open since 2000 and was keen to impress marketing agencies like us. We were not meant to be staying in the hotel. We were in the cheaper hotel near the Coliseum. This was until I went to check Holly Blake into the hotel and the manager insisted that I stayed at the Russie. Alice and I were treated to the most fantastic suite, courtesy of Rocco Forte.

The clients attended the international, which England won with ease, and then invited Alice and me to join them for dinner at another hotel that I had booked, The Hotel Eden. We booked the corner table of the La Terrazza which overlooks the seven historic hills of Rome. It was one of the most scenic places to have dinner in Rome and, thanks to the generosity of Holley Blake, Alice and I experienced this with them. One of their guests was Jason Dalby, who had attended Wells Cathedral School with Alice and her three sisters.

I got to know Rome very well. However, there is one trip that remains particularly memorable. I was invited to fly to Rome by Alitalia and taken to The Hotel Splendide Royal in Rome. I was then treated to dinner before waking the following morning to be taken to some of the most magnificent private palaces in Rome. After a beautiful lunch I was taken to a station in Rome where the Orient Express was waiting to go to Florence. The celebrated train was reborn in 1977 thanks to an entrepreneur and rail enthusiast called James B Sherwood. In 1977 he bought two of the train's carriages at a Sotheby's auction in Monte Carlo. Over the next few years, he spent $16 million locating, purchasing and restoring thirty-five vintage sleepers, Pullmans and restaurant cars. This led to a maiden run from London to Venice and the rebirth of the Venice Simplon-Orient-Express.

I had imagined standing outside the gleaming carriages of the Venice Simplon-Orient-Express as a boy whilst watching old films that featured the train, like *Murder on the Orient Express*. I always imagined travelling in a bygone era. There were very few things I had aspired to do as a boy, but this was one of them. I was going to get a chance to be on the train's overnight trip to simulate what it would be like to go on a long journey. This was odd because the distance from Rome to Florence was only 143 miles and would take less than three hours to travel normally. However, they found a way of travelling through the night and stopping in railway sidings to kill time. As a boy I never expected to sleep on The Orient Express in the same carriage that Winston Churchill had enjoyed a good night sleep. I stayed in a wood-panelled compartment, which during the day provided compact carpeted sitting room with sofa and small table, and by night a bed and a washbasin. I had dinner in the dinning car, dressed in black tie whilst a pianist played to us. We eventually came in to Florence station in the morning and were taken to a private viewing of the Uffizi Gallery.

The Uffizi Gallery is one of the most famous museums of paintings and sculpture in the world. Its collection includes universally acclaimed masterpieces including works by Giotto, Simone Martini, Piero della Francesca, Fra Angelico, Filippo Lippi, Botticelli, Mantegna, Correggio, Leonardo da Vinci, Raphael, Michelangelo and Caravaggio. My highlight was to be taken down the Vasari Corridor, the raised passageway connecting the Uffizi with the Pitti Palace. This was built by Vasari in 1565 and was one of the most astounding architectural masterpieces of its time. It was normally closed to the general public, and the professor who guided me that day got emotional when he entered it, such was the honour to be invited to cross it. He told me that Hitler had had a fondness for the Corridor and the Ponte Vecchio, and spared both when the retreating Germans blew up all of the other bridges crossing the Arno as the Allies advanced on Florence in August 1944. The corridor contains the self-portraits of some of the most important painters in the world and was designed as a path for the royal family, the Medicis, to allow them to observe the crowd below. It was great to visit Florence again and to see *David* in the Academy of Fine Arts. This sculpture by Michelangelo is one of the most remarkable things that I have ever seen. It brought back memories from 1988 of The Basilica di Santa Maria del Fiore, where Neil Back punched me to the ground for dropping a camera.

That night I stayed in the Villa San Michele, a former monastery dating from the fifteenth century. The hotel was on a hilltop surrounded by trees and terraced gardens overlooking Florence. Michael Winner, the film director and producer, was also staying at the hotel whilst I was there, in his capacity as a food critic for the *Sunday Times*. This trip was a superb experience. Sadly I found it difficult to sell some of the contents of this trip. The cost was outside the realms of even our top corporate clients. I felt indebted to the Orient Express for giving me such an experience and did manage to use them for an amazing event for the clients of Prologis.

Prologis was a great client to work for and was led by Alan Curtis who had an expertise in developing large-scale modern logistics developments like Magna Park in Leicestershire, where he had cut his development teeth. He had become MD of Prologis in 1999 and had made the company the undisputed market leader. Prologis did business with a handful of people, the individuals and companies who supplied them with land, architects, lawyers, chartered surveyors and, of course, the occupiers of their buildings. It was my responsibility to ensure that RTL provided these people with unique experiences. Alan became a good friend. In those early days he was very exacting in terms of his requirements. They had to be "money can't buy" experiences. Budgets were never a problem, as long as we got the trip right.

The briefs were no more complex than this at this time. I had got to know that Rick Stein was a rugby lover. Rick Stein was a big name and I convinced his PA, Judy Macdonald, to let me bring Prologis down to Padstow. Rick appealed to our demographic, who were in their mid to late fifties. Alan had a great relationship with his wife Margaret and his was one of the first companies that included partners on their trips. This was one of the recipes for his success. We had to find a way of getting down to Padstow without spoiling the long weekend with a lot of travel. The only answer was to hire a private jet. No-one ever turned down an invitation to the Rick Stein Weekend, which Prologis ran every year since then.

I had never been to Padstow and had never met Rick Stein, but Alan Curtis liked the idea and was willing to take a risk with me. I went on the inspection trip in advance of the event. Alice and I drove down and booked ourselves into the hotel I intended to use, The St Enodoc Hotel. This hotel is in Rock, with views over the Camel Estuary towards Padstow, on Cornwall's rugged north coast. We had been invited to see a private demonstration by Rick Stein in his Seafood School, which he was putting on for guests who stayed in his hotel. We got to Padstow on a water taxi that left from a jetty five minutes walk from the hotel. We didn't know what to expect and were surprised when Rick Stein came out to his forty guests, who sat in rows of stools in front of his demonstration counter. On each of the chairs there was a copy of the menus he was about to cook and people sat bolt upright as if they were going to see the opera. The script was very simple. He demonstrated three dishes and then we compared these dishes to the ones his sous-chefs had cooked in the kitchens at the back of the School for us to taste.

Rick was nervous and Alice picked up on this and posed some questions to him to help through the first few minutes. The atmosphere soon lifted as we were handed, along with Rick, copious glasses of wine from the Tower Lodge Estate, which was located in the Hunter Valley, New South Wales, Australia. Rick had a thirteenth share in the estate. At the end of the demonstration, we were invited to meet Rick. We were very drunk at this stage and Alice uttered the immortal words, "Rick, your demonstration was superb, but you need to work on your delivery." At which point Rick invited Alice and me to his local pub to talk about it. Alice was a speech-writer and in that drunken haze felt that she could truly help the man who was a household name and an accomplished television presenter. He did not take offence and was in a good mood when we walked into the London Inn, a down-to-earth fishermen's local on Lanadwell Street. He was very well known in Padstow and as soon as we arrived a local wag was overheard saying, "Rick Stein in Padstow, well that's a rarity." He ignored this comment and ventured to the bar, where he was immediately approached by a local woman who was in tears and anxious to vent her frustration.

She said "Rick, you're an arsehole, you have put up all the property prices in Padstow and you don't buy Mick's mussels any more." Rick was incensed by the lady's comments and defended himself fervently. Alice appeased the woman, and Rick and the woman posed for a photograph with each other. Rick invited us to join him for a nightcap in the Seafood Restaurant. The restaurant was packed and it was difficult to speak to him without being interrupted by people who wanted his autograph. By the end of the night we were slightly the worse for wear and ended up giving Rick a lift home in our taxi, before we went around the headland to Rock. This was a great night and I knew that Alan Curtis and his clients would love it.

The first trip to Padstow was in 2002 and we spent two nights and three days in the St Enodoc Hotel. We ate and drank ourselves to oblivion, which was one of the criteria for the brief. The other was a visit to the Lost Gardens of Heligan, to please Margaret. The Gardens had been neglected for almost a century when many of the gardeners that had tended them had been killed in the World War I, it was truly amazing to see them be reborn. We finished lunch at the Old Custom House in Padstow on the Sunday and telephoned the pilots of our private jet who were standing by at Newquay Airport. It took forty minutes to get back to the airfield in Bedfordshire. It was difficult to top an event like this, but Prologis were a great client and I came up with a trip where I was able to repay the Orient Express for the superb trip that they had given me to Italy. The event was called a "Taste of a Bygone Era."

I managed to persuade the Orient Express to let me have a carriage on board the Northern Belle Grand Tour. This was marketed to rich Americans who wanted to relive the "land cruise" that was originally established in 1933. This was a cultural journey that allowed the passengers to discover the spectacular scenery of Britain and its unique history. We boarded the Northern Belle at Victoria Station before heading North to Edinburgh. This was a perfect way to travel and enjoy a champagne brunch. We stopped on the way for afternoon tea in the Grecian Halls at Castle Howard. Prologis events were all about food and drink, and when we re-boarded the train we were served dinner before our arrival at Waverley Station. It will be no surprise that upon waking the following morning at The Bonham, a boutique hotel in the West End of Edinburgh we left on a bus to go whiskey tasting. The Glengoyne Distillery was situated in a wooded valley in the southern Highlands of Scotland, close to a small river that flows into the famous Loch Lomond. There was a unique smell in the dark airy warehouses full of oak sherry casks from Spain where the whiskey was laid to mature for ten years or more. They told us a lovely story about the "angel's share", which is the whisky that is lost at a rate of roughly 1–2% a year because of evaporation through the pores of the wooden cask. I had visions of angels coming down late at night to enjoy a glass of Glengoyne.

The trip would not have been complete without yet another banquet, this time in the State Dining Room of the Royal Yacht Britannia. We entered the yacht via the Royal Brow, an honour previously reserved for members of the Royal Family and Heads of State. A Pipe Major played us on board prior to a tour and drinks on board the Royal Deck and views over the Firth of Forth. The Yacht was decommissioned in 1997 and Edinburgh was successful in their bid to become her new home when she was moored in the historic port of Leith. This was a superb experience and a chance to see some of the royal memorabilia still on board. We had a great night on board. The event was finished off the next day with a lunch in the Secret Garden, at the Witchery, a restaurant located at the very top of the Royal Mile, close to the gates of Edinburgh Castle in the heart of the Old Town. I flew back with the clients in a private jet propelled aircraft to Birmingham, having had one of the most indulgent weekends on board two of the enchanting forms of transport which really were a "Taste of a Bygone Era."

Our clients, Prologis, Holley Blake and BSH Home Appliances, did some wonderful events with us during this period. BSH sold brands like Bosch, Siemens and Neff, and were based in Milton Keynes. Once again, as with Alan Curtis at Prologis and Simon Holley at Holley Blake, there was a rugby connection. The Neff sales director was Mike

Jarrett, who was a season ticket holder at the Saints. Mike gave us some superb opportunities to work with him and as a consequence I had some memorable experiences. The first was Neff's Fifteenth Year Anniversary Celebration for their dealers in Dromoland Castle. I became used to hiring small private jets, but for this event Ben Rodber chartered a jet with capacity for 220 people and flew them to Shannon, twenty minutes drive from the hotel. Dromoland Castle, was one of the most famous baronial castles in Ireland. It was the ancestral home of the O'Briens, Barons of Inchiquin, who were one of the few native Gaelic families of royal blood and direct descendants of Brian Boru High King of Ireland in the eleventh century. It is set in over 410 acres of private grounds and is regarded as one of the most impressive and distinguished castle hotels in Ireland. There is a lovely story about Dromoland. The Lord Inchiquin ran the estate as a dairy farm, but was so hard pressed that he had to sell the castle, land and hunting and fishing rights to Mr. Bernard McDonough, an American industrialist in 1962. However, Conor O'Brien, the eighteenth baron, and his family still lived on the estate and continued to farm and run a sporting and leisure business there. We took over the whole hotel for one night and, as we came up the long curving driveway, a lone Irish piper welcomed us to the hotel.

Ben brought in the best Irish ghillies to teach the group fly-fishing in the lake opposite the hotel. Conor O'Brien provided clay pigeon shooting, golf was available on a course designed by Irish golfing legend, JB Carr. Ballymaloe Cookery School provided a cookery demonstration and the French Sommelier Pascal Venaut taught wine tasting. This was the first time I got a true understanding of the complexity of wine and it has fascinated me ever since. This was a very important event for Neff and its Managing Director Uwe Hanneck who hosted, along with Mike Jarrett, the banquet in the Brian Boru Hall in the evening where we created a theme of all things Irish. Jean Butler and Michael Flatley had made Riverdance and Lord of the Dance very popular, which meant that Ben needed to include this in the evening show and hired dancers from these shows.

This was one of the biggest events that Ben Rodber had put on and it ran so well that we were invited by Mike to tender for other work which the agency still does to this day. We were asked to come up with an incentive for a brand called Gaggenau. The brand was so desirable at the time that Raymond Blanc had installed a Gaggenau kitchen in his cookery school at Le Manoir Aux Quat Saisons. It had a huge reputation, so much so that the marketing spiel was, "We don't sell Gaggenau, we allow people to buy it." They were bringing out a fridge that produced clear ice and Ben Rodber came up with an incentive for the dealers to visit the Ice Hotel if they hit their targets.

The James Bond film *Die Another Day* had featured an ice palace, inspired by the real-life Ice Hotel in Jukkasjärvi, Kiruna, Sweden. This inspired Ben to come up with the sales incentive. The actual location of the Ice Hotel was 200 kilometres north of the Arctic Circle in the village of Jukkasjärvi, Sweden. The river Torne River provides the Ice that enables them to build a hotel which has to be rebuilt every year from 30,000 tonnes of snow and 3,000 tonnes of ice. We travelled by plane to Stockholm and stayed there for one night to break up the long journey. I had no expectations before going to Jukkasjärvi. It was different to any location that I had ever been to. We stayed there for two nights, with one cold night in the Ice Hotel and one warm night in the hotel chalets located next door.

There was a great sense of expectation when we arrived. We checked in and were given thermal suits and sleeping bags. As I was changing into my suit with the rest of the group, I noticed one of the women open her suit case to reveal high heals and an evening dress that she had brought assuming that she was going to a formal dinner. She obviously had no idea that for the first night she would not be attending a traditional gala dinner. Instead she would be drinking in the Absolut Icebar made entirely of ice and sleeping on an ice block and a thick mattress, covered with reindeer skins in a sleeping bag, in temperatures between minus five and minus eight degrees Celsius. You had to drink vodka in this bar, as this was the only drink that didn't freeze in these temperatures. Every room in the hotel had a theme designed by artists from all over the world who gathered together in this small village, close to the Arctic Circle, to create an exclusive art exhibition. One of the rooms had an Elvis theme, which was very odd. Every time you breathed, the vibrations would set off sound waves similar to the chords that you would hear in Elvis songs.

In the morning our guests were awoken with a mug of hot lingonberry juice, but this was not enough to convince them to stay another night. There were a lot of very disgruntled guests who, because of the cold, were not enjoying the experience. However, this soon changed when they knew that they would be moving to warm accommodation for the last night. We spent the morning on a dog sled tour. It sounded idyllic, being pulled over the snow banks by a pack of huskies; it was, but some of the group didn't enjoy the flatulence that came from the rear of the dogs. It was all they talked about as they drank coffee by a campfire in this amazing wilderness.

We went to the Ice Hotel in December and at that time of year there is only four hours of daylight in this part of Sweden. This is the best time of year to see the Northern Lights. The Northern Lights, or aurora borealis, are natural phenomena and provided us with an amazing light show. We saw them on an evening snowmobile tour, which lasted three and half hours. We ate supper that night in a Sami (Lapp) tent made of reindeer-skins and sat around a fire inside the tent eating smoked salmon and moose soup, whilst drinking lingonberry juice. The highlight was coming back from the supper for over forty minutes down the frozen Torne River at a speed of sixty kilometres per hour. I was driving a snowmobile with Ben Rodber screaming for me to slow down and the only light that I could see was the Northern Lights above me. What a memory. The trip to the Ice Hotel was far from corporate. It brought people closer together in the same way as the Ghana trip that I organised in 1996 had done. The guests could not stop talking about all they had experienced after they had slept well in the warmth of a chalet. I have never seen so many reindeer skins purchased in the shop before they left.

We grew a very significant business at the same time as having great fun. This was what it was all about. We had six directors and great staff who were all very passionate about what we were doing, and passion is infectious. People buy from passionate people and we were cooking on gas. We out grew Cobden House, the office that Paul had set up, and moved to Church Street, Twickenham. This soon became too small and so we moved to Brompton House, Kew Road, Richmond, which is where the business, now called RT Marketing, is located today.

I have learnt over the years that one of the recipes to successful people is their ability to constantly re-invent themselves. The move down to London was huge, but it was a moment outside the Petersham Hotel and a conversation with Tim Rodber that changed me and our lives forever. Tim had asked me to put together a sales plan, which I had never done before, and I had to enlist the services of another client and season ticket holder of the Saints, Roger Alexander, to help me do this. Roger Alexander was the former MD of the Emerging Markets Group for Barclaycard and I will always be indebted to him for taking the time to help me. I hadn't a clue about how to go about this, but it was very important to the business and our future. At the time it seemed like a huge undertaking. It described how in just five years RTL had achieved double-digit growth year on year, since its foundation in 1996 in Tim's chapel in Milton Malsor. We had evolved a fully integrated marketing communications agency with relationships with ninety clients, five of which were spending in excess of £100,000 and nine additional clients spending in excess of £50,000 with us each year. We predicted that we would make £4 million and this is exactly what we did. In fact, when we did the next review in October 2003 our turnover was £4,458,413.

It was in the cark park at the Petersham Hotel that Tim used some reverse psychology on me. I thought the meeting had gone very well and the results stood for themselves. However, Tim explained that he thought I was the worst word you could use for a woman's anatomy. I can remember the words distinctly. He said that as a rugby player I had the potential to play for England but didn't concentrate on achieving this objective. He then said that I had the potential to do well in business and he didn't want to see me squander this opportunity. He was perfectly clear about what he wanted me to do and he was exactly right. Sadly, on a Friday night in a hotel car park after a good meeting, I wasn't prepared for these remarks and I was slightly pissed off.

The next morning I asked a mate of mine, Michael Smith, whether I might be able to play rugby as a way of getting rid of some aggression and he called Michael Whitfield, the Barnes team manager, who told me to bring my boots along. The last time I had been on the ground we played on that day was for England A in a training session and here I was returning with Barnes Vets. London had a very strong Vets League, made up professional business people with a passion for rugby. Playing alongside Michael Whitfield was a hooker called Wyn James, who worked for Merrill Lynch, in financial management. He introduced Tim and me to Tim Griffiths, the MD of Williams Lea, the firm who purchased RTL in March 2003.

Tim Rodber had repositioned HTL as an outsourced marketing communications agency at the conference held the day before at the Petersham Hotel and when Wyn asked me what I did, I said that I worked in an "outsourced marketing communications agency." Wyn immediately picked up outsourcing and said, "You want to meet my mate, Tim Griffiths." He gave me his mobile number and like any good salesman I followed up the lead on Monday morning. Tim had joined Williams Lea from NatWest in 1984 as a management trainee and pioneered the establishment of Williams Lea FM, and was responsible for securing the company's first outsourcing contract with John Hepburn of Morgan Stanley in 1988. He was also a great lover of rugby. He agreed to have a meeting with Tim and me in his offices in Worship Street, just off Moorgate in the City of London. The meeting went well and Tim Griffiths arranged for his chauffeur to give us a lift back from the City to Richmond, which we both found quite impressive. Tim Griffiths got on very well with Tim Rodber. They seemed to share so many common interests. I can say in all honesty, the next time I saw Tim Griffiths was just a few days before Christmas in December 2002, when I got back form the Ice Hotel with Neff. Tim took me for lunch at Soho House, a Private Members Club in the heart of Soho. He was there to seek my approval, as a founding member of Rodber Thorneycroft Ltd, to purchase the business. Tim Rodber had developed a very strong relationship with Tim Griffiths and they shared a common vision for the future of our business. I gave my approval to enter into negotiations. Tim always did everything by the book and was probably one of the most trustworthy individuals that I have ever met with regard to matters like this.

Tim Rodber's conversation with me in the car park at the Petersham couldn't have been more pertinent. He was responsible for the strategic direction of our business and it was he who came up with an "outsourced marketing communications agency." We realised as a management team that we had to deliver the numbers we were targeting for our fiscal year. Williams Lea agreed to pay a multiple of ten on our net profit pre-tax. I wasn't hugely motivated by money, but when someone wants to buy your business it really does focus your mind.

The next time I saw Tim Griffiths was at the Lainston House Hotel, a seventeenth-century country house hotel in Hampshire. This was an opportunity for him to present his intentions for our business to the other directors and a chance for them to meet them in a more informal setting. They were all successful business people and had a lot of experience in this area, having either acquired or sold businesses. They were a huge help during this period and enabled us to make informed decisions. Some of the directors thought it was too early to sell the business, but some felt the offer was a good one and we should accept it. We took their advice and sold our business in March 2003.

We appointed DFA Law in Northampton to dispose of the business for us and it was relatively straightforward. It doesn't seem possible to think that Tim and I retired from Saints rugby officially at the end of the 2000/2001 season and then less than two years later we were selling our business to a large city firm. RTL was officially founded on the 5th September 1996 by Tim and me, and there wasn't a day that we had stood still. Tim gave us the profile that we needed in the early days and

Paul, David, Lesley and I had managed the business until he was ready to take it in the strategic direction it deserved.

We accepted the offer from Williams Lea despite getting a counter-offer from Nigel Wray and Dominic Silvester. The common denominator for meeting Nigel and Dominic was through rugby. I met Nigel Wray for the very first time at Paddy Johns' Testimonial Match at Ravenhill in 2002. I hadn't been back to this ground since I played in the Kegworth Air Disaster match in 1989. I had been asked by Paddy to play in this match and duly accepted. Johnnie Bell picked me up at the airport and took me to the hotel where Paddy Johns ("the Quiet Enforcer") welcomed us. I was looking forward to playing in the same team as him, but was told soon after arriving that he was in the opposition and they were the full Ulster side.

The match was being used as a curtain raiser before a big match against Leinster, the week after. This was quite a surprise given our back line were all over thirty and included Maurice Field, Alan Tait and Richard Wallace. It was a real pleasure to play in a match like this. I met Nigel in the after-match reception. He was a hugely successful and innovative businessman with directorships in over fifty companies, and yet was very humble. Nigel was the principle shareholder in Saracens Rugby Club and was there to support Paddy, who had played for him before returning to Ulster and his beloved Dungannon. I travelled back on the bus to the hotel after a large night with the Ulster team. We were all asked to sing a song and I sang *Mack the Knife*, the Bobby Darin classic, which went down like a lump of lead. Next up to the front of the bus were Paddy Johns, Willie Anderson and Brian O' Driscoll singing *The Fields of Athenry*. Three generations of Irish Rugby singing this Irish folk song, went down better than my feeble effort.

I met Dominic Silvester by chance coming out of Bank tube station and asked him for directions to Threadneedle Street. Dominic gave me directions and then remembered that we had played rugby against each other during my first visit to Bermuda in 1994, in the Easter Classic. In 1993 Dominic had set up in a business venture in Bermuda to provide run-off services to the insurance and reinsurance industry, which led him to become the CEO of Enstar Group Limited from 2001. He was also a director of Saracens. We remained friends after our chance encounter and he helped me get my head around selling the business. Tim met Nigel and Dominic before the sale of RTL and had taken the view that Williams Lea was the best option for us. We had a boardroom in Brompton House on a mezzanine level in a converted chapel. Williams Lea had their lawyer present, as did we. Tim was keen to close the deal by close of play on the Friday. Justin Barton was the finance director for Williams Lea and he was ensuring that things went smoothly via conference call. In the main contract there were no sticking points, apart from the "death clause" in the contract. The deal breaker for Ben Rodber was an onerous clause, which stated that, if any of us died within three years of signing the contract, any shares that we got in the Williams Lea company would not go to our dependents.

Williams Lea agreed to drop this from the contract for everyone apart from Tim and I. Instead they wrote into the contract that if we died within the first year, then the shares would revert back to Williams Lea. I debated this with Tim and our lawyers. It is comical looking back, but Tim took me aside, like so many of the rugby huddles I had been in with him over the years.

"Are you planning to die over the next year?"

"No."

"Nor am I. shall we sign the contract?"

We then visited our spiritual drinking hole and the pub that served the best pint of Guinness in London, Molly Malone's on the Kew Road, now The Hope.

We would go into Molly Malone's most Fridays after work and this day was no exception. We were joined by Tim Griffiths, Conor Davey and Justin Barton to celebrate the deal. We had a great night listening to Stevie-boy Carroll, as he was affectionately referred to. Steve was a musician/singer who played every Friday night in Molly Malone's and we loved listening to him. He operated an open mic policy during the night for any wannabe singers. On one particular night, Jaspar Burham, a friend of Tim's, had agreed to meet Tim and some other friends for a few beers in Richmond. One of their group was signed to East West records and was just about to bring an album out. The singer approached Stevie in Molly Malone's and asking him whether he could sing two songs from his new album whilst he played an acoustic guitar. There was a stunning girl in the pub at the time and he directed the song at her. *You're Beautiful* from his album *Back to Bedlam* was the first song he sang. The singer was James Blunt. I asked Stevie what he thought of his music and he said, "Very good, but unlikely to be a success". James Blunt sold eleven million CDs world-wide, going number one in eighteen countries. The next time I went into Molly Malone's, Steve was singing James Blunt covers.

I hadn't set up the business with Tim to sell it or make money. I just wanted it to be a success and to have fun making it successful. The by-product of success was money, and I felt very proud of Tim and the rest of the team for what they were able to achieve in a short period of time. It was life changing doing the deal with Williams Lea. The term "selling out" had good and bad connotations. Whilst we still had to hit our earn-out and on-going financial performance, we had picked a financial winner. This allowed me to do three major things – to buy a house and move out of the one bedroom flat I shared with Alice; to treat my dad to a trip to South Africa to thank him and Joy for all of the support they had given me over the years leading up to the sale; and lastly, but most importantly, to get engaged to Alice Victoria Bufton.

Chapter 23

Through the barricades

I planned to take Alice to the Heineken Cup quarter-finals in Toulose on Saturday, 12th April 2003. The Saints were playing and I had ear marked a trip, but this was just a ruse. I had asked her father's permission to take his daughters hand in marriage. I wanted to do it the traditional way, but hadn't expected the response that I got. Edward had been a senior partner in a law firm in Somerset and a rugby player. His first reaction upon hearing my question was not to grant me permission or congratulate me but to ask if I really knew her. It was an odd question but one that I felt qualified to answer. I have a great deal of affection for Ed. He was keen that his daughter and I had thought about the time-honoured tradition of marriage before we entered into it. I had a diametrically different mindset to Ed, being very right-hand brain, and so we battled our way through lunch before he eventually gave me his permission.

Dad and Joy's immediate reaction was happy relief. Finally someone had relieved them of their burden. They were very generous. They offered to sell me Mum's diamond ring at its market value, which was considerable. The sale of the business enabled me to buy it and as soon as I presented them with a cheque they donated this back to the wedding fund. I took that ring to Carcassonne, a walled medieval town in the Languedoc region of southwest France. I had visited this town with my parents during long, memorable summer holidays. Alice and I had flown there and picked up a hire car with every intention of booking into a hotel for the evening in another small walled village called Minerve. I didn't want to propose in Carcassone, although I had taken the ring with me.

It was the weekend of the Heineken Cup quarter-finals in Toulose and as a result a lot of Saints fans had gone out to watch the game. We went for lunch in the central square in Carcassone and sat with mostly Saints fans including Brian Thompson, one of my Dad's great friends and a former sponsor and great supporter of mine. It was hardly the best way to prepare for a romantic weekend. However, the great plan was to get engaged in a restaurant that I can remember sitting in with Mum, in Minerve, called Relais Chantovent, which had beautiful views over the river gorge. As we were walking down the ramparts of Carcassone I suddenly felt Mum's presence, which I hadn't felt since that week after her death in Sicily, sharing a room with Neil Back. The feeling was so strong that I felt compelled to get down on one knee and propose to Alice. She wasn't expecting it, but it was a perfect setting and she agreed to marry me. I telephoned Dad and Joy to tell them the news and where it had happened and Dad replied that Carcassone was one of Mum's favourite places and he had taken her there on holiday before she had passed away.

I told Alice the story of the ring and how my Dad had bought it for Mum, but she felt it was too valuable and hadn't dared wear it and so it had spent most of its life in the safe deposit box of a bank. She loved the history and the ring. I felt that my mum had inspired me with her spiritual presence to ask Alice. We ended up spending the rest of the weekend in Minerve and ate in the Relais Chantovent. It was the first time that I had drunk single vineyard wine.

The owner explained that the wine had been produced from a "terroir" within five miles of the restaurant. The grapes were all from one enclosed area and were harvested at the same time, and fermented in one bunch to ensure its purity. It was a special bottle. It wasn't expensive, but the owner of the restaurant selected it to reflect the moment of our engagement, whilst eating the gastronomique tasting menu. This was the best meal that I have ever had.

The negative reality of "selling out" was that I no longer had autonomy. I couldn't dictate how I planned my day. I had a primary responsibility for RT business development and had to attend all Williams Lea group sales and marketing forums with a view to introducing my new employer to senior level contacts. I had a new boss, Conor Davey, who was a great guy and so the transition was not difficult. He was a former hooker of Barnet Rugby Club, which is where he met Tim Griffiths. Conor was the Group Sales Director and was responsible for much of the new business generated by Williams Lea. I found myself commuting to the city from Twickenham. I couldn't understand why anyone would choose to suffer a daily commute like this. I tried everything I could to avoid the train and the drain. I boarded the train at Twickenham and stood all the way to Waterloo before qeueing alongside some of the most privileged people in the UK to squash myself onto the Waterloo and City Line, AKA the drain. You didn't need to be an expert in body language to sense the tension on the commuters' faces. They hated it as much as I did. I decided to buy a scooter and my route to work took in Richmond Park, Putney Bridge, Parsons Green, Chelsea Harbour and then views along the embankment, beautiful bridges crossing the Thames, the Houses of Parliament and Big Ben, the London Eye and the Bank of England. I got a true perspective of the importance of the Thames when London was a key trading centre during the British Empire. The river is less important now, but the buildings that line its banks are some of the most beautiful in the world. I loved passing the Tate Gallery, Battersea Power Station and Somerset House. I may have been escaping the commute with the rat race, but the scooter commute from Twickenham was a like being part of the grand prix in Monte Carlo. The pressure of the traffic and fellow commuters is immense. Every traffic light is like the starting grid of a big race. Cyclists go first, if they stop at the lights, scooter riders and motorcyclists go second and then those people who choose to drive to work in their cars. The lack of autonomy and the commute weighed heavily on me, but the financial motivation was too strong to ignore.

Tim took on a massive role at Williams Lea. He became the MD of the marketing support services division and was responsible for ensuring we hit our earn-out and on-going financial performance. He became an executive board member, reporting to Tim Griffiths, and his remit grew both in scope and geography as he moved into a global client service role. He eventually moved to the US. We hit our earn-out and whilst this was very important to my long-term future with Alice, it was insignificant compared with what was about to happen.

On the 12th November 2003 my sister died suddenly in her house in Hackleton, Northamptonshire. It was a shattering loss. She left behind two beautiful boys, Ben and Sam, and her long-term partner Simon. I loved my sister very much and her death was completely unexpected. I had lost four significant women in my life in a very short time, my mum, Nicola my sister, Edna my Nan and Marjory my grandma. They had each helped me to become the person I am. They were always there for me and provided me with the values that gave me the building blocks for a remarkable life.

My dad had lost his wife and his mother, and then had to bury his thirty-two-year-old daughter. This is not the natural course of events. My dad spoke at her funeral at Carey Baptist Chapel, Hackleton, on the 21st November 2003 and we sang two of Nicola's favourite hymns, *Make me a Channel of Your Peace* and *Lord of the Dance*, and listened to her two favourite songs, *Through The Barricades* by Spandau Ballet and *We've only Just Begun*, which was a cover sung by The Carpenters. That day I pledged to play a significant role in the Ben and Sam's life, and to help Simon in times of need.

What followed was a strange and terrible weekend for me and I don't know how I got through it. On Saturday, 22nd November 2003, England won the Rugby World Cup, with a breathtaking Jonny Wilkinson drop goal just twenty-six seconds from the end of a thrilling final in Sydney. Martin Johnson became the first player to lead a northern hemisphere side to the world title. We watched the full game at home and then got in a taxi during extra time, to go to Heathrow to board a plane to Florida. Ian Robertson was commentating on the radio in the car for Five Live during the nerve-wracking final moments in Sydney. Daws set up Jonny Wilkinson for the drop goal and Ian could barely control the emotion in his voice as the ball spun towards the uprights, with Rob Andrew shrieking in the background. This was a proud moment for me. I had played in representative sides with eight of the team that started that match and to see them win the ultimate prize and seal their destiny was hugely satisfying. I had experienced the ultimate low and high in the space of twenty-four hours. Dad insisted that I go to Florida in the same way as after my Mum's death he had insisted that I go the Sicily Sevens, "Take advantage of every opportunity, it is what your sister would have wanted".

We had been invited out to Florida by Alice's sister, Emma. Emma was married to Jim Stafford and his family was celebrating Thanksgiving in Florida. This was a chance to get away from the events of the last few days. We flew to Miami and travelled North to Manalapan. This was located south of West Palm Beach on a barrier island surrounded by the Atlantic Ocean on one side and the Florida Intracoastal Waterway on the other. We were visiting the house of Jim's uncle, Bill Ziff, who had brought him and his two brothers up with his three sons Daniel, Dirk and Robert. Bill and his family were very kind, knowing the loss that I had just suffered.

Thanksgiving is a special time for families in America and I felt honoured to be part of their celebrations. They were very sympathetic to my emotional state. The house was a little like a museum with a fully equipped gym that was adorned with original Michael Jordan memorabilia.Bill was very keen on botany and had recreated the grounds of his house and the beachfront as it would have looked before urbanisation. Huge trees that had been transported from all over the US were being irrigated in preparation for planting.

Bill Ziff was a publishing executive who led his family's company to become a forerunner of niche magazines. He was one of the most successful businessmen in America. I was inquisitive about how he had achieved his success. He explained that he had spent most of his life acquiring wealth and the remaining part trying to acquire health. I didn't know this at the time but he had prostate cancer. This pearl of wisdom changed my outlook on life. His house provided everything you could need to de-stress and unwind and we were made to feel very comfortable. His was a very successful family who understood the importance of that family and looking after their well-being. The lesson that I learnt was that many of us neglect our mental, emotional, physical and spiritual well-being in pursuit of a dream that never comes. My grandma had a sign on her kitchen wall, "Today is the day you worried about yesterday that never happened." Most of us neglect the one thing that is relatively easy to maintain, and that is health. Bill Ziff's comments resonated with me so powerfully that I totally changed my thought process from that day on. I wanted to make sure that despite selling the business I made the right life-choices for my family, my friends and my career. Sadly, my sister had made some poor health choices and as a consequence lived a short life. I had many conversations with her about this over the years and I had realised her answers to two questions designed to show how ready she was to change would contain very low scores. For the question, "Out of ten, how confident would you be to change your behaviour?" Nicola would probably have answered, "Two." And to the question, "How important is it to change?" she would also have said a low number. I miss her very much, she was a lovely person, but I know that I could not have made any difference to what happened to her. Her choices meant that she shortened what should have been a beautiful life with Simon, Ben and Sam.

I returned from Florida to the most amazing euphoria surrounding the World Cup, which started with the most well-timed Testimonial Evening held by Matt Dawson, held at the Royal Lancaster Hotel in Mayfair on the 27th November 2009, five days after the rugby world cup final. I can remember Ron Dawson (Matt's dad) and Tony Stratton coming into the office for some advice on his year. The only advice I gave them was to put together a really good testimonial committee for the London event. They were extremely shrewd in holding it after the Rugby World Cup and it was very well supported and broke records in terms of money donated on the evening.

Daws has amazing luck. He told this great story about when the England team were flying back from Australia on the Monday after the final and going through customs' x-ray machines, and they kept going off and he had to keep going back through. He removed his shoes, loose coins, his phone and belt, and yet the machine kept going off. Daws eventually revealed the true reason why it was going off to the customs guards. Around his neck he had his World Cup winning medal. You can imagine how that went down with the Aussies.

The week of the 8th December 2003 was a week of dinners to celebrate the Rugby World Cup. I had decided that at any major event that I attended after Nicola passed away I was going to get autographs from any famous people who were there for Ben and Sam, so they knew that they were always in my mind. I have got them some great signatures. The first dinner I attended that week was at the Grove, put on by Saracens, as a guest of our client Stephen Hemsley, the CEO of Domino's. This was good timing as it was the day that England's Rugby World Cup squad completed an unprecedented day of national celebration with a champagne reception at 10 Downing Street. The day had started with a victory parade in central London, then on to Buckingham Palace to have a team photo with the Queen and her corgis.

A great story was told at the dinner about Dorian West. The players had been briefed about greeting the queen, as there are traditional ways of going about it. Usually the main thing to keep in mind is to be courteous and bow your head. You have to stay quiet unless you are spoken to and Dorian was not prepared to honour these traditions. Dorian was a salt of the earth, working class lad who wanted to honour his roots. Richard Hill recalled how all the players were lined up waiting for the Queen to meet Dorian and anticipating him giving her the royal snub. Disappointingly, he folded at the last minute and gave a small curtsy. On the bus journey through the West End of London, Jason and his teammates enjoyed more than a few beers on board thanks to Tetley. Sadly, they didn't have a toilet on the bus so when Jason was caught short he found himself having to urinate into a champagne bottle under the cover of his teammates. This was fine, but when they arrived at Buckingham Palace to meet the Queen there was no hand basin to wash his hands.

On Wednesday 10th December 2006 I attended Lawrence Dallaglio's Testimonial Dinner at Battersea Park. Lawrence, like Matt Dawson, put on some superb events for his year and this one was no exception. I entered the park on my moped from Twickenham to see a traffic jam of cars waiting to get to the marquee that had been placed there for the Christmas period. Most of the squad was there to support Lawrence and the security around the players was huge. There was still some good banter, none more so than that received by Mike Tindall who was quizzed about his involvement with Zara Philips. He claimed they were "just mates", but it wasn't long before they then moved into a cottage on Gatcombe Park, which is where I had been introduced to her through Land Rover. Lawrence, like Matt, timed the moment to have a testimonial to perfection and raised a huge amount of money. The headline act that night was Kim Wilde, who Lawrence had seen play in an 1980s revival concert in Sydney with The Human League, Belinda Carlisle and Go West just days before the World Cup Final. He convinced her to play at his testimonial and she sang the famous track *Kids in America*.

As the year turned I had to think of the future, which was no longer going to just revolve around me. Alice and I were getting married on 29th May 2004 and I had a wedding, two stag dos and a honeymoon to plan. In the build up to my wedding I really got fed up with those energy sappers (like Hot Chocolate Nigel) who would be negative when I mentioned that I was just about to have the best day of my life. The sort of comments that I would get back would be, "Enjoy your last days of freedom", or, "Make sure you enjoy it because it goes by really quickly". I was determined to prove them wrong and enjoy every element of getting married. I couldn't decide on who to have as a best man, so I chose two best men. Yaser Martini and Jake Richardson. They were responsible for the two stag weekends.

Jake organised a monumental day at out at Franklin's Gardens to see Northampton beat Harlequins on the 26th March in his private box on the half way line. Northampton fly-half Shane Drahm landed a conversion seven minutes into injury time to secure this crucial victory, which set us up for a night in Auntie Ruth's. There were over thirty boys on the lash, including my father and future father-in-law. Yaser was charged with organising the overseas leg of the trip to Marrakech. Marrakech, exotic and mysterious, was only three hours by plane from Gatwick, and La Mamonia Hotel was just fifteen minutes drive from the airport.

The former Moroccan Palace, now a hotel, was set within the twelfth-century ramparts of this ochre city. We had decided that on our first night a five-star hotel was in order. The hotel's idyllic gardens were almost 300 years old. We spent the morning relaxing by the pool until our 4X4 arrived to take us into the Atlas Mountains and its views. We had a driver booked for a two-day trip and headed out, southeast of Marrakech, and after twenty kilometres drive it was like being in a different world. We visited the Berber villages of Aghmat and Dar Caid Ouriki, before arriving in Ouarzazate, the so-called "Gateway to the Sahara". There was a strange and empty feeling to Ouarzazate. We were supposed to be on a stag do, but there was no alcohol served in the restaurant we ate in. The only place that you could get alcohol was in the hotel bar. We entered the bar and it was unusually busy for a small town like this. We didn't realise that this town was a film-making location, with Morocco's biggest studio located just down the road. The crowd we stumbled across was filming *Kingdom of Heaven*, a Hollywood blockbuster directed by Ridley Scott. We ditched our excursion into the Atlas Mountains the next day in favour of a private tour of the set of the *Kingdom of Heaven* film. The set was unbelievable. It had been built at a cost of $13 million dollars and the extras were there in their thousands, depicting Saladin's forces besieging the walls of Jerusalem.

We returned to Marrakech and watched as the Djamaa el Fna square and the medina were setting up. We sat in a roof top café as the square came to life. Monkey handlers, acrobats, snake charmers, fortune tellers, henna artists, smoky and brightly-lit food stalls, storytellers, actors, singers, healers and fakirs were all going about their business. This square was the geographical, cultural and social centre of the medina and had been formerly used for executions, hence its name "Dead Men's Square". Now it is a World Heritage site.

That night we stayed in a simple riad close to the centre and had an early evening drink on the roof whilst storks nested on roofs. It was an amazing sight as they took off and flew above the rooftops. The stork is a holy bird in Marrakech and they are protected by law.

This stag weekend set us up beautifully for an amazing wedding. As a bloke I don't think I'd imagined where I was going to be married. I had reached the tender age of thirty-five and was just pleased that Alice had agreed to marry me. I think in my mind I envisaged a wedding like that of Angus and Laura, at "St John's Church, Stoke Clandon, Somerset" from the film *Four Weddings and a Funeral* and I got just that, Dindar Church, near Wells, Somerset. We had a reception in a marquee in the paddock of Manor Farm where Alice had grown up. I had lived *Four Weddings and a Funeral* in reverse. I had lost Mum, Grandma, Nan, Nicola and attended all of their funerals, and now I was at my wedding. I had lost four very special women in my life and I was marrying Alice who was one of four girls.

Alice and I stuck two fingers up to those energy sappers who had told us to enjoy our wedding day because it goes by so quickly. Instead, of a wedding day we had a full-on wedding weekend. Nothing could have prepared me at the time for the feelings I had as I stood in an ancient church waiting for Alice to arrive, which she finally did fifty-five minutes late. The church was packed and Alice took it all in her stride. As for me, I was a blithering idiot. This was not good because the church was the most important part of the proceedings for Alice. Alice and her three sisters had all gone to Wells Cathedral

School, a musical school, founded in 909 AD. Alice had grown up with some talented musicians and they were all there and performed for us at Dindar. Alice's family was like the Von Trapp family in *The Sound Of Music* and everyone played a part in our day. Alice's three sisters all performed. Emma and Sarah read as Catherine played a trumpet fanfare with Nick Zagni, who had played in the Portuguese Symphony Orchestra. Holly Slater, Alice's best friend, a tenor saxophonist who won the young jazz musician of the year in 1996, played, *The Nearness of You* whilst we were signing the registers, and Tim Rodber was equally impressive organising the ushers and reading at the church. As I stood there in that church, I didn't doubt for a moment what I was doing and that it was a lifetime's commitment. I was married to the most beautiful girl in the world. I had hoped that she would be my wife from the first moment I had met her and my dream had come true. In his best man's speech Yaser said, "Beautiful women fall in love with ugly men in Harvey's World".

We left the church in a vintage car and arrived at our reception. The marquee over looked the Bishop's fields, with direct views of one of the most beautiful cathedrals in the country. It was filled with family and great friends from our past. I visited all the tables and talked to everyone. A conversation that stood out was one that I had with Ben Cohen, who at this time was at the very peak of his fame as a Northampton Saint, England and Lions legend who had just won the World Cup. I was truly honoured to have him there and told him so. He gave me a big hug and congratulated me. A passing comment of his took me back: "They still don't chant my name at Franklin's Gardens." I looked at him in bewilderment; here was a man that had achieved everything, a European Cup, Grand Slam, Lions Tour, World Cup and MBE, and still it wasn't quite enough. I was astonished that this man who I had watched with such admiration and whose ambition still burned brightly desperately wanted his home crowd to chant his name as they had done with me.

I enjoyed every minute of our wedding day, the Pimms flowed, our guests drank 880 pints of bitter and lager, ate Mendip lamb from up the road and we toasted each other with champagne. The band played into the night and everyone was on the dance floor until the very end. I hugged Paul Grayson, as we sang *Hey Jude*, the last song of the night, at the top of our voices. The hog roast the next day was like the scene from every morning after and a great opportunity to see everyone before we departed for our honeymoon in Italy. Ashley Redmond stole the show. He was up all night drinking with some of Alice's mum's neighbours and returned the next morning barefoot in his morning suit.

So there you have it, one becomes two, the most perfect feeling in the world. That day in Dindar Church I had entered into a contract which was binding for the rest of my life. I made a mental note that life would be different and, having always been someone that had done what I wanted when I wanted, I now had to make sure that I now took my wife into consideration. I had entered a different phase in my life. There is something very satisfying knowing that you are committed to someone for the rest of your life and many of the things that had mattered to me before our marriage no longer seemed important.

The other poignant thing about a wedding is that, afterwards, how often do you get to see the guests that you invite to your wedding? It is as if that group of people who you have shared significant moments with in your single life are there to bear witness to this state of transition. The nature of life is such that you will probably never get all those people in the same room again. There is something about a wedding that brings people together. This is not just the food, alcohol and party spirit, but the notion that this is one of the most significant moments of anyone's life and an institution that is not one to be entered into lightly.

Marriage like any decision in life is a risk and not everyone gets it right. I wanted to make sure that I gave Alice no reason to ever doubt my commitment to her. This involves a mind-shift, which fundamentally changed me as a person. No-one gave me a road map of how to manoeuvre myself through this transition. I could only make decisions based on previous experiences. In my dad and mum, I had world-class role models and many of the decisions I make as a married man are based on what I saw throughout the most blissful upbringing that anyone could ever have. My grandparents were also wonderful advocates for marriage. Failure to me would not be living the rest of my life with Alice. I am acutely aware that along the way there are going to be setbacks and challenges, but they are minor in the overall purpose of being married. We used to have this expression in rugby which is, "You've changed", when someone showed unusual characteristics. I did change that day. That doesn't mean that I don't step back into my old world from time to time, even now, but I don't want the same things any more.

Our honeymoon to Italy was a surprise to Alice and something she had always wanted to do. I enlisted the help of Michael Libotte of Fourth Dimension, Italy's leading Destination Management Company, to help me put together a trip of a lifetime and they did not let me down. We wanted to travel all over Italy and I booked us a Jaguar X-type saloon for these journeys. We arrived to pick it up and they didn't have any available, so we were upgraded to a Mazda RX-8. There were very few of these cars in Italy, having only been launched in early 2003. It was a beautiful car to drive through Italy in. We flew in to Milan Bergamo Airport and headed to one of the most beautiful hotels I have ever stayed in on the shores of Lake Garda. The Palazzo Arzaga was built in the fifteenth century and our room had frescoes in the style of Guido Reni, the famous Italian Baroque painter. The palace had previously been used as a monastery. The hotel was privately owned by the Lanni della Quara family and was the perfect retreat for two nights before driving 310 kilometres to Castello di Verrazzano in the heart of Chianti. We travelled right down the middle of Italy, through Bologna and Florence. The Castle of Verrazzano was on a hilltop in the Chianti Classico area, the first grape-growing and wine-producing area in the world to be determined by an official proclamation, made by the grand Duke Cosimo III de' Medici in 1716.

We were staying in a house that the week before had been occupied by Morgan Freeman, the American Actor. There was a strong connection to the United States because the family had produced a navigator called Giovanni da Verrazzano, who was the first European to enter in the bay of New York and as a consequence the The Verrazzano Bridge in New York was dedicated to him. This brought many American tourists to the Castle. Luigi and Silvia Cappellini had acquired the estate in 1958 and had replanted Verrazzano's vineyards.

Whilst we were in Tuscany we visited Siena. I was keen to see the Piazza del Campo where the Palio Horse race has taken place every year since 1644. Only ten horses compete in Palio around the Piazza del Campo and the race is over in around seventy-five seconds. It is a festival that attracts people in their thousands. We travelled from the Castle of Verrazzano 100 kilometres east, to Gubbio in Umbria. This ancient town is on the lower slopes of Mount Ingino. It is rich in history with medieval, gothic and renaissance buildings and a Roman amphitheatre just outside the town. We were having dinner one night in a restaurant when we were approached by an American, who had noticed that we were English and came to chat to us. We were invited back to his wife's family's house for a grappa. We had no idea until we entered their house on the Piazza della Signoria that Rick's wife was an Italian countess and she owned most of the property on the square. I was fascinated by the house, which was a series of inter-connecting doors, full of magnificent works of art including Roman busts taken from the amphitheatre.

We travelled from Gubbio to the Grand Hotel Ambasciatori in Sorrento, which is the hotel that is perched on the cliff overlooking the sea, with a breathtaking view of the Gulf of Naples and Vesuvius. This was a journey of 450 kilometres. I had always wanted to visit the Amalfi coast and places like Positano, which I had seen in the film *The*

Talented Mr Ripley. We visited the Island of Capri and organised a private boat with a captain to take us around the turquoise waters to some of the most secluded bays and other beautiful parts of the island. Our last part of the honeymoon took us a further 300 kilometres from Sorrento to Civitavecchia to board a ferry to Olbia in Sardinia. This was our last destination before flying home. We had indulged ourselves in all that Italy had to offer.

The matrimonial home is a very different place to the house we lived in before we were married. We returned to everyday life and changes needed to be made. One room in our house contained boxes that had been deposited from my life in Northampton. I hadn't had time to unpack them and so, according to Alice, there couldn't have been anything in there that was of any value. To me my boxes contained my life before I met her. You cannot imagine how much joy I got opening the contents to reveal countless memories. The contents of my Dad's attic, three of my own houses in Northampton and "stash" from more than twenty years of rugby were revealed. I couldn't have written this book if I had thrown away these memories. It is one thing keeping rugby shirts, but shorts and rugby socks seem illogical. Jonnie Whitehead's compilation tapes seemed a necessity when they first entered the box, but in 2004 no-one used tape recorders any more and time had taken its toll in this way on much of the contents. The trouser press that had been the height of luxury would never take pride of place in the matrimonial home, despite the enormous practicality of this treasured Christmas present. I had kept a pair of Adidas Flanker boots, which my Dad bought me as a gift for my first match on the wing for an England Colts game. I was the only winger who wore forward boots and when we realised this was soon rectified, Dad had them cut down to size, but sadly they were cut too short and they kept sliding off my heel. Letters from former conquests, programmes from junior school sports day, BAGA Awards, cycling proficiency tests, Boys Brigade Badges, O-level and A-level Certificates, postcards, lots of photographs and old pairs of Church's shoes each had a special place in my heart. The odd thing is that I could recall every name on the Chiltern School Football Team and I hadn't seen them for twenty-seven years. The room of boxes was soon whittled down to an under-eaves space in the attic. I am a serial horder and it was very painful to cleanse my life in this way, but I felt a sense of satisfaction when I was strong enough to let go of my mementos.

The popularity of the world cup players continued throughout 2004 and for none more so than Martin Johnson. His public persona changed the moment he lifted the World Cup in Sydney in front of a television audience of 14.5 million people. I had watched Johno's career with great admiration from the moment he was called down to Twickenham to replace Wade Dooley on Friday 15th January 1992, from the England A hotel. His notoriety allowed him to have nine worldwide testimonial dinners in Singapore, Bermuda, Johannesburg, Paris, London, Auckland, Sydney, Dubai and Hong Kong organised by my old room mate Matt Poole, who he was close friends with from the Tigers days. I attended the event on Tuesday 9th November 2004 at the Fairmount Southampton Princess Bermuda, where 700 guests paid over £300 each to hear Francois Pienaar, JPR Williams, Bob Dwyer and Martin speak. I was playing in the World Rugby Classic for the Classic Barbarians and we were invited to this event.

I sat down with Martin again in January 2005 at an event at Stableford Park in Leicestershire. A law firm called BLP were entertaining Barclays at a senior level, which included the head of UK Banking, Peter Harvey, and thirty of his senior team. They were keen to build a strong relationship with Barclays and decided, through me, to ask Peter and his team what they would like to do. I went to see Peter to discuss ideas with him. He was recovering from Bell's palsy, an illness that causes weakness of the facial muscles on one side of the face. He had originally thought this it was a stroke and it had caused him great stress, and he was keen to make sure that the team he managed didn't go through the same ordeal as him. He agreed that his senior management team should attend this event, aptly named "Peak Performance", which looked at work–life balance and the importance of physical intelligence, which manifested itself in fitness, nutrition, stress reduction and re-generation.

The team who delivered this event were Frank Dick, Michel Roux Jr (the marathon-running chef), and Alice, and Martin Johnson. Frank Dick used a metaphor in his speech, about life being like a "three-lane highway". In the outside lane was your career; in the middle lane your family, friends and environment; and your inside lane was yourself. He said that if any of those lanes cross, it affects the way you perform and most people don't get out of their career lanes unless someone rudely interrupts them (Peter Harvey was interrupted by Bell's palsy). The penny dropped. I had sold my business and received in return a lifestyle that was more like that of Peter Harvey the business man rather than that of Martin Johnson the rugby player. Martin Johnson had been through a huge amount of stress in his life, but appeared to be able to keep the lanes in his "three-lane highway" running in parallel. He had lost his mother Hilary to cancer in 2002, his wife Kay had given birth to their first child and he had led his club Leicester to all the major honours, winning four successive league titles (1999–2002) and two European Cups (2001 and 2002), and England to the 2003 Grand Slam and The World Cup. He was a perfect practical example of how to perform at your optimum, whilst looking after important relationships and managing your health and well-being.

Martin articulated in a simple way the importance of looking after yourself and was very open about the loss of his mother. I sat down with him over a cup of tea and he hadn't changed at all. He was extremely humble about his achievements and I think this is a quality that super performers like him all display. They have nothing to prove to anyone but themselves. We paid handsomely to have Martin Johnson at this event, but for him it wasn't about the money. It was about being part of a team and giving 100%. He stayed with the guests until very late that night and appeared to enjoy a fine meal in the dinning room of one of England's finest stately homes. The content that we delivered changed the delegates' mindsets. Peter Harvey became a good friend and participated some years later in a 900 kilometre, Pyrenees Cycling Charity Challenge, from Biarritz to Perpignan through the Pyrenees raising £68,495.

It was all well and good wanting the lifestyle that I had had as a rugby player, but this was wholly unrealistic. I was living a completely different life to the one I had in Northampton. I now worked in the city and commuted to work. My salary had increased to reflect the level of responsibility that I now had, but I had to report to a boss so I had lost my autonomy. I was charged with selling a "global Marketing outsourcing solution" to Williams Lea's clients that was like Woodrow Wilson's principle of self-determination: great in principle, but appalling in practice. It soon became apparent that few companies were willing to outsource their marketing to Williams Lea, it was too emotive. We had no way of knowing this until we tested it and Williams Lea was willing to take the risk. This didn't stop us selling Rodber Thorneycroft into some major companies, like Scottish Courage, PWC, Deutsche Asset Management, Oracle, Punch Taverns and Investec. It was great to work directly for Conor Davey who, like Tim, knocked the rough edges off me and made me better at my job. We adopted many of their working principles and raised our brand profile in the market place. Tim Griffiths left the core business to run itself. It was even allowed to retain its name. I had a vested interest in making sure that my contribution added to the unbelievable growth curve that Williams Lea was experiencing.

Our settlement for selling RTL to Williams Lea included part cash and part equity. At the time, it was more risky to take shares in Williams Lea than cash. This was because they only vested if Williams Lea were to either float on the stock exchange or be acquired by a competitor. The business had been around since 1820, so the likelihood of anything happening during my service agreement of three years appeared remote or so I thought. I had 27,776 ordinary shares in Williams Lea and how I wished I had taken the whole settlement in equity. The only thing I needed to do to retain these shares was to carry out the duties required of me under the terms of the service level agreement and not be a "bad leaver." I may not have felt passionate about selling outsourcing, but I believed in the senior management team, who were all extremely self-effacing and very approachable. Conor encouraged my slightly unconventional corporate style. He said that I had no place in a corporate environment, but if he needed some one to contact the pope then he would give me a call. I did feel shackled working in a big organisation, but I realised that it was for a finite period of time and to be part of a successful company like Williams Lea was a superb experience The experience was short lived, the global marketing outsourcing proposition was never really part of the core Williams Lea offering. Williams Lea had expanded into Europe and the United States, and I saw an opportunity to help Nigel Wray and Dominic Silvester buy back Rodber Thorneycroft from Williams Lea. I was charged with the responsibility of going to see Tim Griffiths, in his office in Worship Street, to see whether he would consider selling it to Nigel and Dominic. This was a difficult conversation given the fact that Tim had only bought RTL in March 2003 and just two years later we were asking him if he would sell it back to the investors who had interested him in it in the first place. Tim was congenial about the whole proposition and entered into negotiations, which led to the business being sold in August 2005. I was rewarded with a bonus for putting the deal together and was able to retain my shares in Williams Lea and could never be a "bad leaver" under the terms of my service level agreement, because I no longer had any obligation contractually with Williams Lea. There was still no value in the shares, because there was no free or open market in which we could trade them as Williams Lea was still a Private Limited Company, but less than a year after we sold the business to Nigel Wray and Dominic Silvester Williams Lea announced that they had signed an exclusive agreement with Deutsche Post World Net to acquire a majority equity stake in their business. They became the principal investors and offered a huge amount for the shares; happy days.

This was an exciting time for Rodber Thorneycroft; the business was growing very quickly and I was back doing the thing that I enjoyed most, which was selling the core business and attending events. The city was flying and we benefited. In April 2006, I got a call from Dominic Silvester to go to his house in Weybridge for lunch. Dominic is one of life's gentlemen and had been highly successful. He asked me whether I was enjoying Rodber Thorneycroft. I replyed that I was still passionate about the work we undertook, but the environment I was working in was not particularly enjoyable. He was kind to me and said that I was free to leave Rodber Thorneycroft and Nigel and he would back me in anything that I wanted to do. He didn't go into the reasons why they were allowing me to go, but some of the stories he told me about similar situations that he faced in his career will stay with me forever. I walked out of Rodber Thorneycroft's office two days later and set up Harvey Thorneycroft Ltd in April 2006.

I was nervous about setting up again. Starting a new business is very difficult. However, I had a chance to create something I was proud of, on my own. Rodber Thorneycroft, which soon became RT Marketing, was no longer my business. I had been an employee since March 2003 and the chance of having total autonomy was extremely appealing. I had a blank canvass to do anything that I wanted and the full financial backing of Nigel Wray and Dominic Silvester. I inherited some projects, and by default clients who wanted me to deal with them. I set up in my kitchen in Haggard Road and registered a new company. I wanted to prove to myself that I was capable of running my own business. I wasn't bothered by the short-term setbacks that I encountered during those early days. I went back to the basics of running events. However, this time around I had a great deal more experience and contacts.

I carried out a feasibility study on corporate wellness, so I was being paid to research a subject that I had a great deal of passion and interest in. I spent a year looking at the way that leading organisations look after their clients, employees and partner community. I read the leading books in this field by authors like Malcolm Gladwell, Jack L Groppel, Patrick Holford, Jim Loehr, Stephen R Covey, Jim Collins, Seth Godin and Nassim Nicholas Taleb. These people were some of the leading business writers who delivered metaphors around risk, body language, creativity, subconscious and conscious decision making, leadership, teamwork, corporate health, success, stress reduction, nutrition, regeneration fitness and much more. The reading was valuable, but I discovered that none of the authors were saying anything new. They were just using different metaphors to help people resolve modern-day issues. The same subject matter was around during the time of Socrates, Aristotle and Plato. There was obviously a market for this material because many of the authors were in very high demand on the speaking circuit and had best selling books. You wouldn't believe the cost of trying to get these speakers over from the United States. I had an idea: that I would try and recruit the UK equivalents of these authors. I wanted to find people who had interesting stories and who had achieved personal success in different walks of life.

The first person I consulted about this was Frank Dick. He was renowned as one of the country's best motivational speakers. For over fifteen years he developed a range of keynote speech themes, workshop topics and bespoke employee development programes, which he had delivered to some leading organisations. He had been the Great Britain athletics coach in the golden age and had coached some of the best talent in the world, including Boris Becker and Daley Thompson. I had heard Frank speak on many occasions and very often got that hairs-on-the-back-of-your-neck feeling. It was my intention to create an academy of motivational speakers, with Frank at the helm mentoring the other members.

This was a great idea in principle, but in practice it was too difficult to put together. Many of the speakers we worked with were highly competitive and the notion of sharing their material was unrealistic. However, we did manage to find some very interesting people who between them addressed some of the issues that businesses feel are pertinent to them, when in reality they are generic to all businesses. These included names like Alan Chambers (the Polar Explorer), BJ Cunningham (an independent brand marketing expert and keynote speaker), Dr Dorian Dugmore (Director of Wellness International and a Wellness Coach at Adidas UK), James Cracknell (a double Olympic gold medallist), John Harle (the musician) and Sahar Hashemi (the co-founder of Coffee Republic). It also included the crown jewels of British Rugby, Jonathan Davis, Lawrence Dallaglio, Matt Dawson and Keith Wood.

Alice discovered Caspar Berry, who started his career as the lead in the first BBC1 series of Byker Grove, alongside Ant and Dec. He went on to read economics and anthropology at Cambridge where he became a professional film writer. At twenty-five he had a "quarter-life crisis" which he resolved by becoming a poker player in Las Vegas. He returned from the United States and co-founded Twenty First Century Media, an audio visual media company in the North East of England. He was the poker adviser on the James Bond movie, *Casino Royale*. Caspar was like Frank Dick. His speeches were uplifting and made me think differently about my propensity to take risks and over come my fear of failure, which is something I have never been able to shake off.

Caspar's life, like many successful people, was one of re-invention. He used the metaphor of poker as a fun and original way of getting people engaged and to think about business and life. Many of the decisions I made then and make now are based on the knowledge I gained from listening to Caspar. He made me look at fear of failure in a very different way. He defined Hell as dying and the person you meet when you get there is the person you could have been. This resonated with me. I wasn't scared of the short-term setbacks and rejections that I would inevitably come across, but I was afraid of not becoming the person I could be. This was something that has been with me all my life.

Chapter 24

The family man

Someone once told me that you only get on average of seventy summers in your lifetime. When I was setting up my new business I always had this in the back of my mind. Life should be about living and experiences not about money. The by-product of success can often be money, but it shouldn't be the primary driver. Very often people forget this because they get themselves into positions where they are unable to make their own decisions, because their lifestyle dictates that they need to earn a certain figure to maintain the status quo. I felt very fortunate to be in the financial position that I had achieved at such an early age, but it was the experiences that I had gained which were far more valuable to me than any financial returns.

Caspar explained to me the simple economic principle of diminishing marginal utility, which I failed to understand during my A-level in economics at Wellingborough. This simply means that we value that which we have more than that which we could possibly accrue. I was prepared to risk my reputation and time in order to make the new company successful, but not the hard cash that I had accrued. A good principle to adopt when setting up a new business is only spend what you can afford and don't have too many delusions of grandeur.

During this year I met Polly Miller, who highlighted the importance of putting life into perspective. Polly was one of the most inspirational people that I have ever met. Our meeting was serendipity. I wouldn't normally be playing in a mixed netball tournament in Kingston-upon-Thames, and this is where we had our chance encounter. At first I had no idea about what she had experienced. Polly had set up a charity called Dan's Fund for Burns and was looking for some help to raise its profile. It was named after her late husband, who she had met in October 2000, in Bali, Indonesia. They were married two years later at Shamley Green Parish church in Surrey and spent their honeymoon in the Maldives and Sri-Lanka. In the last week of their Honeymoon they joined the Hong Kong Rugby club tour to Bali. Dan belonged to a local rugby team, the Hong Kong Vandals. They were in Indonesia for the annual Bali Tens tournament. It was during the same event two years earlier that Dan and Polly had first met in Paddy's Bar. They had got engaged in Bali.

On the night of 12th October 2002, Polly and Dan went out for dinner with Annika, their bridesmaid, and seven other friends and then on to the Sari Club. Nothing could have prepared them for what was about to happen. Shortly after 11:30 p.m. two bombs were detonated at the Kuta beach which ripped Paddy's Bar and the Sari Club apart. 202 people were killed. Dan was killed instantly in the explosion, together with Polly's bridesmaid and their seven friends. Polly was badly injured and sustained 43% burns. She dragged herself out of the club and ran across the burning roof to safety. She was rescued by Noel Fergusson, an Aussie rules footballer, before being evacuated to an intensive care unit in Brisbane.

I met Polly in 2005 and have never met a more positive person. Alice and I asked her around for dinner and she told me in graphic detail what had happen that night. Polly said that she wanted a game to commemorate Dan's life. Dan had had the motto, "Forever on tour". Alice and I instantly agreed to help Polly. We had no idea how big this event would become, but thought it could be similar to the match I had organised to raise money for the Harry Birrell Scholarship Fund. We assembled a committee of Polly's friends and set up a commemorative day of rugby at St John's College and The University Rugby Ground, Grange Road, Cambridge, on Saturday 9th September 2006.

There was a Sevens tournament through the morning which featured fourteen teams from all around the world, many representing those lost in the bombings. The final was played at the University Rugby

Ground, followed by a full exhibition match between an International Legends XV, coached by Matt Dawson, and an Oxbridge Legends XV featuring a host of veterans of previous Varsity Matches. I was very proud when I ran out with my nephews Ben and Sam, with international legends including Jason Leonard, Scott Gibbs, Nick Beal, Alan Bateman, Tyrone Howe, Darren Garforth, Mattie Stewart and Jon Sleightholme. The tragedy had struck at the heart of the rugby community and they showed their support on this day.

The highlight was the dinner after the match, hosted at St John's College, Cambridge, by Martin Bayfield. I sat next to the principal sponsor, Danny Desmond of Bride Hall, who purchased the Bali Bar in the auction. This was a Mars Bar framed behind Perspex that had been sold around the world to raise money for the victims of the Bali Tens. It had been in one of the kit bags of one of the boys in Bali. Polly had managed to get it to England. At the Singapore fundraiser it was sold for $30,000 and the buyer donated it to the Hong Kong fundraiser where it went for $50,000, before the buyer donated it to a fundraiser in Taiwan. All buyers have their names engraved before they pass it on. The great thing about it is that Mars donate money whenever the Bali Bar is sold and it is displayed in the foyer of their headquarters. Polly raised a lot of money from that evening and from a black tie dinner in London. There was a lot of cash still in the city and people came out in full support of Dan's Fund for Burns. Simon Weston, who survived with 49% burns when his ship, the RFA Sir Galahad, was bombed and set on fire by enemy Skyhawk fighters during the Falklands War, spoke at the dinner and raised the profile of the charity. I was very proud to have got to know Polly and I realised yet again how fickle life can be and why it is so important to live it to the full.

I should have realised that my passion for travel was just about to take a back seat with the news that Alice was expecting our first child. I never missed an opportunity to sell overseas trips and I managed to fit in two superb trips before our baby's due date in February. I had a trip to Rome staying in the Hotel Russie with private tours of the Vatican on the same weekend as Tom Cruise was getting married in

Italy. Many of the guests were staying in the five-star hotels around Rome and he virtually brought the city to a standstill. In the same month, Alan Curtis, one of my clients, wanted to put together a thank you to all those people who had been loyal to him and his company. A *Taste of Bordeaux* was born out of the best of the best Rick Stein events. However, rather than fly to Padstow, we chartered a plane to Bordeaux with Rick Stein.

The location was Les Sources de Caudalie. It was voted the leading small hotel of the world in 2007. In 1990, two former Olympic skiers, Florence and Daniel Cathiard, fell in love with Château Smith Haut Lafitte and its charming eighteenth-century house during a flight over the Bordeaux vineyards. Daniel Cathiard was the founder of the Go Sport chain of supermarkets and sporting goods stores, and Florence Cathiard was Vice-President of McCann Europe. They decided to give up their stressful careers and start a new life by buying Château Smith Haut Lafitte and return it to its former glory.

In September 1993, their daughter Mathilde and her husband Bertrand were taking part in the harvest at Smith Haut Lafitte when they met Professeur Vercauteren, the Head of the Bordeaux Pharmacognosy Laboratory, who was visiting the estate. He noticed the heaps of skins and seeds about to be thrown away during the wine making process and told them they were wasting "a veritable treasure!" The grape seeds contained polyphenols, which when stabilised were treasure troves for the skin. Two years later, in September 1995, the first three products of the Caudalie range were created. Today, Caudalie has thirty-five products and seven oils, and the brand is sold in twenty-five countries. The luck of the Cathiard family doesn't stop there. They observed that a low-lying area in the vineyard produced lower-quality grapes than the rest. A water diviner was called in and they discovered a natural hot spring in that spot. This discovery led to the first Vinothérapie Spa in the world, which then led to them pulling up of the sub-standard vineyard to make room for Les Sources de Caudalie in June 1999.

We had asked Rick Stein where he thought we should go to celebrate the "Best of the best Rick Stein events". He put us in touch with Gavin Quinney who had gone out to live the dream by buying Chateau Bauduc, a seventy-five-acre vineyard near Bordeaux, where he made house wines for Rick Stein and Gordon Ramsay. Gavin was a Bordeaux critic and every year would taste the new wines of the leading five hundred châteaux. He knew everything about the region and was a perfect host. He suggested Les Sources de Caudalie and it was here that I was taught to appreciate Bordeaux. The trip was one of the best events that I have ever organised.

We had dinner and a private tour of Château Smith Haut Lafitte, after drinks at the Cathiard family home. Gavin took us to Chateau Bauduc and talked us through how an artisan vineyard makes upmarket house wines. He then opened his house up for lunch, before we returned to the hotel for a private cooking demonstration by Franck Salein, the Michelin star chef at the hotel, and Rick Stein. The dinner was a selection of Rick Stein's *French Odyssey* dishes, prepared by Franck Salein. Gavin choose the wines. He was given a big budget and they were some of the best wines I have tasted. We drank Batard Montrachet 1999 with the starter, Chateau Palmer with the main course, and Margaux 1998 and Chateau Latour Pauillac 1994. The desert wine was a Chateau Suduiraut 2001 from Sauternes. The "Best of the best Rick Stein trip" was the end of an era. I don't know whether trips like this will ever be repeated.

I knew Alice was pregnant well before we had it confirmed officially. We were in San Francisco visiting her sister and her body had felt different. I stayed an extra week and Alice returned to Europe for a hen weekend in Spain. She had a big first night and felt very sick the day after. She tried to run it off and couldn't. It was then that she thought she may be pregnant with our first child and it was confirmed when she returned. I came home from my trip to San Francisco to this fantastic news. I never thought I would even get married, so hearing news like this, from the person whom I adored, was like a dream come true.

I hadn't a clue that a pregnancy was around forty weeks. I had no idea of the procedure that we should follow. Typically the build up to the birth was a comedy of errors. The first significant point was the nuchal scan. Everybody has a risk of having a baby with a chromosome abnormality, such as Down's syndrome. The nuchal scan is normally carried out between eleven weeks and just under fourteen weeks of pregnancy. We thought it was odd that we hadn't been contacted regarding the scan, but there had been a cock-up between the doctors so we ended up going to a private hospital in Wimbledon.

Twickenham to Wimbledon is about seven miles and it should take twenty minutes to drive there, but not on the night of our nuchal scan. A water main burst on the A3 causing traffic chaos, and we ended up abandoning the car at The Green Man at Putney Heath and walking the rest of the way. The nuchal scan was an important scan to assess the risk of Down's syndrome and to make sure that there were no fetal abnormalities and that the baby was alive and well. It is the time that, if the results are good, you pick up the telephone and tell family and friends your news. The Green Man provided the venue for these telephone calls. There can be no better feeling than making this call to your family.

I told Dad and Joy that we were not going to let the birth of a child change our lives. How naive I was. I watched Alice grow throughout the forty weeks of pregnancy and attended various National Childbirth Trust classes and a home birth class. Alice hated hospitals and would faint at the sight of a needle, and so was desperate for a home birth. I supported her and naively didn't really look into exactly what this would entail. Alice had given me various articles on the benefits associated with home births and the thought of having our first child at home seemed quite appealing. I am not very practical and one of the main responsibilities that I had before the birth was to assemble a birthing pool, which contained eighty gallons of water and had to be kept at a constant temperature. This was to be assembled on our kitchen floor and regularly emptied and cleaned to make sure that it was just right for the big event. There was some pressure associated with this responsibility, which I eventually mastered with difficulty, but it was nothing compared to the pressure of the actual birth. As Alice and I sat down to eat a sausage casserole the night after her due date, we had no warning that she was just about to embark on one of the most stressful nights of her life and I had no idea what to expect. Never in all my thirty-eight years had I had less than seven hours sleep in a night.

As her labour progressed, I timed her contractions with military precision and made the call to the West Middlesex Hospital at exactly the right time. The midwives arrived and Alice laboured through the night. We had no idea that our baby was a back-to-back baby. Some babies lie with their back against their mother's back. The labour tends to take longer if the baby is in this position because getting through the pelvis is more awkward. If a baby is lying this way then this often causes backache during labour. Alice was in massive pain and I spent hours rubbing her back to relieve the pain, whilst listening to a relaxation CD on repeat. It was a surreal experience and despite her pain much more relaxing than being in hospital. This was until the gas and air ran out. Entonox, or gas and air as it is more commonly known, is a 50/50 mix of oxygen and nitrous oxide. Alice used it to dull down the pain of each contraction. It came in a gas cylinder with a pipe coming out of the top which had a mouthpiece attached to the end. We were about twenty hours into the birth and I could not attach the pipe on to the cylinder, so Alice suddenly found herself without any pain relief and made a very rational decision to finish the rest of the birth in hospital.

Four hours later, at 6:45 p.m. on Valentines Day 2007, Scarlett Daisy Thorneycroft was born and this changed my life forever. Nothing could have prepared me for the ecstasy of seeing our child being born. During the course of this book I have described some treasured memories and this is the most precious of all of them. I was thirty-eight years old and had lived a selfish existence as a single man and then as the husband of my beautiful wife. Subconsciously, I changed that day. Life was no longer about me; it was about my family and making sure that I provided them with the opportunities that I had been given to experience the most wonderful life.

I wrote this book for my children to read when they are older. It has taken me over a year to complete and since then Harry Llewellyn Thorneycroft has been born. The birth of Harry in the house next door to where Alice laboured with Scarlett couldn't have been more different. I had a good night's sleep and woke up to find Alice preparing herself for a big day with military precision. She was determined to have her baby at home this time.

The bathing pool had been constructed and emptied and cleaned in preparation for the impending birth. Our midwife, Po Ying, was in control and so was Alice. Scarlett went off with her grandparents and I was running around like a headless chicken. I crashed the car into a small wall and jumped up on our bed basketball style to put something on a shelf and broke that too. I failed to cancel the building control officer who had arranged to inspect our house the morning Alice went into labour and he arrived just as Alice was having serious contractions. I have never seen a bloke pass something so quickly in my life and he was gone before we knew it. In a matter of hours Harry was born on the floor of our basement lounge. Before he was born I didn't care if we were going to have a girl or a boy, but when Harry came out I punched the air as if I was saluting the Gordon Stand at Franklin's Gardens. I had the family that I had always wanted; a beautiful boy and girl with the woman I had loved from the moment I set eyes on her.

I have written this book from the house where Harry was born and have loved every minute of reliving my wonderful journey. I hope that when they are older Scarlett and Harry will pick this book up and feel that there are a few lessons that can be learnt even from people as ancient as your Mum and me. I love you both so very much.